W. DOUGLAS SIMPSON

The
Ancient Stones
of Scotland

ILLUSTRATED

ROBERT HALE · LONDON

9999043515 ✓

936·11

VENDOR

ORD. No.   DATE

5207

30471

TO THE MEMORY OF

SIR DANIEL WILSON, LL.D.

1816–1892

FATHER OF SCOTTISH ARCHAEOLOGY

CONTENTS

ILLUSTRATIONS

HALF-TONES

ACKNOWLEDGEMENTS

The following photographs are Crown Copyright and are reproduced by permission of the Ministry of Public Building and Works: 1, 6, 7, 8, 9, 10, 11, 12, 14, 16, 18 and 20; no. 2 is from a watercolour drawing by Lt.-Col. Jonathan Forbes Leslie at Newton House, by courtesy of Mr. A. Parkin Moore; 3 is from W. Douglas Simpson, *Province of Mar*, and 4 from *Viking Congress, Lerwick*; 5 is reproduced by permission of the Society of Antiquaries of Scotland; 15 by permission of Messrs J. Valentine & Sons; and 17 by permission of the Scottish National Buildings Record.

FIGURES IN THE TEXT

PREFACE

THE purpose of this book is to provide the general reader with a survey, simple, concise and non-technical, yet I hope scholarly, of the ancient monuments of Scotland, covering their whole time-range from the earliest prehistoric tombs and homes down to the extinction of a national building style in the eighteenth century. No account is taken of portable antiquities, except in so far as these, when found in the monuments, help to date the latter and to clarify the purpose or purposes for which they were built and the life that was led or the ritual practised in them. Nor, in general, has account been taken, except for the sake of completeness or necessary comparison, of castles which are yet inhabited and ancient churches still in use. Likewise, the whole field of burghal architecture is left out. Even within these limitations, imposed by the scope and size of the work, the reader into whose hands this book may come may well feel astonishment at the richness and variety that Scotland offers as a field for archaeological study.

In the Preface to a former work (*The Province of Mar*, 1943, p. iii), I made the point that "in a survey extending from Mesolithic times until the fifteenth century, only a charlatan would claim to speak with equal authority about the many and diverse topics handled". The present survey covers not a province but the whole of Scotland, and extends until the eighteenth century. Moreover, in the past twenty years the progress of archaeological research, in all periods, has been prodigious: so that the sheer burden of fact which weighs upon the writer who proposes to sum up the whole, in what can be no more than a *coup d'oeuil*, becomes grievous indeed. I can only hope that this first attempt by a single author, since Sir Daniel Wilson's classic work of a century ago, to present the whole theme of Scottish monumental archaeology within the compass of one volume, will be judged with forbearance and charity.

W. Douglas Simpson

Kings College,
Old Aberdeen.
February, 1965.

THE ANCIENT STONES
OF SCOTLAND

I

The Scottish Stage and
its European Background

SCOTLAND is a small country. She contains no more than, in round figures, 30,000 acres. In the days before the modern large-scale industrial exploitation of coal and iron, Scotland was likewise a very poor country. The greater part, north of the Highland Boundary Fault which crosses the land from Stonehaven in the north-east to Helensburgh in the south-west, is a mass of rugged inhospitable mountains diversified by narrow glens, all composed of hard and ancient rocks, yielding for the most part a soil both meagre and poor. Somewhat similar though less rigorous conditions prevail in the Southern Uplands, below the line of another major geological fracture, the Southern Boundary Fault, which traverses the country between Dunbar on the north-east and Girvan to the south-west. The only large areas of fertile or relatively fertile soil—and these are by no means continuous— are thus found in the Midland Valley, in the broad basin of Strathmore extending thence north-eastward towards the coast at Stonehaven, and in the coastal plains and lower river valleys round the great alcove of the Moray Firth, and terminating in the rich cornlands of Caithness. Even today, despite centuries of intensive cultivation, little more than a quarter of the country is under crops or grass; while of this quarter, again, barely one sixth is arable land. Thus, in terms of human exploitation, Scotland has always been a pastoral rather than an agricultural country.

Scotland is likewise a remote country. She occupies the northern apex of the British Islands, themselves situated in the north-west quarter of the Old World. And whereas England is separated from Europe only by a channel at its narrowest little more than a score of miles in width, Scotland on her eastern flank is sundered from the Continent by some 400 miles of open sea; on the north she fronts the "wild and wasteful waves" of the Arctic Ocean; while westward 2,000 miles of the broad Atlantic separate her from the New World. Moreover, while the most fertile regions of England are those that face the Continent, and therefore both encouraged and eased the path of successive invaders and cultural infiltrations, Scotland is separated from her southern neighbour by the long barren moorlands of Northumbria and the bleak tangled mountains of the Lake District—a circumstance which has tended, throughout the human record, to emphasize the isolation of "Caledonia, stern and wild".

Lastly, Scotland is not blessed with a genial climate. Although extremes of cold and heat are lacking, sunshine is deficient, and the rainfall, particularly on the western seaboard, tends to be excessive. In England, the average annual rainfall is about 32 inches: for Scotland generally, the average may be computed at 47, and only some ten per cent of the total area approaches in lowness of annual rainfall the English average. The variability of the weather is a further disadvantage, and much of the country, notably in the Northern Islands, is scourged by frequent and stormy winds.

Since man first settled in Scotland there have been climatic changes. When the Ice Age came to an end, perhaps about 8,000 years ago, tundra conditions of half-frozen moorland and steppe supervened, in a climate still very cold. Gradually things improved: the winters grew shorter and less cruel, the summers longer and more kindly. Birches and pines began to grow, sparsely at first, amid the tundra—to be succeeded in their turn by regular forests, including alder and some oak. To climatologists this phase is known as the Boreal period. In due course a moister and milder climate began to prevail, marked by an increasing predominance of oak and alder, but also by the growth of great peat bogs, in which the stems of the ancient forest trees, blown down by westerly gales, may still be found embalmed. This is known as the Atlantic period. Still later, the climate changed once more, introducing the colder and wetter conditions that we endure today. At no time, since the last of the valley glaciers relaxed the grip of their icy fingers, can it be said that Scotland has enjoyed a kindly climate.

A country so poorly favoured by nature can never have been other than sparsely inhabited. Even today the population numbers no more than about five millions. By far the largest proportion is now concentrated in the so-called "industrial belt", roughly corresponding to the Midland Valley. Of course in ancient times the population will have been more evenly distributed, as well as much smaller. In the thirteenth century, for example, it is computed that Alexander III ruled over no more than 600,000 subjects. When the first official census was taken in 1801, the figure revealed was about 1,600,000. Nor, for the broad mass of the people, has the standard of life ever been other than a modest one. Before the Industrial Revolution, indeed, the lot of large numbers of Scotsmen was sheer poverty. About the time of the Union in 1707 it is estimated that ten per cent of the population lived by begging—either as "licensed gaberlunzies", like Edie Ochiltree in Scott's *Antiquary*, or as "thiggers and sorners" masterful beggars who helped themselves to what they wanted.

The reader who has accompanied me thus far may begin to wonder, at this point, how a country so remote and so ill-favoured could come to boast an archaeology worthy of having an entire volume consecrated to itself. As a matter of fact, the antiquities of Scotland, in all periods from the Stone Age to the eighteenth century, are at once rich and diverse; and, though small in bulk, they form an important and distinctive part in the *ensemble* of European archaeology—using that term in its broadest sense both chronologically and comprehensively: though it must, thus early, be made clear that the present work is concerned, first and foremost, with what may be described as monumental or structural antiquities, and only incidentally with portable objects—in so far as these elucidate the life that was lived by those who built the various kinds of structures, for the living or the dead, with which we shall have to deal.

Why then should Scottish archaeology offer so rewarding a field of study? For this there are a number of reasons.

One of them is the very remoteness of the country. It is a well-known principle that in a peripheral area, and especially in a Highland area, older racial stocks and cultural patterns tend to absorb, rather than to be obliterated by, newer cultural permeations or immigrant movements. Thus the material relics of such ancient cultures come to be preserved more perfectly than in more central areas where such cultures were absorbed or superseded, and in due course altogether obliterated in times much more remote. A striking instance of this is furnished by the famous prehistoric village of Skara Brae in Orkney. This primitive community was Neolithic in its domestic economy and way of life, yet plainly dates from a period much less remote than the New Stone Age of Southern Britain. Moreover, in a treeless land its clusters of huts were perforce built of stone, instead, of in timber as in the south; furthermore, the local flagstones split readily into slabs or long blocks that could be used in place of planks or posts. Thus nowhere in Britain, perhaps nowhere in Europe, can we find a more vivid picture of a Stone Age village, reproducing in durable materials fitments elsewhere doubtless made of perishable wood.

In the second place, the position of Scotland, at the extreme north-western apex of the Old World, has exposed her to powerful influences from at least three quarters. If her own Southern Uplands and the high Northumbrian moors and Cumbrian fells isolated her from the heart of England, her western seaboard lies fully open to maritime intercourse not only with England but with Ireland, which, owing to her richness in copper and gold, played an important part in the prehistoric economy of Western Europe. From very early times there has been far more seafaring around the British Islands than is often realized. Irish tools, weapons and ornaments were imported into Britain, and across it to the Continent, by well-defined trading routes. Some of these led through Scotland, either by the Clyde estuary and Strathmore, or by the Great Glen, which cleaves the Highlands from Fort William to Inverness. It was by the western sea routes that the Neolithic builders of our chambered cairns reached Scotland, in the course of a long migration which had led them from Spain, *via* Brittany and Ireland, to the remote Orkneys and Shetlands. We do not always realize that one can sail from Gibraltar to the Muckle Flugga—the northmost point of Britain—without ever losing sight of land. By the same coastal route, in times much more recent, the people who were to devise the Scottish brochs, starting from the Severn basin, reached the Northern Isles.

When it is remembered that Ireland and Scotland are parted by
no more than a bare thirteen miles of sea (between Antrim and
the Mull of Kintyre) it will be understood how powerful has
always been the impact of Ireland upon Scotland. To Ireland
Scotland owes not only her name, but much (though by no means
all) of her early Christianity; and we shall find that the churches,
high crosses, and grave-slabs of the Hebrides, right down to the
Reformation, show unmistakable signs of Irish influence. Nor was
the traffic only one-way. Scotland gave as well as received. In the
early seventeenth century, the "plantation" of Ulster by James VI
and I resulted in the building there of a large number of castles
purely Scottish in type.

Again, though to a lesser extent, Scotland lay open to immigration on her eastern front, across the North Sea. Such immigration
may indeed have begun overland, by a circumambient route, so
far back as Mesolithic times, when the southern part of the North
Sea, up to the Dogger Bank, was still dry land. It was no doubt to
such an infiltration, reaching Britain by the land bridge and thence
up the eastern coastal plain, that we owe the traces, on a number of
early Scottish sites, of the influence of the Maglemosean or Forest
Culture of Denmark and the Baltic. At a later time, the very
powerful invasion of Scotland—for it was nothing less—by the
Beaker Folk, towards the end of the Stone Age, undoubtedly
came directly west-overseas from the delta of the Rhine. It is not
too much to say that in the north-eastern knuckle of Scotland the
Beaker Folk of four thousand years ago still form the basic stock
of the rural population.[1]

Thirdly Scotland, at least from the ninth century, was exposed
to extensive colonization from Norway. It is but a short and easy
voyage, in calm summer weather, from Norway to Shetland and
Orkney, and thence by the Pentland Firth to the Hebrides, where
the Vikings, who came to raid and remained to settle, found
scenery that reminded them of their Scandinavian homeland—
scenery that satisfied their "craving for surroundings where something of the old was to be found in their new activities. They
asked for sea and fjord, mountain and hill, the fowling cliffs and
sealing grounds. They needed the pastures, meadows and heather,
to which they had been accustomed in the land of their birth, and
the light summer nights which brooded softly over farm and field

[1] See my *The Province of Mar*, pp. 21–30.

at home in Norway. No sentimental spirit of homesickness lay at the back of all this, but the simple fact that the whole of their mentality, fostered by the toil of countless generations before them, was adjusted to a life in which all these things were to be found."[1]

So it befell that the Norwegians colonized not only the Shetlands and Orkneys, termed by them collectively the *Nordereys* or Northern Islands, but also the Hebrides and the whole western seaboard, which became the so called *Sudereys*, a vast domain itself falling naturally into two parts divided by the Ardnamurchan peninsula. The Sudereys were recovered by Scotland in the Treaty of Perth (1266), after Haakon Haakonsson's failure at Largs three years earlier. Not until 1472 did the Orkneys and Shetlands fall in, as a result of the marriage between James III of Scotland and the Princess Margaret of Denmark, with which Norway, as well as Sweden, was then united. Furthermore, the Norwegians in Viking times extensively colonized the old Celtic Province of Cat, comprising the modern shires of Caithness (Cat-ness, the promontory of Cat) and Sutherland—the "southern land" of Norway.

In all these far-flung domains traces of the former presence of the Norsemen are abundant. The population of Shetland, and to a lesser degree of Orkney, is mainly of Norse descent, and the place names are almost entirely Norwegian. In Orkney the old dialect of Norse, known as "Norn", continued to be used until the sixteenth century, the Shetland "Norn" until a full two centuries later.[2] In the Hebrides, on the other hand, the Celtic population reasserted itself, and here the evidence of place-names points to a mixed breed—the "Gall-gael" of the ancient chroniclers. On the south-west of Scotland, traces of Danish settlement, particularly round the Solway basin, are evident. These immigrants must have come in from Cumbria and Northumberland. In general, it may be claimed that Norse graves and homesteads make a significant contribution to the archaeology of Scotland.

Lastly we have to consider direct penetration of Scotland from northern England, either by the coastal plain or by the passes over the Cheviots at Carter Bar and the Lammermuirs at Soutra—and also, of course, by the seaborne route. There is a growing bulk of

---

[1] A. W. Brøgger, *Ancient Emigrants*, p. 26.

[2] For the third "Norn" dialect, that of Caithness, see Per Thorsen in *The Viking Congress, Lerwick*, July 1950, pp. 230–8.

evidence, though much of it is still obscure, that in this way Scotland was receiving fresh immigrations, and cultural increments, throughout the later prehistoric period: and it was both by land and sea that the Romans carried out their successive attempts to subjugate Caledonia, or to visit her inhabitants with "military execution", from the time of Agricola to that of Stilicho. We shall find that the traces of Rome in Scotland are indeed impressive; and every year adds to their number.

Where Rome had failed with the sword she returned to conquer by the Cross. The earliest Christian mission to the Britons and the Picts, who then dwelt in the land upon which Irish immigrants afterwards bestowed the name of Scotland, was conducted by St. Ninian, who in 397 planted his famous monastery at Whithorn in Galloway. In this neighbourhood some early Christian monuments of Romano-British type remain (p. 107). One or two similar inscriptions survive elsewhere in southern Scotland, where also, and as far north as the basin of the lower Tay, Christian graveyards of uncertain but remote antiquity have been discovered. These monuments and cemeteries serve to remind us that the first current of Christian missionary enterprise flowed out from the Roman Empire and followed the trail already blazed by the legions.

Following the aggressive pattern set by the Romans, the powerful Anglian Kings of Northumbria, seated in the old Roman capital of *Eboracum* (York) and claiming to inherit the position and prestige of the former imperial *Dux Britanniarum*, attempted in their turn to reduce the Celtic North. These efforts foundered in the disastrous defeat of Egfrith of Northumbria at the hands of the Pictish King Brude MacMaelchon at Nechtansmere (Dunnichen in Angus) in 685. Nevertheless, we shall learn that, in the centuries immediately following, the brilliant monumental art of Northumbria exerted a strong influence upon the sculptured stones of Pictland, and that its effects are still traceable on the Hebridean high crosses and grave-slabs of the later Middle Ages.

Meantime the influence of Irish Christianity, coming in mainly by way of Iona, was becoming increasingly dominant with the growing political power of the Scotic kingdom of Dalriada, which in St. Columba's time comprised little more than the present county of Argyll and the adjacent islands. It is thus that we find, in the very heart of the old Pictish kingdom, two Round Towers of Irish type at Abernethy and Brechin.

In the twelfth and thirteenth centuries—the high noontide of Latin Christianity in western Europe—Scotland, under the guidance of her vigorous and large minded Kings of the House of Canmore, opened her frontiers to a full tide of Anglo-Norman cultural penetration, coupled with an administrative overhaul which converted the kingdom, from a loosely-knit congeries of Celtic provinces, into a strongly organized feudal monarchy. This process may be said to have been completed, so far as the Lowland areas are concerned, by the time of the tragic death in 1286 of Alexander III, the last king of the ancient Celtic line. As a result, the whole eastern half of Scotland, from Berwick to the Dornoch Firth, grew to be one cultural province in full communion with England. English masons were imported to build the churches and castles that were the hall-mark of the new order. Thus a Yorkshire master-mason was called in to erect the strange little reliquary church of St. Rule's at St. Andrews. Dunfermline Abbey is plainly the work of mason-craftsmen brought up from Durham; while earthwork or stone-and-lime castles of English types were built by the Scottish heads of great Anglo-Norman baronial families—for example, by the de Vaux at Dirleton; the de Quincies at Leuchars; the de Baliols at Buittle, Red Castle (Lunan Bay) and Dunnideer; the de Comyns at Balvenie and Lochindorb; the de Pollocks at Rothes. Flemish settlers, too, were notable builders of castles. Freskyn the Fleming, the common ancestor of the present ducal houses of Atholl and Sutherland, was the founder of the noble Norman Castle of Duffus in Moray. Collectively all these immigrants liked to call themselves "English", in contrast to the native Gaelic-speaking population. Hence in Scotland today the place-name *Ingliston* is frequently met with hard by the site or earthworks of a Norman castle. English and Flemish settlers were also encouraged to man the burghs which were planted throughout the Lowlands, as a means to foster industry and commerce by the far sighted monarchs, barons and churchmen.

From all this it is apparent that in the twelfth and thirteenth centuries the civilization of Scotland was developing in an English, indeed in a European context. The influence of English ideas and arrangements is apparent also in the frequency with which, through the areas of Scotland that were exposed to the Anglo-

Norman penetration, we find the remains of a Norman castle adjoining an ancient parish church. For it was the Anglo-Norman hierarchy that divided the country up into parishes: and very often the parish was nothing else than the manor of a baron, considered ecclesiastically; while the parish church began as the private chapel of the lord of the manor, placed close beside his castle for the convenience of his household, and the community of his dependents who clustered outside his gate.

As a result of these various processes, by the end of the thirteenth century the stage seemed fairly set for a peaceful union between Scotland and her larger and much more wealthy neighbour. This was indeed a consummation devoutly to be wished. It would have spared both countries three centuries of bitter war, and might well have enabled Scotland to share more fully in that glorious burgeoning of the human spirit which we call the Renaissance. But alas! the death of the little Queen of Scotland—the hapless Maid of Norway—on her voyage from Bergen frustrated the statesmanlike vision of Edward I, greatest of British monarchs, and tempted him, the ambitious, masterful Plantagenet, to the fatal step of seeking to complete by force of arms the work of peaceful amalgamation which had been in full and beneficent progress for well-nigh two centuries. So followed the glorious yet how calamitous struggle for independence, which devastated Scotland for more than seventy sorrowful years, and forms the main cultural divide in her national development.

Hitherto, it can scarcely be said that medieval Scotland had evolved a national style in architecture, art, and literature. But now between her and her southern neighbour there was a great gulf fixed. No longer would the designers of Scottish churches and castles continue to follow more or less the Anglo-Norman pattern. Instead, Scottish builders, under the influence of intense self-centred patriotism, began to develop their own national architecture. When they sought models or craftsmen from abroad, it was rather from Scotland's ally France, to whom she had been drawn by common resistance to Plantagenet imperialism; and still more from the Low Countries, with which Scotland became increasingly linked by commercial dealings. It is therefore from the fourteenth century that we can truly claim that a Scottish national architecture may be seen to date.

Furthermore, the country was now much poorer than in the "Golden Age" of the Alexanders. Before the great war, many of the Anglo-Norman barons owned also estates in England, and could use their wealth to build castles and parish churches and to endow monasteries and cathedrals in the northern realm. The war compelled them to choose their side. Those who elected to stay in Scotland lost their English possessions. The lands that they retained in Scotland, and indeed the fertile portion of the country at large, had been pitilessly ravaged, over and over again, during the long struggle, both by the invaders and by the Scots themselves, in pursuit of the "scorched earth" defensive policy dictated by Bruce. For example, in 1339 the rich country around Perth had been reduced to a desert: not a house was left standing; the starving deer invaded the town; many people died of sheer hunger. It is not under such conditions that architecture can thrive. To make matters worse, the long and cruel war was followed by an equally prolonged period of feudal anarchy. The power of the Crown had been gravely weakened by the large grants of estates which the adventurer Bruce had to make in order to buy or confirm the loyalty of his supporters. On top of everything came the tragic fate of the Stewarts—surely the most unlucky ruling dynasty in the history of Europe. An unparalleled series of sudden and untimely deaths, followed by long minorities, reduced the central government to a farce, and opened the way for civil strife between the great baronial factions. Thus Scotland in the fourteenth and fifteenth centuries underwent something of the same experience which England had briefly endured during the anarchic reign of Stephen. It is true that in the fifteenth century England herself underwent a revival of feudal strife in the Wars of the Roses. But here the crisis was both shorter, and less deep-seated in its social and political origins. It was largely caused by the ease with which the over-mighty baronage, amid the clash between the rival houses of York and Lancaster, could recruit their private armies from the multitude of unemployed ex-service men who were available after the English had been thrown out of France. Sharp while it lasted, the crisis was soon overcome, and the baronage tamed, by the strong hand of the Tudor monarchs. In Scotland the monarchy proved too weak to assert its authority; the political framework of the country and its social organization had been too sorely damaged by the Wars of Independence: and the middle classes were not yet sufficiently numerous, wealthy, or united in purpose to form a separate interest supporting the Crown in its endeavour to restore law and order.

Yet civilization did not perish. History teaches us that it can survive, nay even flourish, amid conditions of chronic internecine warfare—witness the record of ancient Greece, or of the Italian republics in the Middle Ages, In point of fact the fifteenth century was an era of steadily increasing prosperity, in which all classes, save indeed the very poorest, partook. Inevitably therefore it was a great building period. Everywhere was heard the sound of the hammer and the trowel. And equally of necessity, the new, intensely national architecture now being developed was highly militaristic in tone. Every landowner's house, from the petty laird to the great feudal magnate, had to be fortified—a "house of fence", so the term went. It was now that the Scottish barons, great and small alike, discovered their fondness for the "tower-house" which today remains so characteristic a feature of the national scene. Even the churches become in a manner militarized. They display the fireproof vaulted roofs, covered by overlapping slabs of stone, the embattled and sometimes machicolated parapets, and the square defensive towers, which characterize the contemporary castles. The existing monasteries and cathedrals furnished themselves with fortified precinct walls, embattled gatehouses, and frowning donjon towers. The episcopal palaces were refashioned as formidable castles. But the time had now passed—nor indeed was the wealth perhaps available—for the foundation of new monasteries or the large-scale endowment of cathedrals. Piety, and the desire to insure against the hazards of the next world, now took the form of the foundation of collegiate churches, each served by a small corporation of clergy held bound to sing masses for the souls of the founder and those mentioned in his deed of gift. These collegiate churches of the fifteenth and sixteenth centuries form one of the most distinctive and fascinating elements in Scottish ecclesiastical architecture. The patrons of such modest structures were no longer always the great lords: country gentlemen, and burgesses moved by a sense of civic pride, all took a hand in the good work. So busy, indeed, were the thriving burghs in building, re-building, or enlarging their "town's kirks" that an Act of the Scottish Parliament in 1457 directed that every Scottish vessel homeward bound should bring one ton of material for the "church work" of the town to which she was freighted.

It was thus in the fifteenth century, and despite the disorderliness of the public scene, that Scottish medieval civilization may be said to have reached its climax. In describing the highly distinctive features of the churches and castles erected during this busy and bustling time, the pioneer authorities on old Scottish architecture were moved by the special character of these remarkable structures to portray the strange society of which they remain the memorial. The passage to which I refer is so striking that it deserves to be reproduced in full:[1]

> "These structures reveal to us, and picture vividly to the mind, a state of life and society so different from our own, and so full of the picturesqueness of medieval times, that we are inclined to linger over it and dwell upon its peculiarities, as we would upon those of a foreign country we are visiting. We feel in a new element, and stop to enjoy the novelty and variety of the surroundings.
>
> "The feudal pomp and state of the King as he moved from one palace to another, surrounded by a brilliant court and attended by all the distinguished of the kingdom, lay and ecclesiastic, as his ministers and servants, and encouraging by his patronage the poets, artists, and musicians of the day; the great barons in their several castles repeating on a variety of scales the same display, sometimes equalling, if not exceeding, that of royalty in magnificence; the bishops and abbots, in their fortified palaces and monasteries, vying with the nobles in the splendour of their retinues and the number of their armed followers; and every smaller proprietor endeavouring to maintain in his tower of fence, with a few retainers, an independent state—all completely fortified and in a constant position of watchfulness and armed neutrality or actual warfare; the innumerable feuds and constant clash of arms; the frequent movement of bodies of steel-clad troops, or the swift passage of the solitary armed messenger—present a picture so widely different from that of modern times as it is possible to conceive."

Viewed in its totality, all this building activity of the fifteenth century must be saluted as a great and creditable national achievement. Yet it affected only a part of Scotland—the country south and east of the "Highland line", including the coastal plains of Aberdeenshire and the counties bordering the Moray Firth. Within the Highland line dwelt a people speaking, not the Scot-

[1] D. MacGibbon and T. Ross, *The Castellated and Domestic Architecture of Scotland*, vol. IV, p. 29.

tish dialect of the English tongue, but Gaelic, the ancient language of the Celts, and differing radically in their political, economic and social system from their Lowland neighbours. It therefore becomes necessary to look at the monuments of the Highland area, which reflect, in their very different character and art relations, the people of whom they are the memorials.

It is a great mistake to exaggerate the difference between Highlander and Lowlander in ancient Scotland. True, they spoke different languages. But language and race have not necessarily anything in common. It is certain that the Lowland population of Scotland possessed in the Middle Ages, and indeed today retains, a large Celtic element. It is equally certain that the Highlanders were, and still are, a very mixed breed, including a considerable infusion of Scandinavian blood, and retaining also many traces of the successive races that had found their way into Scotland by the various routes which I have indicated, ever since prehistoric times.

It is also a great mistake to regard the old-time Highlanders as barbarians—though their Lowland neighbours, who suffered from their cattle-raiding "down-falls", referred to them as "pestiferous *caterans*" (armed robbers), while foreign observers distinguished them, impolitely, as the "wild Scots". The poverty in natural resources of their country, and its inability to sustain an ever-growing population, indeed imposed upon them a way of life largely made up in plundering expeditions against other clans and against the "Sassenach" who had dispossessed them of nearly all the fertile parts of Scotland. Sir Walter Scott, who so well understood the essentials of Highland history, has put this ancient grievance of the Gael, doubtless with some poetic dramatization, into the mouth of Rhoderick Dhu, in his famous argument with the disguised King James V:[1]

> "Saxon, from yonder mountain high,
> I marked thee send delighted eye,
> Far to the south and east, where lay,
> Extended in succession gay,
> Deep waving fields and pastures green,
> With gentle slopes and groves between:—
> Those fertile plains, that softened vale,
> Were once the birthright of the Gael;
> The stranger came with iron hand,

[1] *The Lady of the Lake*, canto V, vii.

And from our fathers reft the land.
Where dwell we now! See, rudely swell
Crag over crag, and fell o'er fell.
Ask we this savage hill we tread,
For fattened steer or household bread;
Ask we for flocks those shingles dry,
And well the mountain might reply,—
'To you, as to your sires of yore
Belong the target and claymore!
I give you shelter in my breast,
Your own good blades must win the rest.'
Pent in this fortress of the North,
Think'st thou we will not sally forth,
To spoil the spoiler as we may,
And from the robber rend the prey?
Ay, by my soul!—While on yon plain
The Saxon rears one shock of grain;
While, of ten thousand herds, there strays
But one along yon river's maze,—
The Gael, of plain and river heir,
Shall, with strong hand, redeem his share."

Nevertheless, for all their endemic anarchy the Scottish Highlanders had a civilization of their own. In the realm of monumental art, it was by far superior to that of the Lowlands. Lying
for the most part unregarded in the ill-kept West Highland and
Hebridean church yards, sometimes wholly buried under grass
and moss, Scotland possesses a *corpus* of grave-slabs to which there
is no parallel in Europe. The intricate beauty of their interlaced or
floriated designs, retaining as they do many old Celtic motives
combined with Romanesque elements derived ultimately from
Anglian, and through them, still more remotely, from classical
sources, provide a vivid commentary on the point which I made
earlier in this chapter, namely that the remoteness of this western
seaboard has tended to the survival of ancient cultural streams, and
their absorption into newer currents to form a monumental art as
subtle as it is delightful. The same complex characteristics are
found on the glorious High Crosses which still adorn the more
important centres of Hebridean Christianity. Not a few of these
crosses and grave-slabs bear inscriptions, always in competent
Latin and set forth in beautifully carved Lombardic or Gothic
lettering. Nor were the chiefs thus scholarly commemorated

themselves illiterate. The earliest signature to a Scottish medieval charter that we possess is that of Donald, Lord of the Isles, the Highland hero of the "Red Harlaw" (1411). The portable antiquities of the period, such as the beautifully carved whalebone caskets and the massive jewelled brooches, tell the same story of a society whose wealthier members were above all things art-loving, like the La Tène Celtic chiefs of Britain fifteen centuries earlier. The major ecclesiastical buildings of the Hebrides, such as Iona Abbey or Rodil Church, display strong Irish influence; the castles, on the other hand, conform rather to current Lowland design.

Before we leave (for the moment) the Scottish Highlands, let me remind my readers that in such a country something more survives than monuments betraying the persistence, in a peripheral area, of artistic elements belonging properly to times much more remote than the period when the monuments were wrought. Also there survives an archaic *mise en scène* for the drama of human life. The very landscape, the wild untamed aspect of the country, carry us back in our imagination to prehistoric times. Changed beyond recognition, by centuries of civilized inhabitation, may be the face of the Lowlands: but within the Highland area we may still contemplate the material surroundings of early men. Nearly a century ago this was recognized, and set forth in eloquent language, by a distinguished English anthropologist:[1]

"The contemplation of a herd of dark-coloured mountain cattle in the north of this country, of small size and yet with ragged, ill-filled out contours, standing on a wintry day in a landscape filled with birch, oak, alder, heath and bracken, has often struck me as giving a picture which I might take as being very probably not wholly unlike that which the eyes of the ancient British herdsman were familiar with."

Only late and tardily did Scotland respond to the artistic impulse of the Renaissance. As is to be expected, the impulse came from France. French designers and craftsmen were employed by James V at the royal palaces of Stirling and Falkland, where their handiwork can still be recognized. Unfortunately the full participation of Scotland in the European Renaissance was interrupted by the peculiar character of the Scottish Reformation. Once again the opportunity was lost to concert arrangements for a salutary

[1] G. Rolleston in W. Greenwell, *British Barrows*, p. 744.

union with England, based upon their common rejection of the ancient faith. Once again the mischief was wrought by the insensate violence of an English King, Henry VIII, seeking to impose this union by force, through a marriage, dictated at point of pike, between his son Edward Prince of Wales, and the little Mary, Queen of Scots. Once again English brutality drove Scotland, very much against her own long-term interest, into the arms of France. Apart from the frightful devastation that it caused in the country south of the Forth, the "War of the Rough Wooing" marked a turning point, and that for the worse, in the cultural development of Scotland. It was from the Continent, not from England, that the northern realm borrowed her peculiar version of Reformed faith and church organization: a circumstance that resulted in the digging of a fresh chasm between the two British kingdoms, and must take some share in the blame for the great Civil War in the seventeenth century. From our present viewpoint, the important matter is that Calvinism, and English Puritanism that followed in its wake, whatever other benefits they may have conferred upon the Scottish people, were, so far as the realm of art is concerned, an utter disaster. It involved many of her finest medieval churches in immediate ruin, tasteless adaptation, or slow decay by sheer neglect; and, so far as the ordinary parish churches are concerned, it replaced them, all too often, by structures in which plainness was by no means always combined with dignity. Yet we shall find that many of the Scottish churches built in the seventeenth and eighteenth centuries have a certain quality of modest mannerliness that compels our respect, and sometimes indeed evokes our admiration.

In the field of domestic architecture matters went much better. One result of the Reformation was that a large proportion of the patrimony of the old church fell into the hands of the greedy nobles and lairds, whose new-found wealth expressed itself in an outburst of castle building. And one result of the Union of the Crowns was a great improvement in the government of Scotland. The prime cause of this was the removal of the King from control by warring factions among the Scottish nobility, by the militant clergy and by the Edinburgh mob. "This I must say for Scotland", James VI could tell his English Parliament: "here I sit and govern it with my pen. I write and it is done, and by a Clerk of the Council I govern Scotland now, which others could not do by the sword".

From the opposite standpoint we have the lament of the honest Mrs. Howden in *The Heart of Midlothian*:

"I dinna ken muckle about the law; but I ken, when we had a king and a chancellor, and parliament men, o' our ain, we could aye peeble them wi' stanes when they warna gude bairns. But naebody's nails can reach the length o' Lunnon."

The combination of these two favourable circumstances—new wealth in the hands of the ruling classes, and orderly conditions that tempted them to indulge in what was then called "policy"— the building of fine houses and laying out of pleasure gardens— resulted in an Indian summer of castellar construction to which Scotland owes the finest of her secular buildings. But the story of the further development of Scottish architecture, domestic and ecclesiastical, after the Union of the Crowns in 1603, must await a later chapter. For it may be said that that event heralded the termination of Scotland's long-enduring peripheral position in relation to the general cultural development of Western Europe. Henceforward the style of her monuments of all kinds—her churches, her graveyards with their "head-stones" and "table-stones", her country houses, her public buildings and burghal "lands" or tenements, grew more and more into general conformity with prevailing Western European standards—a process interrupted only partially by the "Gothic revival" in the nineteenth century.

From this rapid preliminary survey of our theme, the reader will, I hope, have gathered that the monumental antiquities of Scotland, due to the remoteness of the country combined with various external influences to which at all times she has been exposed, are possessed of a highly individual and deeply interesting character. It is thus that Scotland can show, from every period in her long and turbulent past, monuments unique in character, or at least with no precise parallels elsewhere. Thus from the Neolithic age we have the extraordinary "stalled" cairns of the Orkneys; from the Bronze period the unique type of "recumbent stone" circle, found only in the north-east—in Aberdeenshire and its border lands; from the Iron Age those mysterious and unparalleled structures, the brochs. Then in early Christian times we have the development of Pictish lapidary symbolism, a manifestation of ideographical art to which no parallel is known, and which defies elucidation. The later monumental art of the West Highland slabs and crosses is no less singular than beautiful. In the field of medieval architecture, nothing elsewhere seems quite to resemble the semi-castellated churches of the fifteenth century; while the sacrament houses of the eastern Lowlands form a distinctively Scottish contribution to medieval ecclesiology. Among the castles, the Scottish tower-houses form a series paralleled indeed in the three northern English counties and in Ireland, where similar conditions prevailed: but our Scottish towers far excel these others in numbers, variety of design and picturesqueness of treatment. In the later castellated mansions, equipped for firearm defence, Scotland has made, in her famous "three-stepped" or Z-plan, with flanking towers echeloned at each of two diagonally opposite corners, a significant contribution to the general development of European military architecture. And in the peculiar construction of the iron "yetts" by which the portals of her castles were defended, and the "grilles" by which their windows were barred, Scotland achieved something that has almost, if not certainly, failed to find a counterpart elsewhere.

Thus if our field be but a small one, it is a rich and varied crop, a crop moreover dappled with flowers, in which the reader is now invited to browse.

A NOTE ON CHRONOLOGY

Everybody nowadays is familiar with the grand divisions of prehistoric time into the Stone, the Bronze and the Iron Ages. What is not always fully realized is that these divisions represent sequences, not an absolute chronology. In history, chronology is absolute. Thus when we speak of the fourteenth century, we mean the years between the beginning of 1300 and the end of 1399. In the same way, the Tudor period covers the years from 1485 until 1603. But the Stone, the Bronze and the Iron Ages did not follow on at the same time all over the world. There are indeed tribal communities which still are, or were until quite recently, in the Stone Age. So far as Europe is concerned, the further west and north we go, the later becomes the sequence. A good example of this may be seen at Jarlshof in Shetland, where among a community still living in a Neolithic economy there settled a wandering smith, probably from Ireland, casting swords of a late Bronze Age type. In Caithness we shall find evidence that a population of Mesolithic food-gatherers persisted until well into the local Bronze Age, which itself probably lasted until not so very long before the beginning of the Christian era. Coming to much more recent times, we shall have to note the survival of archaic accoutrement among the Hebridean chieftains in the later Middle Ages. Equally, there are cases in such peripheral areas of the persistence, or perhaps rather the revival, of obsolete fashions in architectural detail: for example, the occurrence of the dog-tooth and chevron in secular buildings of the sixteenth century. But the theory of "retarded work" must not be pushed until it becomes a dogma. The standard authorities on Scottish medieval architecture, David MacGibbon and Thomas Ross, claimed that the transition from Romanesque to Gothic did not take place in the Orkney Islands until the middle of the thirteenth century—an assumption which played havoc with their architectural analysis of Kirkwall Cathedral. But Earl Rognvald, the founder, and his building Bishop, William the Old—an able and munificent prelate, "a good Parisian scholar", and the warm friend and crusading companion of the brilliant Earl —were perfectly able to import first-class craftsmen from the great centres of current Romanesque construction: and the evidence, alike stylistic and documentary, is absolutely clear that both the Romanesque and Transitional or First Pointed work in Kirkwall Cathedral is completely abreast of contemporary fashions. Unfortunately the dogma of time-lag or retarded work was adopted also by the late Dr. Mackay Mackenzie in his book on *The Medieval Castle in Scotland*, and in the volumes of the Scottish Royal Commission on Ancient Monuments which appeared under his editorship. The result has been serious error in the dating of our earliest stone castles. But the Kings of the Canmore dynasty, and the wealthy Anglo-Norman barons who founded or endowed cathedrals and abbeys built in the most up-to-date style of the twelfth and thirteenth centuries, were fully capable of providing themselves with stone castles in the latest contemporary style. Each building, whether castle or church, must be considered strictly and solely upon its own merits, in the light of the documentary evidence available and of an objective comparison with similar buildings of which the exact or approximate date is known.[1]

---

[1] For all this, see Stewart Cruden, *The Scottish Castle*, chap. 2.

II

Primitive Food Gatherers

WHAT are probably the earliest traces of human presence in Scotland were found in 1926 in a group of four limestone caves some 200 feet above the present level of a brisk little burn at Inchnadamph, in remote and wild north-western Sutherland. These caves appear to have been filled with gravel by a marginal stream of melt-water, flowing alongside a glacier which then filled the valley to a height of 200 feet above its existing floor. In the caves were found the bones of Arctic animals, including the reindeer (which indeed survived in northern Scotland until the twelfth century), the cave bear, the Arctic lemming, the lynx, and the Arctic fox. Some of the reindeer antlers had been cut or scratched by man, whose presence was also revealed by burnt hearth-stones, bones burnt or split to extract the marrow, and charcoal. The high antiquity of the bones was shown by their state of fossilization—that is to say, by the degree to which the animal matter had perished or become mineralized. One at least of the caves had been occupied up to a comparatively recent time. In another, associated with the bones of a bear, were found two skeletons which clearly had been interred—but, of course, not necessarily at the time of the earliest occupation of the cave.[1]

Since the present work is concerned with the monumental remains of Scotland, rather than with her portable antiquities, these Inchnadamph discoveries find a place here only in so far as they revealed that in glacial times, in Scotland as elsewhere, man made use of caves for a habitation. Of course we must remember that men have made their homes in caves and rock shelters until

[1] Although the excavations at Inchnadamph took place so far back as 1926, it is a disgrace to Scottish archaeology that no more than a meagre "preliminary report" has been published (*Proc. Soc, Ant. Scot.*, vol. LXI, pp. 169–72).

modern times. The yellow limestone caves overlooking the Loire in the neighbourhood of Tours are still inhabited by folk by no means down-and-out. It is not too much to say that caves were the first real homes of man: something more than merely a shelter against an Arctic climate, or a refuge against wild beasts, but a centre of family life—the germ-cell from which all human society and civilization have developed. There is deep truth, as well as fun, in the way in which Kipling puts the matter in the *Just So Stories*, when in the High and Far Off Times a Woman made the First Home:

"She picked out a nice dry Cave, instead of a heap of wet leaves, to lie down in: and she strewed clean sand on the floor; and she lit a nice fire of wood at the back of the Cave; and she hung a dried wild-horse skin, tail-down, across the opening of the Cave; and she said 'Wipe your feet, dear, when you come in, and now we'll keep house'."

On one point, however, Kipling is wrong. It was the front of his dwelling, not the back, that the cave-man lit his fire. This was to enable the smoke to disperse; also to scare wild animals away, and to prevent them occupying the cave when the family was out.

Two famous early Scottish cave dwellings are the MacArthur Cave and the Druimvargie rock shelter at Oban. Here, at a time when the land was at a level some 34 feet lower than now, Mesolithic food-gatherers made their homes—in the MacArthur Cave until flooded out by a high tide, probably during a storm, although today this cave is a hundred yards distant from the beach and more than 30 feet above it. In both cave dwellings were found hammer stones, tools of flint, bone, red deer antler, and barbed harpoons made of deer horn. These closely resemble similar fish-spears found in a celebrated Mesolithic cave at Mas d'Azil in the Pyrenees. Our two Oban caves were the homes of communities of food-gatherers, strand-loopers of whom traces have been found elsewhere in the Hebrides at what may be termed open-air (perhaps summer) stations. One of these camping sites was on the island of Oronsay, where, driven into a vast pile of limpet and periwinkle shells, were found the post-holes of a semicircular wind-break or temporary shelter, probably made of skins. If this can be accepted as contemporary with the Mesolithic strand-loopers, it could well be the earliest known artificial habitation of man in Scotland. These people lived upon molluscs, crabs, and fish, sea-birds (including the now extinct Great Auk) otter, seal, red deer and wild boar. Necklaces made of perforated cowrie shells were worn: and a lump of ochre suggests that the use of lip-stick was not unknown!

These wandering food-gatherers seem to have entered Scotland by the western seaboard. On the opposite side of the country, in the valley of the lower Dee at Banchory, another camping site, or open station, of Mesolithic food-gatherers has been found, where charcoal and fire-cracked stones revealed the presence of a hearth. These eastern folk belonged to what is known as the Tardenoisian stage of culture, characterized by the extensive use of tiny chipped or pressure-worked flints—the so-called "pigmy" flints—which probably were hafted as teeth in implements of wood or bone, such as might be used like a sickle for cutting edible grasses. Since the charcoal was oak, it may be presumed that these wandering folk were camping on Deeside in Atlantic times (see p. 18). Their date could thus lie as far back as three or four thousand years before the birth of Christ. The Tardenoisians undoubtedly reached Scotland by the eastern route, coming up from northern England, where their camping sites and pigmy flints are found in Yorkshire, Durham and Northumberland.

Thus early in the human record do we find Scotland receiving diverse racial elements, with their distinctive material equipment, alike from east and west—by the front door and by the back door.

But caves, rock shelters, skin tents, and the hearths of wandering folk can hardly be described as "monuments". A much more vivid and definite picture of a Mesolithic community, persisting until times greatly more recent, and burying their dead in monumental constructions, can be formed from some very important discoveries, made a century ago at Keiss, in remote Caithness[1]; and, in more recent times, at Freswick in the same

[1] See S. Laing and T. H. Huxley, *Prehistoric Remains of Caithness*, 1866. This book is usually now referred to for the sake of Huxley's masterly study of the skeletal remains submitted to him, in which he surveyed the whole investigation of prehistoric skull forms in Western Europe so far as it had then been carried. But Laing's own contribution is of the highest interest. Though of course he did not realize it, he was in fact making the first *ad hoc* study of a Mesolithic settlement in Britain. In his rigorous insistence on scientific observation, and on inference strictly controlled; in his clear understanding that cultural stages are sequences, not absolute chronology, and in his grasp of the implications of "retarded development", he was far in advance of his time.

county. Here, on the early post-glacial raised beach, forming a natural terrace of sand and shingle, no more than ten or twelve feet above the present shore, primitive food-gathering communities of longshore squatters persisted, following their own Mesolithic way of life yet not uninfluenced by the more civilized folk inhabiting the fertile cornlands behind. Thus among the graves of these folk at Keiss, one was found to contain the inhumed burial of a tall, long-headed man, who had been laid to rest at full length in a "long cist", or rather stone-lined grave of Celtic or Iron Age type, within a round cairn in the Bronze Age tradition, while beside the occupant had been deposited a kit of tools of Mesolithic character. At another Keiss site a typically Mesolithic kitchen midden was found, on top of which later a broch had been built. Still more remarkably, at a third site, four long cists or stone-lined graves, containing skeletons at full length, were found amid the sand that had overblown the ruins of a broch. It is obvious from these discoveries that the Mesolithic strandloopers survived, little affected either by the Neolithic agriculturists or the Iron Age broch builders, probably until as late as the beginning of the Christian era. The relics found in these pioneer investigations can now be paralleled from Mesolithic times in localities as far apart as the valley of the Tweed; the Victoria Cave, Settle; Low Halstow in Kent; Schleswig-Holstein; Denmark; Sweden; and even East Prussia. At the other site, Freswick Links,[1] two periods of occupation by the longshore men could be identified, the upper level containing, in addition to the usual "kitchen-midden" refuse, scraps of pottery which look like a feeble effort to imitate the sepulchral urns of the Beaker Folk (p. 56), several burials of whom have been found in Caithness.

But the stone-lined graves of these impoverished shore dwellers, clinging to their primitive economy at a time when their more civilized neighbours in the *hinterland* were already building truly architectural constructions, can hardly be regarded as a significant contribution to the ancient monuments of Scotland. It is time, therefore, that we proceeded to consider the tombs and dwellings of Neolithic man. At this stage in our study it may be well to reflect that the step forward from a Paleolithic or Mesolithic to a Neolithic economy was by far the greatest advance ever made

[1] See A. D. Lacaille, *The Stone Age in Scotland*, pp. 185, 266–9, 275.

by the human race during its age-long pilgrimage on this globe. So long as man remained a mere trapper, hunter and a gatherer of small fruits and edible grasses, he must be perforce a wanderer in the wilderness. Under such conditions, his primitive habits could persist almost unaltered for ages, as the relics of the Caithness longshore men have shown us. But the moment that prehistoric man started to raise crops of emmer wheat and barley, he is tethered to the spot. He must tend his little patch of cornland till it ripens; he must guard it against wild beasts and hostile neighbours. To do this he must combine and organize. Hence follows the slow growth of village communities, tribes and states; and in due course, the appearance of monumental constructions, which, be they the abodes of the living or the dead, are the product of combined effort.

III

Homes and Tombs of Stone Age Man

B Y far the most vivid picture available in Britain of the material equipment and domestic economy of a Neolithic community is to be seen at the celebrated prehistoric village of Skara Brae, overlooking the shore of the beautiful Bay of Skaill, on the western side of the Mainland of Orkney. In the course of ages the sea has carried away a large proportion of the village, but seven huts still remain, overlying the foundations of others belonging to at least two older periods of occupation. The huts form a cluster, closely huddled together, and connected by a series of winding, roofed-in and "crazy-paved" alleys, with a small open paved area, or place of concourse, towards the west end of what may be called, with some exaggeration of language, the main street. So far as their surviving remains reveal, all these huts were built of local stone—flagstones, sandstones, or indurated shales. Typically, a Skara Brae hut is more or less rectangular, with rounded angles: the average internal dimension may perhaps be about 15 feet square. The walls are carefully constructed in horizontal courses, the stones being accurately fitted together, but (of course) not laid in lime, or even in clay. In one hut, however, the lower part of the wall had been blanketed with blue clay, as if to form a damp-course. In a number of cases, building slabs were found to be carved with a rudely decorative incised pattern, the most ambitious of these efforts being a band of hatched lozenges separated from each other by double vertical lines. Each hut is entered by a low paved passage through its outer wall, usually from 5 to 8 feet in thickness. Set well back in this passage is a door, probably a slab of stone, but possibly sometimes of whale-bone, let into sockets on either side of the

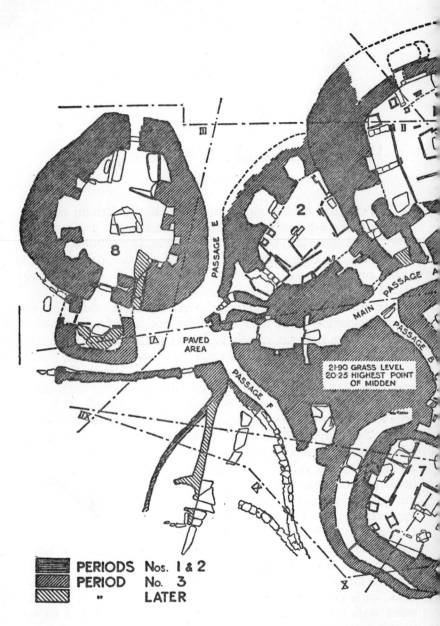

PERIODS Nos. 1 & 2
PERIOD No. 3
    "   LATER

Fig. 1   Prehistoric village at Sk
(By Courtesy, Minis

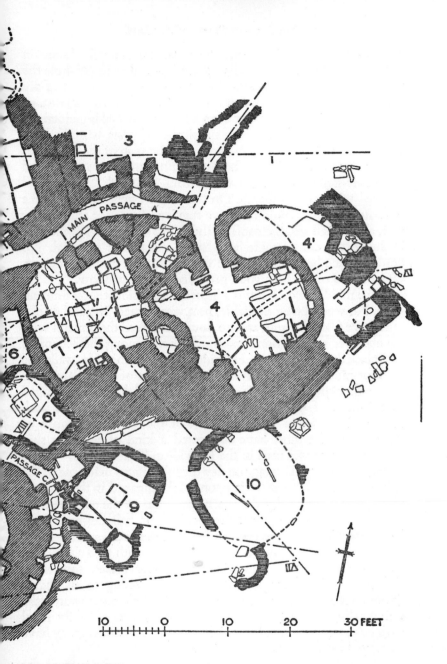

e, Orkney: general plan
ic Building and Works)

passage. In one hut the stone draw-bar was actually found in position; while one of the alley gates retained in its bar-hole the perished remnant of a whale-bone draw-bar. At a height of say 3 or 4 feet the walls of the hut may begin to be corbelled out, or oversail inwards, but in other cases a beehive profile is maintained right from the ground. Since no timber appears to have been available to the villagers, it is likely that the span of the roof, thus reduced by the corbelled or beehive construction, was completed by whale-bone rafters, obtained from stranded animals, and covered with sods or thatch. On that wind-swept site a tent-like covering of skins would not have survived for long; and, in any case, as we shall see, the roofs of the entire village had eventually to support a considerable weight of extraneous material. No doubt in each hut a central hole was left for the smoke to escape. One or two of the huts were provided with a window.

In the middle of each hut is a hearth, and beside it sometimes an oven. No wood being available, peat was burned. Its acrid smoke must have filled the huts, and no doubt endowed the inmates with the ebonized complexion sometimes found among the occupants of "black houses" in the Hebrides. Against the side walls are beds, or rather bunks, skilfully fashioned out of stone slabs. One bed on the right hand side is always larger, and doubtless belonged to the head of the house. These bunks would be filled with heather, bracken, or moss. In front of them are the stumps of stone posts that must have supported a kind of tester or skin canopy, such as was used in the Hebridean "black houses" as late as the last century. During the day the inhabitants made use of the fore-edge of their beds to sit upon while engaged in their avocations. This is shown by the worn condition of the edge, and by the fact that tools and articles, spoiled or half-finished, were frequently found on the floor in front of the bed.

At the back of the hut is a stone dresser, with two shelves. In the walls are various aumbries or keeping places, sometimes shelved, and also privies, with drains connecting to an underground system of sewers, presumably leading out towards the sea. Finally, in the floors are sunk little boxes, carefully lined with clay, as if to contain water. It is thought that these may have been used for the storage of shell-fish.

The westmost hut (which was outside the main gate of the village) is differently arranged from the others, and seems to have served industrial purposes: certainly at one period a chert-knapper had plied his craft here; and masses of clay were found, stored as if for working into pottery.

The entire village was externally buried in its own midden refuse. It is clear that the inhabitants had deliberately heaped this stuff over the whole place—leaving of course a vent above each hut for the peat-reek to escape. Thus the village "must have looked like a great ant-hill with crater-like smoke holes over each dwelling and two or three tunnel-like entries on the flanks".[1] The interiors will have been almost dark: but when the weather was good, the villagers would seem to have worked on top of their mound, as may be inferred from the large number of tools, and articles of various kinds, found all over the surface. It is needless to add that the settlement must have stank to high heaven. Despite the underground sewers, the sanitary conditions will have been appalling. The inhabitants appear to have gnawed their evening meal in bed, and were not above relieving themselves therein! We can only assume that the villagers in course of time developed a certain resistance to disease.

The inhabitants of Skara Brae had no knowledge of metal, nor of tilling the ground. They were pastoral folk, tending their herds of scraggy, long-horned cattle and flocks of little, touzled long-legged sheep. The number of young cattle found shows that as always in olden times, lack of "winter-feed" necessitated a wholesale slaughter in the autumn. The large proportion of bullocks points to the practice of gelding. For the rest, their chief diet consisted of edible shell-fish, but, rather surprisingly, little fishing or seal-hunting was practised; nor was venison often on the menu. The Skara Brae folk made themselves pottery, but in this they were not very expert—possibly because for firing it they had no other fuel than peat. On the other hand they were good at stone work: their axe heads and other implements are quite respectable, and they showed real mastery in carving highly decorated knobbed or spiked stone balls, the use of which is unknown. Many articles of course were made of bone or horn: indeed, the villagers appear to have used no imported material of any kind. They knew not how to weave or spin, and doubtless clad themselves in skins—whence the large number of awls,

[1] *Ancient Monuments*, vol. VI (Scotland)—Ministry of Works, Regional Guides, p. 22.

bodkins and pins found all over the site. For ornament, they made themselves necklaces of sheep bones, teeth of cattle and killer-whales, and walrus or narwhal ivory. Little pots of stone or whale-bone, containing white, blue, red or yellow ochre, permit us to infer that they painted their bodies.

The end of Skara Brae came suddenly. The Bay of Skaill is scourged by fierce south-westerly gales; and one wild day a storm of exceptional severity overblew the village with sand. The inhabitants had to bolt for their dear lives, leaving all their possessions behind. "One woman in her haste to squeeze through the narrow door of her home broke her necklace and left a stream of beads behind as she scampered up the passage."[1]

More recently, another village of the same ancient folk has been uncovered at Rinyo, on Rousay Island, likewise in the Orkneys. Here the huts and their contents were altogether similar to what was found at Skara Brae: but the pottery, as well as numerous sherds in the Skara Brae style, included also, in the older levels of the site, fragments of vessels akin to those found in the chambered cairns which were the burying places of the Neolithic folk in the Northern Isles. In the Skara Brae pottery itself certain decorative elements *en appliqué* recall motives found in Western Europe in the later Neolithic period. Finally, the perforated antler hafts, bone chisels, and some of the stone artifacts remind us of the "heavy kit" of the Forest Cultures of the Baltic lands (p. 21). Thus both Skara Brae and Rinyo belong undoubtedly to the local Neolithic age in the Northern Isles: and confirmation is available from the discovery of an urn of the Beaker Folk (though a late and degenerate one) in the uppermost level at Rinyo.

Despite the vivid beam of light cast by Skara Brae and Rinyo, it is about the dwellings of the dead, rather than those of the living, that we are most fully informed in Neolithic Scotland.

To the western Neolithic folk, who entered Scotland across the North Channel, we owe some of the most imposing monu-

---

[1] V. G. Childe, *Skara Brae* (Official Guide), p. 5. See also his fascinating work *Skara Brae*, published in 1931. There is evidence that in the disaster the villagers lost their flocks and herds; so that when thereafter some of them returned to camp in their abandoned homes, they now had to rely mainly for their food on collecting shell-fish and hunting deer.

ments of any period that our country can boast. These are the "chambered cairns"—family ossuaries in which the individuals of one group or kindred were buried, whether by inhumation or cremation, over a considerable span of generations. We must regard such collective tombs as the burial places of the upper classes, since their construction will have involved a high degree of organization, mechanical skill, and disciplined labour. From the western seaboard these chambered cairn folk spread eastward and northward, by Loch Crinan, the Firth of Lorne, and the Great Glen, reaching by this route the rich country round the Moray Firth, and thence pushing forward to Caithness and the Northern Isles. Others made their way by Loch Awe, Strath Fillan and the Tay Valley to the Eastern Midlands. Different racial strains seem to have been involved in these immigrations, marked by varying styles of chambered cairns. Thus in the south-west, around the broad estuaries of the Solway and the Clyde, we meet with cairns typically long—sometimes as much as 100 feet. A semicircular alcove at one end contains the entrance to the burial chamber, which is rarely more than 20 feet in length. This chamber is carefully built, the side walls corbelling forward until the space between them becomes narrow enough to be spanned by ponderous lintels. Typically, the chamber is divided by septae or partitions, slabs set on edge, yet not reaching up as high as the roof. The pottery associated with the burials in such cairns is usually round-bottomed and bag-shaped. It has been thought that such urns were made in imitation of leathern vessels used perhaps for the ordinary processes of cooking. Stone axes and "mace-heads", leaf-shaped arrow points of flint, and knives of flint or obsidian, are also found. Mostly inhumation seems to have been the practice; and the use of the chamber for successive burials has resulted in the fact that when the cairn is opened the skeletons are found in sorry disarray. Presumably those who made the funeral arrangements were able to scramble across the partitions in the chamber. No wonder the previous burials suffered! Animal bones often accompany the burials—either the remains of funeral feasts, or more probably offerings deposited with the dead as nourishment during their pilgrimage to the world beyond.

It should be added that the cairns themselves are never mere rickles of stones. They are very carefully constructed, often with a kerb of earth-fast stones or a dwarf wall built with slabs. As to the corbelled construction of the burial chamber, a distinguished archaeologist once described this as "a lazy way of avoiding the transport of large cap-stones". Such an assertion betrays a remarkable lack of understanding of a primary condition of human progress. It is precisely by devising such sound economies in the expenditure of labour that man's constructive capacity is developed. The corbelling in a chambered cairn is no more a sign of sloth than is the steel reinforcement that saves many tons of masonry in a modern building. Both are signs of man's increasing mastery of matter.

Up in the far north, in Caithness and in the Orkneys and Shetlands, a very different type of chambered cairn confronts us. Here the cairn may be long, oval, or round. Very often it has alcoves between a pair of projecting "horns" at either end. Sometimes the length of these cairns is enormous in proportion to the size of the burial chamber. Thus the horned cairn of Yarrows in Caithness is no less than 240 feet long: the chamber, at its broader and higher end, has a length of no more than 12 feet! In these northern cairns the chamber is approached by a passage, and is divided by partitions as in the south-western group: only in the north these septae do not meet across the chamber, thus leaving an unimpeded access from front to rear. Side chambers, not unlike the sacristies in a medieval church, are frequent. In the Orcadian cairns, the passage sometimes opens in the side of the cairn, not at its end. One most remarkable cairn, at Taiversoe Tuick in the island of Rousay, contains a two-storied chamber, each with a separate access. Burials in the northern cairns were usually by inhumation, but burning the dead was also sometimes practised. As many as thirty skeletons have been found in a single vault. The grave goods partake of the same general character as in the south-western group, but the pottery is of superior quality, more finely formed and richer in its decoration. There is the same association of animal bones with the burials.

Beyond a peradventure the noblest chambered tomb in northern Europe is Maeshowe on the Mainland of Orkney. Rising from the flat margin of the Loch of Harray like a boss upon a buckler, amid a tract of country teeming with prehistoric monuments, it arouses an anticipation from afar which is quickened into sheer amazement when the interior is penetrated.

Somewhat oval in shape, the mound measures about 115 feet in the longest diameter, and about 24 feet in height. Far out from its base it is enriched by a wide shallow ditch, the material from which was doubtless used to cover the surface of the monument—the substance whereof, it may be presumed, is made of stones. A passage, some 36 feet in length, carefully lintelled over and paved underfoot, but no more than 4 feet high, allows the visitor to crawl into the central burial chamber. This measures about 15 feet square, and is of the usual corbelled construction. Originally it must have been some 16 feet, or even more, in height, but the crown of the vault was removed by the Norsemen who, digging downwards, violated Maeshowe in the twelfth century. The present roof, accordingly, is modern. Opening on the three sides of the central chamber, in front and to the right and left of the entrance, small square doorways, placed about 3 feet above the floor, and once closed with stone slabs, admit to the actual burial cells, small charnel chambers each roofed by a single slab. All these dispositions are in the "common form" of the Orcadian chambered cairns. What gives Maeshowe its unique distinction is the superb quality of the megalithic masonry. The flagstones (in the passage more than 18 feet in length) have all been dressed to an ashlar-like finish, and are fitted together with such accuracy that in some places you cannot push a knife blade into the joints. At each corner of the central chamber, the better to carry the great weight of the corbelled roof, are massive internal buttresses, faced with monolithic slabs no less that 9 feet 8 inches high.

The effect of this sepulchral chamber upon the visitor, when once he has crawled in and stands upright in the centre, is nothing less than overwhelming—though it has abated something of its awe-inspiring mystery since the Ministry of Public Building and Works installed electric light! Clearly this has been the family burial place of a great prince—perhaps a precursor of the *regulus Orcadum* of whom we read in Columba's time.[1] Unfortunately, it has yielded no relics, for (as stated above) Maeshowe was ransacked by Norsemen in the twelfth century. By way of compensation, the tomb-robbers have left on its walls the largest and finest collection of runic inscriptions in the world. These inscriptions, mostly carved with some care, record the removal from the "howe" of treasure, apparently on more than one

[1] Adamnan, *Life of St. Columba*, bk. II, chap. 42.

occasion. Some of the spoilers describe themselves as *Iorsala-farar*, "Jerusalem farers"—i.e., Crusaders. No doubt these were members of Earl Rognwald's crusading party in 1150-51. Again, on 6th January, 1153, as recorded in the *Orkneyinga Saga*[1] Earl Harald and his men "were in Maeshowe while a snow storm drove over them, and two men among them went mad there; and that caused them much delay". As well as the runes, the

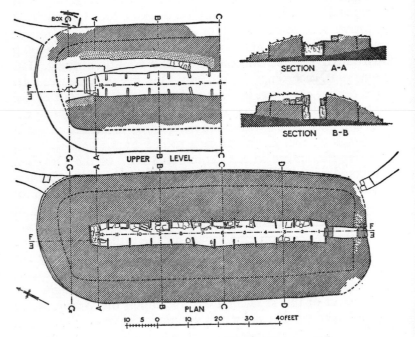

Fig. 2   Chambered Cairn at Midhowe, Rousay, Orkney
(By Courtesy, Ministry of Public Building and Works)

Norse intruders have left spirited carvings of a lion-like monster, a walrus, and a serpent-knot.

Another and highly remarkable type of Neolithic mausoleum found in the Orkneys has been aptly christened the "stalled cairn". The first to be discovered, and the most astonishing of them all, is the famous cairn at Midhowe, on the south-western coast of Rousay. This cairn, now under the custody of the Ministry of Public Building and Works, is protected by a stone

[1] Transl. A. B. Taylor, p. 310.

house, lit from the roof and furnished with a gallery, from which on this windswept site the interior of the cairn can be inspected in comfort. Usually, Neolithic burial places occupy commanding positions, with an extensive outlook: but the Midhowe cairn stands no more than 26 feet above high-water mark, and about 22 yards from the beach, from which it is separated by a low cliff. About a hundred yards to the north-west stand the ruins of the Broch of Midhowe (see p. 87). Thus within gunshot of each other, on this remote Orcadian island, stand two major British prehistoric monuments, separated from each other by a thousand years!

The Midhowe stalled cairn is indeed an imposing structure. It measures no less than 35 yards long and 14 yards in greatest width, forming an oblong with rounded ends. As always, the cairn has been very carefully built. It shows an outer and an inner ring of revetment walling, the latter midway in the substance of the cairn. A considerable portion of the outer wall is constructed of flagstones set in a herringbone pattern. Since the whole cairn structure was probably clad with turf, this decorative masonry could not have been seen. We must presume that it served some ritual purpose. The cairn lies, roughly speaking, north and south, and at the latter end is the entrance. This was found carefully blocked. No doubt the infilling would be removed, and thereafter replaced, on each occasion when a burial was made. The interior of this great ossuary forms a single long gallery, measuring 76 feet in length and about 7 feet in average width. The roof was lintelled. This gallery is divided into twelve compartments by partitions of stone slabs opposite each other, but not meeting, so as to leave a central alley extending the whole length of the interior. Thus are formed twenty-four stalls—for all the world like a long, narrow byre. Seven of these stalls on the eastern side contain a low bench or shelf; and on these were laid most of the burials. Only one skeleton was found in a western stall—whence it may perhaps be inferred that the mausoleum passed out of use before its capacity was exhausted. The skeletons were found in such a disordered state as to suggest, not merely disturbance caused by insensitive undertakers during successive funerals, but also the possibility that, as is not seldom the case among primitive folk, dismemberment had taken place before interment. Mortality was certainly frequent in those early days; the opening of the cairn was a matter of some labour, and perhaps controlled by superstitious taboos, or by the necessity of importing a high-ranking priest. So the corpses may have been saved up!

Bones of the ox, sheep, and various birds suggest funeral feasts. The pottery found with the burials was of the usual round-based Western Neolithic type, known to Scottish archaeologists as Unstan ware, from its first recorded place of discovery in Orkney —and indeed in the British Islands.[1] The only tool found was a flint knife, beautifully wrought.

The excavators of the Midhowe cairn found distinct evidence that it may have originally possessed an upper storey, like the neighbouring cairn at Taiverso Tuick. If so, it must have been one of the most remarkable Stone Age monuments in Europe. Attention has been called to the resemblance between the stalled cairns of the Midhowe type and the plans of certain "long houses" of Neolithic date, with two rows of wooden posts, which have been explored in the Isle of Man and in Ireland. Nothing indeed is more likely than that the abodes of the dead should be copied from those of the living: we may think, for example, of the "house tombs" of Minoan Crete, or the "house urns" of the later Bronze Age in Denmark.

Burial at Midhowe was by inhumation. In all, some twenty-five individuals could be identified—seventeen adults, six teenagers, and two infants. All were of the normal British Neolithic type, summarized as follows by Sir William Turner[2]:

> "Their crania were long and relatively narrow, purely dolicho-cephalic. The face was high in relation to its breadth, the jaw not projecting, the nose narrow. We have no knowledge of the colour of the skin, hair and eyes, but if the conjecture be correct that they were descended from the South European people of the Mediterranean basin, the skin would have been brunette, the hair jet-black, and the eyes black or dark brown."

Not surprisingly, these ancient folk at Midhowe suffered from rheumatism and arthritis. The leg bones show a characteristic flattening, due to the habit of squatting. Their average height may be estimated as 5 feet 3 inches.

The most astonishing example of a chambered cairn in the

[1] In England it is known as Windmill Hill pottery, from the type-site in Wiltshire.
[2] *Trans. Royal Soc. Edin.*, vol. LI, part i, p. 253.

Orkneys is the celebrated "Dwarfie Stone", in a damp and desolate valley of the mountainous island of Hoy. Its special character resides in the fact that it is not built, like the other chambered cairns, of drystone masonry, but hewn from the living rock—or rather out of an enormous mass of red sandstone, 28 feet in length some 14 feet in mean width, and nearly 7 feet in greatest height, which at some remote period has tumbled from the cliffs above. In the side of this block a passage, once closed by a well-fitted stone slab which still lies in front, admits to two lateral cells. Of these, the right hand cell has a shelf at the far end, doubtless for laying the bones upon, just as we found at Midhowe. The left hand cell has been broken into from above, possibly by Viking plunderers. Remarkable enough on its own account, the Dwarfie Stone has become famed throughout the English-speaking world through the part which it plays in Sir Walter Scott's *The Pirate*. It was within the mysterious recesses of the Dwarfie Stone that

> "Norna of the Fitful Head
> Mother doubtful, mother dread"

had her fateful interview with the demon dwarf, Trolld the Powerful, the "Dweller in the Stone".

In the Shetland Isles we meet with a peculiar type of chambered cairn, in outline resembling the heel of a boot, or sometimes like a cocked hat. One of these has yielded a sherd of Unstan ware. Since these "heeled cairns" are not found in the Orkneys, or indeed in Britain, but in their internal arrangements have certain parallels in Ireland, it has been suggested that the folk who built them arrived directly thence overseas, by-passing both the Scottish mainland and the Orkneys.

The western Neolithic folk have also left their characteristic chambered cairns in the Hebrides, where the types of cairn and associated pottery correspond in a broad way to those of the south-west. One remarkable cairn, at Unival in North Uist, deserves mention even in this brief sketch. The chamber was on the east side of the cairn, and, reached by a short passage, was multangular in outline. Set against its southern side was a shallow cist of thin slabs. This cist was an original feature of the chamber. About all this there is nothing very special. What renders the excavation of the Unival cairn important is the way in which, by careful observation, it was found possible to infer the ritual followed in the successive interments. The cist formed the actual burial place. The dead were inhumed, accompanied by the usual western Neolithic urns. After each burial the body was allowed time to decompose. Thereafter the cist was purified with charcoal, perhaps also with the idea of driving the now disembodied spirit from the tomb. On each occasion when a further funeral took place, the bones and urns of the last occupant were then taken out and piled against the walls of the chamber.

A special type of cairn confronts us at the north-eastern end of the Great Glen—in the valleys of the Ness and the Nairn, with an outlying group in Strathspey. The most famous of these is the group of three cairns at Clava, beside the battlefield of Culloden. They are circular in plan, with well-built kerbs, and contain central chambers likewise circular. In two of the cairns access to the chamber is gained by a passage, but the third has no entrance, and must presumably have been used, once only, as the burial place of some notable chief. Round each cairn is, or was, an outer circle of free-standing monoliths, and these increase in height towards the south-west—a peculiarity which we shall find recurring in the stone circles of Aberdeenshire. Unfortunately the potsheds found in the Clava cairns have perished: but it may well be that this group, though inheriting the "passage grave"

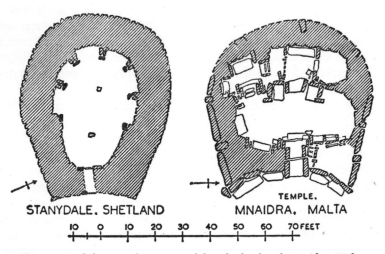

STANYDALE. SHETLAND   TEMPLE.
                            MNAIDRA. MALTA

10 0 10 20 30 40 50 60 70 FEET

Fig. 3   Neolithic temples at Stanydale, Shetland and Mnaidra, Malta
(*By Courtesy, Ministry of Public Building and Works*)

tradition, should be assigned rather to the Bronze Age than to the Age of Stone.

In a class by itself, among the Scottish monuments of the Stone Age, stands the "Neolithic temple" at Stanydale in Shetland. This remarkable structure may be described as pear-shaped, except that instead of the upper apex of the pear there is a concave façade, so that the outline of the whole resembles an exaggerated version of the "heel cairns", with which there is an obvious connexion. The Stanydale structure, however, is much larger than the cairns, measuring 65 feet in length. Also the interior chamber, reached by a passage opening in the incurving front, is of great size (39 feet by 22 feet) and possesses a series of six alcoves, or "side chapels" of very careful construction. In the centre of the area are two post-holes, indicating that the edifice had a wooden roof. Remains of the rotted posts were found in these holes: and perhaps the most astonishing thing about Stanydale is that the wood was found to be spruce. This tree is not on record in Scotland before the sixteenth century; and it has therefore been conjectured that the timber reached Shetland as drift wood from North America. Fragments were found also of pine wood, a tree which even today does not grow in Shetland. Potsherds scattered over the area included wares assigned to the later Neolithic period; portions of a Beaker; and decorated pottery of the High Bronze Age.

The excavator of Stanydale called attention to the strong similarity between it and the well-known temples of Malta and Gozo. The resemblances cannot be denied, and while the structure may well have been used for burials, as indeed our own churches often have been, it is difficult to escape the conclusion that here at Stanydale we have the veritable ruin of a Stone Age temple. Since it was discovered, a similar "temple", with the addition of a forecourt (strongly suggestive of a ritualistic function) has been excavated on the Isle of Whalsay. Beside it was a building of a different though kindred construction, showing evidence of domestic use. This has been thought to be the priest's house.

IV

The Bronze Age and its Monuments

AS in the case of their Mesolithic predecessors, we can hardly believe that the earliest farmer colonists of Neolithic times, entering the country from east and west, can have been numerous enough to have bulked large in the make-up of the Scottish people. The first really intensive settlement of Scotland took place at the close of the Stone Age, probably about 2000 B.C. About that time, the whole lowland region betwixt Tweed and Spey was colonized, in large numbers, by a new race that came directly west-overseas from the delta of the Rhine, and made their landfalls on the sandy beaches or in the mouths of the rivers. Particularly in the north-eastern "knuckle", from Dee round to Spey, the colonization was dense: so much so that the movement, albeit protracted, may in bulk result be not unfairly described as an invasion—comparable to the later settlement of the Anglo-Saxons in Britain. In marked contrast to their Neolithic predecessors, the new settlers were sturdily built, with bullet heads and square jaws. They inhumed their dead, for the most part singly, in short stone cists, usually not more than 3 feet 8 inches long. The skeleton is thus found in a flexed position, and alongside it is a characteristic grave pot, from its shape known as a beaker. Tools and weapons of flint and stone are also found, and occasionally such specialities as archers' wrist guards and handsome jet or amber necklaces. A funeral rite of some kind is indicated by a handful of charcoal often found in short cist graves.

After the Beaker Folk had been settled in Scotland probably for a few generations, two changes of cardinal importance occurred in their economy. First came the use of Bronze. As neither copper nor tin is found, to any significant extent, in

Scotland, the new and always precious metal had to be imported —principally from Ireland. The second change was the introduction of cremation, which became general in the High Bronze Age. The ashes of the dead were gathered into a large vessel, shaped like a plant pot, and known as a cinerary urn. Very often the urn was inverted over the deposit. Large numbers of such urns have been reported from the habitable areas of Scotland; yet the total number preserved is considerably less than that of the beakers. But it would be wrong to regard this as evidence of a decline in the population; for the cinerary urns, being often found loose in the soil, sometimes in groups as "urn fields", and lacking the protection of a stone cist, are apt to be destroyed, by the plough or the gravel-digger's tool, at the moment of discovery.

The characteristic sepulchral memorials of the High Bronze Age are the round cairns and the stone circles. No monuments are more typical of our Scottish skyline than the great round cairns which must surely mark the resting places of Bronze Age chiefs, and usually yield the cinerary urns of that period. On the lower grounds, but sometimes also associated with the great cairns, smaller burial mounds occur in groups, doubtless the graves of humbler folk. These are often associated with hut circles, stock pounds, cultivation terraces, and other signs of primitive occupation. Even more characteristic of the period are the circles of standing stones, popularly known as "Druid Circles". These usually yield cinerary urns of the Bronze Age, though some at least of their sites are known to have been first occupied by the Beaker Folk, or even by Neolithic people; while others again appear to have continued in use until the beginning of the Christian era. A type of stone circle, practically restricted to the region between the Dee and the Spey, is marked by the presence, almost always on the south-west sector, of a massive recumbent stone set between two flankers.

Let us look first of all at some of our Scottish Bronze Age cairns.

Close to the parish church of Collessie in central Fife, a large round cairn was excavated in 1876 and 1877, with remarkable care for the period, and the results were recorded with unusual precision. The cairn, which stands at a height of 200 feet above sea level, had already been in part removed to make way for a road. When complete it will have measured about 120 feet in diameter: but round much of its surviving area a kerb of earth-fast stones was found inside the mass, which the excavators thought represented the original base of the cairn—the stones having slid down over it in the course of ages. In that case the diameter of the cairn might have been about 70 feet. Its height before excavation was about 14 feet. Near what would have been the original centre a short cist was found, resting on the old ground surface, and containing the fragmentary remains of an inhumed skeleton, alongside which was a fine beaker. "This one burial was all that was discovered in the cairn, and it was apparently the burial for which the cairn was constructed." When the cairn had been mostly removed, it was noticed that the natural ground surface beneath it was covered over with burnt patches, as if some rite of purification by fire had been performed before the cairn was built. Nay more, under the cairn (and of course prior to its construction) two burial pits were found. One of these contained ashes, associated with the fragments of a beaker. Here therefore we seem to have one of the very few recorded instances of a beaker associated with a cremation. The other pit was much more interesting. It likewise contained a cremated burial, but without a beaker. Along with the burnt bones lay a bronze knife-dagger which had not been passed through the fire. Traces of the wooden sheath, which had been covered in cowhide, with the hair outwards, were recognized; and the pommel of the haft had been enriched by a gold fillet with repoussé ornament.

On the glebe land of Kilmartin, Argyllshire—a district exceedingly rich in prehistoric remains—a large but partly ruined cairn was explored in 1864 by Canon Greenwell, in his day a renowned investigator of barrows. Towards the south-western side of the cairn mass were two concentric rings of earth-fast stones, about 2 or 3 feet in height, and placed from 3 to 4 feet from each other. In the centre of the area thus enclosed was a short cist, containing an unburnt body, a jet necklace and an urn of the food-vessel type. This kind of funeral ware comes in time between the beakers and the cinerary urns: it is squatter and broader than the former, and is peculiar to the British area. Near the true centre of the whole cairn a second cist was found, likewise containing an inhumed burial and a food vessel. Another cairn on the same glebeland was found to contain a cist of unusual length, two of the end stones of which bore incised sculpturings. One of these depicted eight flat axes of Early Bronze Age type, while the other displayed what has been conjectured to be a highly stylized picture of an open rowing boat with its crew.

At Mill of Williamston, in Culsalmond parish, Aberdeenshire, on the site of a large cairn which had long previously been removed, a wooden coffin, fashioned from the split portions of a large oak tree, was discovered, containing an urn, which, from the description, was probably a food vessel. Such "tree burials" are more common in the lands surrounding the Baltic—particularly in Denmark: but a number have been found in Britain; and one of these, the famous Gristhorpe burial near Scarborough, carefully excavated and recorded so far back as 1834, contained a typical short cist skeleton, wrapped in hide held in place with a bone pin on the breast, while among the other grave goods was a bronze knife-dagger like the one from Collessie. There is therefore no need to invoke a settlement from Denmark to account for our British tree-burials. It should be noted that our Scottish example was a wooden cist, not a tree-trunk coffin.

The variety is immense of the Bronze Age burial cairns or barrow which have been explored, with care, greater or less, throughout Scotland: and the foregoing particulars must therefore be regarded as no more than a meagre selection from the more outstanding examples. But just as Christians have often buried their dead within churches, so we find interments of the Bronze Age in structures which beyond doubt were devised in the first place as temples. Such are the stone circles which, in their several varieties, remain the most characteristic monuments of the Bronze Age in Scotland.

In this matter of stone circles Scotland is a classic land. On 15th June, 1692, Professor James Garden, of the Chair of Theology in King's College, Old Aberdeen, addressed a letter to John Aubrey, the famous English antiquary—after whom the "Aubrey holes" at Stonehenge have been named—in reply to a query from the latter as to "circular monuments in Scotland". In his answer, Professor Garden gives a clear and (so far as it goes) an accurate description of some of the "Recumbent Stone" type of stone circle, so frequent in his neighbourhood. About one of these circles, at Old Keig on middle Donside, he writes as follows:

"I have only one thing more to add, which was written to me a few days since from the country; viz. that some persons who are yet alive declare that many years since they did see ashes of some burnt matter digged out of the bottom of a little circle, set about with stones standing close together, in the centre of one of those monuments which is yet standing near the church of Keig in the shire of Aberdeen."[1]

This may well be the earliest authenticated instance of the exploration of a stone circle in Britain. Professor Garden makes it clear that the burnt matter was recovered from a feature which, as modern excavation has shown not only at Old Keig itself but at other circles of the Recumbent Stone type, seems to have been a characteristic of this class of monument: namely, the presence within the circle of standing stones of a low and flat ring-cairn with a central hollow or open space. Usually this ring-cairn does not occupy the precise centre of the circle, but approaches near to the great recumbent stone and its two flankers, which group is always in the southern, and usually in the south-western, sector of the circle. Sometimes the ring cairn is, as it were, "fended off" from the recumbent stone by a kind of platform of boulders. It has often been noticed that the upper surface of the recumbent stone tends to be flat and horizontal. In his latest pronouncement on the subject, Professor Childe commented:[2]

"it would therefore provide a good 'artificial horizon' for observing astronomical phenomena, such as the heliacal rising or setting of a star, that were used by the priestly astronomers of Oriental antiquity for the correcting of the Calendar."

If there be any truth in this conjecture, then it becomes hard not to think of the "fender" in front of the recumbent stone as a kind of altar-pace. Thus we seem to be coming back to the older idea, once associated with the popular term "Druid Circles", that these mysterious structures were places of worship. And furthermore, as Professor Piggott has well remarked, "an open sanctuary is appropriate to a sky-god"[3]: so we are also getting back to the astronomical theories about origins of our stone circles which were so stoutly championed, at the end of the last century, by Sir Norman Lockyer.

[1] *Archaeologia*, vol. I, p. 342.
[2] *Ancient Monuments (Scotland)*, published by the Ministry of Works, p. 30.
[3] *British Prehistory*, p. 119.

A remarkable feature about the Recumbent Stone circles is that the standing stones increase in height towards the recumbent stone and its flankers in the south-western sector. We have already noticed this peculiarity in the Clava cairns. At Stonehenge, the most famous of British megalithic monuments, the climax is also towards the south-west. All this can be no coincidence; but what secret of ancient ritual is involved therein we shall perhaps never know.

Now that old ideas about the astronomical purpose of our stone circles seem again to be coming into favour, it is well that old errors should not at the same time be revived. Doubtless the enthusiasts who gather each Midsummer Day to watch the sun rise at Stonehenge will never be persuaded that the sun does not now rise on that morning over the "Heel Stone", and that it certainly did not do so in prehistoric times. But a much more weighty objection to the idea that Stonehenge was arranged to observe this special day was set forth by Lord Abercromby, who pointed out that in no known religion, ancient or modern, does the worshipper turn his back upon the interior of the temple, church, or mosque, and reverence his God by looking back through the open door.[1] From this consideration, Lord Abercromby, accepting the theory that Stonehenge was dedicated to the worship of the Sky-God, drew the inference that the high ceremony for which the temple was devised was not the summer but the winter solstice—when sunshine and heat, the Sky-God's gifts, both fail. If there be any truth in this, and bearing in mind the fact that our Recumbent Stone circles are likewise aligned towards the south-west, it could be that Lord Abercromby's conjecture is right, and that, in a northern land where the winter darkness and the winter cold are long and deep, the shortest day of the year was celebrated with appropriate ritual: a service doubtless of mourning, but yet in the sure conviction that the Sun-God would revive again—a matter of prime consequence to a primitive agricultural community.[2]

[1] Lord Abercromby, *Bronze Age Pottery*, vol. II, p. 94.

[2] Such a mournful observance must necessarily have involved a corresponding springtime festival of rejoicing over the re-birth of the Sun-God. This may have been the origin of the ceremonies once observed throughout Scotland on "Beltane Day", usually the first of May. It may not be without significance that in at least one case, at Tillybeltane in Perthshire, these rejoicings were associated with stone circles. See *Jamieson's Scottish Dictionary*, ed. J. Longmuir and D. Donaldson, vol. I, p. 161.

One of the most imposing of British stone circles is the Ring of Brogar, on the Mainland of Orkney, Here, within a shallow fosse, stands an immense megalithic circle, no less than 340 feet in diameter, and still retaining twenty-seven pillars, of which the tallest now rises 15 feet above the grass. Originally there would have been about sixty stones. On one of them has been incised an inscription in runes.

But of all our Scottish stone circles none excels, in weird impressiveness, the Standing Stones of Callanish, on a desolate moorland in the Isle of Lewis. Here we find a circle 37 feet in diameter, consisting of thirteen tall pillars, grey and hoary with lichen. This is approached from the north by an avenue of pillars, 27 feet wide, extending for a length of 270 feet, and now containing nineteen stones. To the south the avenue is continued, but shorter now and reduced in width: there remain here only six stones. On either side of the circle extends a "cross-arm", composed in each case of four stones. Within the circle is a chambered cairn, which was found to contain a cremated burial; and, at the west side of this, opposite the entrance to the chamber, rises the tallest pillar of all, 15 feet 7 inches in height above present ground level.[1]

Here again, bearing in mind Professor Piggott's dictum, it is impossible not to think of this great megalithic complex except in terms of ritual. We imagine the chambered cairn as the burial place of a priest-king, and the stone circle, with its stately avenue of approach, as erected afterwards to serve the purpose of ancestor worship by his successors. But what sort of ritual did they carry out in so impressive a temple? Once more old conjecture comes back into the picture; and we recall an observation made more than a century ago, by one who knew Callanish well:

"That the position was chosen and laid down from astronomical observation can easily be determined by visiting the spot on a clear night, when it will be found that by bringing the upper part of the single line of stones extending to the south to bear upon the top of the large stone in the centre of the circle, the apex of that stone coincides exactly with the pole-star: this is more readily done from

[1] The Ancient Monuments Commission speaks of a second cairn impinging on the eastern margin of the circle: but there is no mention of this when the site was cleared in 1857–8, and the slight mound now visible gives no warrant for being described as a cairn.

the south line being on sloping ground, so that looking along the line upwards to the higher level of the centre stone is very much the same as taking an observation through the incline of a telescope."

Among the temple-tombs of Bronze Age Scotland none exceeds the sheer complicated length of history, and none has been explored with more painstaking skill, than Cairnpapple in West Lothian. On a rounded basaltic hill no less than 1,000 feet in height, commanding a magnificent view over the Firth of Forth, and far beyond, including the Bass Rock, Schiehallion and Goat Fell, there was laid out, towards the end of the Neolithic Age, a temple consisting seemingly of small stones, arranged in an irregular arc open towards the west.[1] Within this, cremated burials were made. By the Beaker Folk this shrine was enlarged to twice its size, the original stones being taken out and replaced by a circle of a couple of dozen larger standing stones, set out on a different centre, and enclosed by an outer bank and inner quarry-ditch, with entrances north and south. What may be the primary burial within this new temple was a rock-cut grave, enclosed in a stone setting and containing a full-length inhumation with two beakers and a couple of indeterminate wooden objects. In its turn this great temple was demolished to make way for an Early Bronze Age burial cairn, in which were two cists, one containing a skeleton with a food vessel, the other a cremation, not inurned. In the High Bronze Age this cairn was doubled in size, and within the additional area were deposited two burials, beneath inverted cinerary urns. In each was found a pin of hartshorn, which had passed through the fire. Doubtless these pins had fastened the shroud. Finally, it is claimed in the Early Iron Age, four inhumed burials, at full length, were made between the cairn and the eastern sector of the rock-cut ditch.[2] Thus, in one form or another this astonishing combined sanctuary and shrine must have

[1] There is doubt whether the holes which defined this arc are the sockets for standing stones, or merely ritual pits, such as have been found elsewhere in British Neolithic sanctuaries. Professor Piggott, the excavator of Cairnpapple inclined to the latter view. I have followed the opinion of the late Professor Childe.

[2] Since this group of rock-cut tombs, made for three adults and a child (probably a family) are oriented, we cannot exclude the possibility that they may have been Christian. Early fourteenth-century pottery was found upon the site: and it is conceivable that a refugee household may have occupied the ruined cairns during the troubles of the Wars of Independence.

remained in use, more or less continuously, at least for a couple of millenia!

From the particulars that have been given, in this and in the preceding chapter, about our Scottish megalithic monuments—chambered cairns and stone circles—it must have become apparent to the reader that all the various varieties are closely connected, and that both the cairns and the circles partook of the dual character of temples and tombs. If, for example, the Clava cairn which has no passage can be conceived as undergoing a process of flattening down, with the resultant gain in importance of its surrounding circle of standing stones, we should have something very like the Aberdeenshire stone circles with their central ring cairn. In the same way, the "heel-cairns" of Shetland plainly share a common theme with the temple at Stanydale. At Callanish the stone circle, with its obviously ritualistic avenue of approach, is centred upon a chambered cairn. The south-western recumbent stone of the Aberdeenshire circles shares in a ritual axis which is the *Leitmotiv* of Stonehenge, the greatest of all British prehistoric temples; and we have found reason to suppose that the ritual for which these structures were designed was the commemoration of deaths, and its concomitant, the worship of ancestors. All are connected, in some way or another, with the nether world. Perhaps the modern archaeologist, pursuing his rigid classification of the different types of cairns and circles, is apt to forget that, just as our modern churches are often also burial places, so there is no fundamental distinction between the ancient cairns and circles of standing stones.

Ritual motives, too, have plainly inspired the "stone rows" or settings which are common in Caithness, and may be regarded as a pale reflection of the magnificent alignments of Carnac. And it is no less clearly a long forgotten ritual that has dictated the carving, on many of our standing stones as well as on boulders and live rock surfaces, of those mysterious "cup-marks" and "cup-and-ring-marks" in which some folk have fondly thought to detect star-charts. So far as Scotland is concerned, the one thing that we know for certain about them is that they are characteristic of our Bronze Age.

From the temples and dwellings of the Bronze Age dead we now turn to the far less frequently surviving abodes of the living.

Skara Brae: interior of Hut No. 1

Auquhorthies Stone Circle, Aberdeenshire

Earth-house,
Kildrummy,
Aberdeenshire

Broch of Mousa,
Shetland

Of these, our space will permit us to deal with no more than two examples.

Reference has already been made (p. 57) to hut circles. These are found in most parts of Scotland, surviving mainly on the high grounds where they have escaped obliteration by the plough. Quite commonly they are found in considerable groups, so as to form villages. Typically, a hut circle consists of a circular or oval ring of mingled stone and earth, usually about 3 feet thick and surviving to a height of perhaps 2 or 3 feet, and enclosing an area which may measure anything between 20 and 30, or even 35 feet in diameter. Quite commonly an entrance may be traced, and this is often on the south or sunward side. The interior may be paved, and usually contains a hearth. It is to be presumed that the superstructure was made of wattle and daub, or, it may be, of skins stretched upon a framework. Such primitive habitations may date from almost any period, until well within historic times. But in a group of hut circles at Muirkirk in Ayrshire potsherds were found which enabled the period of their occupation to be determined as the Early Bronze Age. Some of these were fragments of beaker, others more resembled Peterborough ware. Other relics found in one of the circles included pot-boilers, a hammer-stone, knives and scrapers of flint or chert, a jet armlet and a saddle-quern. These circles were situated at a height of 700 and 900 feet above sea level. Probably the settlers were attracted by the fertile limestone soil. In the largest circle a central hole was found, which had housed an oaken roof-post.

For the most vivid picture of a Bronze Age settlement in Scotland we must go to Jarlshof, on Sumburgh Head at the southern tip of Shetland. This place derives its name, and its earlier renown, from the part which the sixteenth-century ruined mansion on the spot plays in Sir Walter Scott's novel, *The Pirate*. Modern excavation has revealed that beneath and around this former home of the Bruces of Sumburgh lies what has been justly described as one of the most remarkable archaeological sites in the British Isles. A Bronze Age village was succeeded by a settlement of the Early Iron Age, including one of those enigmatic structures, the brochs, which we shall have to look at in a subsequent chapter. Later still came immigrants from Norway; in the thirteenth century the site was occupied by a substantial farmstead; and finally, before 1592, the notorious Earl Patrick Stewart built here the House

5

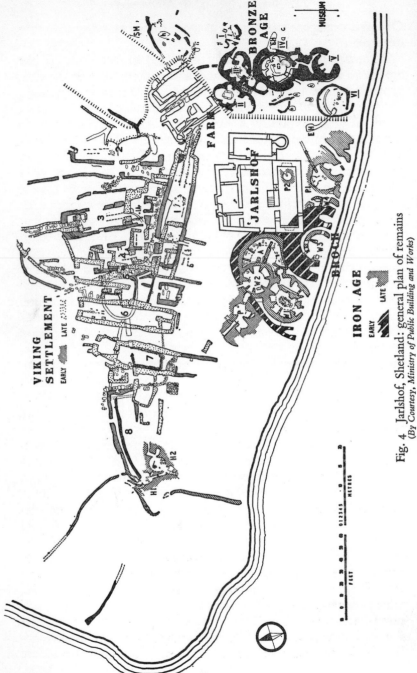

Fig. 4 Jarlshof, Shetland: general plan of remains
(By Courtesy, Ministry of Public Building and Works)

of Sumburgh—re-christened by Sir Walter Scott with the more high-sounding name of Jarlshof, which, already thus celebrated in literature, has now become familiar to archaeologists all the world over.

For the moment we are concerned only with the Bronze Age settlement. A group of six houses, enclosed by a boundary wall, was uncovered, but not all of them were inhabited at the same time. They may be described as ovoid huts of massive construction, containing a central hearth and a series of alcoves or cubicles in the walling round about. No doubt the roof was of turf, with a central vent for the peat reek. Here, once again, we have to note the resemblance between the dwellings of the living and the dead: for these Jarlshof huts have many points in common with the chambered cairns of the Northern Isles. The inhabitants were sheep and cattle farmers, but they also grew some bere—a primitive form of barley—and eked out their diet by cockles, limpets and mussels, cod and other sea fish, varied by wild fowl and seal. The pottery made by the earliest settlers may be described as belonging to the Unstan tradition of Neolithic ware. Later on, they made themselves vessels of clay or soapstone, more akin to normal Late Bronze Age types. They ground their grain in saddle querns; used shovels made of slate, or of the shoulder blades of oxen, for keeping the all-pervasive sand at bay: and made their kit of working tools, large and small, from the materials to their hand—bone, stone, and doubtless drift-wood. From access to bronze they were of course far removed, and for the greater part of its history the earliest settlement at Jarlshof must have exhibited a virtually Stone Age economy. But, wonder of wonders!—towards the end of this first phase in the story of Jarlshof an Irish bronze-smith settled among them, and made for his customers axes, swords, daggers, pins and gouges, of which the moulds have been recovered from the ruins of his workshop. What tempted him to this remote and backward community? Had the market for his wares been destroyed by the introduction of iron further south? How much bronze did he bring with him, and was he able to replenish his supply? We should dearly like an answer to these questions: but all is forever wrapt in the silence of the sand which, in the end, as at Skara Brae, overwhelmed this earliest settlement on the West Voe of Sumburgh.

V

The Coming of Iron: Earth-houses, Crannogs, Hill-forts

ACCORDING to the latest view, the use of iron became general in Scotland probably sometime after 200 B.C. No more than bronze was the new metal brought in as weapons in the hand of conquering invaders. Nevertheless, it is certain that, all through the later Bronze Age and the earliest part of the Age of Iron, Scotland was receiving constant fresh streams of racial immigration. It is equally certain that, by the time of the Roman invasion in the first century of our era, the upper strata of the population at least were of Celtic stock—though the mass of the inhabitants doubtless continued to be the descendants of the chambered cairn builders, the Beaker Folk, and the various immigrants who had found their way north, by east or west, during the long centuries of the Stone and Bronze Ages.

With the Iron Age, the monuments of the living, for the first time, bulk larger than those of the dead. Iron Age burials in Scotland are comparatively few in number. The dead were usually interred at full length in long cists, and the graves are poorly furnished. By contrast, the dwellings of the living became of great importance; and now, for the first time, we are confronted with massive and formidable works of defence. The reasons which impelled the Iron Age inhabitants of Scotland to erect such astonishing structures as the earth-houses, the crannogs or lake dwellings, the hill-forts of earthwork or stone, and above all the brochs, provide us with some of the most difficult and fascinating problems of Scottish prehistory.

The two chief regions in which *souterrains*, or earth-houses, are found in Scotland are Angus and Aberdeenshire. In every case where these subterranean structures have been carefully explored they are found to have been adjuncts to a hut-circle above ground. Typically, the Scottish earth-house takes the form of a long and usually curving gallery, built with drystone walls, which in their upper parts are corbelled forward on either side until the space between becomes narrow enough to be roofed over with massive lintels. Sometimes, particularly in Angus, these earth-houses branch out into lateral galleries, and indeed may assume quite complicated patterns. They were not mere cellars, as hearths, food-refuse, and other indications of habitation are found in them, and two Aberdeenshire earth-houses boasted a chimney. The relics found in them fix their date as about the first or second century A.D. Roman coins, pottery, and nick-nacks, doubtless imported in the course of trade, are frequently found in them, and two earth-houses, one at Newstead in Roxburghshire and another at Crichton in Midlothian, are partly built out of stones taken from a dismantled Roman building. Native relics found in the earth-houses include massive enamelled bronze armlets of Celtic design, but belonging to a type peculiar to Scotland.

Nor can the earth-houses have been refuges from an enemy; for the presence of the hut above ground would lead to the discovery of the *souterrain*, which then would become a death trap for its inmates. Now the Roman historian Tacitus, in his description of Germany, tells us how some of the inhabitants there were accustomed to dig caves in the earth, into which they retired in winter. Certain of the tribes whom Tacitus classed as Germans are now known to have been of Celtic or partly Celtic stock: and it is probable that the underground dwellings of which he had heard were earth-houses similar to those constructed by their Caledonian kinsmen. Dark and cheerless such an abode may have been; but we must remember that, in fine weather at least, the inhabitants would be out and about as long as daylight lasted. Certainly our Scottish earth-houses are wonderful pieces of construction: yet one cannot but recall the witty remark of a famous French archaeologist, who, on being conducted through one of them, observed that it passed his understanding how a people clever enough to build such a structure were not also clever enough to remain outside them once they were built. And it was a Scottish antiquary who remarked, *apropos* of the Aberdeenshire earth-houses, that the alleged lack of a sense of humour among the peasantry of that county could be due to the fact that, when one of their earth-house dwelling ancestors cracked a joke, he had to handle his neighbour's cheek to feel the resultant smile!

Another type of habitation, very characteristic of the Scottish Iron Age, is the crannog or lake dwelling. Here again, such constructions must not be construed too narrowly in terms of defence. In those early days, the mountain slopes and braes were densely clothed with forest; along the lake margins the narrow strips of land were liable to flood, so the inhabitants perforce erected their settlements on piles—by which ingenious device they were enabled to use the whole available area of flat land for stock-breeding and corn raising, as well as to engage in fishing on the lake and hunting in the woods. Moreover, it seems fairly certain that, in Galloway and Ayrshire at least, where the oldest of our lake-dwellings seem to have been located, some of them were built rather in bogs than in open water. Elsewhere, and particularly in the Highlands, crannogs continued to be used, and even to be built, all through the Middle Ages.[1] No doubt in most cases the defensive advantages of lake dwellings would not be wholly absent from the minds of their founders: but so far as concerns the south-western or oldest group of Scottish crannogs, which alone have been subjected to anything like systematic exploration, the scarcity of warlike gear found among the relics suggests that the lake dwellers enjoyed in the main a peaceful existence.

As a classic example of a Scottish crannog of the Early Iron Age, we may briefly consider the Lochlee crannog, near Tarbolton in Ayrshire, which was carefully, though incompletely, excavated

[1] "In the year 1580, in order that he might be able to subdue the insolence of the Lochaber men, Mackintosh caused an island in the loch commonly called Loch Lochy, to be constructed, which was called Alan-darrach, that is, the oaken island: for it was built on wooden beams; and while he was engaged on this, he had 2,500 men along with him in Lochaber, from the 29th day of May to the 21st day of August. In that island he placed a garrison, and while it was there, all the people of Lochaber were very submissive and obedient to their superiors; but as soon as the island was broken down they relapsed into their wonted rebellion and mischief."—MacFarlane's *Genealogical Collections* (Scottish Hist. Soc.), vol. I, p. 242.

A sixteenth century crannog, at Eadarloch in Loch Treig, was very fully explored, with most interesting results, by the late Prof. James Richie. See *Proc. Soc. Ant. Scot.*, vol. LXXVI, pp. 8–78.

in 1878-79. The locality is of special literary interest, because the farm on which the lake dwelling stands was tenanted, from 1777 until his death there in 1784, by William Burns, jointly with his two sons, Robert the poet and Gilbert. At Lochlee were written some of the earliest and most famous of Burns's songs, such as *The Death and Dying Words of Poor Maillie*, and *Death and Dr. Hornbook*. As to the farming at Lochlee, the poet described it as part of his "uphill gallop from the cradle to the grave".

In Burns' time the loch covered about nineteen acres, and the crannog appeared only as a small, bird-haunted island in the summer time, whose artificial origin was guessed by nobody. About 1838 the lake was drained, and at that time two dug-out canoes and some wrought beams were discovered. But the Swiss lake dwellings were still unknown to antiquaries, and it was not until a second drainage scheme was being carried out that the systematic exploration of the crannog was taken in hand.

The construction of the crannog was found to consist of layers of unbarked tree trunks (mostly oak or birch) laid in transverse order, all pinned down by piles arranged in circles and morticed into a framework of horizontal beams disposed both circularly round the crannog, and radially through its mass like the spokes of a wheel. Round the exterior of the mass was a broad stockade, forming "a strong binding framework to the whole island". The platform of the crannog was reached by a timber gangway. It appears to have supported a single dwelling, 39 feet square, floored with thick oaken beams. This house contained four successive hearths, a feature which suggests the gradual sinking or compression of the crannog. Outside the dwelling, but, surprisingly, upon what may be described as the courtyard, the excavators found a large midden. The whole mass of the crannog, including the hut platform, measured 10 feet deep. Its surface area may have had a diameter of say 100 feet. In such a dwelling the fire-risk must have been great; and the excavators found that it had several times been burned, which need not of course imply a hostile hand.[1]

[1] In some of the North Italian lake dwellings, conflagration layers recur in such regular sequence as to have prompted the suggestion that the inhabitants may have used this method of spring cleaning. When the lake dwelling grew too insanitary and vermin-ridden, the owners burnt it down to the water's edge and started again!

The Lochlee crannog is remarkable for the number and variety of the relics that it yielded. Unfortunately at that time conservation methods were in their infancy, so many of the articles found, particularly those made of wood, have since perished. As might be expected, wood played a large part in the domestic economy of the lake dwellers. Objects of this material included bowls, dishes, plates, a ladle, a large trough, implements resembling clubs and swords, a mallet, a hoe, pins and pegs of various kinds, three dug-out canoes, a paddle, and an oar, Bone was also much used. From it were fashioned chisels, awls, burnishers or smoothers, and spoons, and finger rings; while hartshorn was employed to make hammers, picks and pointed tools of various kinds; and horn, bone and wood alike provided handles for the iron implements, which included a gouge, a chisel, knives, a punch, a saw, a hatchet, a pickaxe, a ring or ferrule, an awl, two spear heads, five daggers or knives, and a curious three-pronged implement that may have served some culinary purpose. Very remarkably, only a single nail was found. A flat-bladed implement of bronze much resembled a modern paper-knife. Hammer stones were made of water-worn pebbles; there were whetstones of a hard argillaceous rock, stone rubbers and rotary querns, and a net-sinker. A greenstone axe[1] and three finely worked flint tools remind us that the use of stone cutting implements did not cease with the "Age of Stone". Spindle whorls were fashioned of clay or stone: and the inhabitants made themselves ropes of withies and mats of moss. Their shoes were of leather, with copper "tackets". Some of the ladies wore jet armlets, and blue and red pigments were in use. Contact with the Roman invaders was proved by the finding of Roman pottery, glass beads, a bronze pin, and fibulae or ornamental brooches of bronze; but the essentially Celtic character of the crannog civilization was revealed by a bridle bit of bronze and iron, as well as by a board made of ash, beautifully ornamented with "Late Celtic" incised

[1] In the famous lake-village at Glastonbury in Somerset, which was occupied during the centuries immediately preceding the Roman conquest, two stone axes were found. The excavator considered that "these specimens of axes were brought to the site by the inhabitants not so much possibly with a view to using them as implements as for some superstitious reason. For centuries they were considered to be thunder-bolts, and regarded with veneration because of some medical or other occult virtue attached to them."—A. Bulleid, *The Lake Dwellings of Somerset*, p. 65.

designs. The Romano-British objects may be dated to the second century; and that this was, broadly speaking, the epoch of the south-western lake-dwellings is confirmed by discoveries else-where—notably at the Hyndford crannog near Lanark, where some forty sherds of Samian ware were dug out. The dwellers in Lochlee grew corn or barley, kept herds of cattle and pigs, and flocks of sheep, rode on horses, and hunted the red deer, the roe deer and the wild boar. Many of the animal bones had been split to extract the marrow.

From the foregoing summary the reader will infer that the lake dwellers were in no sense an uncivilized folk, and in the con-struction of their abodes they displayed a high degree of engineer-ing skill.[1] The discovery of so elaborate a prehistoric settlement on ground farmed, sixteen centuries later, by Robert Burns recalls an observation made by Sir Daniel Wilson, the father of Scottish archaeology. Sir Daniel of course knew nothing about the Lochlee crannog, and was thinking not of lake-dwellings but of earth-houses when he penned the following thought-provoking sentence[2]:

> "How striking is the contrast between the artlessness of the Ayrshire cottage that served, with its straw roof, to satisfy the wants of one of the great master-spirits of all times, and the labour and ingenuity expended in producing these retreats of the Scottish aborigines."

Since the last war a crannog of Romano-British date in Milton Loch, Kirkcudbrightshire, has been explored with scientific pre-cision. It comprised a circular platform put together in the usual manner, and connected by a timber gangway with the shore; while on the opposite side a small harbour, or boat pen, had been enclosed by piling and stonework. On the platform was a circular hut, apparently containing a square inner room as at Lochlee. This room was lightly built of wattling, and had a central clay hearth, laid upon stone slabs. Among the few finds was an enam-elled dress-fastener, dated to the second century A.D.; and very

---

[1] The average reader of this book may find it difficult to envisage life upon a lake-dwelling. He will find an imaginative portrayal of a Romano-British crannog—Inch Crindil in the Black Loch near Stranraer—in Sir Herbert Maxwell's entertaining yarn, *A Duke of Britain*.
[2] *Prehistoric Annals of Scotland*, 2nd ed., vol. I, p. 112.

remarkably, the head and stilt of a wooden plough—perhaps the earliest recorded from Scotland.

Whatever may be thought about the earth-houses and crannogs, there can be no doubt as to the warlike purpose of the hill-forts, which are the most impressive monuments of the Scottish Iron Age. With such structures, as Professor Piggott has said, begins the story of military architecture in Britain. Sometimes constructed of earthwork, more often of dry-stone walling, sometimes vast in size, complicated in design, and devised with great tactical ingenuity and consummate engineering skill, these astounding defensive works, appearing so suddenly amid the "peaceful rusticity" of the native hut-circle villages, present many baffling problems to the student. Unfortunately very little has been done to solve these problems in the only way possible, by scientific and thorough excavation. Some have thought to explain them in terms of the well-known Celtic addiction to clan or tribal warfare: but in many cases these massive structures are situated too close to each other to permit us to believe—on the assumption indeed that they are more or less of one date—that they could have been the refuge of rival communities large enough to command the human resources requisite to construct such formidable undertakings. In central Aberdeenshire, the location of the group of massive hill-forts which straddles the county has prompted the inference that they may be the response of the inhabitants to the Roman invasions. That they were permanently occupied is hardly credible, if only because of the height of the mountain summits which they crown. The hill-fort on Tap o'Noth, for example, is 1,855 feet above sea level: that on Bennachie crowns a peak rising to a height of 1,698 feet. So far as excavation goes, the evidence seems clear that our Scottish hill-forts belong to the Iron Age. In a number of them, Roman relics have been found: one fort, Ruberslaw in Roxburghshire, had some Roman stones built into its walls; while at Clatchart Craig, near Newburgh in Fife, a chunk of Roman masonry was found in the main rampart, which can have come only from the neighbouring Roman legionary fortress and harbour installations at Carpow on the Tay. Few of our hill-forts seem to have had a regular water supply, a circumstance which suggests that they were not designed for permanent occupation, but rather as a temporary refuge for the inhabitants with their flocks and herds. Upon an emergency, enough water for a few days could be carried up in skins and vessels of wood or earthenware. In the Welsh hill-forts, which are now known to have been constructed during the Roman period, amphorae or Roman wine jars have been found, which clearly were used for storage purposes.

In a number of cases the dry-built walls of our hill-forts were disciplined by an ingenious system of bonding timbers, so as to prevent the collapse or down-slipping of the weighty mass. Such walls are described by Caesar in his account of the Conquest of Gaul: he calls them *muri Gallici*, Gallic walls. If in such a wall the bonding timbers catch fire, either by hostile hands or as a result of the accidental conflagration of the wooden or wattled huts inside, then under certain conditions a forced draught and a very high temperature can be engendered on the windy hill-top— with the result that, if the stone be suitable, it may be partly melted into slag-like masses, in which are seen the impressions of the burnt logs. Thus were formed what for long have been known as "vitrified forts". Scotland is the classic land for such structures, since it was in the Highlands that they were first noticed, excavated and most carefully described by John Williams, "mineral engineer", in his epoch-making little book, published in 1777.[1] About forty-five of these vitrified forts have been recorded in Scotland: there are a few in England and Wales, one or two in Ireland; and on the Continent they are known in France, Germany, Czechoslovakia and Hungary. In a number of cases, such as Abernethy in Perthshire, where a fort built in the Gallic manner has not been set on fire, the voids left in the wall by the decayed logs have been found. Such a method of construction, whereby a dry-stone wall is laced with bonding timbers, was of course an early invention. It is also widespread: for example, Fort Chitral on the old North-west Frontier of India, which in 1895 stood a famous siege, was built in this manner.[2]

[1] *An Account of Some Remarkable Ancient Ruins lately discovered in the Highlands and Northern Parts of Scotland*, 1777. When the first copy of the MS was sent to a London bookseller, it was rejected as a fiction!

[2] "The walls are made of coarsely-squared timbers, some 4 inches by 4 inches, laid horizontally between layers of stones embedded in mud mortar . . . The long timbers are strengthened in position by short cross-pieces, similarly made of inflammable pine wood, which stick out some few inches from the wall like stumpy almonds from the surface of a plum pudding. At the corners of the

How immense was the effort involved in building such a *murus Gallicus* may be gauged from the fact that for the vitrified fort of Finavon in Angus—one of the few that has been excavated with reasonable completeness and precision—it has been computed that 250,000 cubic feet of stone and 100,000 cubic feet of timber will have been required. Under natural forest conditions, the timber might represent some 50 acres of woodland.

Although so little excavation has been done upon our Scottish hill-forts, much care has been bestowed upon their ground-surveying and air-photography—notably in the counties so far covered by the Royal Commission on Ancient Monuments. Several different kinds or groups of hill-forts have been recognized; but to set forth the details of this provisional classification would go far beyond the scope of the present work. It is clear that in more than one case the fort has undergone alteration or reconstruction—a fact which points to successive occupations, perhaps over a prolonged period. No more can be said than barely to mention the stone-built farmsteads, enclosed by a ditch and a rampart of stone, which occur in the area south of the Forth, and have been shown to have been occupied during the Romano-British period. Upon the whole, it seems clear that no single explanation will suffice to account for the origin and distribution of our Scottish hill-forts.

In his description of Gaul, Caesar distinguishes between *vici* or open villages, *castella* or camps of refuge, and *oppida* or *urbes*, fortified towns. In Scotland, Caesar's *vici* will be represented by our hut settlements, including the earth-houses. The *castella* will

---

towers, where the long lateral timbers overlap, they are often fixed together by a clumsy tenon and mortice, and jut forth several inches beyond the uneven walls. Projecting knobs are therefore to be found all over the fort, but particularly close together upon the towers. A monkey would find them convenient steps to climb anywhere, while a little Chitrali could follow him in most places. "The immense amount of wood in the towers, where the intervening layers of masonry are only a few inches thick, is not all disclosed to the view. For there is an inner pine-wood frame corresponding to that seen from without, separated from it by about a foot of rubble. In very dry weather it would be almost sufficient to light one of these structures with a torch to make it blaze like a blast furnace." Sir George S. Robertson, *Chitral: the Story of a Minor Siege* (ed. 1905), p. 231. See the illustrations at p. 348, and in G. J. and F. E. Young-husband, *The Relief of Chitral*, p. 128.

be our hill-forts. *Oppida*, hill-towns, are represented in Scotland only by such sites as Traprain Law in East Lothian and Kaimes Hill in Midlothian. Kaimes Hill we know was occupied in the third century: but the only Celtic *oppidum* so far explored in Scotland is the famous hill-top town of Traprain—one of the most notable prehistoric and proto-historic sites in Britain, at present being ruthlessly quarried away for road metal by the East Lothian County Council! Traprain Law is known throughout the archaeological world by reason of the great hoard of Roman silver found there in 1919. This however was an interpolation, hastily buried on the hill by raiders after the *oppidum* had been abandoned, early in the fifth century. The Celtic hill-town provides us with more than enough of interest on its own account. Within a substantial stone rampart enclosing some 32 acres, the township contained numerous huts of wattle and daub, each with its hearth. Some of the better-class buildings were of squared woodwork, held together by iron nails and holdfasts. The native relics found in remarkable profusion resemble those from other centres of our Celtic civilization. There are brooches, pins, buttons, dress-fastenings, and harness-mountings of bronze, sometimes enamelled and sometimes silvered; bracelets, pins, rings, and other ornaments of jet; beads of glass and amber; glass bracelets, or armlets, sometimes enamelled; tables for a game of chance; coarse native pottery; and a large quantity of miscellaneous domestic utensils and tools in stone, bronze and iron. Local arts and crafts are amply vouched for by moulds used to cast dress-fasteners and such like minor objects. Agriculture is represented by sickles and a hoard of barley. The part played by female hands is indicated by numerous spindle-whorls in earthenware, stone or jet. But alongside these objects of native manufacture there is also a considerable admixture of Roman relics. These comprise pottery, including sherds of the famous Samian ware; portions of Roman glass; and a goodly number of coins, which had evidently been the currency of the inhabitants. Also among the Roman objects found was a beautiful folding spoon of bronze; and—most remarkable of all—a *stylus*, or iron pen for writing on wax. One is tempted to believe that the language and script of the imperial race were finding their way with the coins and nicknacks into this Celtic township; a supposition for which confirmation seems to be forthcoming in a potsherd upon which the letters I.R.I. had been inscribed in the Latin alphabet apparently after the vessel of which the fragment formed a part had been broken. This is in no way unlikely, since the legends on ancient British coins and other evidence prove that Latin was understood in the south of England before the Roman conquest.

VI

The Brochs and their Builders

WITH the brochs, Scottish prehistoric archaeology reaches its climax. They are unique in all the world. Their evolution, the circumstances which gave them origin, and the purposes that they were designed to serve, alike remain obscure—despite much careful excavation and a great deal of earnest thought and vigorous debate.

Typically, a broch may be described as a hollow round tower of carefully built dry-stone masonry. A good average internal diameter at the base might be given as 32 feet; but, as it rises, the circumference of the tower is gradually reduced, so as to give a conical profile: the bell-shape of the Broch of Mousa (Shetland) is probably due to settlement. There seems little doubt that the brochs were all lofty structures. The present height of Mousa— the only broch that has survived substantially complete—is 43 feet; that of Dun Carloway (Lewis), little short of 40 feet; while the two Glenelg brochs (Dun Troddan and Dun Telve) are known to have been once rather higher than the latter figure. The entry into the courtyard is narrow, low, and well defended, with a stone-slab door held in place against a check by stone or wooden bars received into slots on either side. One or more cells occur at ground level, roofed over on the so-called "false vault" or corbelled system—shaped in section like an old-fashioned bee-skep. Round the interior of the broch, at a height varying from 4 to 12 feet, runs a scarcement, which supported a kind of verandah, the post-holes of which may remain in the courtyard floor. This floor is usually paved, and contains a central hearth. Often there is also a well or cistern. In one or two cases we find a second scarcement, higher up the tower. But the most remarkable

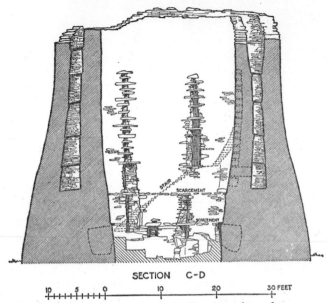

SECTION   C–D

Fig. 5   Broch of Mousa, Shetland: section through tower
(By courtesy, Ministry of Public Building and Works)

feature about the brochs is the way in which the thick walls of
the tower are built hollow above the ground level, with a central
void roofed over by tiers of stone lintels, carried all round the
building. In this way are formed a series of mural galleries, one
above the other: but since owing to the conical exterior shape of
the broch, the walls, which may be 15 or 16 feet thick at base,
decrease in thickness the higher we go, it is obvious that only the
lowest galleries could have served any practical purpose, whether
for storage or for habitation. Clearly this singular method of
building was devised to secure economy in stone and labour:
moreover, each successive gallery roof formed a building platform for the next stage, so that scaffolding was eliminated—a
prime consideration in a land where timber was scarce. At
intervals round the interior of the tower occur a series of vertical
window-like openings, one for each gallery, and of course decreasing in size with the successive contraction of the galleries. These
openings must also be regarded as a device for economy in
material, and reduction in the weight of the whole mass, which
otherwise might result in settlement, such as has in fact taken

Kirkmadrine,
Wigtownshire

Dunnichen, Angus

Aberlemno, Angus

Kildalton, Islay

Kisimul Castle, Isle of Barra

place at Mousa. Often, indeed, these voids rise vertically above
the lintelled opening of a basal cell, and in such cases are plainly
designed to relieve the pressure on the latter. From the courtyard,
sometimes from the entrance passage opposite the guard cell,
rises a narrow stair, which curves round inside the wall of the
broch in a gently winding ascent, traversing each gallery in turn,
until it finally emerges upon what will have been a fighting deck
upon the wall-head. It is most unlikely that the brochs were
roofed over.

The above description is, of course, a generalized one. No two
brochs are exactly alike. Moreover, there are regional differences:
for example, in the Hebrides, basal galleries are found, but these
are seldom present in the Northern Isles. There are other
differences between the brochs in the two areas.

It is evident that in the brochs we are confronted with a highly
specialized type of defensive dwelling, devised and carried out
with consummate skill. As Joseph Anderson put it, more than
eighty years ago[1]:

". . . the concentration of effort towards the two main objects of
space for shelter and complete security was never more strikingly
exhibited, and no more admirable adaptation of materials so simple
and common as undressed and uncemented stone for this double
purpose has ever been discovered or suggested. Perhaps there is no
characteristic of the typical structure more remarkable than the
extreme constancy of its essential features. The uniformity of plan
and construction is so unvarying among all the known examples
that there exists no means of tracing the development of the form
through a series of primitive or immature stages."

Since these words were written, some have thought to see a
connexion between the brochs and a class of prehistoric forts in
the Hebrides which have been termed "galleried *duns*".[2] These
resemble the brochs in having lintelled galleries within their walls
and entrances defended in a manner more or less similar to that
in the brochs: but differ from them in their larger area, irregular
plan, and lack of height. Such galleried *duns* have been claimed as
the primitive precursors of the perfected broch: but this conten-
tion was decisively rejected by no less an authority than the late
Professor Brøgger, who forcibly maintained that "it is in the

[1] *Scotland in Pagan Times: the Iron Age* (1883) p. 204.
[2] *Dun* in Gaelic means a fortified site.

nature of things final that one must naturally look for origin within the area where the broch is most strongly and densely represented, not on the outskirts".[1] On this view, the Hebridean galleried *duns* will represent, not the genesis of the broch idea, but the final stage in its degeneration, as manifested in a marginal area remote from the special circumstances (whatever they were) of the centre of origin. And, on Professor Brøgger's view, this centre of origin will have been the Orkneys, the earliest seat of consolidated Pictish power, a rich and populous land which had for long held a pre-eminence of dry-stone construction, due clearly to the splendid building material that it yields in its Old Red Sandstone flags. Let us not forget Maeshowe, which, though a thousand years older than the brochs, and finer built than any of them, in more than one of its constructional features anticipates the technique of the brochs.

When all is said and done, the broch design remains so standardized as to prompt the suggestion, made by more than one investigator, that the conception was a single one, evolved in the mind of some highly gifted master of construction. Such an idea is perhaps somewhat hard of acceptance in these modern days, when the "comparative method" of classification, and the dogmas of evolution and typological development have been pushed to a point where there is little room left for the individual genius thinking out something new on his own. Yet the history of military invention during two world wars may well inspire us with a different view. And the archaeologist should remember those extraordinary, highly specialized military training camps of the Vikings, the *Trelleborgen*, which appear so suddenly in Denmark in the tenth century.

It appears likely that very few broch towers stood alone. Certainly many of them were enclosed by formidable outer defences, like the curtain walls and fosse surrounding the keep of a medieval castle. In one case at least, the Broch of Clickhimin (Shetland) careful excavation has shown that this curtain wall is older than the broch. Within the curtain wall may be found a warren of hut foundations, often assuming a bewildering complexity, as at Gurness and Midhowe (Orkney). In most cases these hutments seem to date from a later period, after the broch tower had ceased to be occupied. Sometimes the interior of the tower

[1] A. W. Brøgger, *Den Norske Bosetningen På Shetland-Orknøyene*, 1930, p. 97.

itself is found to be crowded with such secondary constructions.

The relics found in the brochs are very numerous, and give us a clear picture of a population busily engaged in farming and weaving. Querns, both of the older saddle and newer rotary types, carding combs of bone or hartshorn (used to pack the threads on to the loom) whorls, pots and dishes, and other vessels of handmade pottery or whalebone, whale-bone lamps, double edged combs for personal use, whetstones, bone dice, and iron tools of various kinds are among the objects commonly found. Roman pottery, saucepans and ladles, brooches of bronze or silver, and an occasional coin fix the general period of the northern brochs in the first and second centuries of our era.

The distribution of the brochs raises problems of extreme importance. They are most frequent in the Northern Isles and in Caithness and Sutherland. A second broch area is found in the Hebrides, with the adjacent coasts of Ross and Inverness. Quite outside the main broch area, thus seen to be in the north and west, two brochs are found in Angus, one in Perthshire, one in Stirlingshire, two in Selkirk, one in Berwickshire, and one or two in Galloway. In all, there are probably some 500 certain cases of brochs in Scotland. A noteworthy fact is that all brochs stand on good farm land.

The archaeological evidence is clear in fixing, within broad limits, the period of the brochs—though it must be remembered that the earlier excavators failed to distinguish between relics contemporary with the broch itself, and relics associated with the secondary structures built subsequently in and around the tower. Moreover, it is becoming clear that more than one strain is involved in what may be described as the "broch culture". Nevertheless, the combined evidence of archaeology and distribution maps points to the conclusion that the broch type was fully evolved and in active use during the second century, at the time of the Roman penetration of Scotland from the south. Just as the distribution of Roman forts and camps in Scotland indicates an occupation diminishing in intensity, and finally petering out, before it reached the Great Glen, so in the reverse direction the distribution of the brochs reveals another and contemporary invasion, or perhaps rather an infiltration, of Celtic war-lords coming from the Northern Isles: occupying the adjoining parts of the mainland with diminishing intensity as far as the Great Glen; and beyond it, in sporadic fashion, reaching as far south as the semi-Romanized buffer states on the imperial frontier. Who, then, were these broch-building intruders from the north? There can, I think, be only one answer. They were the ancestors of the people afterwards known in history as the Picts, whom our ancient authorities describe as having entered Caledonia overseas from the north.

It has been considered by more than one archaeologist that the astonishing correspondence between the relics found in our northern brochs and those which are characteristic of the Somerset lake-dwellings—the "Glastonbury culture"—can best be explained on the theory that upon the disruption of that culture (probably by the Belgic invaders in the first century B.C.) some of the lake-dwelling chiefs made their way northwards by the traditional western seaboard route, and established themselves as a dominant aristocracy, the "broch lords", in the Northern Isles.[1] Such circular *duns* as Dunburgidale in Bute and Ardifuar in the Crinan district, resembling in some of their features both the brochs and the Cornish circular forts like Chun Castle, could well mark stages in this northward migration from south-western Britain. In 1944 the late Professor Childe acutely surmised that the remarkable record, preserved by a fifth-century Roman historian, that the Orkney Isles were added to the Roman Empire in the course of the Claudian conquest may embody the recollection of an authentic fact, namely that the broch builders, having recently arrived from a part of Britain which had long been in close touch with the Roman Empire, on the news of his invasion of Britain sent an embassy to Claudius, as so many of the southern Britons had done during the invasions of Julius Caesar.

Against whom did the "broch lords" find it necessary to defend themselves in such formidable castles? Against the natives whom they found in the Northern Isles? Against each other, in the incessant clan warfare endemic in Celtic societies? Against sea-borne raiders, seeking captives for the Roman slave market? Against their southern neighbours, the Caledonians embattled in their massive hill forts? And how can we explain the fact that brochs are sometimes found so close together as almost to elbow

---

[1] But see a cautionary statement on this matter by Professor Piggott in *The Problem of the Picts*, ed. F. T. Wainwright, pp. 59–60.

each other?[1] To all these questions no certain answer can be given. For their solution more spade-work, in the most literal sense, is the only way towards providing a key.

The scale of this book does not permit me to offer even the briefest description of the few brochs, such as Midhowe and Gurness in Orkney, or Skitten in Caithness, which have been excavated with modern scientific precision. Nevertheless, something must be said about the remarkable broch at Torwoodlee in Selkirkshire, which was investigated with great care in 1891, and again in 1950-51. Situated upon a lofty site overlooking the Gala Water, about two miles above Galashiels, this broch lies far to the south of the normal broch area.[2] Its special importance consists in the fact that it brings the broch lords, coming down from the north, into direct contact first with the native hill-fort builders and then with the Roman invaders pushing up from the south. To begin with, the broch—a large one, with a courtyard diameter 40 feet—was found to have been built within the ramparts of an Iron Age hill-fort; and that the broch is an interpolation was shown by the way in which its ditch had been cut into the defences of the fort. Nay further, within the area of the broch tower were discovered the post-holes and fragments of the wattling and daub of one of the circular huts belonging to the hill-fort. Within this hut, and elsewhere inside the area of the hill-fort so far as this was investigated, no Roman relics were found. The only objects that could be referred to the fort dwellers were one or two sherds of coarse native pottery and the upper stone of a rotary quern. Upon the whole, it seemed to the excavators that the hill-fort probably dated from about the beginning of the first century A.D., and that the fort had been abandoned before the building of the broch. Whether the broch lords had driven out the hill-fort folk is not so clear.

About the broch itself the remarkable feature is the large number and variety of the Roman relics that it contained. These comprised quantities of potsherds, including much of the fine Samian table ware, pieces of amphorae or wine jars, used for general storage purposes, and coarse culinary pottery of various types; part

[1] In Rousay six brochs are found within a total distance of four miles: at Keiss in Caithness is a group of four within a square mile.

[2] There is a second broch, the Bow Broch, some two miles further up the Gala Water, but within the county of Midlothian.

of a glass armlet, and fragments of glass
bottles, bowls and jugs; a terret and an
enamelled stud, both of Romano-British
types; and a silver denarius of Titus (A.D.
79-81). All this Roman material can be
firmly dated to about A.D. 100. Professor
Piggott, who conducted the more recent
excavations on the site, considers that these
Roman relics must be loot from the fort at
Newstead, which we know was stormed,
sacked, burned and wrecked by the Caledonians just about that time. It would
therefore appear that the broch lords of
Torwoodlee may have had a hand in its
destruction.

The Romans returned to Newstead when
Lollius Urbicus re-occupied southern Scotland prior to the building of the Antonine
Wall about A.D. 143. Then the heavy hand
of imperial vengeance fell upon the broch
lords at Torwoodlee. During the recent
excavations, the tower was found to be
overthrown, and its materials cast down
into the ditch, with a systematic, ruthless
thoroughness which left no doubt in the
mind of Professor Piggott that it was the
work of Roman hands. Most extraordinary
of all, a cist containing the skeleton of a
young woman was found among the debris,
in circumstances which made it clear that
the burial must have taken place during
the work of demolition. Did the Romans

force the broch lords and their women folk to destroy their
own tower? And did one of the women die upon the job—
perhaps under the lash of a Roman slavedriver, even as the children of Israel were beaten by their Egyptian taskmasters? To these
questions we shall never know the answers. But the fact that the
woman was so carefully buried in a massive stone cist surely
suggests that she was a person of consequence. Could she have
been the wife or widow of the chief of the broch tower, com-

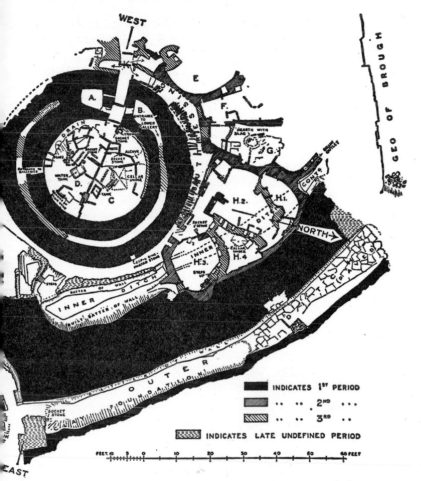

Fig. 6 Broch of Midhowe, Rousay, Orkney: general plan
(*By courtesy, Ministry of Public Building and Works*)

pelled to bear a hand in the destruction of her home? Dimly across the centuries we seem here, perhaps, to glimpse an instance, dramatically poignant, of the forced labour against which Calgacus in his famous speech protested with such bitterness: "Our bodies and hands they wear and consume, in paving of bogs and of woods, with a thousand stripes and indignities."[1]

[1] Tacitus, *Agricola*, chap. XXXI: from the magnificent translation by Sir Henry Savile (1598).

We must now take another look at Jarlshof in Shetland, that famous prehistoric site of which some account has been given in chapter IV. Here, probably in the first century A.D., the broch lords took possession of the old Bronze Age village—perhaps by then derelict and half overblown by the all-pervasive sand. Within a stout curtain wall the newcomers built themselves a massive round tower of the usual broch type. A good half of this tower, and of the oval courtyard attached to it, has now been removed by the sea. Probably the broch was early deserted, and partly in ruins, when fresh occupants built within its courtyard a group of what are known as "wheel-houses"—circular dry-stone huts with radial partitions, not unlike the cross-section of an orange or a grapefruit. Even into the interior of the ruined broch itself was, in the end, inserted one of these curious structures. They belong to a kind of Iron Age dwelling commonly found in the Hebrides, also in Caithness, where they are known as "wags". Such wheel-houses had a bee-skep roof, of stone or divots, with a louvre or smoke vent above the central hearth. The radial partitions did not, of course, extend right across the building, and the side compartments or cells which they formed were lintelled over at a height from 8 to 10 feet above the floor.

Can these Jarlshof wheel-houses have been erected by the successors of the original inhabitants of the settlement—herdsmen, crofters and fisher folk as before—reoccupying their old home after the departure or extinction of the broch lords? Still later, other huts, of simpler fashion, were built further out towards the north-west. This final Celtic village at Jarlshof survived until the "*papae*" or first Christian missionaries set foot in the Shetland Islands. This we know from an eighth-century Celtic cross, with expanded terminals, found in one of the latest huts. Finally, about the year 800, arrived the Norsemen—peasant farmers faring forth west-overseas. But this is a tale to be told in a later chapter. All in all, the pre-Norse settlement at Jarlshof must have persisted, in one form or another for a full two thousand years.

VII

The Roman Invasions

WE enter Scottish history, it has been said, in the track of the Roman legions. The first precise date in the history of our land is A.D. 80, when Julius Agricola, the most famous of all the Roman Governors of Britain—thanks to the noble biography written by his son-in-law, the great historian Tacitus—in the course of a vigorous forward policy overran Scotland as far as the River Tay, where he planted a legionary fortress, probably occupied for little more than a year or two, at Inchtuthil, near the point where that river emerges from the Highlands. The first inhabitant of Scotland whose name is known to us is Calgacus, the Caledonian war-lord, who was defeated by Agricola at the great battle of Mons Graupius in the year 84. The site of this famous conflict is still unknown: but one thing is certain, that it was far further north than was imagined by those two doughty disputants, Sir Arthur Wardour and Mr. Jonathan Oldbuck, when they wrangled so fiercely over the authenticity of the Kaim of Kinprunes. The furthest north known Roman permanent fort, at present recorded only from air survey, is at Cardean in Angus, twelve miles north-east from Inchtuthil. But beyond this a chain of marching camps—the nightly bivouacs of a Roman army on active service—extends onwards through Aberdeenshire and Banffshire to the shores of the Moray Firth. These camps belong to more than one period. Some of them may represent the Agricolan invasion: others, that of the Emperor Septimius Severus, who between A.D. 208 and 211 conducted a massive punitive expedition, by sea and land, against the unruly Caledonians, and is said to have penetrated farther north than any of his predecessors. Excavation has shown that he made use of two naval bases in what is now Scotland, one at Cramond on the Firth of Forth, and the other at Carpow on the Firth of Tay, which for the time indeed became a legionary fortress.[1] Still later, about the year 300, another Emperor, Constantius Chlorus, appeared in person in Britain, and conducted important operations against the northern clans, now lumped together by Roman chroniclers under the general name of "Picts". At this time the naval base at Cramond was reconditioned. Further vigorous offensives against the Picts, and their new allies, the Saxon raiders from across the North Sea, and the Scots from Ulster, were carried out, by naval and military forces acting in combination, under the command of Theodosius the Elder in 368, and again by Stilicho in 395.

The story of all this activity is summed up, in one of the best known Histories of Scotland, in a chapter entitled "the Roman episode". When we reflect that the Romans were in occupation of southern Britain during as long a period as that which separates the Scotland of Queen Mary and John Knox from the Scotland of today, and that during the whole of that time they were exerting their influence upon our land, alike in war and peace, it must be allowed that the Roman "episode" was a pretty considerable one. It was only, however, during a comparatively limited period, from the building of the Antonine Wall, betwixt Forth and Clyde, in or about the year 143, until its final abandonment probably about 196, that the Romans were in continuous effective military occupation of what may conveniently be described as the Southern Uplands. Nevertheless, structural remains of the Roman period surviving in our country are both numerous and impressive. Broadly speaking and summarily considered, they fall into four main categories: marching camps, permanent forts, roads and signal stations. In general, it may be said that there is little or nothing about them peculiar to Scotland: they represent the uniform or standard practice of the Roman War Office,

[1] The Roman name for Carpow was *Horrea*, "The Granaries": and the designation indicates that this port served as the main supply base for the campaign of Severus, as also for those of his predecessors. The Roman army lived mainly on grain, and it has been estimated that a legion would consume about 500 bushels a week, i.e., in those days the crop of upwards of 70 acres. Immense stores of corn must have been brought up into Scotland during the Roman invasions. See Professor Piggot in *Roman and Native in North Britain*, ed. I. A. Richmond, pp. 23–5.

whether the works concerned are on the Tay, the Rhine, the Danube, the Euphrates, or in any other frontier region of the great Empire. In this sense, then, they are hardly part of our native antiquities, and therefore they will be described as briefly as possible in this little book. In a category by itself, however, stands the Antonine Wall; and of this wonderful structure something in detail must be said.

And first as to the marching camps. No Roman force, large or small, operating in hostile territory, ever failed to entrench its nightly bivouacs. Had such a salutary precaution been followed by British forces in our colonial campaigns, some great disasters might have been avoided—for example, in the Zulu War.

Typically, a Roman marching camp is rectangular on plan, with rounded angles. It may have either four or six gates, corresponding usually to the gridiron pattern of streets which ran between the rows of leather tents in which the soldiers slept. In an open space in the centre stood the tent or tents of the commanding officer and his staff; and of course, if the force included cavalry, there were lines for the horses. Spaces were reserved for the baggage; and there were slit trenches for latrines, cooking stances (usually behind the ramparts), and all other such installations as would be necessary even for a single night's encampment. The "laager", if we may call it so, was defended by a bank and ditch, the former crested with a palisade, provided by the stakes of which every infantry soldier carried two. The gates were protected in one of two ways. One method was by a *titulus* or short earthwork traverse, to check an inrush—much like the barriers erected outside the gates of our country school playgrounds, so as to prevent the children rushing out on to the road and being run down by passing traffic. The other method was to construct a *clavicula*, or claw-like projection, either outward or inward (occasionally both), which would have the same effect of preventing a hostile inrush.

Such, then, was the standard plan. But the Roman army suffered less than usual from the rigidity which is apt to be the bane of the military mind. So, where the terrain did not permit it, or where deviations from the rectangular scheme were dictated by the need to secure advantageous ground, the outline of the marching camp might become highly irregular. Nevertheless, in such cases it is always made up of straight sections: circular camps are never Roman. Also the angles are invariably rounded: a rectangular entrenchment with sharp angles can likewise never be regarded as Roman.

When they occur in what is now cultivated ground, marching camps can seldom be seen on the surface. Long ploughing has levelled the banks and filled up the ditches. But the development of air photography has recorded scores of long forgotten Roman bivouacs: for under suitable conditions the track of the obliterated ditch is clearly seen as a dark crop-mark. For an example of a great Roman marching camp, which, lying in what is today uncultivated moorland, is still clearly visible, we may glance at a famous example, Raedykes near Stonehaven. Here, almost the entire outline of the camp, bank and ditch, may be traced out on the ground, with a full appreciation of the masterly way in which its plan has been adapted to a highly irregular *terrain*. Moreover, it was the first marching camp in Scotland to be tested by modern scientific excavation.

The camp at Raedykes covers an area of 93½ acres; and, making every allowance for the extreme irregularity of the ground, has clearly been the bivouac of a large force, possibly twelve or even fifteen thousand men. Its outline is highly irregular. The east and south fronts are almost straight; but there is a deep re-entrant on the north, forming an acute north-eastern salient; while the western front is deflected wherever necessary to suit the irregular ground. Nevertheless, it is clear that the engineer has done his best to achieve the standard layout, with six gates, three pairs of opposites, in the normal Roman style. All the gates are defended by *tituli*. The excavators distinguished two varieties of rampart and ditch: a heavy rampart, formed out of the upcast of a deep ditch, and a shallow ditch associated with a slighter rampart largely composed of loose boulders gathered from the surrounding moorland. It has been contended that the heavier rampart and deeper ditch were devised to front dangerous ground: but this seems unrealistic, since surely a Caledonian force of any size could move freely round the perimeter and attack the camp from any quarter. A more likely view might be that the camp was never finished.[1]

[1] This is the opinion of Mr. David W. Reece, lecturer in Humanity in the University of Aberdeen, who has made a special study of Raedykes.

The deeper form of ditch is of the kind which the Romans called *fossa fastigata*—V-shaped, faced with puddled clay, with a vertical slit-trench in the bottom. In addition to facilitating drainage, such a trench was an important aid to the defence of the camp. It would not be easy for a Caledonian who had won his way into the ditch to cast a javelin or launch a sling-stone with his feet at a quarter to three! Bank and ditch form one continuous slope, so that no foothold is offered to an assailant who seeks to climb over the palisade.

Raedykes camp has yielded a complete chariot, or cart wheel, the hub of another and the axle-ring of a third, as well as two spears, a helmet and a mallet: but all these articles, with the exception of a hub found in the modern excavations, have now been lost. Thus they cannot be dated; nor has the site yielded any coins. We do not therefore know to which of the Roman invasions our camp should be assigned.

South of the camp a long line of bank and ditch, so far unexcavated but Roman in character, probably indicates an annexe for horses or baggage. It is therefore possible that the laager at Raedykes was intended to remain in use for a compaigning season. Perhaps it is worth noting that from the highest point of the site Stonehaven harbour is visible. We know from the narrative of Tacitus that Agricola's fleet and army kept in touch with each other as they advanced northward into Caledonia; and excavation has already indicated that Severus likewise used both naval and military forces in his great punitive expedition. But it would be a mistake to imagine that, in seeking a date or dates for the line of marching camps stretching northward from Strathmore through Mar into Moray, we are limited to a choice between Agricola and Severus. For example, we know nothing of what campaigning in the north may have taken place during the second major advance of the Romans, which culminated in the building of the Antonine Wall, and consequent stabilizing of the frontier on the Clyde-Forth isthmus. All is meantime doubtful, and we must patiently await the result of future excavations.

In contrast to the marching camps, a Roman permanent fort (*castellum*) is almost always laid out upon a rectangular plan, with rounded angles—in shape like a playing card. The reason for this greater uniformity, or adherence to the standard plan, is obvious.

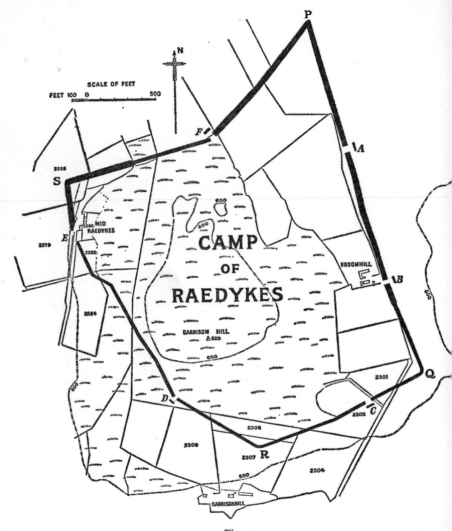

Fig. 7
The Roman marching camp at Raedykes, near Stonehaven, Kincardineshire
(*By courtesy, Society of Antiquaries of Scotland*)

The permanent fort was built at leisure on a selected site, by a military force in full control of a conquered country. Its purpose was to provide secure and comfortable quarters for a detachment whose duty it was to control a stated district or a vital tactical position, such as the crossing of a river or the debouchure of a mountain pass: whereas the marching camp had to be laid out on whatever ground where the operational unit was overtaken by night, physical exhaustion or the failure of supplies, and therefore its designers had little choice of site.

For the rest, a Roman fort corresponds closely to the theoretical scheme of the marching camp—except of course that it is of more permanent construction. Its ramparts were of turf, usually on a stone base: later they were wholly of stone, sometimes with an earthen *banquette* behind. Outside the rampart there is always a berm, or short level platform, in contradistinction to the continuous slope made by the profile of bank and ditch in the marching camps: for the permanent rampart, whether of stone or turf, was heavy, and would be liable to slide down into the ditch, were there not an interval of undisturbed soil between them. Internally, the *castellum* was laid out upon the usual standardized gridiron plan. In the centre was the headquarters building (*principia*), containing a long hall and a suite of offices, as well as the shrine (*sacellum*) where the regimental standards were laid up. Under the *sacellum* is sometimes a sunk vault for the treasure-chest. To one side of the *principia* is the commandant's house (*praetorium*). This was provided with central heating. Further out are the granaries, easily distinguished by their floors raised upon sleeper walls, so as to be damp- and vermin-proof, as well as by their heavy buttresses, indicating a massive fire-proof roof of stone or tiles—for if the granaries were set ablaze by incendiary arrows (such as were found in the Bar Hill fort on the Antonine Wall) then the garrison would indeed be in evil case. Regular rows of barracks filled up most of the rest of the space within the ramparts: but in the case of a larger unit there were always storehouses, workshops, and a hospital. In the hospital of the Agricolan fort at Fendoch, near the mouth of Glenalmond in Perthshire, it was noted that on one side were small rooms for serious cases. There we see that those wise old Romans were fully abreast of what is now becoming the most up-to-date principle in modern hospital design. The buildings within the fort might be either of timber, or timber framing

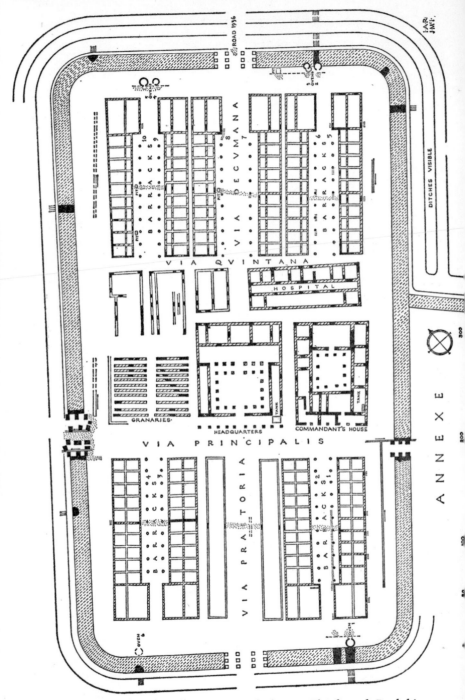

Fig. 8   The Agricolan Fort at Fendoch, near Glenalmond, Perthshire
(*By courtesy, Society of Antiquaries of Scotland*)

with a wattle and daub infilling, or of good stone masonry. Outside the fort, sometimes inside as well, was a suite of baths, which would serve as a social centre for the garrison, their families and the civilian hangers-on who are always attracted by the presence of a standing garrison.

The size of such a fort of course depended upon the strength of the garrison. Thus at Inchtuthil on the Tay, systematic excavation, now almost completed after a decade of work, has revealed the full plan of a legionary fortress covering fifty acres or thereby, the headquarters of an army corps of more than 5,000 men, comprising all arms—infantry, cavalry, field artillery[1] and the necessary technical, medical and administrative services. Antiquarians await the final report of the Inchtuthil excavations with bated breath: for it is probably the only known site of a legionary fortress in Europe which is unencumbered by modern buildings, so that a complete and scientific exploration of the whole area has been possible.

Most of our Roman forts in Scotland, however, are of much smaller dimensions. They were designed to house a cohort, a unit nominally 500 or 1,000 strong, in practice probably comprising respectively about 480 or 800 men. In the exploration of such sites Scotland holds a proud position. The excavation of the fort at Birrens, in Dumfriesshire—the Roman Blatobulgium—in 1895 has been described, by one pre-eminently qualified to judge, as resulting in the "mapping out of the internal arrangement of a typical Roman *castellum* with a completeness that had no parallel in this country in its day".[2] Still more epoch-making was the excavation of Newstead near Melrose (*Trimontium* of the Romans), where the meticulous thoroughness of the work conducted by Dr. James Curle between 1905 and 1910, and the enormous number of the relics found, resulted in giving to the world the most complete picture so far available of "a Roman frontier post and its people".[3] But at Newstead and elsewhere, the remains exposed were filled in again, so as to preserve them in the soil for

---

[1] The horse-drawn spring guns of a Roman army in the field are depicted on Trajan's column.

[2] Sir George Macdonald in *Proc. Soc. Ant. Scot.*, vol. LXXIII, p. 254.

[3] The title of Dr. Curle's classic work, published in 1911. The speed with which this magnificent volume was produced makes the more recent archaeologist envious.

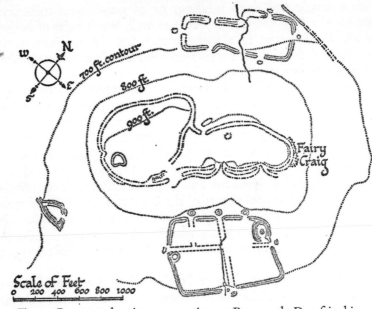

Fig. 9   Roman and native constructions at Burnswark, Dumfriesshire
(*By courtesy, Oxford University Press*)

future generations[1]: with the result that, on the site of most
excavated Roman posts in Scotland, little or nothing is now visible
above ground. It is only at certain places such as Birrens, Lyne in
Peeblesshire, and Ardoch in Perthshire, that the outer defences
are still distinct. And here we recognize a feature peculiar to the
Roman forts in northern Britain, namely the multiplication of
ramparts and ditches. At Birrens there are no less than six ramparts,
each with its corresponding ditch. Clearly the Roman soldiery
had as wholesome a respect for a Highland charge as had their
successors who faced the fury of the clans under Montrose,
Dundee and Charles Edward Stuart.

The Romans were the greatest road–builders of all time. Their

---

[1] At Rough Castle and Castle Cary, two *castella* on the Antonine Wall
excavated early in this century, the remains were left open for the benefit of
visitors. They have thus disintegrated through weathering and mischief. At
Newstead, where all the foundations were carefully buried again, a second series
of excavations, conducted with more modern expertize, has resulted in an
important clarification of the complex history of the site.

vast empire was literally held together by its road system; and under the *pax Romana* Latin civilisation, and in due course the Christian faith, were able to spread, peacefully and in silence, into every corner of western Europe. Much attention has been paid by scholars to the Roman road system in Britain, and by no means least in Scotland: so far as at present known, it will be found fully set forth in the splendid Ordnance Survey Map of Roman Britain.

A first class Roman road may be as much as 25 feet in breadth, though 16 feet is a good average. It is constructed with a heavy bottoming of large stones, covered by a cambered surface of rammed gravel or small pebbles. There are gutters or drainage channels on either side, and culverts are provided where required. Rivers were crossed by fords, staked or stone bedded; or, if necessary, by wooden bridges, sometimes carried on stone piers.

At one time or another, a considerable number of sections of Roman roads in Scotland have been exposed, either accidentally or by archaeological research. A good example was laid bare at Collielaw, near the *castellum* of Castledykes in Lanarkshire. Here the road, constructed in the standard way, and having a heavy kerb and the usual ditches on either side, was 19 feet wide. The ditches had been made water-tight by a lining of clay. The best known example of a Roman bridge in Scotland was found at Summerston, in Dumbartonshire, where the Military Way associated with the Antonine Wall was taken over the River Kelvin, east of the *castellum* at Balmuildy. The bridge appeared to have had a stone pier, resting on piles, and having a cut-water at least on the upstream side. Probably the bridge itself was constructed of trussed timber work.

Since the portion of Scotland occupied by the Romans was essentially a military area, it became necessary to secure the road system, and to facilitate rapid communication between the garrisons linked by the roads, by an elaborate series of signal stations. Smoke signals of course would be used by day, fire signals at night. On the sculptured panels of Trajan's Column and the Column of Marcus Aurelius we may see pictures of such signal stations on the Danube frontier. A chain of signal stations has been discovered along the line of the great Roman road between Strageath and Perth: others have been found on the Antonine Wall, and along the Roman roads in Annandale and Nithsdale; as well as one within the rampart of the native fort upon Eildon

Hill North, overlooking the Roman garrison at Newstead. Typically, they consist of a shallow circular ditch, intended for drainage, not defence, enclosing a wooden tower of which the corner post-holes and sleeper trenches alone survive. The tower is usually about 11 feet square, and no doubt was fairly high.

Of all the Roman monuments in Scotland, by far the noblest is the Anonine Wall. Unfortunately its surviving remains lie in the central industrial belt of Scotland—a belt moreover, which is at present in course of undergoing rapid development. The amount of destruction has already been appalling; and much of what survives is in imminent danger. But some of the finest stretches of the Wall, and two of its *castella*, Rough Castle and Castle Cary, are now in the custody of the Ministry of Public Building and Works; and every effort is being made to awaken, in the minds of the landowners, farmers, local authorities, and industrialists concerned, a due sense of their responsibility for the preservation of so outstanding a portion of our national heritage.

The Roman Wall in Scotland was constructed, in or about the year 143, by the Governor of Britain, Quintus Lollius Urbicus, to the order of the Emperor Antoninus Pius. The Wall extends for a total length of 37 miles, between Bridgeness on the Forth and Old Kilpatrick on the Clyde. It occupies a superb position, alike tactically and scenically, overlooking on its eastern sector the Carse of Falkirk and the Midland Valley, and in its central and western sectors confronting the Kilsyth Hills, Campsie Fells and Kilpatrick Hills. Striding for the most part high along the southern escarpment of the Midland Valley, it is given additional protection east and west, by the Rivers Carron and Kelvin, and by the broad marshlands through which in Roman times the former river made its way towards the Firth of Forth. Thus the views obtained *per lineam Valli* are magnificent. Nobody can walk along it without feeling a constant thrill as he finds himself traversing what was intended in the second century to be the final frontier in Britain of the greatest, and upon the whole, the most beneficent Empire that the world has known.

For most of its length, the Wall itself was built of turves. Thus when a section is cut across, the regular dark lines of carbonized vegetation are seen, pencilling, as it were, both faces of the section.

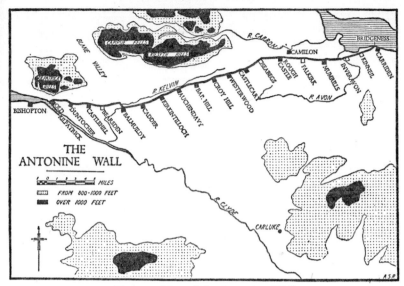

Fig. 10 Map of the Antonine Wall
(*By courtesy, Glasgow Archaeological Society*)

As far as Falkirk, however, the Wall is made of compacted Carse clay, or, at some places, of rammed earth sheathed in clay. The rampart, whether of sods or clay, stands upon a substantial stone base, with outer kerbs of squared blocks, and provided when necessary with culverts. Where the Wall descends a slope, this stone foundation is sometimes built with steps, so as to afford anchorage for the turf superstructure. The latter was 14 feet wide at base, but both faces sloped inwards, so that at the summit, thought to have been about 10 feet high, the Wall will have been something like 6 feet broad—that is to say, allowing room for two armed men to pass each other. The wall-head was doubtless finished with a wooden platform, protected towards the outside by a breastwork of timber, or perhaps of gabions. Outside the Wall was a ditch, cut through earth or rock as the case may be. This ditch was, in general, about 40 feet wide, and at least 12 feet deep. It was, as usual, V-shaped, sometimes with the drainage slot or channel at the bottom. (See p. 93.) Sometimes the lips of the ditch were revetted with stonework. On the outside of the ditch was a low and broad mound composed of the upcast. While not high enough to afford cover to the assailants, the inner edge of this upcast mound of course prolonged the slope of the ditch down which they would have to scramble under a hail of missiles from the Wall. Between Wall and ditch was the usual berm (p. 95), varying from 20 to 100 feet in width.

To the south of the Wall was a Military Way, linking the garrison posts from sea to sea. Of these posts—oblong *castella* of the usual type, but varying in size—thirteen so far are known. Probably there was originally one *castellum* for every 2 miles of the Wall. All except two were built, like the Wall itself, of turf or clay upon a stone foundation: but at Castle Cary and Balmuildy the walls were of stone. Under two of the forts which have been excavated—Croy Hill and Bar Hill—remains have been found of the small entrenched posts, called *praesidia* by Tacitus, which were laid out by Agricola, who first, in the year 81, placed garrisons across the isthmus. In addition to the *castella*, the Antonine Wall was provided with patrol posts or fortlets, as well as with signalling platforms.

Although the Wall was garrisoned by auxiliary cohorts, the great structure itself, built it would seem with astounding speed, was the work of detachments seconded from all three legions stationed in Britain: the Sixth from York, the Twentieth from Chester, and the Second from Caerleon-upon-Usk. We know this from the distance slabs which the working parties built into the structure to record, with a pride surely justified, the lengths accomplished by each squad. So far, seventeen of these distance slabs have been dug up; and their discovery had led to various ingenious, if hardly convincing, theories as to the organizational way in which the undertaking (*opus Valli*, as the Romans called it) was carried out. One thing at all events seems certain, that the Wall and its associated works was built from east to west. Air survey has identified fourteen temporary camps along the Wall, which no doubt were occupied as quarters by the troops engaged on its construction.

It is estimated that the garrison of the Antonine Wall amounted to some 10,000 men. The reader must be clear in his mind as to the precise purpose which the Wall was intended to serve. It was not to be defended, from end to end, by closely ranked men, like the curtain walls of a beleaguered castle or town. Such a conception would have called for an enormous garrison, and in any case would have been hopelessly unrealistic. If serious danger approached the Wall, the garrisons of its forts would receive ample notice. Throwing open their northern gates, they would march forth to meet the foe on the plain field of battle, *more Romano*. The purpose of the Wall was rather to provide garrison quarters and an emplacement for what was intended to be the definitive frontier of Rome in Britain; to serve as a springboard for punitive operations when these were called for; and, perhaps most of all, to impose an obstacle to cattle raiding and to provide, at selected checkpoints, for customs control in the ever-increasing flow of trade between the Roman Province and the unconquered North.

The sectors wherein the Wall and its ditch can be seen to best advantage today are the following:

(1) between Polmonthill Cottage and Farm, where, though the Wall is hardly visible, the ditch makes a grand appearance.

(2) in the private grounds of Callendar Park. Here the ditch remains open for a length of some 600 yards and to a depth sometimes as much as 9 feet, while both the Wall itself and the upcast mound on the outer lip of the ditch are quite distinct.

(3) East of Watling Lodge—the best-preserved portion of the ditch, which is here about 40 feet wide and 15 feet deep: in other words, practically, in its original state. This magnificent exposure, about 350 yards in length, is now under the charge of the Ministry of Public Building and Works, The northward view, over the Midland Plain towards the Kilsyth Hills, gives one an unforgettable impression of an Imperial Frontier. The education of no Scotsman is complete until he has visited this site.

(4) In Tentfield Plantation, east of the fort at Rough Castle. Here the ditch appears to great advantage. A short stretch of the Military Way is exposed about 600 yards east of Rough Castle: it is here no less than 280 feet distant from the Wall, which at this point has a salient.

(5) West of Rough Castle, where the ditch is well preserved and the Wall survives to a height of about 5 feet. This sector, with the fort, is now under the guardianship of the Ministry of Public Building and Works.

(6) In Seabegs Wood another sector is under the guardianship of the Ministry. Here not only are the line of the Wall, ditch, and upcast mound all conspicuous, but the track of the Military Way, about 40 yards to the south, may still be traced.

(7) Upon both sides of Croy Hill, where the ditch is particularly

striking. On either side of the Croy Hill Fort, it is hewn out of the living rock, but at one point, close east of the fort, the labour seems to have been too much even for Roman soldiery, and an 80 foot stretch of the ditch was never quarried. An eighteenth-century writer, however, could not bring himself to believe in such a failure of the legions, and surmised that this portion of the ditch had filled up again through "vegetation of the rock"!

(8) In the cemetery at New Kilpatrick two stretches of the stone base of the Wall, here 15 feet broad, are exposed to view, each with a culvert and one with a "step" down the slope.

(9) Another stretch of the stone base, with a culvert, is exposed to the west of the fort in Golden Hill Park, Duntocher.

As to the forts, of the two in the custody of the Ministry of Public Building and Works, that at Rough Castle is now in the active process of development by the Ancient Monuments Division of the Ministry. Its earthworks have always been the most impressive of any *castellum* on the Wall; and when the work of clearance and consolidation is complete, Rough Castle will be one of the most impressive Roman sites in northern Britain. The small fort occupies a site of great strength, and was defended by powerful earthworks. A remarkable feature is the series of ten rows of defensive pits (*lilia*) arranged in chequer-pattern outside the Wall. These were probably the handiwork of Agricola, and were partly buried by the upcast mound of the Antonine Ditch. Within the fort, excavations in 1902–3 recovered the foundations of stone buildings, including the *principia*, *praetorium*, and a granary. At the south gate the pavement was deeply worn into ruts by wheeled traffic. Outside the fort to the east a large entrenched annexe contained a suite of baths. The relics found were scanty, but included the fragment of a life-size imperial statue and a stone recording the building of the *principia* by the 6th Cohort of Nervians. This unit originally came from the Lower Rhineland.

At Torwoodlee we saw Roman and native in Caledonia coming into sharp hostile contact. An even more dramatic picture of such an armed confrontation is furnished by the remains on Burnswark Hill. On top of this commanding summit, which rises to a height of 940 feet, "from whence is seen a vast prospect of an extended country on all sides", to quote the words of "Sandy" Gordon,

who first described the site in 1726[1]—are the well preserved
remains of a large hill-fort, formidably defended. On either side,
north and south, is a Roman camp. In the southern camp, the
three northern gates are covered, not by the usual *tituli*, but by
circular platforms about 60 feet in diameter. These have all the
appearance of emplacements from which slings might bombard
the fort. Confirmation of this idea was found during excavations
in 1898, when numerous *glandes*, or leaden sling bolts, were found
in the southern camp and on the slopes below the hill fort. Some
of the latter showed flattening by impact. Lastly, round the hill
are distinct though incomplete traces of lines of communication.
It is hard to escape the conclusion drawn by an eighteenth-
century parish minister, who surmised that the two camps "were
at first formed by the Romans besieging a body of the ancient
Britons, who had occupied the summit of the hill". Now in the
north-east corner of the southern camp is embodied an older
Roman work, a small square fortlet, belonging to a type of which
other examples such as Durisdeer and Tassiesholm, have been
excavated in Annandale. These fortlets are of Antonine date, and
this is confirmed by the pottery found in the Burnswark fortlet.
Therefore the two large camps and associated earthworks investing the native hill-fort would seem to be later than that period.
Can it be that we are here in touch with the campaign of Severus?

---

[1] *Itinerarium Septentrionale*, p. 16. It is unnecessary to remind Scott lovers
that this is the "large folio" that so delighted Monkbarns on his journey in the
"Queensferry Diligence". It was the first work specifically consecrated to the
study of Roman military remains in northern Britain.

As to the astonishing view from Burnswark, we may quote from Colling-
wood Bruce, *The Roman Wall*, 1st ed., p. 356:

"From this elevated summit, the mountain ridges which are scattered over
no fewer than six of the Scottish counties can be descried; looking eastward
the Nine-nicks of Thirwall are in sight; southward, the familiar forms of
Skiddaw, Saddleback, and Crossfell rise into view; to the south west, the
craggy peaks of the Isle of Man arrest the attention in favourable states of
the atmosphere; and, not unfrequently a long black streak, on the distant
verge of the ocean, indicates the position of Ireland."

From every point of view, Burnswark is one of the outstanding archaeological
sites in Britain: and the complete excavation of its works, native and Roman,
with modern techniques, is greatly overdue.

VIII

The Early Christian Monuments

O UR Christian faith was the last and greatest gift of the dying Roman Empire to the young nations that came out of her loins. While it may no doubt be true that the majority of the inhabitants of Roman Britain remained pagan to the end, there is ample evidence of an active, vigorous, and well-organized Christian Church throughout the fourth century. And the first mission sent out to the Picts of the unconquered north was simply an extension, beyond the frontier line of Hadrian's Wall, of the Church within the Western Empire. This was the mission of St. Ninian, who about the year 400 planted the first Christian Church in what is now Scotland at *Candida Casa*, now Whithorn in Galloway. Little is known about St. Ninian, or the earliest history of his foundation, and much controversy has raged over the scope and nature of his work. But it is certain that in the fifth and sixth centuries *Candida Casa* was an important centre of evangelizing activities not only in Britain but in Northern Ireland; and material remains survive of the Ninianic mission in the group of early Christian tombstones still preserved at Whithorn and the associated site of Kirkmadrine, as well as in other very early Christian monuments and cemeteries to the south of the Forth-Clyde isthmus. Not only so, but recent excavation has recovered, under the remains of the medieval priory at Whithorn, of the foundations, it can hardly be doubted, of *Candida Casa* itself, the "White House" of St. Ninian.

These foundations indicate a building with walls 3 feet 4 inches thick, laid in clay in the most ancient manner of the Celtic Church. The little chapel was 15 feet wide, but its length is unknown. No-where do the walls survive to a height of more than 3 feet.

Externally, the dark local flagstones had been covered over with a cream-coloured plaster, thus strikingly confirming Bede's statement that Ninian built "a church of stone, after a custom strange to the Britons", and that it was known as the White House (*Candida Casa*). As Dr. Ralegh Radford, the excavator of Whithorn, has justly observed:

"The discovery of a light-coloured plaster on the face of the masonry inevitably recalls Bede's description of *Candida Casa*, the white house, so called from its church of stone. Dry built structures of the dark native stone were not unknown in the district, and a church of this type would hardly have caused the fame which Bede's words suggest. It was the white covering which distinguished the original church of St. Ninian and the discovery near the centre of the monastery of a primitive building treated in this manner justifies the deduction that it is indeed the white house named after St. Martin that has been found, the little church in which the shrine of St. Ninian lay for so many centuries."

Not far away from the site of the *Candida Casa* was found the oldest Christian monument in Scotland. It is a rough-hewn stone bearing a Latin inscription, in an early Christian formula, recording the burial place of a man called Latinus and his daughter, and telling us further that the monument was set up by his grandson Barrovadus. This stone dates from the fifth century, and may well commemorate a member of St. Ninian's flock. At the ancient church site of Kirkmadrine, in the Rhinns of Galloway, further memorials of the earliest Christian mission to our land survive in the form of three tombstones bearing Latin inscriptions accompanied by the famous Chi-Rho monogram, formed by a combination of the two first letters of our Saviour's name (Ch+r) as written in the Greek alphabet. One of these stones commemorates three priests, or perhaps bishops, named Ides, Viventius and Mavorius. Crosses of a very early type, the oldest dating back to the seventh or eighth century, have also been found, inscribed on the rock face or carved upon stones, in St. Ninian's cave, on the coast about 3 miles from Whithorn.

So far as Scotland is concerned, here indeed, in this remote corner of the country, we stand at the cradle of our Faith. In all Scotland there is no more hallowed spot than Whithorn. Since the fifth century upon this site the Christian message has been continuously proclaimed, and Christian worship conducted according to every variety of observance that has successively prevailed in Scotland: for the Premonstratensian Priory and later Cathedral Church of Galloway overlies the foundations of the *Candida Casa* of St. Ninian; and upon the claustral buildings of the medieval priory stands the present parish church, erected in 1823. Here, if anywhere in Scotland, one recalls the command given by Jehovah to Moses of old: "put off thy shoes from off thy feet, for the place where on thou standest is holy ground."

The most famous early Christian monastic site in Scotland is undoubtedly Iona. This is largely due to the vividness with which we can realize the material aspect and equipment, the daily routine, inward life and spiritual outlook of its Celtic monks, from the information furnished to us (for the most part quite incidentally) in Adamnan's fascinating account of its great founder, St. Columba—a book written within a century, or very little more, after the founder's death. Unfortunately, we are never likely to know much about the lay-out and buildings of the Columban monastery at Iona. On no less than six occasions it was destroyed by the pagan Vikings: and what of its foundations may have survived all these catastrophes is now buried beneath the Benedictine Abbey, so splendidly restored in our own day. Yet careful excavation has disclosed the line of the monastic precinct, marked out by a bank and ditch: on Torr Abb, the Abbot's Hillock, which overlooks the medieval abbey from the west, a small cell has been found, which may well have been Columba's sleeping place; the remains of other cells have also been discovered, together with the post-holes and sleeper trenches of a large rectangular building, probably the refectory.

On Eileach-an-Naoimh, in the Garvelloch Islands at the mouth of the Firth of Lorne, the remains of an early Celtic monastery built of stone are carefully preserved by the Ministry of Public Building and Works. The ruins include beehive cells, a chapel, and a graveyard: but unfortunately some of these structures were occupied for agricultural purposes until modern times, and it is not always easy to distinguish the ancient work from comparatively recent alterations. Farther north, on the Isle of Canna, the very perfect remains of a small Celtic nunnery survive, unaltered, to await excavation. We can still see the cashel or stone enclosing wall, the well-house, the mill, and various cells: but no trace of a chapel is now visible above ground. In the now drained bed of

Loch Chaluim Chille—"Columba's Loch"—in the Isle of Skye, we find the well-preserved remains of a small Celtic monastery, including a tiny unicameral church or chapel, a cashel containing two *domunculae* or dwelling places for the monks, and a stone-paved causeway leading across to the monastery from the shore. But to see the best preserved example of a Celtic monastery in Scotland we must journey far northward to the Orkneys. Here, on the storm-beaten promontory known as the Brough of Deerness, towering to a height of a hundred feet above the restless waves, survive the complete installations of a large monastic community, including a small chapel and the foundations of at least a score of huts, in appearance strikingly resembling those uncovered by excavation at the Anglian monastery of Whitby in Northumberland. There is also a well, or perhaps rather a cistern. The root of the promontory, by which alone the place can be approached, is protected by a strong cashel wall. No early Christian site in all Scotland would better repay excavation than the Brough of Deerness. As late as the seventeenth century, in spite of all that Puritanism could do, the place continued to be a resort of pilgrims, from every isle of the Orkneys. "Barefooted, on hands and knees, they climbed with difficulty to the top by a path that only admitted one at a time to ascend. Once at the top, with bent knees and hands clasped, they proceeded three times round the chapel appealing to the 'Bairns of Brough', and every now and then throwing stones and water behind their backs."[1]

By far the most interesting monuments of the Celtic Church in our country are the sculptured symbol-stones of Pictland. They are almost entirely restricted to the limits of the ancient kingdom of the Picts—that is to say, to the country north of the Forth and Clyde and east and north of the area, roughly corresponding to the modern Argyllshire, which in the fifth century A.D. was colonized by intruding Scots from Ulster (see p. 21). Nothing like these monuments is known anywhere else in the whole wide world: and, despite much study, the meaning of "Pictish symbolism" remains the grand unsolved problem of Scottish archaeology.

[1] J. R. Tudor, *The Orkneys and Shetlands*, p. 278. Who were the "Bairns of Brough", and what was the legend connected with them, seems to have been forgotten.

Comparative study of these monuments has shown that they may be grouped into three classes, and it has been found possible to establish, within broad limits, a relative chronology for each class.[1] The resultant scheme may be set forth as follows:

Class I (before A.D. 700)—unshapen and undressed monoliths with incised symbols only.

Class II (between A.D. 700 and 900)—slabs roughly tooled and shaped, having in addition to the symbols a cross of Celtic pattern, and often elaborate figure groups; the sculpture now being in relief, and the symbols and cross alike enriched with more or less complex ornamentation in the school of Celtic art. Where the figure subjects can be identified, they are found to be portrayals of themes drawn from Holy Writ, or from the vast and ever increasing mass of allegorical or mythological ideography which was current throughout Western Europe during the early Middle Ages.

Class III (from about A.D. 900 to the extinction of native Celtic art by the Anglo-Norman infiltration in the twelfth and thirteenth centuries)—slabs on which the symbols have disappeared so that there remains only the Celtic cross, carved in relief and often sumptuously decorated.

As to the symbols, some of these, notably the famous "elephant" are obviously highly stylized animal forms, whatever the beast that they may have originally been intended to portray. Others, such as the "crescent and V-rod" and the "double-disc and Z-rod" seem, as incised in outline on the oldest stones, to be as purely abstract in significance as the diagrams of Euclidean geometry. But when we find these seeming abstractions re-appearing carved in relief and elaborately decorated with Celtic ornament, on the stones of Class II, the conviction is irresistably borne in upon us that they possessed a real existence, as objects plaited in wicker work or leather, or wrought in metal. And proof of this is forthcoming in an actual symbol—the "crescent and V-rod", wrought in bronze, which was found in Fife: but, as if to mock us with a further puzzle, on its back are incised two other symbols, the "double-disc and Z-rod" and the "beast's head"! The symbols

---

[1] The tendency among modern scholars is to push back the antiquity of the three classes as originally proposed by Dr. Joseph Anderson. A conspectus of the various dates now being argued out will be found in *Proc. Soc. Ant. Scot.*, vol. XCII, pp. 54-5.

have also been found inscribed on objects of metal or bone, and rudely carved upon natural rock surfaces—in some cases, in caves known to have been occupied by hermits in early Christian times.

Even on the oldest class of the sculptured stones, the symbols exhibit a precision of outline and fixity of form which makes it clear that they must have had a long evolutionary history behind them before the fashion set in of graving them on pillars. And that this fashion originated in Aberdeenshire, or, more precisely, in the Garioch and Lower Mar, is strongly suggested by the fact that something like one third of the total number of stones of this oldest class are found in that area. Into the previous evolution of the symbols we get a glimpse in a stone disc, incised with the "double-disc and Z-rod", found at Jarlshof, though unluckily not in a stratified context: also—though again in an undated level— at the Broch of Burrian in Orkney, which yielded, among many other relics of normal broch types, the metatarsal bone of an ox upon which have been scratched the "crescent and V-rod" and the "mirror-case" symbols.

Upon the whole, it seems most likely that the symbols were personal emblems, denoting the social status, perhaps the profession, of the individual or individuals presumably commemorated by the momuments—though it is well to remember that in very few cases indeed has a burial been found in association with a symbol stone. Difficulty has been felt in the commemoration of a person's social status upon a monument otherwise anonymous. But this is to impose a modern way of thinking upon the mentality of a far distant and more primitive society. In ancient times one's status was more important than one's name, the preservation of which was a matter for the deceased person's kindred. It is probable that the purpose of these monuments was to protect the grave by setting forth the symbols of the rank of its occupant. This seems to have been the case in Scandinavia, where the runic inscriptions on gravestones record the name of the "rune-master", not of the person whom the stone commemorates.[1] And that this was equally so in Celtic Scotland, we may learn from an early Buchan charter, in which a Celtic Mormaer of that Province grants a portion of land, one of whose boundary marks is stated to be *crux medici*—"the doctor's cross". The name of the doctor had

[1] See H. Shetelig and H. Falk, *Scandinavian Archaeology*, p. 244.

not apparently been preserved: what remained important was his professional status.

Although it would seem that the practice of graving "Pictish symbols" on stone monuments originated in Mar or the Garioch, the hard, intractable igneous and metamorphic rocks of that province arrested the burgeoning of the new art which flourished so gloriously in Angus and Moray, the sandstone provinces on either flank. Nothing can exceed the sheer unearthly beauty of the sumptuously decorated slabs of Class II which occur in such profusion in Strathmore. And how much do they teach us, with all their richness in figure subjects, about the daily life of that gifted, powerful, tenacious and deeply interesting people, the Picts, who by an unhappy chance have left us so few literary memorials of themselves that a modern scholar can bewail "the silence of the Picts"! But if the Pict is silent in literature, he comes indeed to life upon his sculptured stones. A distinguished Scottish antiquary has set this important matter forth in a memorable passage:

"Though the details of these diagrammatic human figures are treated in a conventional manner, there can be no doubt that the costume, the weapons, and other accessories, are those of the country and the time. In this aspect of their character, as illustrative materials of unwritten history they are as valuable as the seals and the monumental effigies of later times. They illustrate the most ancient life in Scotland of which we have any illustrations. They show it in its common as well as in its ecclesiastical and military aspects. They exhibit the dress of the huntsman, the warrior, the pilgrim and the ecclesiastic. They furnish representations of the forms of the chariot, and the ship, the housings and harness of horses, instruments of music, arms of offence and defence, the staff of the pilgrim and the crozier of the ecclesiastic. Such implements and weapons of the period as the axe, the knife, the dirk, the sword, the spear, the shield, the bow, and the cross-bow, are all represented, and, so far as I know, no other representations of them exist. Customs and fashions of which there is no other distinct evidence are also represented. For instance, we learn from a comparison of all the different representations that the horsemen of that period rode without spurs or stirrups, cropped the manes and tails of their horses, used snaffle-bridles with cheek rings and ornamental rosettes, and sat upon peaked saddlecloths: that, when journeying on horseback, they wore peaked hoods and cloaks, and when hunting or on horseback, armed, they wore a kilt-like dress, falling below mid-thighs, and a plaid across the shoulders; that they used long-bows in war, and cross-bows in hunting, that their swords were long, broad-bladed, double-edged, obtusely pointed weapons with triangular pommels and straight guards: that their spears had large lozenge-shaped heads, while their bucklers were round and furnished with bosses; that they fought on foot with sword and buckler, and on horseback with sword, spear and shield; that when journeying on foot they wore trews or tight-fitting nether-garments, and a plaid loosely wrapped round the body, or a tight jerkin with sleeves, and belt round the waist: that they wore their hair long, flowing and curly, sometimes with peaked beards, at other times with moustaches on the upper lip and shaven cheeks and chin: that they used covered chariots or two-wheeled carriages with poles for draught by two horses, the driver sitting on a seat over the pole, the wheels having ornamental spokes: that they used chairs with side arms and high, curved backs, sometimes ornamented with heads of animals: that their boats had high prows and stern-posts: that the long dresses of the ecclesiastics were richly embroidered: that they walked in loose, short boots, and carried croziers and book-satchels. Such illustrations of the life and habits, the arts and industry, the costumes and arms of the Celtic inhabitants of Scotland are nowhere else to be found. We grudge no expense to obtain fragments of similarly sculptured representations of the ancient art of other countries wherewith to enrich our museums: but the wealth of unique materials which exists in our own land for the illustration of Celtic art and national history is still left, scattered and unprotected, to decay and perish."[1]

But the sculptured stones do more than preserve to us the material life of those who wrought them. They also afford us precious glimpses into the mental and spiritual outlook of the Pictish people. In sharp contrast to the early Christian monuments of the Scotic area on the other side of the country, the crosses on the Pictish slabs never depict the figure of the Crucified. Thus on the noble wayside stone at Aberlemno, in Angus, we see two

[1] Joseph Anderson, *Scotland in Early Christian Times* (Second Series), pp. 122–5. Since Dr. Anderson's book was published in 1881, many of the early Christian monuments of Pictland have been gathered into museums for preservation, while the others have been afforded the varying degrees of protection provided by the Ancient Monuments Acts. Nevertheless, the ignorance and indifference of the educated public in Scotland to their incomparable heritage in Pictish art remains as invincible as ever.

It should be noted that, as Dr. Anderson himself admits, the evidence for the portrayal of the cross-bow on the sculptured stones is doubtful.

angels bowed in grief on either side of a splendid High Cross: we feel that the Saviour of mankind is hanging there, yet His figure is absent. It looks as if something in the Pictish *ethos* forbade these ancient sculptors to portray the contorted, broken and tormented body of our Lord as He hung upon the shameful Cross. Perhaps their keen Celtic imaginations had a more vivid grasp of the true horrors of crucifixion—as portrayed, for example, with such stark reality, in Lewis Grassic Gibbon's novel, *Spartacus*, rather than in the cold calm of our modern stained glass windows.

Again, it has been noted that in the whole range of Pictish figure sculpture there is no trace of anything obscene. This is in marked contrast both to classical art—for example, we may mention the shocking portrayals so often found on Roman Samian ware—and also to the indecencies which we find, sometimes in the most hallowed surroundings, in the Gothic sculpture of the Middle Ages.

On one or two of our Pictish stones, inscriptions in Roman lettering occur: but, except that they seem to record the names of the persons commemorated, little has been made of these. There are also, in various parts of Scotland, inscriptions in the ogham alphabet, a form of Celtic script usually thought to be of Irish origin: but here again, although the key to the ogham alphabet is preserved in the *Book of Ballymote*, no success has hitherto been attained in the decipherment of our Scottish examples. Probably this is due to our ignorance of the language, or languages, spoken by the Picts. The most famous Celtic inscribed monument in Scotland is the Newton Stone in Aberdeenshire. On the front of this is an incised inscription in six lines of debased Roman cursive writing; while on the left edge is an ogham inscription in two vertical lines. Here again, decipherment has baffled scholars; but it now seems clear that the two inscriptions are quite separate, the oghams probably having been added later. In other words, we have not here to deal with one of the bilingual inscriptions, in Latin and Celtic, so commonly found in Wales.

At Brechin in Angus and Abernethy in Perthshire, Scotland possesses two precious examples of the Round Towers which are such characteristic monuments of the Celtic Church in Ireland. Our two Scottish Round Towers are outward and visible signs of the infiltration of the Columban Church into the ancient centres

of Pictish Christianity, during the period following the union
of Pictland and Dalriada in 843, under the Scotic hegemony of
Kenneth MacAlpin and his successors. They are in fact, outliers of
an Irish group, erected by the Celtic clergy as refuges for themselves and their holy things during the Viking invasions: and, in
time of peace, serving as belfries, and as landmarks indicating afar,
to weary travellers, the position of the hospitable monastery. The
older of our two Scottish Round Towers is the one at Brechin.
It can be dated, on fair documentary evidence, to the period
990–1012; and with this its stylistic characteristics perfectly accord
in the ascertained chronology of the Irish Round Towers. The
door shows the typically Irish inclined jambs and arched head cut
out of a single stone. The double pellet border on the raised band
is found on the doors of some of the Irish Round Towers and
churches, as well as on certain high crosses in Ireland. Over the
arched doorway is a sculptural Crucifixion, a subject common in
Ireland but (as we have noted), never found in Pictland. Our
Saviour's legs are uncrossed in the Irish manner, derived ultimately from the Eastern Church. One of the ecclesiastics on
either side of the door carries a T-shaped pastoral staff of Coptic
pattern, while the other has a *bachuil* or Celtic crook.

The Abernethy Round Tower is clearly later than the one at
Brechin. Moreover it does not appear to be all of one date: for
the lower twelve courses are in a grey freestone, while the rest of
the tower is built of yellow stone. The doorway is quite plain, of
Irish type, with sloping jambs and arched head, all surrounded by
a plain broad, raised band. The belfry windows, however, are of
pronounced early Norman fashion, and this portion at all events
of the tower can hardly be earlier than the first half of the twelfth
century.

Our two Scottish Round Towers must therefore be construed
as outliers, as intruders of an Irish culture into Pictland. Now on
the western side of Scotland—the area exposed to Irish influences
—we find a sequence of early Christian monuments, quite distinct
from their contemporaries in Pictland. Within the confines of the
former Scotic kingdom of Dalriada the Pictish symbols are
absent: and while crosses graven on a slab are frequent, as in
Pictland, the characteristic monument of the Early Christian
period in Dalriada is the free-standing cross, with its arms linked

by a "ring of glory". These High Crosses, as they are termed, doubtless served various purposes: to commemorate clerics of distinction; to mark out monastic boundaries; or to serve as preaching stations, round which the faithful, or prospective converts, might gather. Thoroughly Irish in character, and richly ornamented in complex Celtic patterns, interspersed with scenes from Holy Writ or Christian mythology, these early High Crosses are the precursors of the numerous West Highland free-standing crosses belonging to the later Middle Ages, some account of which will be given in a later chapter of this work. Alas! of the early Christian High Crosses themselves only two examples survive intact: St. Martin's Cross at Iona, and the superb Kildalton Cross on Islay. Both may be assigned approximately to the tenth century.

With the conversion, by missionaries from Iona, of the Anglian kingdom of Northumbria in the seventh century, northern England came under the influence of Irish ecclesiastical culture. In the country north of the Trent, which was less thoroughly Romanized during the imperial occupation, there is evidence that the fine native Celtic artistic tradition was never fully submerged beneath the dull and mediocre, uniform Roman provincial culture of the West. With the collapse of Roman power in the fifth century it revived; and under the stimulus of Irish Christianity it blossomed forth into the magnificent Anglian civilization of Northumbria, with its marvellous artistic achievement in sculpture and illuminated work, as illustrated by the Bewcastle Cross and the Lindisfarne Gospels; and with its massive scholarship, of which Bede is the choicest flower. This dominant Anglian art in its turn exercised a profound influence upon the later development of ecclesiastical sculpture in Pictland. Many of the elaborate decorated slabs, assignable to the ninth century or later, display Anglian motives, and the few free-standing crosses in Pictland, such as that at Dupplin in Perthshire, are of Anglian types. And it is to this period of artistic dominance from Northumbria that Scotland owes its two grandest monuments of Early Christian art: the St. Andrews tomb-shrine and the Ruthwell Cross. Space forbids us to embark upon a description of the St. Andrews tombshrine, which has truly been described as "ranking among the finest examples of Dark Age art in Europe".[1] But something

---

[1] S. H. Cruden, *The Early Christian and Pictish Monuments of Scotland*, p. 12.

must be said about the Ruthwell Cross, now preserved inside the parish church of that name in Dumfriesshire. No nobler monument of the Early Christian period exists anywhere within the bounds of the erstwhile Western Empire. It can be considered only in conjunction with the almost equally famous Bewcastle Cross in Cumberland.

An analytical study of the art relationships discernible in these two splendid monuments shows clearly how they form a most instructive archaeological commentary upon the composite sources of the Northumbrian Christianity that gave them origin. The Scotic or Irish archetypal element in that Christianity is revealed in the panels of interlaced pattern on the Bewcastle Cross, a form of ornament which the Anglian sculptors borrowed from Celtic art, and also in the Roman lettering on both crosses, which is neither Latin nor Gaulish in type, but belongs to the distinctive Hiberno-Saxon school. For the Anglian element, or racial foundation, speak the form of the Ruthwell cross-head, the Anglian runes on both crosses, and particularly the famous poem inscribed in runes on the Ruthwell Cross, in which, with a thoroughly Teutonic and indeed largely pagan spirit, the Cross itself describes its part and emotions in that greatest of sagas, the tragedy of Our Lord's Passion:

> "Then the Young Hero, who was mightiest God,
> 　　Strong and with steadfast mind,
> Up to the Cross with steps unfaltering trod
> 　　There to redeem mankind.
> I trembled, but I durst not fail,
> I on my shoulders bare the Glorious King.
> They pierce my sides with many a darksome nail,
> And on us both their cruel curses fling."[1]

Anglian feeling also appears in the skill with which animal, and especially bird life, is displayed upon the two monuments. And lastly, the Roman Church influence, that was making itself felt with emphasis in Northumbria after the Synod of Whitby in 664, comes out strongly in the vine-leaf ornament and in the beautifully sculptured figures, which are entirely classical in inspiration. Indeed, the feeling of this figure sculpture on both crosses is Byzantine or Hellenistic rather than Romanesque, and reminds us that, at the time when the two crosses were, in all

[1] Transl. T. Hodgkin, *Political History of England*, Vol. I, p. 243.

probability, set up, the dominating figure in the English Church was Theodore of Tarsus, Archbishop of Canterbury from 669 until 690.

In a category by itself, among the early Christian monuments of Scotland, stands the famous Sueno's Stone at Forres. Our old friend "Sandy" Gordon, who first described it in 1726, enthusiastically claims that "it far surpasses all the others in magnificence and grandeur, and is, perhaps, one of the most stately monuments of that kind in Europe". And in modern times, so sober an archaeologist as Joseph Anderson could salute it as "unquestionably the most remarkable monument in Britain". This magnificent stone is no less than 23 feet in height above present ground level: it is 3 feet 9 inches broad and 1 foot 2 inches thick at the base. On the front is a splendid wheel cross, occupying with its plinth five-sixths of the height of the monolith. The remaining portion, below the cross plinth, displays five figures now no longer identifiable, and below these again a row of figures concealed by the stepped base built by Anne, Countess of Moray, in the early eighteenth century to uphold the monument. On the wheel-cross itself the ornament is weathered out: but the entire length of the shaft, and the panels on either side, are enriched with diversely patterned plaitwork. The edges of the slab display foliaceous enrichment and interlaced beasts—both signs of Anglian influence—as well as figure sculpture. On the back of the slab is an astonishing array of closely marshalled military scenes: infantry and cavalry in martial posture or arranged in actual combat, rows of headless corpses laid out as if for counting—the whole set forth with a deliberate ruthlessness that reminds one of Assyrian bas-reliefs, and has no parallel among the Celtic monuments of Britain and Ireland.

In the middle of this grim sequence is carved an object shaped like a flat-topped or truncated cone, with a door at ground level in front. This door has sloping jambs in the Celtic manner. Dr. James S. Richardson, to whose sharp and highly trained eye Scottish archaeology owes so much, has suggested that this subject is the portrayal of a broch. Upon the whole, it seems hard to escape the conclusion that all this sculpture on the reverse of Sueno's Stone depicts an actual historical event—a victorious battle which the monument was erected to commemorate. That it was a victory over Norse invaders is suggested by the name

"Sueno's Stone", attached to the monument since immemorial times. And that a broch played its part in the campaign is noways unlikely, for we know from the Sagas that the Broch of Mousa figured in events in 900 and 1153, in which latter year it stood a siege.

In these grim scenes on the reverse of Sueno's Stone we seem to be confronted by the cold ferocity of an Asshur-natsir-pal— something wholly alien from the peppery but kindly Celts. Does Sueno's Stone preserve for us something of the intense hatred aroused in Scottish breasts by the *furor Normannorum*? To this subject we shall require to address ourselves in the next chapter.

IX

The Norsemen: Their Homesteads
and their Graves

"*A furore Normannorum libera nos, Domine*—from the fury of the
Norsemen, Good Lord, deliver us!" Such was the petition, of
fearful import, that was added to the Church's litany during those
terrible years, in the ninth and tenth centuries, when the pagan
Vikings were harrying the western seaboard of Christian Europe.
It was upon the churches and the monasteries that the hand of the
heathen spoiler fell most heavily; for these were stored with
treasures of every kind, the gifts of generations of pious benefactors. Since the churches and the monasteries were likewise the
homes, indeed almost the only homes, of literary traditions, it was
natural that in their chronicles these centres of culture and learning,
which suffered most from the Viking raids, should be the most
shrill in their protests. Here, for example, is what an Irish annalist
has to say about the northern sea-robbers:

"They built fortresses and landing ports all over Erinn, so that
they made spoil-land and sword-land and conquered-land of her
throughout her breadth. They ravaged her chieftainries and her
privileged churches and her sanctuaries; they rent her shrines and
her reliquaries and her sacred books; they demolished her beautifully ornamented temples: for neither honour nor mercy for right
of sanctuary, nor protection for Church, nor veneration for God or
for man was felt by this furious, ferocious, pagan, ruthless,
wrathful people."

Of course the indignation of the churchmen was natural, and
no one should minimize the enormous damage wrought by the
Viking onslaughts to the reviving culture of Western Europe

under the Holy Roman Empire. Nevertheless there is another side
to the story, particularly in Scotland. For, well before the great
Viking raids began, the Northern and Western Islands, and the
rich cornland of Caithness had been settled, not by armed sea-
robbers, but by poor yet free-born peasant immigrants from
south-western Norway, driven out by the pressure of over-popu-
lation in a homeland offering but scanty sustenance, and seeking
west-overseas new settling grounds where they could ply their
accustomed pursuits of agriculture, stock-breeding, hunting, fishing, sealing, whaling, fowling and trapping. How extensive was
this peasant colonization may be inferred from the fact that,
according to the most reliable estimates, practically all the ancient
place-names in Shetland and Orkney are Norse; while in Lewis
Norse place-names outnumber the Celtic by four to one, and in
Skye by three to two.

It is thus a mistake to speak of the Norse homesteads at Jarlshof,
to which we must now turn our attention, as a "Viking settlement". They are the dwellings of a village community of poor
and peaceable peasants, farmers and fishermen; and what is true
of Jarlshof is equally true of the Norse homesteads found elsewhere in Scotland. A great Norwegian scholar has pointed out
that the Norse settlement in Scotland "was not a military conquest
but a relatively peaceful and gradual colonization. Great collections of swords, spear-heads, battle-axes and other weapons, like
those found in the neighbourhood of London, York or Durham,
have never come to light in Orkney, Shetland or Caithness".
Elsewhere the same writer says of the Norse settlement in Scotland
that "it was a movement of the peasant youth, and not the work of
pirates or Vikings".[1]

The Norse house laid bare at Jarlshof in 1934 was the first
of its kind to be discovered in Britain, Built originally in the early
ninth century, it underwent enlargement at both ends. In its
original form it measured about 70 feet long by 20 feet in greatest
breadth. It was built carefully of compacted earth, faced outside
and inside with drystone masonry; the angles were rounded. The
house had a roof of timber and turf, supported upon a row of
posts along each side of the interior. It contained two rooms, a
parlour and a kitchen, the former having a kind of low dais or

[1] These quotations are from the late Prof. A. W. Brøgger's book, *Ancient
Emigrants: a History of the Norse Settlements in Scotland*, published in 1929.

sitting bench along both sides. Possibly the inmates slept upon these benches. In the centre of the parlour was the hearth, or "long fire". The kitchen had a fireplace and oven. Since this house, the oldest of the group, as also the first to be discovered, was laid bare by Dr. A. O. Curle, other seven have been exposed, and doubtless more await the spade. All the group underwent much alteration during the long period, extending down to the twelfth or thirteenth century, in which our Jarlshof village continued to flourish—due probably to the excellent fishing opportunities provided in Sumburgh Bay. We get an interesting glimpse of the community in a charming episode related by the *Orkneyinga Saga*, which tells us how Earl Rognwald, being shipwrecked in Shetland in 1148, disguised in a white cowl and cloak, took an old fisherman from Sumburgh out in a boat, the earl managing the oars while the fisherman plied his calling. The couple narrowly escaped being swamped in Sumburgh Roost, but regained the village in safety. Thereupon they divided the day's catch, but the disguised earl gave his share to the poor folk who had crowded down to the beach. As he turned to depart, he slipped and fell on the wet foreshore, whereupon the crowd, led by a well dressed woman, mocked him for his clumsiness and his unsuitable garb. But the good Earl, who had a pretty gift for rhyming, reduced the jeering crowd to silence by the following impromptu versicle:

> "The Silken Dame
>   Mocks my attire.
>   Too loudly she laughs!
>   'Tis ill knowing an Earl
>   In fisherman's garb.
>   But early in spring
>   Valiantly I
>   Over the billow
>   Rowed the oak ship."

Since Dr. Curle's classic discovery at Jarlshof, similar Norse houses have been investigated at Freswick in Caithness. One of these contained a bath-room, equipped for a steam-bath such as used to be employed, until quite recent times, in Finland. Readers of the sagas will remember how much the old Norsemen enjoyed the practice of bathing. Thus in King Sverre's Saga we hear more

than once, during the civil wars that disturbed his reign, of men
being surprised in the bath houses. On one occasion no fewer than
fifty men were thus nearly trapped; while on another the King
advises his followers, before making an attack on Nidaros (Trondheim) "to wait until their foes were mostly in the bath-houses".
Can the Norwegians have learned the agreeable practice of steam
bathing from compatriots who had served in the Varangian
Guard at "Mickle-garth" (Constantinople)?

The largest complex of Norse houses so far known in Scotland
is the group now in process of excavation by Dr. Ralegh Radford
at Birsay in Orkney, the capital residence of the mighty Earl
Thorfinn in the eleventh century. One of these houses, provided
with a steam-bath and also with a centrally heated parlour, may
have been part of Earl Thorfinn's palace.

From the homes of the Norse settlers in Scotland we turn now
to their graves. About these the astonishing thing, for which no
really satisfactory explanation has so far been suggested, is their
fewness. In accordance with the scheme of this book, we are of
course only concerned with those Norse burial places which exhibit monumental features. Many cairns and grave mounds which
have been claimed as Norse are more probably of Celtic origin. It
is unsafe to classify such a cairn or mound as Norwegian merely
because it now bears a Norse, or what is claimed to be a Norse
name. Only one or two examples of undoubted Norse graves,
embodying structural features, may be mentioned in this brief
survey. In the famous Norse cemetery at Pierowall in Westray,
dating from the ninth century, at least three of the graves were
ship burials in the old Viking fashion. The grave goods recovered
from the cemetery "included swords and other weapons, pairs
of the bowl-shaped brooches which show that an interment has
been that of a woman, combs, bracelets, knives, needles, sickles
and beads". Generally speaking, in spite of the ship burials, the
graves must be accounted those of a fishing and trading population, rather than of Viking pirates. Pierowall is the Hofn of the
Orkneyinga Saga, "the harbour *par exellence*, the best and only real
harbour in the Orkney Islands, with the old shipping life with its
shallow boats". A single Norse grave was discovered in 1888 at
the Bay of Skaill, near Skara Brae. It contained a massive stone
cist in which a man had been laid at full length, accompanied by

his spear and knife, as well as by an arrow, a whetstone and
a bone comb, of characteristically Norse type, still in its
decorated case of bone. This grave has been dated to the eighth
century.

On the links at Ackergill, in Caithness, a remarkable group of
Norse graves was investigated in 1925 and 1926. Typically, they
consisted of rectangular cairns set within a kerb of flagstones.
Each cairn contained one or more long stone cists, and over the
whole pile was deposited a top layer of white quartzite pebbles.
One cairn differed from the others in being circular in plan. Of the
rectangular cairns, one contained three cists, each with an inhumed
skeleton; in another, the long cist was divided by a central partition, on either side of which lay a skeleton, male and female
respectively—doubtless a husband and wife. A curious feature is
that the bodies of the couple had been buried, in the old Scotch
phrase, "heids and thraws"—i.e., with the heads and feet lying
in opposite directions. The only relic found came from a female
skeleton in the circular cairn. It was a bronze neck chain, of
Norse workmanship, dating from the tenth century. The cist
in this cairn contained four interments, two men advanced in
years, the young woman who wore the chain, and another young
person of unknown sex. Probably these were members of a single
family.

In 1963 one of the most richly furnished Viking graves ever
found in Scotland was unearthed at Westness in Rousay, a place
often mentioned in the *Orkneyinga Saga*. The burial was that of
a woman, obviously a lady of high degree. Two large shoulder-
brooches, of the familiar Norse "tortoise-shell" pattern, were
found. These are of bronze, richly ornamented. They date the
burial approximately to the middle of the ninth century. There was
also a splendid Celtic long-pinned brooch, silver-gilt, perhaps of
Irish origin, and dating from about a century before the Viking
brooches. Furthermore, the grave included a bronze-gilt mounting in the form of an animal, probably from a casket of metal,
wood, or whalebone, or perhaps from a book binding. Other
objects included a bone comb and a string of beads of stone and
glass, which may have linked the shoulder brooches across the
lady's breast.

For real Viking graves, in the proper sense of the word, we
must go to the Western Isles. These lay athwart the main route

of the sea-robbers seeking the rich spoils of the Celtic Church in Ireland. Thus the Hebrides became a Vikings' lair: In the tenth century it is recorded that there were here "many Vikings and war-kings". Here therefore the graves are not those of peasant immigrants, but of warrior aristocrats, who came to plunder and sometimes stayed to farm and trade. Needless to say, warlike gear forms a major element in the grave goods, but there are also farming implements and even scales and weights—for your Viking was ever a keen trader, who sold in one place what he had looted in another. In most cases, the burials had been covered by a simple mound of mingled earth and stones.

We shall conclude this brief sketch of the Norwegian monuments in Scotland with a word or two about one of the most remarkable, though perhaps the least spectacular of all—the Law Ting Holm in the Loch of Tingwall, near Scalloway in Shetland. Here in the old Norse days was held the *Alting*, or Supreme Court of the Shetlands. "To this place came people from all the Shetland Islands in their sailing craft, to bring complaints and petitions and demands, and to fulfil pledges. Here public discipline was meted out, here all great matters were dealt with. It was the root of the Shetlanders' unity and self-confidence: it was the vital nerve of the free peasant society." The neighbouring town of Scalloway, the ancient capital of the Islands, takes its name, "the haven of the booth", from the temporary shops that were set up by those who came to cater for the wants of the udallers or freemen who assembled, under the chairmanship of the Great Fowd, or chief magistrate, of Shetland, for the annual meetings of the *Alting*. The site is a green promontory, once an island, at the northern end of Tingwall Loch. Formerly the island was reached by a causeway, probably originally a series of stepping stones: the area of the island was walled round, and the stone seats of the Fowd and his court officials remained until they were broken up in the eighteenth century for agricultural purposes.

This is indeed a place of ancient and hallowed memories. No member of the First Viking Congress, held in Lerwick in 1950, will ever forget their visit to the Holm on the evening of 9th July, when, amidst a spectral mist, with the viewless ghosts of the old Norse looking on, Professor Einar Ol Sveinsson, of the University of Reykjavik, delivered an almost rapt address in the Icelandic tongue. It is on occasions and at places such as this that the historical imagination takes fire; and certainly all the company left the Holm with a heightened sense of all that Scotland owes to the Norse element in her heritage.

X

The Anglo-Norman Penetration:
Castles, Churches and Burghs

WE have now reached the period of the Anglo-Norman
penetration, or rather infiltration, of Scotland, under
the auspices of the far-seeing and large-minded kings
of the House of Canmore. In Chapter I something has already
been said about this great movement, the result of which was to
bring the half-Celtic, half-Norse realm of Scotland into full
comity with the European body-politic and Latin civilization of
the High Middle Ages. The Anglo-Norman infiltration affected
not only the Scottish mainland but also the Northern and Western
Islands which still belonged to Norway, and the western seaboard
then largely under Norse domination. The Norwegian Earls of
Orkney and the Hebridean chiefs or *reguli*—kinglets, as they are
often styled in the ancient records—were no longer Viking sea-
robbers but men of wealth, culture and vision, in full contact with
European civilization, capable of importing, for their architectural
undertakings, mason-craftsmen of the first rank from the major
centres of Romanesque and Gothic art. Thus it is to a great Norse
Earl that we owe Kirkwall Cathedral, the noblest monument of
Norman architecture in Scotland; while our first stone castle
whose date is definitely known is Kolbein Hruga's tower on the
Orcadian island of Wyre, still locally known as "Cobbie Row's
Castle", and stated in the *Orkneyinga Saga* to have been built
about the year 1145. So also the only Norman stone keep at
present known to exist in Scotland proper is Castle Sween in

Knapdale, whose name perpetuates its Scoto-Norse founder[1]: while at Dunstaffnage in Lorne was built, early in the thirteenth century, a stone castle of *enceinte*, and beside it a chapel, the latter of which is, in its own smaller way, as rich and delicate an example of First Pointed Gothic as anything at Elgin Cathedral.

It is to the Anglo-Normans that we owe the division of Scotland, for ecclesiastical purposes, into parishes, each provided with its church served by a priest maintained partly by tithes and partly by the pious gifts of the faithful. These parishes were grouped into dioceses, each presided over by a bishop seated in his cathedral church. Likewise to the Anglo-Normans we owe the introduction of the monastic orders, who built those beautiful abbeys, which, now in their sad ruins, form the loveliest monuments of our Scottish Middle Ages. Furthermore, it was the Anglo-Normans who imported the feudal castle, the private stronghold or embattled residence of a baron exercising seignorial jurisdiction over his tenantry. Very often the new parishes were simply the manor of a Norman or Normanized Celtic magnate considered in its ecclesiastical context; and the parish church began as the private chapel of the lord of the manor. Hence the reason why, time and again, we find the remains of a Norman castle hard by an ancient parish church.

Lastly, the Anglo-Normans, and the keen Flemish traders who followed in their wake, founded our Scottish burghs. These were the first towns properly so called in our country: for neither Celt nor Norman dwelt in towns as we understand them. A medieval burgh was a deliberate act of town planning, founded in the interest of trade and public order by a feudal superior. If the founder were the king, the town would be a royal burgh, usually enjoying exceptional privileges; if founded by a baron, the town was known as a burgh of barony. The Church also was a notable founder of burghs. Thus Aberdeen was a royal burgh, dependent on the King's castle: Old Aberdeen an ecclesiastical burgh of barony, founded by the bishop in the immediate neighbourhood of his cathedral. Examples of burghs founded by monastic houses are Arbroath, and Newburgh-in-Fife.

Thus the characteristic monuments bequeathed to us by the

---

[1] It is however right to say that the late Professor W. J. Watson derived the name of Castle Sween not from the Norse Sweyn but from the Gaelic Suibhne. In any case, the family were of Celto-Norse origin.

Jedburgh Abbey, Roxburghshire: in choir

Elgin Cathedral, Morayshire: east end

Middle Ages in Scotland are (1) the feudal castle; (2) the parish church; (3) the cathedrals; (4) the monasteries; and (5) the burghs. About each of these something must be said, very briefly, in the present and following two chapters.

When we think of a Norman castle, the image is apt to arise in our minds of a great stone tower, like the Tower of London or the well-known keeps at Norham, Bamburgh, Hedingham and Rochester. But even in England, and far more so in a poor country like Scotland, the typical Norman castle was a thing not of stone and lime but of timbered earthwork. We may see pictures of them, as going concerns, on the Bayeux Tapestry. Such a castle consisted of a moated mound, flat on top and surrounded thereon by a palisade enclosing a wooden tower. The Norman name for such a structure was a *motte*. If the castle were an important one, to the *motte* would be attached a *bailey* or courtyard, likewise enclosed by a palisaded bank and a ditch, and sheltering the wooden subsidiary buildings of the lord's household. In such cases we describe the *ensemble* as a "*motte* and bailey" castle.

Such castles were in no sense provisional. They were solidly and durably constructed, and were very difficult to attack. If destroyed, only the wooden buildings would perish, by fire or by being pulled to pieces; and these could be quickly and cheaply replaced in a land then richly forested. Sometimes the *motte* is wholly artificial, made out of the upcast from the ditch.[1] At other times, particularly in a heavily glaciated country like Scotland, which is full of morainic mounds, the *motte* has been carved out of a mass of fluvio-glacial detritus. Numerous examples of such earthwork castles are found in those parts of Scotland, particularly in Galloway and up the eastern plainlands, which were early settled by the Anglo-Normans. A few specially fine examples may here be mentioned, such as the Mote of Urr, in Kirkcudbrightshire; the Bass of Inverurie, the Peel of Lumphanan and the Doune of Invernochty, all in Aberdeenshire[2]; and Duffus Castle

[1] *Motte* and moat are really the same word, signifying alternatively the ditch and the material heaped out of it. In the same way, the word *dyke* may mean either a ditch, as usually in England, or a wall, as more commonly understood in Scotland.

[2] The various names attached to this group of Aberdeenshire *mottes* are interesting. "Peel" is derived from the medieval Latin word *palus*, a stake,

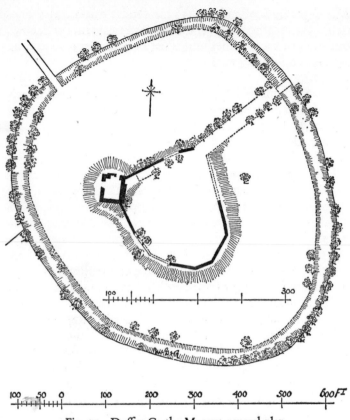

100 |·····|····| | | 300

Fig. 11   Duffus Castle, Moray: general plan
(By courtesy, Aberdeen University Library)

100 _ 50 0   100   200   300   400   500   600 FT

in Moray. This last castle shows, in a manner truly startling, what
could happen when stone buildings were later imposed upon
artificial mounds. About the year 1300, during the English occupation, a stone tower was built upon the *motte*, and stone walls
replaced the stockade round the bailey. The tower has split in
two, and one half of it has slid body-bulk down the *motte*: while
large sections of the bailey walls have similarly subsided. Duffus

reminding us of the palisade by which the mound was crested. "Doune", from
the Celtic word *dun*, a fort, tells us that when the great *motte* of Invernochty
was made in the twelfth century, Gaelic was still the only language of the
common folk in Strathdon. The word "Bass" means an upstanding mass, as
in the Bass Rock.

Castle, the original seat of the great family of Moray, now represented by the ducal houses of Atholl and Sutherland, was in existence in 1151, when David I resided there while engaged upon the foundation of Kinloss Abbey.

Of Norman stone keeps one only is known to have survived in Scotland. This is Castle Sween in Knapdale, already mentioned above. It belongs to the English type best represented at Colchester, in which the area of the keep exceeds its height. Later the keep,

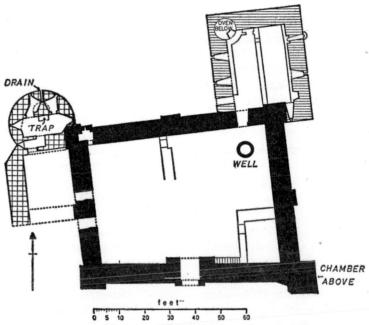

Fig. 12   Castle Sween, Knapdale, Argyll: general plan
(By courtesy, Glasgow Archeological Society)

having possibly been destroyed by fire, was gutted and turned into a small courtyard castle, to which was added a fine stone tower-house of the thirteenth century, while a round flanking tower of the same date was built at another corner. Castle Sween was held against Bruce by a brother of the Lord of the Isles, but surrendered after a "strict siege". It was finally destroyed by "Colkitto" Macdonald during his invasion of Knapdale and Kintyre in the Royalist cause in 1647. Castle Sween is commemorated in a heroic Gaelic poem, referring apparently to an attempt, about the year 1311, by its owner, John MacSween, who adhered to the English side, to recover his patrimony by a naval expedition based upon Ireland:

> "Tryst of a fleet against Castle Sween, welcome is the adventure in Inis Fail [Ireland]: horsemen travelling the billows, brown barks are being cleansed for them. Tall men are arraying the fleet, which swiftly holds its way on the sea's bare surface: no hand lacks a trim war-spear, in battle of targes, polished and comely."

Upon the remote island of Barra, in the Outer Hebrides, Scotland possesses her most perfect example of a stone castle dating from about the year 1200. The Barra group of islands was much used as winter quarters by the Viking raiders "by reason of their distance from land to the south and west, and consequent immunity from surprise attack; and also by reason of their exceptional harbour, with sheltered approaches from both east and west".[1] Such conditions would persist throughout the Norse occupation of the Hebrides, and fully explain the building, on an island in Castlebay, of a formidable stone castle in the most up-to-date style of the age. From time immemorial "Kisimul Castle, our ancient glory" has been the seat of Clan MacNeill, whose Chief is at present, with the co-operation of the Ministry of Public Building and Works, restoring it as a habitable dwelling.

Kisimul Castle occupies the whole area of the sea-girt rock upon which it is perched. It consists of a tall, strongly built square keep, four storeys in height, unvaulted as is often the case with early towers, and rising from a bold and out-spreading plinth. To this keep is attached a curtain wall, following the outline of the rock platform, and on its longest straight front strengthened with semicircular buttresses, almost ranking as embryonic towers. Both keep and curtain have battlements of a twelfth- or thirteenth-century type, and both were garnished with timber hoardings, or oversailing galleries from which the wall-heads were defended. The putlog holes for the beams, and the scarcements on the inside of the walls, upon which these galleries rested, are still perfectly preserved, and admirably illustrate the system of wall-head defences which was usual in western Europe in the early thirteenth century, before the introduction of stone parapets resting upon

[1] Sir Lindsay Scott in *The Viking Congress, Lerwick*, 1960, p. 212.

corbels. The existing buildings within the courtyard, which were comparatively modern, have been largely rebuilt in the recent restoration. In 1643 the castle contained a private chapel, wherein the rites of the Roman Church were still practised, in defiance of the Presbytery.

The MacNeills of Barra took themselves very seriously. It is recorded that after the Chief had finished his midday meal, a herald ascended the high tower of Kisimul Castle, and, after a flourish on his trumpet, proclaimed to all the world: "Hear, ye people, and listen, ye nations! The MacNeill of Barra having finished his dinner, all the princes of the earth are at liberty to dine!"

As a result of the treaty imposed in 1156 by Somerled, Lord of Argyll, upon Godred the Black, the Norse King of Man and the Hebrides, Ardnamurchan became the dividing point between the northern and the southern Hebrides, the latter falling to Somerled, while the Norseman retained the former. Probably after this division, which left a deep mark on the subsequent history of the western seaboard, another early stone castle was erected near the Point of Ardnamurchan. Mingary Castle consists of a hexagonal wall of *enceinte*, adjusted to the outline of the peninsulated rock on which it stands, and having both a landward and a seaward entrance. Here also, as at Kisimul, we note the provision for a timber hoarding: and where the old hall backed upon the curtain the latter is pierced by lancet windows of unmistakably First Pointed date. The battlements are of the same early type as those at Kisimul. Due to its important strategic position, Mingary Castle bulked large in later West Highland history. The most famous event in its colourful record was its siege and capture by Colkitto Macdonald in 1644. During the "Forty-five" the castle was garrisoned by Hanoverian troops, and the principal building now visible within the thirteenth-century walls is a barrack of that date.

With Mingary must undoubtedly be classed the romantically situated ruin of Castle Tioram in Moidart. Here we have the same massive untowered wall of *enceinte*, adjusted to the contour of the island site: the same early form of battlement, and the same regular and well-thought-out provision for timber hoardings. At Castle Tioram a square tower was added in the fourteenth century, and another, smaller tower, picturesquely turretted in the

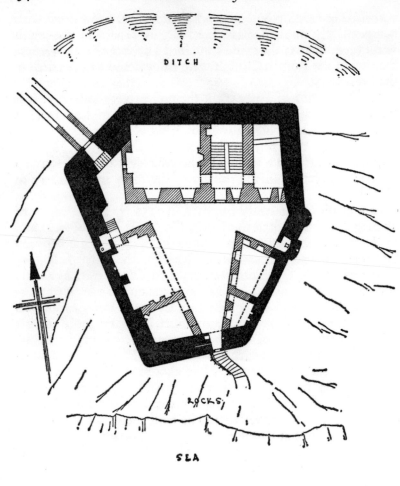

Fig. 13   Mingary Castle, Ardnamurchan, Inverness-shire
(By courtesy, Glasgow Archaeological Society)

later Scottish style, about the year 1600. Like its neighbour Mingary, Castle Tioram had a wild history extending from the fourteenth to the eighteenth century, when it was finally burnt during the "Fifteen".

Undoubtedly the most famous of this early group of stone

castles on the western seaboard is Dunstaffnage, at the entry to the Firth of Lorn, near Oban. True, its fame is largely due to the legendary part assigned to it in the early history, or pseudo-history of the Scotic Kingdom of Dalriada, and to the tales that associate it with the Stone of Destiny: yet it has an authentic and stirring record of its own, dating from its siege and capture by Bruce in 1308 down to the two Jacobite risings in the eighteenth

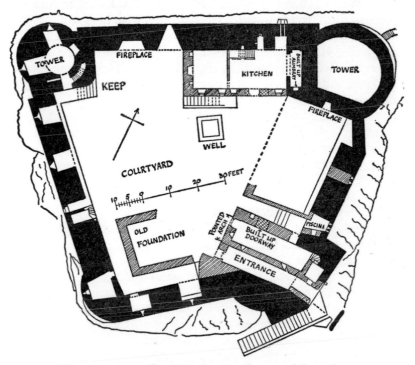

Fig. 14   Dunstaffnage Castle, Argyll: ground floor plan
(By courtesy, Aberdeen University Library)

century. From an architectural standpoint the castle and its attendant chapel, as indicated already, form a subject of the highest interest. Like the others of its group, the castle consists of a great wall of *enceinte* adjusted to the contour of its rock; but here there are three round towers and a projecting gatehouse, much altered in the sixteenth century. The original windows in the curtain wall are pointed lancets, and a small mural oratory is lit by a pair of these, decorated with boldly cut dog-tooth ornament obviously

from the same hand as the very rich First Pointed chapel, which
stands about 160 yards distant from the castle.

Lastly among the group comes Inverlochy, occupying an important strategic position sentinelling the south-western outlet of
the Great Glen, hard by its successor, Fort William. Inverlochy
Castle was the principal stronghold in Lochaber of the great
Anglo-Norman family of Comyn. A naval battle was fought
beneath its walls in 1297. The castle, built on a level site, forms a
rectangular or rather trapezoidal enclosure, with high and massive
curtain walls. At each angle is a round tower, large and boldly
projected, rising from a broad spreading plinth. The north-
western tower is bigger than the others, and formed the *donjon*
or keep. All the towers are pierced with long arrow slits of a
thirteenth-century type. There are two entrances to the castle,
opposite each other, a land-gate and a sea-gate. On the three
landward sides was a wide ditch, running out on either flank
into the River Lochy. Beneath the walls of Inverlochy Castle
Montrose gained his celebrated victory over Clan Campbell on
2nd February, 1645.

What is the significance of this astonishing group of early
castles on the western seaboard? To those described others may
be added for which there is no space here, such as Duart in Mull
and Dunvegan in Skye.

Chiefly, of course, these castles stand for the arrival of the
Anglo-Norman penetration upon our western coastline, and the
cession of the Isles by Norway in the Treaty of Perth, 1266. The
fact that they have survived, in such remarkable completeness,
down to our own time, is due to two causes.

In the first place, this group have escaped the general destruction which overtook our early stone castles during the Wars of
Independence. It was the practice of the Scots to overthrow such
buildings when they were recovered from the English, and to
rely for defence upon the natural difficulties of their country—its
mountains, forests, swamps and lakes—and upon a "scorched
earth" policy. Hence on the eastern side of Drumalban we have
few remaining examples of stone castles dating from before the
Wars of Independence, and these for the most part survive only
in fragments of dismantled structures embodied in the rebuilding.
For example, in the two great royal castles of Edinburgh and

Stirling, if we except the little chapel of St. Margaret in the former, no masonry older than the fourteenth century now appears to exist. But on the western seaboard there is clear evidence that the policy of Bruce was not to dismantle the castles of his enemies when captured, but to place garrisons in them. For example, we are expressly told that after the capture of Dunstaffnage, the King

> "a gud wardane thair-in set
> And betaucht hym bath men and met,
> Swa that he thair lang tym mycht be
> Magre thaim all of that cuntre."

Documentary evidence makes it clear that the reason for this reversal of castle policy on the far side of Drumalban was the King's constant fear of an effort by his implacable enemies, the House of Lorn and their kinsmen the Comyns, to restore themselves with the aid of English naval power based on Ireland.

In the second place, it seems clear that these early castles, having thus survived the struggle for independence, owe their continued preservation in a relatively unaltered state to the fact that, being in a remote and backward part of the country, they were less exposed to being remodelled or extended in accordance with new architectural fashions and new standards of defence and domestic comfort. In fact, many of them on their rock-girt stances were incapable of being extended in any form. Once built, such castles as Kisimul, Dunstaffnage, Mingary and Tioram could never be anything else than essentially a great wall of *enceinte* with or without a keep and flanking towers.

We turn now from the castles to the parish churches of the twelfth and thirteenth centuries. Since Scotland was always a poor land, we cannot expect here anything like the rich and beautiful country churches with which England is crowded. Nevertheless, both wealth and taste existed in certain areas, and one or two of our Norman parish churches, notably Tyninghame in East Lothian, Dalmeny near Edinburgh, and Leuchars in Fife, are in their own way as fine as anything in England. During the twelfth and thirteenth centuries, the entire eastern lowlands of Scotland, up to and including the Northern Isles which then belonged to Norway, formed one cultural province with England, and were exposed to the same architectural influences. Many of the Anglo-

Norman settlers, like the de Quincy family to whom we owe Leuchars Church, held lands in both kingdoms, and were therefore able to import mason-craftsmen from the great building centres in the south. The Norse chiefs, as we have already noted, were equally cosmopolitan in their architectural outlook. Thus it occurs that at Orphir, in Orkney, we find the only example in Scotland of a circular Romanesque church, inspired obviously by the Church of the Holy Sepulchre at Jerusalem. Unfortunately, only a fragment of this unique structure remains, since the greater part of it was demolished in 1757 to provide materials for a Presbyterian preaching-box. Only a small segment of the round nave survives, together with the semicircular vaulted apse. Stylistic details would seem to indicate a late eleventh-century date for the building.

Modern investigation has recovered the complete plan of the first cathedral of the North Isles—the "Christ's Kirk" founded soon after 1050 on the Brough of Birsay by Earl Thorfinn the Mighty, a powerful ruler who had visited the Holy Roman Empire and had obtained pardon for his sins, which were many, at the hands of Pope Leo IX. He died in 1065, and was buried in his cathedral at Birsay. It was quite a modest structure, consisting of a nave with a western tower (perhaps never completed), a short chancel, and a semicircular apse. As originally built, the chancel opened directly out of the nave, in the Irish manner. Later, a narrow chancel arch was inserted, together with semicircular alcoves for altars in the two eastern angles of the nave. Later still, the apse was abandoned and walled off, and the high altar transferred to the chancel. Immediately north of the little cathedral are the foundations of the bishop's palace.

Earl Thorfinn's "Christ's Kirk" shows us that, owing to the intercourse between the Norse dominions in the Northern Islands, the Hebrides, and Ireland, the influence of Irish Romanesque made itself felt in the earliest ecclesiastical buildings of the Orkneys. This is still more apparent in the remarkable church of St. Magnus on the island of Egilsay. It consists of a nave, a chancel, and a tall western round tower which, though incorporated in the church, declares to the eye its kinship with the free-standing Irish Round Towers.[1] The chancel is vaulted, and opens directly from the nave in the Irish manner. Above it, again in the Irish manner,

[1] See *supra*, pp. 114–5.

is a dwelling house for the priest. In addition to an entrance at ground level, there is an upper door from the nave into the tower, and the jambs of this are somewhat inclined in the Irish fashion. There seems no reason to doubt that this church was the scene of the martyrdom of St. Magnus on Easter Sunday, 16th April, 1115.

Returning now to Scotland proper, we have first to note a very early specimen of Romanesque church architecture, long before the Anglo-Norman infiltration, in the tall tower of Restenneth Priory in Angus. Not only is the whole tower, except for a late medieval spire, extremely primitive in masonry and detail, but the lower portion is evidently older than the upper. It has been suggested that we have here a western porch which has been heightened into a tower, in the same way as happened at such early Northumbrian churches as Corbridge and Monkwearmonth; and that the porch may be a remnant of the church "built in the Roman manner", for which the Pictish King Nechtan MacDerile, in the year 710, sought masons from the Saxon monastery at Monkwearmonth.

Norman architecture is easily recognized by its air of massiveness, broad shallow buttresses, heavy round arches and characteristic decoration, such as the cushion or scalloped capital with its square abacus, the chevron, billet and "beak-head" mouldings, and, in the richer churches, a profusion of figure and animal sculpture, often very barbarous in style. If the doorways or windows are deeply recessed, the mouldings are not worked on a continuous slope, but arranged in a series of square steps, or "orders". Arcading is often used, both outside and inside the building. Where a Norman church is built of ashlar, the stones are usually square on face, and the jointing, particularly in early examples, is often wide.

An early and dated example of Norman Romanesque in Scotland is the famous Church of St. Rule at St. Andrews, which has been shown to have been erected, probably as a reliquary church, by Bishop Robert (1126–59), with the aid of masons imported from Yorkshire. The church consists today of a chancel and a very tall western tower, 108 feet high; the sanctuary and the nave have disappeared. In its great height and megalithic masonry the church retains early characteristics, derived from Anglo-Saxon and, more remotely, from Celtic traditions. Similar very tall towers of about the same period, are found in the parish churches of Dunning and Muthil in Perthshire, and Markinch in Fife. The Muthil tower was originally free-standing, like the early Norman tower, later heightened, which is now incorporated in Dunblane Cathedral.

In addition to Dalmeny and Leuchars, already mentioned, Norman parish churches, though more or less altered, are still in use at Duddingstone, near Edinburgh; Kirkliston and Uphall in Linlithgowshire; Cruggleton, Wigtownshire; Monymusk, Aberdeenshire; and Birnie, Morayshire. Also restored and in use are the celebrated chapel of St. Margaret on the Castle Rock of Edinburgh and the Reilig Orain at Iona, which, as might be expected, betrays strong Irish influence. For the rest, parochial architecture of the Norman period survives only in bits and pieces: here a door or a window, there a chancel arch, sometimes a tower embodied in later work. But at St. Blane's, Kingarth, in the Island of Bute, we have a very interesting ruined parish church of fine Norman workmanship, with a richly decorated chancel arch. What lends particular interest to this beautiful ruin is the fact that the Norman work in the chancel appears to embody remains of a more primitive church, dating perhaps from the eleventh century. Kingarth has an ecclesiastical history going back far into the Celtic past: a monastery was founded here by St. Blaan, who died in 590.

Lastly, a word about the burghs. No old Scottish burgh retains any secular building going back to Norman times: though Aberdeen has the distinction of possessing important remains, absorbed into later work, of the only cruciform Norman parish church in Scotland. No doubt, then, and long afterwards, the houses of the burghers were built of wood, or of clay and wattle work. It is a great mistake to imagine that the men of the Middle Ages were ignorant of what we now call "town planning"; but to enter into this fascinating subject would be to go far beyond the scope of the present work. Attention may however be called to the early town-plan of the royal burgh of Forres, probably a foundation of the good King David I. Here we see how the town in effect forms the bailey of the royal castle on its *motte*: we notice the position of the "town's kirk", as usual a little aside from the "stour" of the central market street: the regular gridiron planning of the street system, and the walk (like the Roman *intervallum*) left free all round the inside of the ramparts, of palisaded earthwork doubtless, by which the town was defended. Here indeed is town planning, forthright and purposeful, not unworthy to take its place beside the *villes neuves* and *bastides* of medieval France. Forres, it is clear, was designed to have a garrison of soldier-burgesses, Norman, Saxon and Flemings no doubt, planted by the Canmore dynasty as a deliberate act of royal policy in the heart of the recalcitrant Celtic Province of Moray, which fiercely cherished its allegiance to the rival House of Macbeth.

XI

The Age of Abbeys and Cathedrals:
I—The Monasteries

THE great architectural revolution in western Europe, which replaced the Romanesque style with its semicircular arches by the earliest development of Pointed or "Gothic" architecture, had its origin in the Isle de France about the middle of the twelfth century. This revolution was dictated by necessities purely structural. Striving always to build churches ever larger and loftier, the architects of that period were increasingly embarrassed by the difficulty in vaulting over areas of different size. Whether in the nave and chancel or in the aisles, bays square on plan could always be conveniently vaulted by intersecting barrel-shaped groins. But in the side aisles it was often convenient to have the bays oblong on plan. Hence the arches spanning the nave must rise to a height greater than those of the side walls, spanning the compartments of the aisles. To raise the side arches by "stilting", i.e. by carrying the arch up vertically at first from the capitals on either side, encountered an insuperable difficulty in managing the intersection of the groining of the side vaults. This problem was overcome by the introduction of the pointed arch. Whereas the height of a semicircular arch is always half its span, that of a pointed arch can be raised without any relation to its span. Hence the desired flexibility was achieved, and oblong groined vaults could be handled as easily as vaults square on plan. The elasticity thus achieved in the management of vaults rapidly communicated itself to other departments of the building. Being a form in itself so beautiful, the pointed arch soon spread from vaulting to doors, windows, niches—indeed to voids and recesses of every description. At the same time the mouldings became lighter, more varied, and more graceful: new forms of enrichment, above all the dog-tooth, so characteristic of "First Pointed" Gothic, were evolved; the pointed bowtell superseded the heavy round members of Norman moulded work; the square capital gave place to a circular form, and foliage, vigorous though still conventional in design, was carved upon the capitals, seeming as it were to be thrusting upwards against the weight which the capitals were designed to bear. The heavy square or cylindrical Norman piers gave place to piers of "clustered" form, corresponding to the richly diversified series of deeply cut arch-moulds above. The portals were similarly diversified and enriched, and as the style developed their mouldings, instead of being arranged in a series of "orders" successively recessed, came to be wrought upon a broad sloping surface, often with shafts from a single stone and wholly detached from the wall-face. The external buttresses became narrower and more boldly projected than the broad shallow pilasters of Norman work: they have frequent offsets, may be chamfered at the angles, and rise into gablets or crocketted finials. The lancet windows, as the style matures, tend to be grouped together under a pointed general arch, and the "tympanum", or space between this arch and the heads of the lancets, is pierced by a trefoil or quatrefoil opening, forming what is known as "*plate*" tracery. As the style advances, the lancets themselves become trefoiled, and the earliest patterns of true tracery, always geometrical in design, make their appearance. Lastly, in the greater churches that noblest creation of the Gothic style, the tall spire, makes its appearance to crown the edifice and point upwards towards Almighty God, to whose honour and glory the church was raised.

Something indeed about the soaring quality of the new Gothic style must surely have appealed to an age of intense religious fervour. For the twelfth and thirteenth centuries, the high noon-tide of Latin Christendom, were one of those rare periods in which the spirit of man, as in Athens of the fifth century before Christ, seems to undergo a mystic burgeoning, and seeks its highest satisfaction in consecrating all its energy and talents to paying tribute, with everything that wealth and craftsmanship can provide, to those unseen sources from which all human progress is derived. "Look around you", said a Benedictine monk of the twelfth century to the craftsmen of his time—"Look around you, and survey the fabric of creation. It is the work of an artist, of the supreme artist who has made all things beautiful in their season. He has gifted you too with a portion of His own nature and has formed you an artist; and you are bound in service to Him to exercise your creative gift and make the most of your affinity with what is beautiful. In the name of religion take up the brush and tongs and mallet, and spare not cost or labour till the House of God that you build and adorn shall shine like the very fields of Paradise!"

Very specially the twelfth century was the age of the founding of monasteries. In the prevailing religious fervour of the age, kings and great barons found their account, as an expression of their piety and to secure their welfare in the world to come, in founding and endowing monastic houses, the inmates whereof were held bound, by the deed of gift, to pray for the souls of the patron, his kindred, and other persons named by him. To such motives we must ascribe the establishment in 1115, by Alexander I, of a house of Augustinian Canons regular at Scone, and another of the same order on an island in Loch Tay, in 1122; while his brother, the good King David I, whose pious depletion of the royal revenues by monastic foundations caused a successor ruefully to style him "ane sair sanct for the crown", was the founder of the monasteries of Kelso and Melrose in Roxburghshire, Dundrennan in Galloway, Newbattle in Midlothian, Holyrood near Edinburgh, and Urquhart and Kinloss in Moray, besides being a lavish benefactor of existing houses, such as Coldingham in Berwickshire and Cambuskenneth near Stirling. William the Lion was the founder of the great abbey of Arbroath in Angus. Where the King set the example, his great barons hastened to follow suit. Thus Hugo de Morville founded Dryburgh in Roxburghshire, and Kilwinning in Ayrshire; and David, Earl of Huntingdon, a brother of William the Lion, founded Lindores in Fife. All the leading monastic orders were recipients of this pious generosity. Thus Coldingham, Dunfermline, Urquhart and Iona were Benedictine foundations; Paisley was Cluniac; Dundrennan, Melrose, Newbattle, Sweetheart in Galloway, Deer in Aberdeenshire were Cistercian. A notable feature of Scottish monasticism is the number of houses—Arbroath, its dependency

"Yett", Blackness Castle, West Lothian

Lincluden Abbey, Kirkcudbrightshire:
tomb of Princess Margaret

Melrose Abbey: "nodding ogee"

Fyvie in Aberdeenshire, Kelso, Kilwinning in Ayrshire, Lesma-
hagow in Lanarkshire (a daughter house of Kelso), and Lindores
—which belonged to the Tironensian Order: while still more
remarkable was the fact that Scotland possesses the only three
Valliscaulian houses—Pluscarden in Moray, Beauly in Inverness-
shire, and Ardchattan in Argyllshire—ever founded outside the
parent country, France. All these were monastic houses strictly
so called. The Augustinian Canons regular, or Austin canons as
they were usually called in Britain—otherwise known as Black
canons from the colour of their robes—were a sort of intermediate
body between the monks or "regulars"—so called because they
lived under a *regula* or rule of their order—who had no cure of
souls and therefore no parochial responsibilities, and the secular
or parish clergy: for a canon regular, not belonging to an "enclosed order", could serve the parish churches which might be
impropriated to his monastery. Augustinian houses were well
represented in Scotland: notable examples are Jedburgh in
Roxburghshire, Holyrood, St. Andrews, and Inchmahome on its
island in the Lake of Menteith. Another order of canons regular,
the Premonstratensian, or white canons, have left us some important monasteries, such as Whithorn and Dryburgh.

In the foregoing paragraph we have enumerated no more than
the leading conventual houses founded in Scotland during the
twelfth and thirteenth centuries. Having regard to the comparatively slender resources of the country, the whole effort represents
an astonishing achievement of combined piety and policy; and the
surviving ruins of these beautiful buildings—the loveliest of all
our ancient monuments—impress us as nothing else in Scotland
can, with a sense of the glory of the Middle Ages. To the modern
observer, our ruined abbeys often seem to stand for a way of life
for which a materialistic society may feel scant sympathy: yet,
leaving aside the religious arguments in favour of the monastic
life, we must never forget that these great institutions were
deeply interwoven with the social and economic life of medieval
Scotland, and played a great part in the development of her
civilization.

In the first place, the revenues of the monasteries were to a
large degree spent among the people by whose labour these
revenues were mostly created. The monastic houses were permanently resident landlords, and the evils of non-residence, of

absentee landlordism, which ever since the Middle Ages have formed such a baffling problem of rural economy, were largely absent from the monastic estates. To a considerable extent, the rents of the monastic lands flowed back to those who paid them. Secondly, the monastery was a landlord that never died. Thus its tenants were seldom liable to changes in ownership and to the feudal casualties or payments due on such occasions to the crown or other superior, and to the new owner. Thirdly, upon the whole (though with considerable exceptions) the monasteries were easy landlords. The immemorial power of custom, transmitted uninterrupted by changes of ownership, resulted in the monastic tenants acquiring, in course of time, most valuable common rights. Fourthly, the monasteries were great employers of labour, pioneers in the arts and crafts, in agriculture, land drainage and stock-raising. And lastly and by no means least, the monastic houses played an important part in the life of the community by the hospitality which they exercised. At a time when inns were few and far between, the gates of the monastery were open, day and night, to the stranger, of whatever rank, who sought shelter and refreshment.

Of course, human nature being what it is, not all monks or every monastery always acted up to the high ideals of their profession. Nevertheless, and despite all John Knox's coarse abuse, there is not much evidence of serious or widespread disorders in our Scottish monasteries even during the period of their decline —nothing, certainly, had the spirit of the age been different, that could not have been cured by wise and timely reform. And though the modern mind may sometimes find it hard to appreciate the values for which the monk stood, monasticism is too widespread among many faiths and in many lands for any candid inquirer to doubt that it answers to something very deep in human nature. Nor is it without significance that, midway in this materialistic twentieth century, two medieval monasteries in Scotland are in course of restoration to serve the needs of a religious community—one, Benedictines of the ancient faith; the other, an outgrowth from the Presbyterian Church, which has sometimes been regarded as standing at the opposite pole from Roman Catholicism and all its works.

When the word Abbey is mentioned, there naturally rises

before our minds the vision of a great church. Yet it is the cloister (Latin *claustrum*) which is the essential of the monastery: for a monk is a member of a society who by their vows are cloistered (*clausi*), that is, shut off from the world within the bounds of their cloister garth, so that, removed from the world's distractions, they may spend their time in study, and in prayer for the souls of the founder and benefactors of their house. Let us therefore now betake ourselves to the cloister of a typical Scottish monastery and inspect in order the buildings that enclose it: eking out our study, in the case of features ruined or awanting here, by reference to other abbeys. For this purpose we select Dryburgh Abbey, which, in addition to being, in the opinion of many, the loveliest monastic ruin in Scotland, possesses also the most complete suite of conventual buildings north of the Tweed.[1] As we have already noted, Dryburgh was a Premonstratensian house—the first of that order in Scotland. Its founder, in 1150, was Hugh de Morville, Constable of Scotland—a nephew of one of the murderers of Becket.

In northern Europe, generally, the cloister stands on the south side of the nave of the abbey church, which shelters it from nothern blasts and acts as a reflector for the rays and warmth of the sun. But in some cases, where conditions of the ground, and in particular drainage requirements or the convenience of a water-supply, might dictate, the cloister is found on the north side of the church. Scottish examples of this aberration are Melrose, Iona, and Balmerino, a Cistercian house in Fife. At Dryburgh the claustral position is normal. We take our stand then within the cloister garth, close beside the south transept of the church.

The cloister was once surrounded by an open pillared arcade, but of this nothing now survives except a few of the corbels which supported its lean-to roof. The north walk of the cloister, catching the sun, was the study place, where in the fine weather the learned among the canons would spend part of their time reading or copying manuscripts. At the east end of this north claustral alley the visitor will notice a wall-press, in which the books prescribed for studying or copying, lent out from the

[1] More of the conventual buildings indeed is preserved at Inchcolm, but so much has been rebuilt in the later Middle Ages, and in so highly aberrant a manner, as to make this monastery untypical.

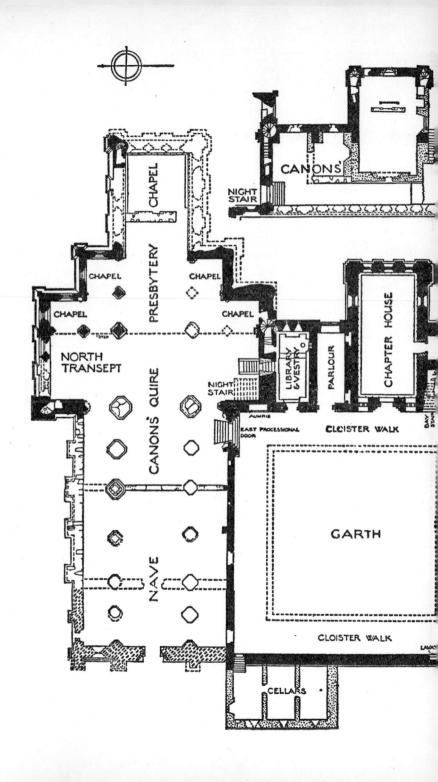

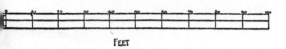

FEET

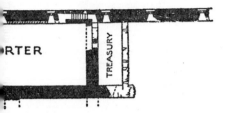

•RTER

TREASURY

■■■ LATE 12TH AND 13TH CENTURY
▨▨▨ 15TH CENTURY
▦▦▦ 16TH CENTURY
▨▨▨ 18TH CENTURY

Fig. 15 Dryburgh Abbey,
Berwickshire: general plan

(*By courtesy, Ministry of Public
Building and Works*)

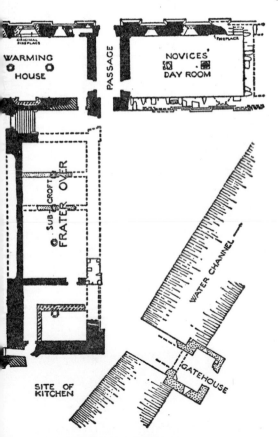

ORIGINAL
FIREPLACES

WARMING

HOUSE

PASSAGE

NOVICES'

DAY ROOM

FIREPLACE

SUB-CROFT
FRATER OVER

WATER CHANNEL

GATEHOUSE

SITE OF
KITCHEN

library, were kept when not in use. The library itself is the first apartment which we encounter as we pass from the northern round to the eastern cloister walk. It is vaulted, so as to be fire-proof. At a later date, the library seems to have been converted into a small side-chapel.

Next to the library comes a vaulted passage, known as the slype, or sometimes as the parlour, because here, and here only according to the strict interpretation of the monastic rule, could a monk have intercourse with visitors from the outer world. This passage also served as a means of communication with the canons' cemetery, which lay to the eastward. At Dryburgh the slype has been converted into a private burial place.

The next room, a large and important one, is the chapter-house. Here the canons assembled daily to hear the reading of a chapter from the Rule of their order. Hence the name "chapter-house"; but the room was used also for discussions about the business of the monastery, for the intimation of news, and for the enforce-ment of discipline. It will be noted that on either side of the door are two large unglazed openings, like windows. These enabled lay-brethren, and any others who might be summoned, to hear the deliberations of the canons from the cloister walk. All round the chapter-house is a stone bench, upon which the canons sat. The Abbot and his principal colleagues occupied the eastern bench, the importance of which is emphasized by a stone wall-arcade.

Next to the chapter-house is the day-stair by which during daylight hours the monks ascended to their sleeping quarters. Beyond this again comes the calefactory or warming house, in which at certain seasons the canons could enjoy the luxury of a fire. This was a handsome room, vaulted upon a central line of pillars. The fireplace was midway in the east wall, so as to distri-bute its heat equably over the room. In some respects, the monastic calefactory answered the purpose of a modern academic common room. Still further to the south, outside the outer wall of the southern claustral range, is a passage, and beyond the latter stretches the day room of the novices, also provided with a fire-place. The novices' quarters were reached by a passage at the south-east angle of the cloister garth.

Over the whole of the eastern range, as far south as the cale-factory, stretched the "dorter" or dormitory of the canons, with the novices' dormitory beyond it, over their day room. At the far, or southern end of the whole range must have been the "rere-dorter" or latrines, but of these nothing has survived. At St. Andrews, Melrose, Deer and Crossraguel we may still admire the conduits which tell of the monks' care for sanitation.

The south range of the claustral buildings is entirely taken up by the "frater", that is, the refectory or dining-room. This was above vaulted cellarage with central pillars. It was entered by a stair at the western end, and in the west cloister walk is a lavatory at which the canons washed their hands before going up for a meal. To the westward, beyond the frater, were the kitchens.

The western side of the cloister was originally closed only by a screen wall: later against part of this a row of storage vaults was built.

Here therefore we find a habitation as rigidly organized for a communal, disciplined life as a Roman fort. Nothing like such standardized and purposeful planning had in fact been seen in Scotland since the Romans left.

We now enter the Abbey church. Albeit greatly ruined, this has been a noble fane. It consisted of a nave with side aisles; a central tower flanked by north and south transepts with eastern chapels; a presbytery; and at the east end a Lady Chapel. The western half of the nave was used by such laymen who might attend the services: the rest of the nave, and the "crossing", or space under the tower, was occupied by the stalls of the canons, while the officiating clergy discharged their duties at the high altar in the presbytery. Into the south transept descended the night stair, by which the canons came down from the dorter to attend the nocturnal service.

The church was entered by a great western portal, and there were processional doorways at either end of the nave, communicating with the cloister. The east processional doorway is a magnificent specimen of Transitional work, with monolithic nook-shafts, carrying four orders of rich and deeply undercut mouldings, including a splendid trail of dog-tooth. The arch is semicircular, like that of the chapter-house doorway. So is the arch of the great western door of the nave, although it dates from the early fifteenth century. Herein is illustrated a remarkable peculiarity of Scottish Gothic, namely the persistence with which the round arch is retained throughout all periods down to the extinction of

Gothic art in the seventeenth century. The lateness of the west doorway in Dryburgh Abbey church is shown in the high and narrow bases and the absence of capitals—the mouldings, which include two rows of very beautiful four-leaved flowers, widely spaced, being continuous on jambs and arch.

In this brief survey of Dryburgh Abbey we have confined our-selves mainly to the functional purpose of the various buildings. The glory of their architecture must be seen to be appreciated. Much of the work dates from the Transitional period between the Norman and Gothic styles: what survives of the Abbey church is mostly in the purest and most vigorous First Pointed architecture, but the nave was largely rebuilt after the destruction of the Abbey by Richard II in 1385. The last days of the Abbey as a sacred place form a story of extreme pathos—all the more because of the absence of a violent termination to its life with the advent of the Reformation. Gradually, one by one, the White Canons died off amid the ruin of the ancient faith; no novices presented themselves to replenish their diminishing number, until at last came the day when the sweet music was hushed, the stately ritual forgotten, the memory of ages of bygone piety spurned by the secular possessors of the beautiful site.[1]

Features of the monastic *ensemble* lacking at Dryburgh can be supplied from other Scottish monasteries. The cloister arcade, carefully restored from the ancient remains, is best studied at Iona; also at another Hebridean monastery, the Augustinian Priory of Oronsay; and at Inchcolm Abbey, an Augustinian house on an island in the Firth of Forth. At the Cluniac house of Paisley the north and west cloister walks have been renewed. In the Cistercian Abbey of Deer (Aberdeenshire) we have the ground plan of the infirmary, occupying its usual position well apart from the cloister garth. Here the sick monks were tended, also those recovering after bleeding, which usually took place four times a year, in February, April, September and December. Inmates of the infirmary were allowed concessions in diet, and also a fire. At Melrose remains the infirmary of the lay brethren. Both here

[1] By 10th June, 1600, the last monk of Dryburgh was "decessit". An honourable feature of the Scottish Reformation is the humane treatment of the monks. They were provided with pensions, and allowed to live on, no doubt in a purely secular fashion, in the conventual buildings, in so far as these were not required for his own purposes by the Commendator.

and at Deer we have the Abbot's house—best exemplified, however, at the Tironensian Abbey of Arbroath. Every monastery had its precinct wall, a feature which survives impressively at Sweetheart, the last Cistercian house to be founded (in 1273) in Scotland; and on an even grander scale, with many a round tower, at the Augustinian Priory and metropolitan Cathedral of St. Andrews. At Sweetheart and St. Andrews the precinct wall encloses some 30 acres. At Dryburgh a small gatehouse still survives, but in no wise comparable to the formidable fortified gatehouses at Arbroath, St. Andrews, and Crossraguel—the last a Cluniac house in Ayrshire. These castellar gatehouses speak to us, in no uncertain terms, of the militarization of Scottish life after the Wars of Independence—a development from which even Holy Church was not exempt, as we shall find in a later chapter.

Although it would perhaps be wrong to use such a term, for example, as "Cistercian architecture", it is certain that the great monastic orders developed their own fashions in building. By their Rule the Cistercians were bound to build and furnish their churches as plainly as possible, with low towers and no soaring spires. Sculpture, painting and stained glass were alike sternly forbidden. Yet gradually this bleak puritanism was abandoned, and the most ornate monastic church in Scotland is the Cistercian Abbey of Melrose, as reconstructed after its savaging by Richard II in 1385. The earliest Cistercian churches had a short chancel and a long narrow aisleless nave. This characteristic plan had its influence on other Orders: it is seen in Scotland at the Valliscaulian Priory of Beauly. The Cistercian Abbey church of Deer was originally of this design, though a north aisle was added later— it being impossible to provide also a south aisle, owing to the cloister. From England this primitive plan was introduced into Scandinavia at Lyse Kloster near Bergen, the first Cistercian house in Norway, a daughter of Kirkstead; and so made its influence felt on the earliest stone church architecture on the Scandinavian North. Thus we find it in the Norse Cathedral of Gardar (Igaliko) in Greenland: and, *via* the Norse occupation of the Hebrides, it appears in the remarkable little church, *Teampull Mholuidh* (St. Moluag's Church) at Eoropie in the Isle of Lewis— in medieval times a famous sanctuary, known in local tradition as "the Cathedral".

A peculiarity of the Cistercian plan is that the frater tends to be placed north and south—i.e., projecting at right angles from the southern claustral range. This seems to have been done to allow more room for the kitchens at the south-west corner, which had to provide not only for the monks themselves, but for the lay-brethren, who were specially numerous in the Cistercian Order. These had their own refectory in the western range. At Melrose and Dundrennan the frater lies north and south, but at Deer it lay east and west in the Benedictine manner.

In contrast to the early Cistercians, the Tironensian Order, so fully represented in Scotland, were zealous patrons of the arts and crafts—employers of masons, carpenters, smiths and painters. It is thus no accident that the ruins of our Tironensian houses include the noblest specimens of monastic building in Scotland. Earliest of them is Kelso in Roxburghshire, the most tremendous fragment of Romanesque architecture left to us—towering above the little town "like some antique Titan predominating over the dwarfs of a later world". Little now remains but the Abbey church, and this survives only in fragments. It is of particular interest because the plan had western as well as eastern transepts, with a tower over both the crossings. The same plan is found at Ely and Bury St. Edmunds: it is derived from the Carolingian and Ottonian minsters of the Rhineland. Kelso Abbey was founded by David I in 1128. Another great Tironensian house, Kilwinning in Ayrshire, was founded, some thirty years later, by the same munificent nobleman, Hugh de Morville, to whom we owe Dryburgh. Here again the fragments that remain, in the early First Pointed style, are noble in conception and refined in execution. At Kilwinning, as at Kelso, there seem to have been western transepts. In Arbroath Abbey, founded in 1178 by William the Lion as a daughter house of Kelso, Scottish Tironensian architecture achieves its climax. Its west front, of late Romanesque, and the south transept, in the First Pointed style, are unsurpassed by anything in Scotland. Over the great western doorway was a tribune or elevated gallery, opening both to the outside and the inside, upon which a choir would sing the "Glory, Laud and Honour" during the Palm Sunday procession. Similar tribunes existed at St. Andrews and Holyrood.

Arbroath Abbey was dedicated to St. Thomas of Canterbury, and the tale of how this came about is typical of the motives which could lead to the foundation of a medieval monastery. In the general rebellion of the English barons which followed upon Becket's murder, the Scottish King, William the Lion, himself a great English landowner, took part. Invading England, he was captured at Alnwick (13th July, 1174). On that same day, Henry II, hurrying back from the continent to cope with rebellion and invasion, knelt in abject penance before the martyr's shrine, and suffered his royal back to be scourged by the monks. So deeply struck was William of Scotland by this coincidence that, on his return from captivity, he founded in 1178 the Abbey of Arbroath, dedicating it to Saint Thomas, Archbishop and Martyr:

> "In the honoure of Saynt Thomas
> That Abbaye that tyme fowndyt was
> And dowyt alsua rychely
> Thare Monkis to be perpetually."

Of Scottish Cistercian houses the most famous beyond doubt is Melrose. Most of the existing buildings date from after the great destruction by Richard II in 1385; but the original dispositions seem in the main to have been preserved. Here there was a second cloister, set apart for the lay brethren. These were largely occupied with industrial work, carried on in the western range of the monastic cloister. To secure the quiet of the latter, the workshops were shut off, in many Cistercian houses, by a solid wall, forming what is known as "the lane". The foundations of this feature are well preserved at Melrose. Tiled tanning pits survive to teach us something of the multifarious activities carried on in this quarter of the monastery. The twelfth-century work surviving at Melrose partakes of the bleak simplicity of early Cistercian architecture, in marked contrast to the florid style of the later reconstruction.

Much more of the early Cistercian work remains at Dundrennan. Combining Romanesque and Gothic elements, and pervaded by an austere yet graceful simplicity, the presbytery and transept in particular well illustrate the continued Cistercian desire for restrained design: whereas the chapter house, dating from about 1300, illustrates the later quest for decoration. The site is typically Cistercian, apart and lonely: for the Rule of that Order prescribes that its monasteries "shall be built not in cities nor in castles nor in villages, but in places remote from the concourse of people."

Of Benedictine houses we shall mention only two: Dunfermline and Coldingham. Dunfermline, where seven Kings of Scotland, including Malcolm Canmore with his saintly Queen Margaret, and King Robert the Liberator, lie buried, began as a small royal chapel dedicated to the Holy Trinity, erected by Margaret about the year 1070. Her modest edifice comprised a short nave and a western tower, to which a chancel and apse were added not long afterwards. The venerable foundations of these pristine buildings now lie beneath the nave of the great Benedictine Abbey founded by Margaret's son, David I, in 1124. This was the first Benedictine house in Scotland. The nave, still in use as the parish church, is the finest piece of Norman architecture left to us in Scotland. It is obvious that the mason-craftsmen who built it came from Durham. In the course of the thirteenth century a greatly extended chancel was provided, including an eastern Lady Chapel to which the remains of Malcolm and Margaret were transferred. But all this work, except the foundations of the Lady Chapel, has long since disappeared, and its place is now occupied by a parish church built in 1818–21. Of the claustral buildings, portions of the dorter, rere-dorter, frater, kitchen and guest-house remain. These all date from the reconstruction of the conventual buildings that followed upon their demolition by Edward I in 1303. What remains of these buildings is in the finest Decorated style, and shows that here at least architectural skill and mason-craftsmanship had not declined during the long war. As is well known, the guest-house range was converted by James VI into a palace for the use of his Queen, Anne of Denmark; and here, in 1600, was born their son, the ill-fated Charles I.

Coldingham in Berwickshire was another Benedictine house, a daughter of Durham, but the date of foundation is uncertain. Here the principal surviving portions are the north and east walls of the chancel, embodied in the parish church. These are in the purest and most vigorous early First Pointed style, and the way in which the triforium and the clear storey are combined displays striking originality. Little now remains of the conventual buildings: but partial excavation had revealed that these were attached not as usual to the nave, but to the chancel. Further spade work may provide a key to this anomaly: but perhaps the cloister was laid out in dependence on an earlier and smaller church, occupying the site of the present chancel, which must date from about 1200.

In a short sketch like the present, it is, naturally, impossible to give anything like a conspectus of the monastic ruins of Scotland. Reference, however, must be made to the remarkable Romanesque "underslung triforium" at Jedburgh Abbey. A great medieval aisled church has its internal elevation built up in three stages. First there is the main arcade, lofty and resting on massive piers. Above this is the triforium or blind storey, a second but lower arcade, affording access to the space under the aisle roof, in case the latter required repair. The darkness of its voids provided an excellent contrast to the interior wall faces of the church, which in the Middle Ages were always richly coloured. Finally we have the clear storey, a row of small windows designed to illuminate the roof. At Jedburgh the main piers are carried right up above the triforium, whose arches are thus, as it were, slung across between them. A similar device—and it is aesthetically most effective—is found at Oxford Cathedral.

At the Valliscaulian Priory of Pluscarden, we have the finest example of a night-stair in Scotland. This feature, and the architecture of the south transept into which the stair descends, so forcibly resemble the corresponding portions of Hexham Abbey in Northumberland as to make it almost certain that mason-craftsmen were brought thence to Pluscarden. At the third Scottish Valliscaulian house, Ardchattan Priory, where the remains are partly embodied in a modern mansion, we have one of the two surviving Scottish examples[1] of the reading pulpit in the frater, from which passages out of Holy Writ, or from some edifying book, were read to the monks while they dined. At Inchcolm we have our only example of an octagonal monastic chapter-house; while at Cambuskenneth Abbey, an important Augustinian house near Stirling, is a detached belfry tower, a major thirteenth century-feature without parallel in Scotland, but recalling that at Chichester Cathedral.

An interesting feature that is bound to strike the explorer of our monastic ruins is the fact that in so many cases, while the north wall of the nave and other parts of the church have been more or less pulled to bits, the south wall is usually better

[1] The other is at Dunfermline.

preserved. The reason for this is that while, on the dissolution of the monastery, the church became expendable and was usually converted into a common quarry for all who had house or barn or byre to build in its neighbourhood, the claustral buildings often continued to be occupied by the Commendator or new lay proprietor, who would lay out the cloister garth as a garden—for which the south wall of the nave would be retained, both for shelter and for growing fruit trees against it.

We may fitly conclude this chapter by reproducing the beautiful verses in which Wordsworth has translated the Latin sentence usually inscribed in some conspicuous position within a Cistercian monastery:

> "Here Man more purely lives, less oft doth fall,
> More promptly rises, walks with stricter heed,
> More safely rests, dies happier, is freed
> Earlier from cleansing fires, and gains withal
> A brighter crown."

XII

The Age of Abbeys and Cathedrals: II—Cathedrals and Parish Churches

IN the later Middle Ages Scotland was divided, for ecclesiastical purposes, into twelve dioceses. Of these the northmost was the diocese of the Orkneys, with its cathedral at Kirkwall. Until 1468 the Northern Isles belonged to Norway, and Kirkwall Cathedral was subordinate to the Archdiocese of Trondheim. On the Scottish mainland the dioceses were: Caithness (including the modern county of Sutherland), with its cathedral at Dornoch; Ross, whose cathedral was at Fortrose; Moray, with its cathedral at Elgin; Aberdeen, Brechin, St. Andrews, Dunblane, Dunkeld and Glasgow, each having its cathedral church in the town from which the diocese took its name; Argyll, where the seat of the Bishop was at first on the island of Lismore, but in 1507 was transferred to the Benedictine Abbey of Iona; and Galloway, where the cathedral church was also the Premonstratensian Abbey of Whithorn. St. Andrews Cathedral, the metropolitan church of Scotland, was, as such, from 1472 the seat of an Archbishop; in 1500 Glasgow also was elevated to archiepiscopal rank.

More fortunate than the Abbeys, a Cathedral Church, or at least a part of it, could still serve as a place of parish worship, particularly if it stood in a sizeable town. To this fact we owe the preservation, intact, of two splendid Scottish Cathedrals, Glasgow and Kirkwall. These buildings do not therefore come within the purview of the present work; neither does the tiny Cathedral of Lismore, of which the chancel survives as the parish church of the island. At Aberdeen and Brechin all but the nave was allowed to fall into ruins or was carted away piecemeal; the nave in both cases being retained as the parish church. Brechin Cathedral has been restored, and its very beautiful chancel partly rebuilt, in modern times. At Dunblane it was the nave which fell into ruin, and has now been restored: a notable feature here is the early Romanesque tower, once free-standing but now embodied in the nave. By contrast, the nave of Dunkeld Cathedral remains a roofless ruin, while the chancel, which shows some fine work of the thirteenth and fourteenth centuries, has been restored and is now in use as the parish kirk. The nave and north-west tower, a notable piece of fifteenth-century architecture, will come up for discussion in Chapter XIV. Dornoch Cathedral was very largely rebuilt in 1835–36, but still retains some important early features, notably the piers of the crossing, which have double abaci, somewhat resembling the dosseret or "pulvino" found on Byzantine capitals.

As befitted its status, the metropolitan cathedral of St. Andrews, which also was an Augustinian Priory, was the largest church in Scotland, with an over-all length of 391 feet. Its present fragmentary state is the more to be regretted because of the high architectural quality of what survives—that is to say, parts of the east and west gables and of the choir and south transept, together with the south wall of the nave. Excavation has revealed the entire outline of the church, as well as of the claustral buildings, of which portions of the eastern range, and of the frater on the south, still make a fair show amid the prevailing desolation.

Of the beautiful cathedral church of Ross at Fortrose there survive only the south aisle of the nave and the undercroft of the sacristy or chapter house. These, however, are mostly works of the fourteenth century, and do not fall within the purview of the present chapter.

Most of the existing work at Whithorn cathedral is also late; the most important early survival is a richly decorated Norman doorway, which had been re-set, apparently in the early seventeenth century, in the south wall of the nave.

Thus among our ruined cathedral churches, with which alone we are concerned in this book we are left with the High Church of Moray, "the lanthorn of the North", as the supreme example of Scottish church architecture in the great building period of the thirteenth century.

Let us look then at Elgin Cathedral as now it stands in melancholy yet majestic ruin. Broken though it is, its plan may still be understood. It is of the usual cruciform shape, comprising a nave with double aisles and north and south porches; twin western towers having a superb portal and window between; transepts, above which rose the great central tower, 198 feet in height; choir with aisles and presbytery; and a detached octagonal chapter-house north of the presbytery. The total internal length of this splendid church was about 264 feet.

The first point of general interest is the strong French feeling that pervades the whole. To begin with, the double aisles of the nave are purely French: elsewhere in Britain they are found only at Chichester and Manchester. The effect produced by such a nave must have been one of vast spaciousness, rather than the long perspective at which medieval builders usually aimed in Britain.

Then again, the great western towers with their simple, un-broken vertical lines, and the splendid deep portal between, are quite French in character. And what holds of these larger features holds also of the smallest detail, and in the work of almost every period. Thus, the arch-mouldings of the door into the south transept—which is the oldest part of the church—exhibit an escallop ornament of very French aspect. The close political con-nexion between Scotland and France after the War of Indepen-dence is well understood, and we shall have to mark its influence upon our later Scottish architecture: but here we have French influence dominant as far back as the thirteenth century. In this there is no cause for wonder. The "Auld Alliance" goes back to William the Lion, who in 1168 joined with Louis VII of France in common suspicion of Plantagenet imperialism. And Alexander II, in whose reign Elgin Cathedral was founded, married in 1239 Marie de Coucy, daughter of the foremost French baron of his time.

The oldest work in the cathedral appears in the south transept. It belongs to the transition between Romanesque and Gothic, and may well be part of the church of the Holy Trinity that is known to have stood on the site before the cathedral of Moray was transferred hither in 1224. The exterior of the south transept is a remarkable and highly abnormal piece of work, in which we find round arches *above* pointed ones, though the whole gable is manifestly of one date. Soon after the foundation in 1224 may be placed the lower portions of the western tower, and a little later on their upper storeys and the grand portal between. But the central pier and two inner arches of the portal, as well as the great window in the gable above, were all inserted when the cathedral was restored after its wanton destruction by the "Wolf of Badenoch" in 1390.

The bases of the nave arcade are of thirteenth-century profile, but those in the aisles, together with what remains of the outer aisle walls and windows, for the most part betoken the fifteenth century. But there is stylistic evidence that at least the three eastern bays of the south outer aisle go back to the late thirteenth century. Probably the decision to provide the double aisles was taken when the cathedral was restored, and (as it would seem) enlarged, after a disastrous fire in 1270. That the double aisles were an afterthought is apparent from the fact that they are not contained within the spread of the western towers, so that buttressing is needed to close them in; also a pilaster of the south transept has been hewn away to admit the aisle wall, so that its upper part is left "in the air". Against the west towers the mark remains of lean-to roofs that had spanned older single aisles. The outer south aisle was roofed with a series of gablets, in a fashion common in France, but (so far as I am aware) known in Britain only at Stokesay Castle and in the great hall of Winchester.

Probably after 1270 were erected the choir and presbytery, in a very rich style. The vaulting of the Lady Chapel in the south aisle was built in the fifteenth century. It should be noted that prior to the reconstruction after 1390 no part of the cathedral, save the basements of the western towers, was vaulted in stone; but there was a timber vault in the presbytery, the track of which can be seen upon its gable. The strong and massive western towers with their vaulted basements, are open neither to the nave nor to the aisles. They could have played no part in the ritual life of the church. Each is entered at ground level only by a door which could be strongly secured: and the upper storeys of both were reached by a single narrow door and steep spiral stair at the south-west corner of the nave. It seems clear that these western towers were designed to serve, if need be, as places of refuge— a precaution well justified by the wild history and recent pacification of the ancient Pictish Province of Moray.

The chapter-house is a very beautiful and deeply interesting structure. Its shell is of the thirteenth century, but after the disaster of 1390 it was cased inwardly, with new masonry, when also narrower lancet windows were inserted and the central pillar and exquisite vaulting built. The latest portion of the cathedral was the great central tower, which was erected in 1538, after a predecessor had fallen. But the days of church building were over. The noble cathedral which had taken three centuries to complete, lasted just three decades in its final state. Then the work of spoil-ation began. In 1568 the lead was stripped from the roofs, and the latter, thus exposed to the weather, collapsed in 1637. Three years later the General Assembly ordered the rood screen to be broken up. On Easter Day, 1711, came the final catastrophe, when the central tower crushed the north transept and the nave beneath its falling mass. Thereafter the ruins remained a common quarry for the neighbourhood, until in 1807 the slow awakening of conscience and a better taste led to the first measures for the cathedral's protection.

So bald an outline description of the noblest of Scotland's ruined fanes can give little idea of the glorious richness and exceeding beauty of its architecture. In a letter to King Robert III, reporting its destruction by the Wolf of Badenoch, the afflicted Bishop describes his cathedral as "the special ornament of the realm, the glory of the kingdom, the delight of foreigners and stranger guests; an object of praise and glorification in foreign realms by reason of the multitude of those serving and the beauty of its ornament, and in which we believe God was rightly wor-shipped; not to speak of its high belfries, its sumptuous furniture and its innumerable jewels." The poignancy of this letter is the more affecting when we recollect that the King to whom the Bishop thus appealed was a brother of the ruffian who had burned the cathedral!

Before we leave Elgin Cathedral one highly interesting detail must be mentioned. The east end of the church, a noble and richly decorated late thirteenth-century composition, consists of two tiers each of five pointed windows, with a large rose window in the gable. Now in the two tiers of lancets, each of them is framed in a tall rectangular panel formed by slender projecting fillets, horizontal and vertical. So rigidly is this framework conceived that the vertical fillets are carried through the bases and caps of the lancets. The whole thing strikes one with the irresistable impression that the design has been copied by the masons from an architect's elevational drawing in which the fenestration had been set out within a scheme of superimposed rectangles. Those who have studied the sketch book of Wilars de Honcort, a great French architect of the early thirteenth century, will have noticed how every kind of delineation, including the figures of men and animals, is schemed out within a geometrical framework. *"Li ars de iometrie le commande et ensaigne"*—"the art (or discipline) of geometry commands and teaches us"—so Wilars himself comments in his Preface. It is fascinating to find in this Scottish cathedral how the precept of the French master has been obeyed.

Every ruin says *"J'accuse"*: none more reproachfully than the ruin of a building erected to the glory of God. The shattered remains of Elgin Cathedral survive today as a sad reminder of the unhappy turn taken by the Scottish Reformation. Had it been possible to preserve the peerless church; to adapt its worship, and the various social services connected with its organization, to modern needs; and to retain its ample revenues for such benign purposes—for example, for the spread of education among the common people which Knox himself so passionately desired— then Elgin today, with its attractive situation, rich and lovely countryside, and kindly climate, could have been the Durham of the North.

Much as we admire our glorious cathedrals and abbeys, there is another side to the medal. In all too many cases these splendid structures were built out of the spoil of the parishes. This arose from what a Scottish historian has well described as "the curse of impropriation". Everywhere the local magnates, in whose hands lay the right of presentation, found it to their advantage, for their soul's weal or for political ends, to grant out their patronage to the great monasteries or cathedral chapters. The latter naturally strove to draw the maximum advantage out of the parochial revenues. Thus the spiritual care of rural districts too often came to be left in the hands of starveling vicars; and under these circumstances, talent in the medieval church tended to gravitate towards the cathedrals and monasteries, while the parish priest, upon whom fell the real burden of catering for the spiritual needs of the people, degenerated correspondingly. There can be no doubt that in the end the system of impropriation was fraught with great evil to the Roman Church, and bore a large share in the causes of her downfall. Nevertheless, in the great period of religious fervour during the twelfth and thirteenth centuries, there is no evidence that, in Scotland at least, much harm had so far been caused by the practice of impropriation. On the contrary, alongside the stately cathedrals and abbeys there was an intense activity in building, rebuilding or enlarging parish churches from end to end of the country. Thus, in the Diocese of St. Andrews alone, no less than 140 parochial churches were consecrated between the years 1240 and 1249. Not a few of these churches which have been lucky enough to survive until our own day are buildings of much elegance, and even beauty—upon which the patron, be he the local feudal magnate or a distant cathedral or monastery, has clearly stinted neither money nor taste. Let us look briefly at one or two of these parish churches of the thirteenth century.

Airth Church, in Stirlingshire, was granted to Holyrood Abbey in 1128. Its ruins show us something of the other side of the story in this matter of impropriation. The distant Abbey did not always neglect its dependent churches; and there is much to be said for the remark of a modern historian, who has pointed out that "in exchange for a considerable share of the tithes of the parishes bestowed upon them", the monasteries "secured the maintenance of a Christian ministry in places where powerful landholders would not have been either regular or exact in paying their alloted proportions of what was necessary for that object". So at Airth there is no reason to doubt that the superior character of the oldest portion of the ruined parish church is due to its connexion with the wealthy and powerful Abbey of the Holy Rood—all the more so as the remains of Holyrood Abbey show a sense of style which has entitled its west façade to be authoritatively acclaimed as "one of the finest early medieval compositions in Britain". At Airth we find a very beautiful late Norman Transitional frag-ment, consisting of two cylindrical piers with foliaged capitals and square abaci, supporting a plain arch of two orders, slightly pointed. Clearly the twelfth-century church had a northern aisle to its nave, and must have been a notable structure. The beauty of the work is enhanced by the lovely golden colour of the sandstone out of which it is built.

No medieval monument—indeed no ancient monument what-ever its date—should be considered without reference to its surroundings. The ruined parish church of Airth stands within an *ensemble*, which, despite all modern demolitions and "improvements", gives us perhaps a clearer picture of a small burgh of the olden time than can be found anywhere in Scotland. Anciently the place was of considerable importance, and in 1511 James IV constructed here a harbour and dockyard for his new fleet—a playing counter which that ambitious monarch was determined to produce in support of his claim to take part in the then fashionable game of "Grand Monarchy". The medieval burgh, which dates back to William the Lion, lay mostly within the grounds of Airth Castle: the present village represents an extension dating from the end of the seventeenth century. Picturesquely embosomed amid orchards and gardens and stately trees, Airth is now a delightful and deeply interesting example of an old-world village still retaining much of its ancient character, with its narrow, irregular, cobbled lanes, market cross, and quaint houses having corbie-stepped gables, forestairs, pantiled roofs, and heraldic enrichment. Hard by the ruined parish church is the stately castle of Airth, still inhabited, and dating from the thirteenth century, with a stormy history during the War of Independence —though no part of the present complex structure seems to be as old as that period. Here, then, we have a striking example of the close association of feudal castle and parish church which (as we have seen) is so characteristic of medieval manorial dispositions. In the later portions of Airth Church the tradition of fine building work has been consistently maintained. The Transitional remains are built into the burial aisle of the Bruces of Powfoulis, which bears the date 1614. The Elphinstone Aisle was erected in 1593, as appears from a dated coat of arms. The Airth Aisle was built towards the end of the fifteenth century. It contains the effigy of a lady, wearing a coif and draped with a coverlet. At her feet crouch two quaintly-wrought hounds. A picturesque tall square belfry tower is inscribed IVLYTHE 15, 1647. In the graveyard are no less than three "mortsafes", dated 1821, 1832 and 1833.

At St. Kentigern's, Lanark, we have the ruin of another fine aisled parish church dating from the thirteenth century. A stately arcade of five lofty pointed arches, resting on piers alternately cylindrical and octagonal, a rich First Pointed doorway, and chancel arch somewhat plainer in style, are the principal remaining features of this important church, which, like Airth, was impropriated to a distant monastery—in this case Dryburgh Abbey. Externally the aisle wall is broken only by a plain stringcourse, which breaks upwards to form a hood-mould for the lancet windows, in a manner which is as simple as it is satisfactory.

Most Scottish medieval parish churches, however, were uni-cameral, without any division, other than a rood screen, between nave and chancel, the whole being then under one span of roof. A fine example is the church of Auchindoir, in Aberdeenshire. It possesses an exceedingly rich Transitional doorway, semicircular-arched, with bold roll and hollow mouldings and a hood-mould of large and vigorous dog-tooth. The capitals have square abaci, and are carved with the characteristic stiff-leaf foliage of about the year 1200. There is also a fine lancet window in the north wall, serving to light the altar. The beautiful sacrament house belongs to the sixteenth century.

Next we select for notice the ancient parish church of Cowie, which now forms a conspicuous ruin on the coast north of Stone-haven. Cowie Church was consecrated by the Bishop of St. Andrews on 22nd May, 1276. As so often was the case, it began as a private chapel of the lord of the neighbouring Castle of Cowie, of which only the foundations remain. The church was of the usual long, narrow, unicameral Scottish pattern, 70 feet by 18 feet internally. Its outstanding feature is the east gable with three lancet windows, the central one slightly taller than its neighbours, and the whole forming a composition which, though simple, is a model of cultured grace.

We have already remarked that in the course of the thirteenth century the First Pointed style of Gothic architecture, alike in castle and in churches, penetrated to the Atlantic seaboard. Mention has been made of the exquisite little private chapel adjoining Dunstaffnage Castle—a little gem which, small though it be, is as rich and scholarly a piece of design as the contemporary work in Elgin Cathedral. At Skipness in Kintyre, adjoining the fine early castle, is St. Brendan's Church—earlier than, and not to be confused with, the private chapel, dedicated to St. Columba, which the lord of Skipness provided for himself within the cincture of his castle, and of which a small portion, with three narrow round-arched windows, is embodied in a later curtain wall. This private chapel is mentioned in a charter of 1261, by which its owner, following the prevailing trend, impropriated it to Paisley Abbey. St. Brendan's Church is a fine thing, of the usual Scottish long and narrow, unicameral plan, measuring over all 27 feet in breadth by no less than 87 feet in length. Two of the doorways are pointed and the third round-arched—all having good simple First Pointed doorways: the side windows are narrow lancets, while the east window is of two pointed arches beneath a pointed general arch, the space between the heads of the two lancets forming a lozenge-shaped void, so as to provide an incipient form of tracery.

Upon a conjoint view of the First Pointed ecclesiastical architecture of Scotland—whether in monasteries, cathedrals, parish churches or private chapels—we must acknowledge that, despite the grievous destruction which all four classes of building have suffered, what remains is sufficient to show that, making all due allowances for the small scale of most of these edifices, Scotland was none the less well abreast of the standard achieved in England and France during the high noontide of the medieval church. So far as the parish churches are concerned, the number of these erected in Scotland during the First Pointed period, if we may judge from their surviving remnants, was comparatively small. No doubt this is partly due to the fact that a large number of our parish churches had been founded in the twelfth century, and therefore will have been built in the Norman style. Even today, the remains of Norman work in our ancient parochial churches are much more numerous than those belonging to the First Pointed style.

One of the most remarkable ruined parish churches in all Scotland is to be seen at the quaint old-world Aberdeenshire village of Kincardine-o'-Neil, once a burgh of barony. In the Middle Ages this was a place of importance, for at this point the Cairnamounth road, the principal communication from Strathmore through Mar into Morayland, crosses the Dee. Here accordingly Thomas the Durward, the local feudal magnate, early in the thirteenth century built a bridge over the river; and in 1231 his son, Alan—afterwards the uncrowned King of Scotland during the minority of Alexander III—erected at Kincardine-o'-Neil a hospital for the relief of poor wayfarers crossing the mountain pass. In the midst of the village we now see a large roofless church, architecturally far superior to the normal parochial place of worship in medieval Scotland. In particular, the north

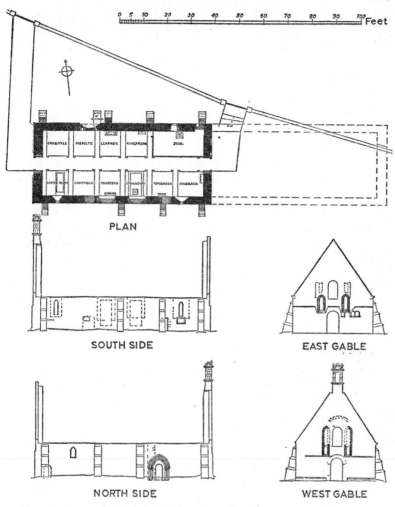

PLAN

SOUTH SIDE

EAST GABLE

NORTH SIDE

WEST GABLE

Fig. 16 Kincardine O'Neil Kirk, Kincardineshire: measured drawings
(By courtesy, Aberdeen University Library)

door, a richly moulded Gothic portal of unusual size, has a quality of delicate, almost feminine loveliness which at once catches the beholder's eye. Probably it dates from early in the fourteenth century—a period when, due to the War of Independence, not much fine building was going on in Scotland. The west gable contains two First Pointed lancets, and there are two more in the east gable: but these last have evidently been re-inserted from elsewhere. Old records show that the church was once much larger than the present ruin: and excavation has revealed the foundations of an eastern extension, giving the building an over-all length of 148 feet. On the *outside* of the present east gable are three aumbries or wall-presses, and above this the gable is traversed by a scarcement for a floor. Over this again, on either side of the two inserted windows, are the sides of two original windows, *opening into the church*. There can be little doubt that the eastern (now demolished) portion of the building contained the hospital, a two-storeyed annexe of which the upper room will have formed the dormitory, in which bed-ridden inmates could hear the services through the westward opening windows. A somewhat similar structural association of hospital and chapel is known in Belgium: and of course the combination of church and living room is not infrequent, as at Egilsay already mentioned, or at the preceptory of the Knights Templar at Torphichen in Midlothian.

No doubt when the eastern limb was demolished two of its lancet windows were preserved and built into the present east gable. It is said that the demolition took place early in the seventeenth century. This would be under the rule of the cultured Bishop Patrick Forbes, who under the Caroline Episcopacy did so much to improve the church buildings and standard of worship in his diocese. He would be a likely person to attend to the preservation of these windows when the hospital portion of the combined edifice was taken down.

XIII

The Castle in the High Middle Ages

IN a previous chapter we noted how the stone-and-lime castle was introduced into Scotland in the twelfth and thirteenth centuries, and how it has come to pass that some of the best preserved of these early stone castles are found today on the north-western seaboard. In less remote parts of the country, however, Scotland still retains some fine examples of the elaborate castles of *enceinte*, with their lofty curtain walls and bold flanking towers, which were erected during the "Golden Age" of Alexander II and Alexander III, "that Scotland left in luf and le".

Of these one of the most remarkable is Rothesay Castle in the Isle of Bute. Here we have a great circular curtain wall, strengthened by four stout round towers, all built of finely-coursed ashlar masonry. Though the towers have been claimed as later additions, there is no reason to doubt that the ring-wall at least represents the Rothesay Castle which sustained a famous siege by the Norsemen in 1230, of which we have a vivid account in *Haakon Haakonsson's Saga*. Having failed to storm the castle, the assailants hewed their way through the stone wall with axes. Part of the curtain wall on the eastern side shows signs of much disturbance and rebuilding out of its old materials: and it is more than likely that this was the point where the Norsemen breached the wall. In the reign of James IV a large forework was added in front of the entrance, containing a barbican-passage below a suite of royal apartments. At the same time the adjoining sectors of the curtain were heightened in rubble-work, in such a way as to seal up the original parapet and battlements, which are thus happily preserved, like a valuable fossil in a geological stratum.

On the opposite side of southern Scotland, at Dirleton in East

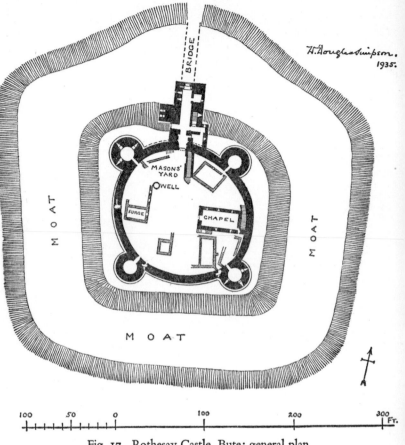

Fig. 17 Rothesay Castle, Bute: general plan
(*By courtesy, Aberdeen University Library*)

Lothian, important remains survive of another fine thirteenth-century castle, which was partly demolished by the Scots when they recovered it from the English, who had captured it in 1298, after a famous siege. What escaped this "slighting" was subsequently incorporated in a reconstruction that followed quite different lines. The remnants of the original castle are built of fine cubical ashlar, and comprise a group of three towers—arranged round a small courtyard or private close. Together these towers form a composite and self-contained residence for the lord of the castle, belonging to a type for which the name of "clustered donjon" has been proposed. This is usually regarded as a development of the fourteenth century; well known English examples being the donjons of Alnwick and Skipton. But a *castellum de Dyrlton* is on record about 1225, as a stronghold of the powerful Anglo-Norman family of de Vaux; and if (as has been contended) the existing thirteenth-century work dates back so far, then we would appear to have here the earliest example of a clustered donjon in Britain.

The later work at Dirleton includes a fine hall of the fifteenth century, and a handsome early Renaissance house built by the Ruthvens in the reign of James VI. The castle was finally dismantled by the Cromwellians in 1650. It is now one of Scotland's loveliest ruins, set within a spacious pleasance or flower garden in the heart of the quaint old-world hamlet of Dirleton, with its seventeenth-century church and village green. A feature of the pleasance is the ancient bowling green, surrounded by venerable yews.

The conception, which ruled castellar construction in the twelfth and thirteenth centuries, of a donjon or keep-tower, conceived as a *dernier ressort* and therefore sited usually in the remotest corner of the *enceinte*, reached its climax in Scotland at the castle of Bothwell, on the Clyde above Glasgow. When complete, the mighty cylindrical donjon of this splendid castle can have been surpassed in Britain only by that of Conisborough on the Yorkshire Don. Unfortunately half of it was thrown into the Clyde by its owner, Sir Andrew de Moray, when he finally recaptured it from the English in 1336. Over walls no less than 15 feet in thickness, the donjon measures 65 feet in diameter above its spreading base: and the surviving half still stands to a height of 90 feet. Its masonry is the most superb, carefully coursed and closely jointed, polished ashlar: and all the architectural details, such as doors and windows, are in the high Gothic style of the later thirteenth century. From its own courtyard the donjon, which stands in the extreme corner of the site, backing on the steep slopes formed by a crook of the river, was isolated by its own proper moat, lined with vertical walls of hewn stone.

The original scheme of the castle proposed a large courtyard, enclosed by walls of enceinte with round and square towers and a gateway between two round towers. In accordance with the usual medieval practice, the foundations of the whole were set out, but

Fig. 18   Bothwell Castle, Lanarkshire: the donjon
(By courtesy, Aberdeen University Library)

nothing more was completed before work was interrupted by the
War of Independence, saving the donjon and the wing-walls
closing in its moat. This is why in the records of that time the
castle is referred to as "the Tower of Bothwell". In the fourteenth
century the castle became the chief seat of the Earls of Douglas,
the most powerful family in Scotland. The reconstruction carried
out by the new owners utilized only the southern portion of the
enceinte as originally laid out. The great southern curtain and
south-eastern tower must be assigned to Archibald, fourth Earl of
Douglas and Duke of Touraine; and proof of his connexion with
the "Auld Ally" may be seen in the very French character of the
superb machicolated coronet of the south-east tower. To about
the same date belong the very beautiful chapel and the great hall
—though the upper portion of the latter, with its remarkable row
of ten high windows, was reconstructed about 1500. Modern
excavation of Bothwell Castle has recovered by far the largest
collection of medieval pottery so far found on any Scottish
site.

Certain famous sieges in the thirteenth century, notably that of Château Gaillard in 1203-4, exposed the weakness of the donjon theme. In the tumult of a storm, it was not always possible for the garrison, from their various fighting-posts in the other towers and round the curtain walls, to escape into the donjon. Also the underlying conception of such a castle after all is defeatist: it acknowledges the likelihood that, sooner or later, the *enceinte* will be mined, or scaled, or the gateway forced, when naught will remain for the garrison but to escape, *if they can*, into the keep, there to await the slow agony of starvation. So as the thirteenth century advanced, the idea of a donjon was gradually given up. Or rather, the donjon was brought forward to the entrance and combined with its towers so as to form a "keep-gatehouse". This was a much more aggressive posture, in which the lord or castellan found his "action-station" not tucked away in the rear but in the forefront of the defence, at the post of greatest danger—for all through the Middle Ages the gateway remained the weakest point in a castle, where the assailants had a better chance of winning entry than by scaling or breaching the walls.

We can see this new conception of the castle plan strikingly illustrated in the Aberdeenshire Castle of Kildrummy. The annals of this "noblest of northern castles" are inscribed in Scottish history, in letters of blood and fire, from the Wars of Independence to the first Jacobite rising in 1715, which was launched from within its walls. The castle consists of a great wall of enceinte with round flanking towers, one of which, at the extreme north-west corner of the site, is much larger than the rest, was vaulted on all floors and therefore fireproof, and contained its own water-supply. The "Snow Tower", as it was called, thus forms the donjon of the castle. But in the south front is a powerful gatehouse of the new fashion. In its plan and architectural detail this gatehouse corresponds closely to that at Harlech Castle in North Wales: it is obviously somewhat later than the other towers of the castle, from which the twin gatehouse towers have a different profile. Edward I's famous architect, Master James of St. George, who came from Savoy and designed Harlech as well as other North Welsh castles, was employed also upon Plantagenet fortifications in Scotland. At Torphins, on his way south from Kildrummy by the Cairnamounth road in October, 1303, Edward I made a payment to Master James of St. George of £100 sterling—a sum equal to at least £10,000 in modern value.[1] It is more than likely that this was for his services in building the keep-gatehouse.

The handiwork of the great Plantagenet is otherwise fairly visible at Kildrummy, but the architectural history of this famous castle is too complicated, and also in some respects too puzzling, for further discussion here. A notable feature is the chapel gable, projecting very unusually from the east curtain, with its three simple and solemn lancet windows dating from before 1250. Another remarkable feature is the sunk passage, or stairway, partly hewn out of the living rock, leading down to a cistern tower and postern gate at the foot of the northern bank. This again reminds me greatly of the "Way from the Marsh" at Harlech.

Not all the secular buildings of stone and lime erected in Scotland during this period were great fortresses like the castles which we have been discussing. At Rait Castle, near Nairn, we have a valuable example of a lightly fortified manor house built during the English occupation. This castle was the seat of two brothers, Sir Gervaise de Rait and Sir Andrew de Rait, who were prominent supporters of Edward I in a part of Scotland fiercely opposed to his rule. The building consists of a long hall, raised upon unvaulted cellarage, with the kitchen and offices, apparently in a timber annexe, at the lower end, while at the upper or dais end of the hall were the lord's private rooms in a round angle tower. Only the first floor room in this tower is stone-vaulted. The entrance, at the lower or screens end of the hall, is a large pointed Gothic portal, slotted for a portcullis: being on the first floor, it must have been reached by a timber staging, perhaps with a movable bridge. This door is out of scale with the rest of the building, and looks as if it had been designed for a larger castle: in fact, it much recalls the portal of the gatehouse at Dunstanburgh Castle, Northumberland, dating from 1313. Other details of Rait closely resemble corresponding work, assignable to the English occupation, at Kildrummy, as well as in the stone tower imposed upon the *motte* at Duffus Castle, near Elgin.[2] Another unvaulted hallhouse, dating from the Edwardian period, may be recognized at Morton Castle in Nithsdale—though in this case the hall is

[1] This payment has recently been discovered by Mr. Arnold J. Taylor, H.M. Chief Inspector of Ancient Monuments, who has kindly permitted me to quote it.

[2] *Supra,* p. 130.

Fig. 19 Kildrummy Castle, Aberdeenshire: the chapel window, interior
(*By courtesy, Aberdeen University Library*)

combined with a regularly defended gatehouse. Morton Castle was ordered to be dismantled under the terms of the treaty of 1357, whereby David II was released from an English prison: and agreably to this stipulation, we find that, while the hall-house or domestic portion of the castle seems not to have been damaged, one half of the gatehouse has been deliberately removed.

A highly interesting, if somewhat fragmentary, example of English domestic architecture dating from the Plantagenet occupation is provided by the oldest portions of the lovely ruin of Hailes Castle, near Haddington. At that time the manor belonged to the Northumbrian family of Gourlay, and the cubical ashlar masonry of the earliest work in the castle, with its characteristic use of "closers", is typical of contemporary Northumbrian architecture. Moreover, the original building appears to have closely resembled the fortified mansion of Aydon Castle on Tyneside. It consisted of a hall, relatively short in proportion to its breadth, having a kitchen at the lower end and at the upper end a cross-wing containing the lord's private apartments, thus giving the house a T-shaped plan. Both castles occupy "bank-side" sites, and in both the "aspect" of the hall, with its axis lying east and west, is the same. Like Aydon, during the frontier wars of the fourteenth century, Hailes was transformed from a stone hall-house into a formidable castle; and in both, the conversion was achieved by including the hall-house in an extended courtyard, stoutly walled and with a large and bold tower at the upstream apex.

As has been indicated above, the normal disposition of a medieval hall-house, be it of timber or of stone, comprises a central *aula* or hall, with the service department at its lower end and the lord's suite at the upper. If for security reasons such a disposition is up-ended, the hall-house then becomes a tower-house.[1] Such was in fact the origin of the wooden towers that crowned the early *mottes*, as well as of the so called Norman stone keeps. In Scotland we have seen that at least two Norman keeps have survived until our own time; and that tower-houses continued to be built in the thirteenth century, alongside the great castles of *enceinte*, is shown by two well-authenticated examples,

---

[1] So also the multi-storeyed tower-blocks of flats which are sprouting up to-day in our larger towns are nothing else than streets up-ended.

Dunnideer Castle in Aberdeenshire, and Yester Castle in East Lothian.

Dunnideer Castle, one of the two chief strongholds of the old royal Earldom of the Garioch, is on record in 1260 as the seat of Sir Joscelyn de Balliol, a brother of the founder of Balliol College, Oxford. At a height of 876 feet above sea level, on the top of an isolated hill and within the remains of a vitrified fort, stands the gaunt ruin of an unvaulted square tower, one wall of which, pierced by a ruined Gothic window, forms a conspicuous landmark over a wide area in central Aberdeenshire. Largely built from the spoil of the prehistoric rampart, the masonry of the tower is banded rubble of a characteristic thirteenth century type. There is therefore no reason to doubt that the tower represents the *castrum de Donidor* mentioned in 1260.

At Yester we have the remains of a large mount-and-bailey castle. Partly into the side of the *motte*, in the same way as was done at Clun Castle and Guildford Castle in England, a large rectangular keep was added in the thirteenth century. Only the basement of this tower now survives. It takes the form of a pointed vault, constructed of fine ashlar, and strengthened with massive chamfered ribs. This is the celebrated Goblin Ha', which a reliable fourteenth-century Scottish historian tells us formed the basement of a *donjon* built by Sir Hugh de Gifford, Lord of Yester, who died in 1267. Connected with the tower-basement are two subterranean passages, likewise built of fine thirteenth-century ashlar. One leads down by a steep stair to a well, the other conducts outwards to a postern at the base of the *motte*. One of the finest remnants of the thirteenth-century military architecture in Scotland, the Goblin Ha' has been immortalized by Scott in the Host's Tale in *Marmion*:

> "Of lofty roof, and ample size,
> Beneath the castle deep it lies:
> To hew the living rock profound,
> The floor to pave, the arch to round,
> There never toiled a mortal arm,
> It all was wrought by word and charm."

At Drum Castle in Aberdeenshire we have another fine late thirteenth-century tower-house, still inhabited. The battlements, which survive unaltered, much recall those at Kisimul Castle.

Rectangular towers of this kind continued to be erected throughout the next century, when the anarchic conditions prevalent during the Wars of Independence rendered such edifices, with their brutal defensive simplicity and stark economy of materials, peculiarly suited to the social circumstances of a violent and impoverished time. We shall here describe briefly two of these fourteenth-century tower-houses, Lochleven in Kinross-shire and Threave in Galloway.

In the minds of everybody, Lochleven Castle is for ever associated with the deposition and captivity of Queen Mary. Yet the castle has a long and eventful history both before and after that event. It stood a memorable though unsuccessful siege at the hands of the English in 1335, when the assailants sought to drown the castle by damming the River Leven, which issues from the Loch. There is no reason to doubt that the rectangular tower-house, and the oldest portions of the stout curtain wall which encloses the "barmkin" or courtyard, were in existence at that time. The tower is quite a small one, measuring only 36 feet 6 inches by 31 feet 6 inches, over walls about 8 feet thick. It contains five storeys. The lowest is a cellar, the next a kitchen, above this is the hall, and on top of that the solar or lord's private room. Over all was a garret storey, containing a common sleeping apartment or dormitory. The tower entrance opens directly into the hall, that is to say at second floor level, over 15 feet above the ground outside. It must have been reached by a lofty ladder, if not by some external staging, of which, however, there is now no trace. From the hall a spiral stair leads down to the kitchen, which is vaulted, so as to be fireproof; while the kitchen in turn communicates with the cellar on the ground floor by a trap-door in the latter's vault. The cellar contains a well, and now has an outside door at ground level, but this has been converted from an original loophole. The kitchen also has a hatch communicating with the hall above, so that provisions could be hoisted up to the hall without using the stair. From the hall, this stair continues upwards to the tower-head. For the rest, the tower-house is well fitted up. Hall and solar have fireplaces and seats in their window bays: the solar is further provided with a mural closet and a privy, and the bedroom is equipped with the latter convenience. In the solar is a small but neatly furnished oratory.

Nothing could be more spartan than the domestic arrangements of this compact little tower-house. Yet, though simple, they are complete and admirably thought out; and in no sense is the tower a primitive structure. Round the garret ran an open parapet, carried forward on simple corbels, and at three of the angles are round turrets. It is noteworthy that, with true Scotch economy, no turret is provided at the fourth corner, which was within the barmkin, and therefore less exposed to attack. Though plain, the architectural details are good, and the masonry is excellent squared and coursed rubble, with large corner-stones, carefully dressed. Oyster shells have been freely used as pinnings.

The round tower attached to an angle of the curtain wall is an addition of the sixteenth century, and is pierced with wide-mouthed gunloops. Within the barmkin are remains of a hall, kitchen, and offices, all probably of that period. Still later, doubt-less, are the foundations of a bakehouse outside the curtain wall.

Threave Castle, on an island site like Lochleven, but a far greater structure, was built by "Black" Archibald the Grim, third Earl of Douglas and Lord of Galloway, some time after he ac-quired the latter lordship in 1369. It is a large and tall, stern-looking tower, measuring 61 feet in length and 39 feet 4 inches broad, over walls 8 feet thick. The tower survives to a height of fully 70 feet, and contained five storeys, each comprising a single room. The basement, which was not vaulted, formed a storehouse, with a well or cistern: the first floor, containing the kitchen, was spanned by a great vault which carried the pavement of the hall, while above the hall were two unvaulted storeys of living rooms, the topmost one covered by a flat defensive roof, supported by massive timber struts let into sloping chases provided in the side walls. The entrance was at the kitchen level, i.e. on the first floor: there was also an upper door from the hall, leading across by a drawbridge to the wall-head of the gate-house tower in the en-closing curtain wall. From the kitchen a spiral stair in a corner of the tower led to the upper floors. It is unnecessary here to describe in detail the interiors, which are well fitted up. A puzzling feature is the presence, round the outside wall-heads of a triple row of putlog holes arranged chequer-wise, while behind these, all round the summit in the thickness of the wall, runs a horizontal cavity, as if for a massive sleeper joist. It has been thought that these features represent the provision for a hoarding or timber war-head, such as we have seen at Castle Kisimul: but the putlog holes, if such they be, do not communicate with the sleeper void, and it is not at all clear what purpose the whole outfit was desired to serve.

Threave Castle is famous for the siege that it sustained at the hands of James II during the Douglas rebellion of 1455, when the "great bombard", known as Mons Meg, and now at Edinburgh Castle, was dragged down to Galloway to batter its defiant walls. The outer curtain and angle towers are loopholed for hand guns, and perhaps were erected, or reconstructed, when extensive repairs were ordered for the castle after the disaster of Flodden in 1513. "The Threave", as it is locally styled, stood its final siege (a long one) in 1640, during the Civil War, and after its capture by the Covenanters was ordered to be "slighted". It is now a gaunt and lonely ruin, sombre and forbidding, symbolizing not inaptly the stern power of the "dark-grey" lords who ruled Galloway from within its walls.

Such castles as Lochleven and Threave teach us that during the fourteenth century the tower-house, which in the later Middle Ages would be so characteristic a feature of the Scottish scene, was already becoming a favourite type of baronial residence, even in the case of the most powerful magnate of his time—for such was Archibald the Grim. That the kings themselves were content to follow the new trend is strikingly revealed by the royal castle of Dundonald in Ayrshire. This most remarkable ruin illustrates, in a unique manner, the switch over from the keep-gatehouse type of castle, introduced as we have seen during the Plantagenet occupation, to the new fashion of a tower-house—the ancestry of which no doubt should be traced back to the old Norman stone keeps.

Dundonald Castle crowns the summit of a rocky hill, a commanding site that has been occupied from an early date, as appears from the earthworks, probably prehistoric, by which the medieval castle is enclosed. Since the first half of the thirteenth century Dundonald belonged to the Stewarts of Scotland; and old writers affirm that there was here a castle which was recovered from the English by Angus Og, Lord of the Isles, a staunch supporter of King Robert Bruce.[1] The existing remains show that this castle consisted of a large rectangular keep-gatehouse, facing westwards, with two solid bastion towers projecting on either side of the

[1] Though Scott prefers to call him Ronald, he is the hero of *The Lord of the Isles*.

portal. In rear of the keep-gatehouse was a walled courtyard, on this steep and lofty site apparently unprovided with flanking towers. Thus in its original form Dundonald Castle will have much resembled the inner ward, or primary structure, of Criccieth Castle in North Wales, or Harry Avery's Castle in County Tyrone. At some period after its recovery for Bruce, or perhaps in the Second War of Independence, this Edwardian castle had been destroyed, in accordance with the usual Scottish practice.

Thereafter the castle must have remained a wreck until it was reconstructed, in the new fashion of a tower-house, by Robert II (1371–90), the first Stewart king, who made Dundonald his favourite residence, and died within its walls. His reconstruction is vouched for by the interesting suite of heraldic shields still visible on the tower. Nearly the whole of what had been the upper part of the front of the original keep-gatehouse was rebuilt: but the ashlar base of one of the old bastions still remains, and the position of the other is quite distinct. So is the built-up portal; and within the present tower-house the stubs of the lateral walls enclosing the entrance passage are clearly identified, showing that the passage had the normal width of 9 feet—enough to admit three men-at-arms abreast. The inner or eastern portal of the entrance passage was likewise built up, but leaving a narrow doorway for admission to the basement of the new building. Above the infilling of this rearward portal, on the inside of the building, the track is plainly visible of the vaulting of the passage.

More of the Edwardian structure has been embodied in the eastern front, including the original entrance to the keep-gate house, a fine pointed doorway on the first floor. This now became a window, while in the south gable at this level a new entrance door was provided for the tower-house, with a guardroom on one side and a spiral stair on the other, conducting to the upper floors. What survives of this stair is beautifully built of sandstone ashlars, accurately wrought to the course of the stair. This could well be a remnant of the original structure.

By this reorganization the castle was, as it were, turned about, so as to face east instead of west. The main structure, formerly a keep-gatehouse in the forefront of its *enceinte*, now became a tower-house in rear of its barmkin. As thus remodelled, Dundonald is the largest of Scottish tower-houses, its over-all measurements being 81 feet 8 inches by 40 feet.

To judge by its surviving portions, the Edwardian keep-gate-house had been built of sandstone ashlar. The new tower-house was constructed in rubble work of dark grey whinstone quarried on the site: but many sandstone ashlars from the earlier building have been re-used, just as they came to hand.

As befitted a royal palace, the principal feature in the remodelled castle was the great hall on the third floor. This must have been a noble *salon*; but unfortunately its upper portion was removed in 1644 to provide materials for the neighbouring castellated mansion of Auchans—itself now a sorry ruin. The hall was covered by a lofty pointed barrel vault, to the surface of which massive moulded ribs springing from richly carved corbels showing the characteristic scroll-moulding of the fourteenth century. There are wall-ribs, cross-ribs and diagonal ribs all in the manner of a groined vault: but since there are no groins, and the profile of a plain pointed barrel vault was maintained throughout, it is obvious that the whole system of corbels and ribs serves no structural purpose. It is purely decorative—the first example of a practice which, as we shall see, becomes common in the latest phase of Scottish Gothic, alike in castles and churches.

On 1st November, 1773, Dundonald Castle was visited by Johnson and Boswell, in the course of their immortal tour. Johnson, so his companion relates, "to irritate my old Scottish enthusiasm, was very jocular on the homely accommodation of 'King Bob', and roared and laughed till the ruins echoed." Yet while Dundonald Castle might well arouse the derision of the English sage, acquainted with the spacious splendours of Windsor and Hampton, its great hall, measuring 60 feet 6 inches by 25 feet 6 inches, and with its fine vaulted roof rising to a height of 25 feet, must have been an impressive apartment; and, even in its despoiled condition, the castle as a whole possesses a full share of the arresting quality that always marks a rugged, massive ruin set on a high and commanding stance.

Although the conception of a tower-house as the most favoured pattern for a baronial residence, even for so great a lord as Earl Archibald the Grim, was becoming more and more predominant in the fourteenth century, it must not be thought that the alternative theme of the castle of *enceinte* had been wholly discarded. On the contrary, about the same time which saw the erection of

Threave Castle the Douglases built for themselves at Tantallon in East Lothian one of the most imposing *enceinte* castles to be seen anywhere in Britain. An older castle on the site is on record about 1300; and a solitary foundation, bearing no relation to the existing fabric, is probably a remnant of this earlier castle, which (we may presume) perished during the Wars of Independence. The existing castle, first mentioned in 1374, was doubtless built by William, first Earl of Douglas, who had obtained the lordship a short time previously. All readers of Scott's *Marmion* will recall the poet's brilliant description:

> "And sudden, close before them showed
> His towers, Tantallon vast;
> Broad, massive, high, and stretching far,
> And held impregnable in war,
> On a projecting rock they rose,
> And round three sides the ocean flows.
> The fourth did battled walls inclose
> And double mound and fosse."

"Three sides of wall-like rock, and one side of rock-like wall," so Hugh Miller described the castle, whose impregnable strength is summarized in the pithy old proverb: "Ding down Tantallon— mak a brig to the Bass!"

Conformably to the outline of its peninsular site, the castle exhibits in front a single enormous lofty curtain wall, straddling the headland. In the centre is the tall rectangular Mid Tower or gatehouse; and from this the huge wall stretches outward and backward till it reaches the cliff, where it terminates, at either end, in a large circular tower. The Mid Tower is pierced at ground level by a vaulted entrance passage, defended by a portcullis and three pairs of folding gates, of which the innermost pair closed against the courtyard. Above this, the Mid Tower contained four full storeys. It is clear that this formidable structure was designed not only as the gatehouse, but also to provide a complete, self-contained residence for the lord or castellan, who thus has the entrance to the courtyard under his own control: and since the inner pair of folding gates closed against the court, he could hold out not only against the enemy in front but also against treachery in his rear. The floor over the entrance passage formed a fighting deck, from which the drawbridge, portcullis, "murderholes" and other defensive tackle were worked. Above this was

the lord's hall, and overhead two more storeys contained his private rooms. Ample sleeping accommodation for the lord's *familia*
or personal household was available in the chambers hollowed out
in the two frontal projections and tall oversailing turrets of the
tower. These chambers are far from being mere cells. Such is the
scale of the building that in the circular turrets they measure no
less than 12 feet 8 inches by 7 feet 7 inches. Their domestic
character is shown by the fact that their small windows are neatly
fitted with stone seats.

East and west, on each side of the courtyard, are the remains of
domestic buildings, but only the western range is still intact. As
originally constructed, it contained two great halls, one above the
other, the "laich hall" and the "lang hall". It is obvious that in this
mighty castle of Tantallon we have a highly specialized structure:
and it is our business to understand what purpose its designers had
in mind.

In the fourteenth and fifteenth centuries the Douglases were the
perfect example in Scotland of a too-powerful baronial house, the
head of which imposed his will by means of the private army of
"jackmen" or liveried retainers whom he kept in his pay. In the
days of the earlier feudalism, there had been, as a rule, no standing
garrisons in the larger castles. If war approached, the baron defended his home by calling up his feudal tenantry who dwelt
around him. But such tumultuary levies, ill-equipped and worse
trained, and bound only, as a rule, to forty days' service in the
year, were of little use for the "total" and specialized warfare of
the later Middle Ages. So everywhere in western Europe the
kings in their national contests, and the great barons in their incessant private quarrels or revolts against the Crown, came to rely
upon professional soldiers whom they hired. For this, money was
found by commuting the military service hitherto owed to these
barons by their tenantry. Of course, quarters for the new mercenaries had to be provided: and this meant, *for the first time*, standing
garrisons in the larger castles. Whereas in former days such castles
would contain, in time of peace, no more than the lord's *familia*
or household staff if he were in residence or in his absence a care-
taker or two, henceforth they must provide accommodation for
a compact body of professional troops. Now the presence of these
mercenaries would always be inconvenient and sometimes dangerous: for they did not owe the tenurial loyalty or natural allegiance

of vassals, and were at all times liable to be seduced by their employer's enemies.[1] Hence, for reasons alike of privacy and safety, the great barons of the fourteenth and fifteenth centuries took care to provide their castles with self-contained residences for themselves and their personal retinue. And it was plain commonsense that this self-contained residence of the lord should include the main entrance of the castle, which the lord could thus retain under the control of his own trusted servants. Here, then, we see the *ultima ratio* of the keep-gatehouse of the later *enceinte* castles.

A little study will show how completely the castle of Tantallon answers to these new requirements.

We have seen that the great gatehouse is not merely a strongly fortified tower of entry, but it also provides a self-contained, secure, well appointed and noble residence for the lord or castellan. Let us now look again at the principal range of domestic buildings on the left or western side of the courtyard. It contained two halls, the "laich hall" on the ground floor and the "lang hall" above it. In Scotland the almost universal practice was to build the great hall on the first floor, over cellarage. Here at Tantallon we have a ground floor hall, with a second hall above it. The inference is unmistakable. The lower hall will have served for the jackmen or paid retainers of the Douglas. Note that it has a central door and a central fireplace, a most unusual feature in a medieval hall. Obviously there was here no division into screens, body of the hall, and dais for the high table. It is a barrack hall, a messroom, nothing more. By contrast, the upper hall is approached, in the normal way for a festal hall, at the screens end up a broad open stair of state, and is entered through an ornate portal. It will have been used, in peaceful times, by the Douglas and his household. But when war approached, the lord's or constable's post was surely in the keep-gatehouse—the mighty Mid Tower— on the "action front", and with the entrance passage in his own safe keeping.

[1] In the ninth chapter of *The Monastery*, Sir Walter Scott has given us an excellent account of these "military retainers", who "conducted themselves with great insolence towards the industrious part of the community—lived in a great measure by plunder and were ready to execute any commands of their masters, however unlawful". Christie of the Clinthill in that novel—"true both to nature and to history", as John Buchan observes—is the perfect portrait of a Scottish jackman.

This new, untoward, and final manifestation of the feudal
system has been termed "bastard feudalism", as being in a sense
the illegitimate offspring of the old age of the real thing. All over
western Europe, and as far east as the castles of the Teutonic
Order in Old Prussia, bastard feudalism exercised the most profound change upon the castle plan. In Scotland, Tantallon is an
early example; and even more completely is the new theme
realized in the contemporary castle of Doune, built by Robert
Stewart, Duke of Albany, Regent of Scotland during the captivity
of James I. Elsewhere I have described this splendid castle, re-
roofed and (though uninhabited) well preserved by its noble

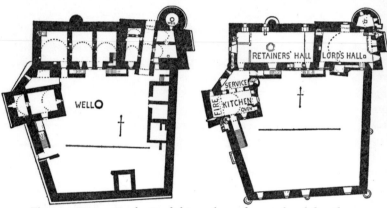

Fig. 20   Doune Castle, Perthshire: plans of ground and first floors
(By courtesy, Moray Estates)

owners, as "the highest achievement of perfected castellar construction in Scotland". Here, side by side, we have a mighty and
complex keep-gatehouse, forming in itself a complete and well-
appointed residence for the ducal owner, and a separate suite of
quarters for a standing garrison. The keep-gatehouse has its own
water supply, and could be defended equally against the castle
courtyard as against foes outside. The whole group of buildings,
lord's quarters and retainers' quarters, is massed frontally on the
only possible line of attack; while behind, the castle tails off, as it
were, into a mere curtain wall, against which were built, or at
all events planned, comparatively minor buildings. Apart from
the obvious advantages, from a military standpoint, of this frontal
massing, it satisfied the requirements of what may be called scenic

architecture, a matter to which the castle builders of the later Middle Ages were by no means indifferent. To a greater or lesser degree, every castle must be considered as a parade of pride in stone, expressing the feudal power and social predominance of its owner: and certainly the brow beating frontal of Doune Castle brazens forth the arrogance of an over-mighty subject in accents that no one can mistake.

According to the standards of the Middle Ages, a curtain wall more than 40 feet high was regarded as *sturmfrei*, to use a compact and expressive German term: i.e. free from the risk of escalade. The point is that a scaling ladder more than 40 feet long was too heavy to manhandle, and, even if successfully placed against the curtain, too wobbly for climbing. Then the wall walk of a curtain 40 feet or more in height could be mastered only by means of a drawbridge dropped from the fighting deck of a "belfry", or wooden tower on wheels brought up against it. This was the way in which the English captured Bothwell Castle in 1301, and the Scots in 1337. At Doune the curtain wall is 40 feet high; but here the contours of the ground would not permit of such a wooden tower being wheeled against it. Hence the curtain walls can fairly be regarded as *sturmfrei*. At Tantallon, facing level ground and thus more exposed to a frontal assult—particularly if the assailants succeeded in filling up the ditch—the curtain wall reaches a height of no less than 50 feet. Tantallon and Doune, representing the climax of castellar construction in Scotland, speak to us not only of the new problem created by "bastard feudalism", but also of the formidable siegecraft of the later Middle Ages.

In our rapid survey of Scottish castellar construction during the High Middle Ages, we must not forget that since 1266 the Hebrides formed part of Scotland. We have already seen that even during the Norse ascendancy the western seaboard and the islands were by no means closed to Anglo-Norman influences, and that the greater chiefs were perfectly able to build themselves castles and churches in the most up-to-date style. Naturally they were still better able to do so after the Treaty of Perth, by which Norway ceded the Hebrides to Scotland. Nothing can be more misleading than the idea that the successive changes in architectural style drifted, as it were, slowly across the country from east to west, and that the succession is inevitably later in the Western Isles. Of course it is true that old fashioned styles, in architecture as in other things, will tend to linger on in peripheral localities: but it is a mistake to draw from this conclusion that *all* work of early aspect in the Hebrides is necessarily later than similar work on the mainland. "Retarded work" is indeed to be expected in minor buildings and monuments which would be carried out by local talent for local patrons. But a big man, or a man with important mainland connexions, would always be able to command the services of mainland craftsmen whose work would be executed in the most up-to-date manner of their time.

So it comes about that in the remote island of Coll we find what may fairly be described, although its scale is *bijou*, as perhaps the most complete example of the classic type of medieval castle to be found anywhere in Scotland. Breachacha Castle—"the Castle of the Dappled Field"—was visited by Johnson and Boswell in 1773. Both were fired with the place: Boswell wrote that "it was more entire than any that I ever saw, and reports that 'Mr Johnson examined all this remaining specimen of ancient life with wonderful eagerness'." Here is how a sixteenth-century writer describes it:

> "ane castell callit Brekauche, quhilk is ane great strenth be reason of the situation thairof verie neir to the sea, quhilk defendis the half thairof, and hes three walls about the rest of the castell, ane thairof biggit with lyme and stane, with sundrie gude devises for defending of the tower. Ane uther wall about that within the quhilk schippis and boittis are drawin and salvit. And the third and uttermost wall of tymber and earth, within the quhilk the haill gudes of the cuntrie are keipit in tyme of troubles or weiris."

Of the outermost rampart of timbered earthwork—the "barres hold", as such a defence is called in medieval Scottish writings—not a vestige now remains, though an air survey might reveal its track. But it is clearly shown, with its palisade, on Blaeu's map, dated 1654. For the rest, the castle exhibits, in singular perfection, albeit on a very small scale, all the devices and contrivances current in the military and domestic architecture of the later Middle Ages. The plan, with its central tall keep-tower or *donjon*, its inner curtain and flanking tower screening a hall, the outer curtain, and the external palisaded envelope, is that of a first-class

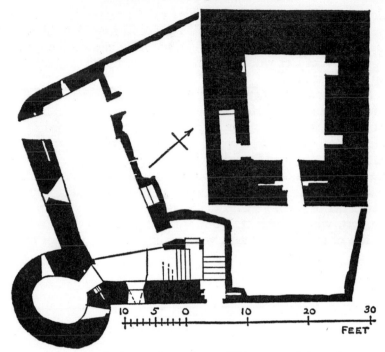

Fig. 21   Breachacha Castle, Coll, Argyllshire: ground floor plan
(By courtesy, Aberdeen University Library)

medieval castle in miniature. All the details of its defensive and domestic arrangements—the battlements, turret and wall-walk of the keep, its main entrance on the first floor, the cleverly considered stair-head arrangements; the vaulted roof and battlements and spreading base of the round tower; the *mâchicoulis* over the two gates in the main curtain; the corbelled privies on the curtain wall—each and every particular about the castle is abreast of the most advanced conceptions in the secular architecture of the time. True, the scale is that of a vignette, and the execution is unlearned enough. One gets the impression that the master-mason was a man of high professional status, well skilled in all the up-to-date conventions of his art, but that he was compelled to employ them here on a much smaller scale than he was used to; also that he had to make do with local workmen, unversed in the niceties of the best masoncraft of the time. That the master-mason was acquainted with the art of castle building on a larger scale seems clear from the way in which in this small "house of fence" he has assembled all the paraphernalia of a major fortress. A local craftsman, we may be sure, either would not have known about these "gude devises", or would have made no attempt to employ them on a scale so small.

From soon after 1431 Coll was the seat of a branch of Clan MacLean. But long before that time, it had been granted by King Robert Bruce to his staunch adherent, Angus Og, Lord of the Isles. Upon the whole, it seems probable that this powerful magnate, at a time when English naval intervention upon the western seaboard was a danger to be reckoned with, will have been the most likely man to build a small but up-to-date fortalice upon his island fief of Coll. Perhaps the master-mason was sent up from Tarbert, where from 1326 onwards King Robert, for the same reason of maritime defence, was building himself a major castle.

XIV

A National Style in Church and Castle Building

BROADLY speaking, it may be true to say that, up to the outbreak of the disastrous war with England, Scotland had hardly evolved a national style of architecture, either in church or in castle building. In the twelfth and thirteenth centuries the country, or at least the lowland portions of it as far north as the Dornoch Firth, formed one cultural province with England, and partook generally in the Anglo-Norman building fashions, and, less directly in those of France. Thus there is nothing specially Scottish about the work of these centuries in Glasgow and Elgin Cathedrals or in Dryburgh Abbey. In the same way such castles as Kildrummy and Bothwell can hardly be classed, in any real sense, as Scottish buildings; they take their place among the contemporary examples of military construction in Western Europe. Many of the great Scottish barons, who were the builders of the castles and parish churches, the founders of the monasteries and the benefactors of the cathedrals, possessed broad acres both in Scotland and in England. They moved freely from one country to another, with no consciousness of crossing a hostile frontier: and it is clear that in the building undertakings which they sponsored in Scotland they imported freely craftsmen from the southern realm.

But all this was changed by the outbreak of the great war. Joseph Robertson, in his classic essay on "Scottish Abbeys and Cathedrals", has eloquently portrayed the dire effects of this calamitous struggle:

"The tide of civilization, which for two centuries had flowed northward without check, was now to be stayed—was even to be rolled back. . . . The first note of contest banished every English priest, monk and friar from the northern realm. Its termination was followed by the departure of those great Anglo-Norman lords— the flower of the Scottish baronage—who, holding vast possessions in both countries, had so long maintained among the rude Scottish hills the generous example of English wealth and refinement. Then it was that de la Zouche and de Quincy, Ferrars and Talbot, Beaumont and Umphraville, Percy and Wake, Mowbray and Fitzwarine, Balliol and Cumyn, Hastings and de Coursi, ceased to be significant names beyond the Tweed—either perishing in that terrible revolution, or withdrawing to their English domains, there to perpetuate in scutcheon and pedigree the memory of their rightful claims to many of the finest lordships in Albany, and to much of the reddest blood of the north.

"The consequences of this crisis, so far as regards ecclesiastical architecture, were twofold. Henceforth comparatively few buildings arose in the north, and these, with one or two exceptions, were on a meaner scale. In the second place, England now become an hereditary enemy no longer supplied models for the sacred edifices beyond the Tweed, which received instead the impress of the new ally of France."

No doubt this forthright statement, like many pioneer pronouncements, is couched in terms too absolute: yet its substantial truth is not to be gainsaid; and, if we add the Low Countries to France as the source from which Scotland henceforward tended to draw some of her architectural inspiration, it fairly depicts the change that, from the fourteenth century onwards, came over the practice of Scottish building. Just as in vernacular literature the national poets—Barbour, Wyntoun and Blind Harry—reveal the new spirit of intense and passionate, self-centred nationalism, so it is with the churches and castles. Among the castles the tower-house, at whose growth in favour we have already glanced, now becomes the favourite type of residence, both for the magnates and for the "lairds" or smaller landowners. At the tower-houses we shall look more fully in the next chapter. The militarization of Scottish life invaded even the churches. Many of these built in the fifteenth century have a half baronial appearance. They are furnished with the battlements, crow-stepped gables, heavy ribbed vaults, and pack-saddle roofs of the contemporary castles. This castellar effect reaches its climax in the Preceptory Church of the Knights Hospitallers at Torphichen in West Lothian.

By the fourteenth century the pattern of piety, in Scotland as in England, was changing. Probably there were more than enough monasteries in the country, and it is likely that prejudice against the monks, and envy of their vast possessions—emotions so marked during the Reformation—were already making themselves felt. So the magnates, instead of founding fresh monasteries, or adding to the endowments of the old ones, took to establishing, usually in the neighbourhood of their castles, collegiate churches, each served by a college or small body of secular clergy, who by the deed of foundation were held bound to sing masses and chant prayers for the soul of the founder of the college, and of such persons as might be named in his deed of gift. In this way not only were many new collegiate foundations planted, but in a number of cases existing parish churches were promoted to collegiate rank. So it happens that a number of these collegiate churches of the fifteenth century still survive in parochial use. Built in the new and intensely national style of architecture of the time, they form a distinctive and highly interesting element in the ecclesiastical monuments of Scotland. Of collegiate churches still doing duty as parish churches we may mention Bothwell near Glasgow (1398); Corstorphine near Edinburgh (1444); Crichton, Midlothian (1449); Cullen, Banffshire (1543) and Biggar, Lanarkshire (1543) as favourable examples. During the fifteenth century some of the larger burghal churches, such as St. Giles', Edinburgh, St. Michael's, Linlithgow, and St. Nicholas', Aberdeen, were raised to the status of colleges. Of all our Scottish collegiate churches, the most remarkable beyond doubt is Roslin in Midlothian, founded about 1446. Its choir—all that was ever built—is still maintained as a private chapel. The astonishing exuberance of ornament, which has made Roslin Chapel so widely famed, is probably unparalleled in the whole field of Gothic architecture, anywhere in Europe. The student of medieval masoncraft and carving will find here an inexhaustible field of study and a source of unending delight.

A characteristic specimen of these fifteenth-century collegiate churches may be seen at Dunglass in East Lothian. Here an older chapel of the Virgin Mary was converted, shortly before 1451, into a collegiate establishment by Sir Alexander Hume, an ancestor of the Earl of Home, whose eldest son bears the title of Lord Dunglass. The foundation comprised a provost, two other priests, and four boy choristers. A manse and orchard were provided for each of the clergy, and suitable stipends were assigned to all seven members of the college. In 1544, Dunglass Castle (now vanished) and the church were held against the English, and after its capture the whole village was "spoiled and burned". Probably the church suffered on that occasion, though its almost all-stone construction would make it hard to burn. Later on, with a fine sense of the fitness of things, it was converted into a stable, as nowadays we see surplus churches turned into garages; and for this purpose a door was hacked down from the sill of the east window, and the interior mutilated and misused in various ways.

The church, now maintained as a ruin by the Ministry of Public Building and Works, is cruciform on plan, with a central tower, and a sacristy on the north side of the choir. It is splendidly built of yellow sandstone ashlar, and the roofs of all four sections of the structure, as well as the sacristy, have high pointed waggon vaults covered with stone slabs, in the manner of the castles of the period. The crossing, however, is unvaulted, and the low tower had a wooden helmet. There are three doorways, one on each side of the nave and a priests' door on the south side of the choir. Inside the latter, in the south wall, are the piscina and sedilia, and in the north wall is a sacrament house. The tower arches are lofty and pointed, and are carried on elaborately sculptured carved caps. All the detail, outside and inside, is very rich and of the highest quality; and the tracery of the windows partakes of the flamboyant character which later Scotch Gothic borrowed from the Low Countries. Over the priests' door a shield displayed the arms of the founder, and above this a canopied niche doubtless contained a figure of the patron saint. A feature of the church are the arched tomb recesses in the transept and sacristy gables. Evidently the founder desired the college to be the burial place of his family.

Another fine collegiate church, long disused but now maintained by the Ministry of Public Building and Works, is Seton near Prestonpans, on the east side of Edinburgh. This church was made collegiate in 1492, and the work of rebuilding was completed by the Lady Janet Hepburn, widow of the founder's son, the fifth Lord Seton, who fell at Flodden in 1513. The nave indeed was never built; and what we have, therefore, is the central tower, north and south transepts, and a choir ending, as often in late

Scotch work, in a chevet or five-sided apse—an idea borrowed from the Continent. On the north side of the choir is a sacristy. The choir has a pointed waggon vault, decorated with moulded transverse and diagonal ribs, which serve no structural purpose. It is the same mode of ornamental treatment which we have already noticed in Dundonald Castle. In the crossing, however, there is a genuine groined vault, with an "eye" for hoisting the bells into the tower. The roofs are, or were, stone-slabbed, as at Dunglass. The windows have the usual flamboyant tracery of the period. Internally the decoration of the church, though rich, is coarser than that of Dunglass. In the choir are the fine effigies of the third Lord Seton, the founder of the college, and a lady, perhaps his mother. A charming feature of Seton Church is the stone broach spire. Its apex, noted a sixteenth-century writer "wants little of compleiting"; and so it remains today.[1]

By far the loveliest of our Scottish collegiate churches is Lincluden, beautifully situated in the angle where the Water of Cluden meets the River Nith, a long mile north-west of Dumfries, but within the Stewartry of Kirkcudbright. This is perhaps the finest surviving piece of Decorated Architecture in Scotland.

About the year 1164, Uchtred, son of Fergus Lord of Galloway, established at Lincluden a Benedictine nunnery; but in 1389 Archibald, third Earl of Douglas, surnamed "the Grim" (whom we have already encountered at Threave Castle), suppressed the establishment, upon the pretext that the nuns had become disorderly. In place of the nunnery, and using its endowments, he founded a college of secular canons, consisting finally of a provost, eight priests and twenty-four bedesmen. The Romanesque nunnery church was swept away, though the foundations of its nave and some moulded fragments of twelfth-century work survive. In its place was built a new church, consisting of a nave with a south aisle, a south transept, and a chancel. North from the chancel extended the college buildings. Architectural and heraldic evidence combine to make it clear that the church is the work of Archibald, fourth Earl of Douglas, Marshal of France and Duke of Touraine —one of the foremost, if also one of the most unlucky, captains of his time. He was known in Scotland as Archibald *Tyneman*—

[1] The complex history of Seton Church has been deployed in masterly fashion by Mr. Stewart Cruden, H.M. Inspector of Ancient Monuments for Scotland, *Proc. Soc. Ant. Scot.*, vol. LXXXIX, pp. 417-37.

"the loser"—because of the number of unsuccessful engagements in which he fought. In the last of these, the fatal battle of Verneuil, he fell (17th August, 1424). Tribute to his military fame is paid in Shakespeare's *Henry IV*:

> "Renowned Douglas, whose high deeds
>   Whose hot assaults, and great name in arms,
>   Holds from all soldiers chief majority,
>   And military title capital,
>   Through all the Kingdoms that acknowledge Christ."

In 1390 he had married the Princess Margaret, daughter of Robert III. Her beautiful tomb at Lincluden is an integral part of the chancel, and moreover was designed as the resting place for them both, since the tomb-chest has room for two effigies. But her heroic husband lies in Tours Cathedral; and so the Princess Margaret slept alone beneath this glorious monument, with her effigy and inscription above. To the eternal shame of Scotland, this is the only surviving tomb of her ancient royal line, until they removed to England, where better care was taken of their resting places. Alas! her remains did not escape violation, for the tomb was ransacked and her bones scattered by treasure seekers in the eighteenth century. One shield on the tomb bears the arms of Annandale, which was granted to Earl Douglas in 1409. The building of the chancel can therefore be securely dated to between 1409 and 1424.

Of Lincluden College it has been truly said that "the remaining portions are of great beauty, possessing a delicacy and richness of detail unsurpassed by any of the churches of the Decorated period in Scotland". The sheer breath-taking loveliness of the ruins is enhanced by the durable quality of the warm red Permian sandstone of which they are built, so that the delicately chiselled ornament is in wonderful preservation. The lofty canopied altar-tomb of the Princess, with its wealth of Gothic enrichment and heraldic blazonry, gives its tone to the whole chancel, which in addition possesses an exceedingly beautiful piscina and sedilia, and is lit by windows ample and nobly conceived, of which the cusped tracery, now unhappily destroyed, has been in the full exuberant style of the Decorated period. The Latin inscription on the royal tomb, obviously an afterthought, incised beneath the canopy when she alone, after years of widowhood, benevolent and be-

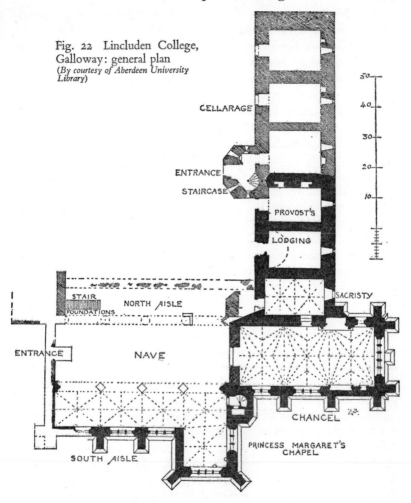

Fig. 22 Lincluden College, Galloway: general plan
(*By courtesy of Aberdeen University Library*)

CELLARAGE

ENTRANCE

STAIRCASE

PROVOST'S

LODGING

STAIR FOUNDATIONS

NORTH AISLE

SACRISTY

ENTRANCE

NAVE

CHANCEL

PRINCESS MARGARET'S CHAPEL

SOUTH AISLE

loved throughout the bounds of Galloway, came to be buried here in 1450, may be rendered thus: "Here lies the Lady Margaret, daughter of the King of Scotland, formerly Countess of Douglas and Lady of Galloway and Annandale." Above is the touching prayer, likewise incised: ALAIDE: DE: DIEU.

The chancel comprises three bays, without aisles, and the first room of the northward wing formed the sacristy, entered by a very rich doorway. Three bays of quadripartite vaulting, with ridge, cross, diagonal and tierceron ribs, spanned the chancel.

Above this was an upper chamber, covered by a pointed barrel-vault with false ribs, in the manner which (as we have seen) was characteristic of the time. The floor of this upper chamber was of timber, resting on corbels on the side walls.[1] No doubt the roof will have been of the usual stone-slabbed construction, borne upon the pointed vault.

A most valuable feature of the Lincluden ruins is the rood-screen, closing in the western end of the chancel. Unhappily it is badly wasted, but the carven subjects, executed with unrivalled delicacy and spirit, included the Annunciation, the Birth of Our Lord, and Adoration of the Magi, the Visit of the Shepherds, Simeon and Anna, and Jesus in the Temple.

The south transept is likewise in a rich style of architecture, corresponding in a general way with that of the chancel. It contained a chapel, founded in 1429 by the Princess Margaret in memory of her husband. Of the nave, nothing now remains except two bays of its south aisle, each with a traceried window, and once covered by quadripartite groined vaults. Perhaps this was all that was built, since the foundations on the north side, and at the west end, seem to belong to the nunnery church. The sacristy is groin-vaulted in two bays: and beyond it, to the north, are two cellars of the Provost's lodging. The remainder of this building, including the stair-tower, is an addition or rebuild of the sixteenth century. All the other claustral buildings have disappeared. A remarkable feature about Lincluden College, and one highly characteristic of the fifteenth century, is the profusion of heraldry upon the walls, without and within. Among the numerous carved pieces preserved on the site is the reredos of the high altar, displaying among other subjects no longer identifiable, figures of St. Paul, St. John the Evangelist, St. James the Less, and St. Thomas.

Nothing can here be told about the colourful history of Lincluden College. But one circumstance cannot be omitted. In 1460 it became the refuge of the indomitable Margaret of Anjou, "that fiery and ambitious mind", Queen of Henry VI, with her young son Edward, the ill-starred Prince of Wales. At Lincluden the royal fugitives were entertained by Mary of Gueldres, the widow-

[1] It seems impossible that the two systems could have co-existed. Probably the groined vault was never completed, no more being built than now survives, and the pointed vault, with its timber loft, was substituted.

ed Queen of James II. Nor must we omit to note that here, at Lincluden, one of his favourite haunts, Burns composed his famous song, "Ca' the Yowes to the Knowes":

> "Yonder Clouden's silent towers
> Where at moonshine midnight hours
> O'er the dewy bending flowers
> Fairies dance sae cheerie."

But we have not yet exhausted the antiquarian interest of this fascinating place. Close south-west of the ruins are the remains of a Norman *motte*, with its outer defences of bank and ditch. In the days of the college the *motte* was terraced and probably surmounted by a pavilion or pleasure tower. To the north, and abreast of the college buildings, is a square sunken area where an astounding discovery was made while the ruins were being conserved by the Ancient Monuments Department:

> "One autumn morn a workman of the Office of Works, standing on the mote, looked down on this space all covered with frost and was astonished that the hoar had brought up a wonderful pattern on the soil. He hastily pegged out that pattern, and in due course that level space was excavated. It brought to light a medieval garden of remarkable design, exactly like the pattern of the frost."[1]

By far the most famous example of Decorated architecture in Scotland is the church of Melrose Abbey. This noble ruin has been so often described and illustrated, and its beauties celebrated in poetry and prose, that it would be superfluous to offer even the briefest description in the present work. Almost all of the abbey church that survives dates from the restoration carried out during the fourteenth and fifteenth centuries, after the savage destructions of the monastery by English troops in 1322 and 1385. As rebuilt, the church was vaulted throughout, a feature paralleled in Scotland only at Holyrood. During the earlier part of the reconstruction period, the country in which Melrose is situated was under English suzerainty, and we are therefore not surprised to find in the presbytery tracery of thoroughly Perpendicular design, obviously inspired by York Minister—indeed it has been plausibly suggested that the east window was designed to fit stained glass imported ready-made from York. By contrast, the south

[1] The herbarium of the College is on record in 1559.

transept window is of characteristically French Flamboyant character: and its *provenance* seems to be confirmed by the two remarkable inscriptions in which, following a practice extremely rare in the Middle Ages, the master mason has commemorated himself. The second of these inscriptions, which has aroused vehement discussion, is as follows:

JOHN : MOROW : SUM : TYM : CALLIT :
WAS : I : AND : BORN : IN : PARYSSE :
CERTANLY : AND : HAD : IN : KEPYNG :
AL : MASOUN : WERK : OF : SANTAN :
DROYS : YE : HYE : KYRK : OF GLAS
GW : MELROS : AND : PASLAY : OF :
NYDDYSDAYLL : AND : OF : GALWAY :
I : PRAY : TO GOD : AND : MARI : BATHE :
& : SWETE : SANCT : JOHNE : TO : KEPE :
THIS : HALY : KYRK : FRA : SKATHE :[1]

Two features in Melrose Abbey Church cannot be omitted even in so brief a notice as the present. One is the use, in some of the canopied niches in which the building is so rich, of what has been aptly termed the "nodding ogee". The ogival head of the canopy leans outward from the plane of the wall of buttress, as if the niche were making one a bow. It is a whimsical and altogether charming mannerism. The other feature is the profusion and beauty of the figure sculpture. One statuette in particular, a figure of the Virgin Mary with the Holy Child in an elaborately decorated canopied niche high up on one of the buttress-pinnacles on the south side of the nave, might be saluted by not a few as the loveliest piece of figure sculpture in the whole range of Scottish medieval architecture.

It must not be imagined that all the mason-craftsmen who wrought this lovely work at Melrose were foreigners. No one but a Scot could have carved the curly kail enrichment on some of the capitals at the eastern end of the nave. These capitals are strikingly paralleled in the oldest surviving work in the ruined crossing of St. Machar's Cathedral, Aberdeen, dating from the time of Bishop Alexander Kyninmund (1355–80). It has long

---

[1] On the south-east buttress of the transept is a grotesque little figure of a mason with his chisel and mell. This could be a caricature of John Morow. The other inscription spells his name as Morvo. It has been "Frenchified" as Moreau.

been a tradition in the oldest Aberdeen Lodge of Freemasons that the Lodge was founded by a mason, John Scott, who came from Melrose to work at Aberdeen.

Of Melrose Abbey Church in general it has truly been said:

"No building in Scotland affords such an extensive and almost inexhaustible field for minute investigation and enjoyment of detail as this. Whether we consider the great variety of the beautifully sculptured figures of monks and angels playing on musical instruments, or displaying 'the scrolls that teach us to live and die', or turn to the elaborate canopies and beautiful pinnacles of the buttresses, or examine the rich variety of foliage and other sculptures on the capitals of the nave and the doorway and arches of the cloisters; or if, again, we take a more general view of the different parts of the edifice from the numerous fine standpoints from which it can be so advantageously contemplated, we know of no Scottish building which surpasses Melrose either in the picturesqueness of its general aspect, or in the profusion or value of its details."

Another important Scottish monastery which was rebuilt in the fifteenth century—probably after destruction during the Wars of Independence—is Crossraguel in Carrick. This was a Cluniac house, a daughter of Paisley. The plan of the Abbey Church is remarkable. It is a long narrow unicameral structure, ending, after the common late Scottish pattern in a three-sided apse. Probably the division between nave and choir was made by a wooden screen: but later, doubtless in consequence of a decrease in the number of monks (who by the Reformation numbered only eleven), the nave seems to have been abandoned, and was shut off by a stone partition, with a door, strongly barred, leading into the chancel. Of the conventual buildings the principal remnant is a fine rectangular chapter house, groin-vaulted upon a slender pier. The militarization of Scottish life during the fifteenth century is revealed in the formidable gatehouse that guards admission to the Abbey precinct, and still more by the mighty keep-tower, in itself a regular fortalice, which adjoins the Abbot's house. The Abbots of Crossraguel had the privilege of minting their own coins, now prized as collectors' pieces. The roasting alive of the Commendator, or lay abbot, in 1570, by the Earl of Cassilis, known locally as "the King of Carrick", with a view to forcing him to sign away the monastic lands, is one of the savage tales of Scottish history.

Another major Scottish church which was largely rebuilt in the fifteenth century is Dunkeld Cathedral, so beautifully situated on the bank of the broad and ample Tay, with a background of wooded and heather-clad, rocky hills. The see of Dunkeld was founded by Alexander I in or about the year 1107. The chancel, long, narrow, unaisled and unvaulted, has been almost entirely restored and is now used as the parish church: but it retains some good First Pointed work. The groin-vaulted rectangular chapter house on its north side is a later addition. It has for centuries been the burial place of the ducal house of Atholl. The nave remains a majestic ruin, and is wholly a work of the fifteenth century. It is aisled, and the pointed arcades rest on plain cylindrical piers, not unlike those, of the same period, in St. Machar's Cathedral, Aberdeen. The triforium is round-arched, with traceried infilling, while the clerestory windows, likewise provided with flamboyant tracery, are of pointed form. So are most of the aisle windows, but one at the west end of the north side is flat topped, a peculiarity noted also at two other Perthshire churches, Dunblane Cathedral and St. John's Kirk, Perth. Only the south aisle appears to have been vaulted. Like the Cathedral of Aberdeen, Dunkeld has a south porch. The western front of the Cathedral is high abnormal. The pointed doorway, richly moulded, was later provided with an extra "order", if so it may be called, for it is a mere thickening of the wall on either side, with an almost plain arch above, designed in order to provide space for a tribune or gallery overhead. The great west window over this gallery has been enlarged, with the queer result that it does not occupy a central position in the gable, its pointed tip being to one side of the small rose window in the apex. The rose itself is not directly beneath the finial on the gable, though it is centred with the entrance door. At the northwest corner of the nave is a very fine square tower, lofty and massive, with a groin-vaulted base, upon the side walls and severies or compartments of which may be seen important remnants of medieval painting. Dunkeld Cathedral contains two altar tombs of particular importance. One is the fine monument of Bishop Robert de Cardeny, who died in 1436, and is recorded to have built the nave as far up as the "blind storey". The other is that of the "Wolf of Badenoch", the destroyer of Elgin Cathedral. The most famous ruler of the diocese was the poet Gavin Douglas, the first British translator of the *Aeneid*:

"More pleased that, in a barbarous age,
He gave rude Scotland Virgil's page,
Than that beneath his rule he held
The bishopric of fair Dunkeld."

Despite the outward turbulence of Scottish public and private life in the fifteenth century, it is clear from all our evidence that the period was one of great and steadily increasing national prosperity. We have already seen in the foregoing brief portrayal of ecclesiastical architecture during this period, that the fifteenth century was a great church building period. Equally so was the case with the castles, the fortified dwellings, great and small, of the landowner. Both in castles and in churches, the prevailing theme is the dominance of the warlike. It is in fact the age of militarism in architecture (see *supra*, pp. 27–8).

One of the best known, and most accessible, of the major Scottish strongholds dating from this remarkable period is the famous Castle of Craigmillar, on the outskirts of Edinburgh—a ruin for ever associated with some of the darkest and most dubious events in the reign of the ill-fated Queen Mary. Long ago, Hill Burton remarked of Craigmillar that "there is, perhaps, no other instance in Scotland of a family mansion so systematically built on the principles of fortification in the fifteenth and sixteenth centuries". The nucleus of the castle is a great L-shaped tower-house dating from soon after 1374. This answers to the donjon, withdrawn to the rear of the site in the manner of a thirteenth-century castle, yet overlooking and commanding the whole. The devious and well-defended approach to its entrance and principal apartments is quite in the manner of that time, and faintly reminds us of the elaborate devices of Krak des Chevaliers or Carcassonne. The machicolated curtain wall of 1427—the best preserved example of this kind of defence in Scotland—corresponds to the wall of *enceinte* of such a castle, and the outer walls recall *les lices* or "the barriers", as the outermost enclosure, often palisaded, was called in Plantagenet times. The buildings within the courtyard portray the advanced ideas of domestic comfort in the sixteenth and seventeenth centuries: the western range, in its present form reconstructed in 1661, is an excellent example of Renaissance planning and detail. A fifteenth-century chapel and a pleasance of the time of Charles I complete the picture of a great house which spans the whole transition period from the High Middle Ages until modern times. And what the castle is, it looks. Seen from the north, it has a formidable aspect, as if bidding defiance to the housing scheme that stealthily creeps up towards it across what so recently were green and pleasant fields. Silhouetted against the southern sky, the great bulk of the buildings, echeloned in cubic masses, is most commanding. From the opposite side, the effect of its lofty central tower and frowning curtain walls, rising sheer from the cliff, is equally impressive. Few structures with so composite and piecemeal a development behind them present such a semblance of compact unity and concentrated strength.

In the fifteenth century the Church, as we have learned, was as highly feudalized and militarized as the lay baronies. Nowhere is this fact more startlingly apparent than in the Palace of the Bishops of Moray at Spynie, near Elgin—the most magnificent remaining episcopal residence in Scotland. It appears to have begun, in the fourteenth century, as a more or less rectangular enclosure screened by massive curtain walls. On the north side was the great hall. Opposite it was a handsome chapel, and at three of the corners were projecting square towers. Early in the fifteenth century an ornate gateway, quite English in style, was inserted in the east curtain. It consists of an elliptic arch, provided with a portcullis, and framed by two buttresses supporting semi-hexagonal oversailing turrets, between which, above the portal, is an oversailing parapet pierced with "murder holes". Bishop David Stewart (1461–76) having quarrelled with his powerful neighbour, the Earl of Huntly, excommunicated the Gordon chief, who retaliated by vowing to "pull the bishop out of his pigeon-holes". In his turn the bishop retorted by building himself a dovecot which might well have daunted any nest robber. David's Tower, as it came to be known, was completed by the next Bishop, William Tulloch (1477–82). It is the fourth largest tower-house in Scotland, measuring 62 feet 5 inches by 44 feet 3 inches, and about 73 feet in height to the parapet walk, with walls in the basement 11 feet thick. The last Roman Catholic Bishop was the dissolute Patrick Hepburn (1535–73)—a man whom no Reformation could dislodge and nobody could reform. To the end of his days he maintained himself in Spynie, providing against all eventualities by piercing its walls for cannon, and securing his position by the landed interest which he gathered round himself through wholesale grants of the Church's patrimony to his supporters.

In some ways the most remarkable of the major fifteenth-century castles in Scotland is Ravenscraig on the Fife coast at Kirkcaldy. This castle was begun by James II in 1460, and left half completed on the death three years later of his widow, Mary of Gueldres, to whom it had been assigned as a dower-house. The special interest of this castle resides in the fact that it represents a detail in the response of Scotland, under the driving power of an energetic and far-seeing monarch, to the new conditions of warfare created in the fifteenth century by the introduction of battering ordnance and the development of organized national navies. In fact it appears to be the first castle in Britain to be systematically designed for defence by cannon. Straddling its sea-girt promontory, the main building of the castle, with its two massive round towers, is essentially an *ouvrage de contre-approche*. Clearly it shares a common theme with the mighty "new mantle" or "great bulwark" erected after 1479 by Count Oswald von Thierstein at his castle of Hohkoenigsbourg in Alsace. It has long been recognized that this astonishing structure was built under Burgundian influence: Mary of Gueldres was a Burgundian princess, and it is known that craftsmen and technicians from that country were employed in Scotland after her marriage to James II.

The greatest builders of castles and palaces were, of course, the kings. The royal castles of Edinburgh and Stirling, and the palaces of Holyrood and Falkland, are buildings of the highest importance: but, being still in use, they do not come within the purview of this survey. Something, however, must be said about the splendid ruin of Linlithgow Palace, which, in the final form that it achieved, early in the seventeenth century, is beyond doubt the most purposeful piece of planning in the whole range of old Scottish domestic architecture:

> "Of all the palaces so fair,
>   Built for the royal dwelling,
> In Scotland, far beyond compare
>   Linlithgow is excelling."

The present building was begun by James I in 1425, carried

forward intermittently throughout the fifteenth century, and re-organized by James V under his master-mason, Thomas French, whose name betrays his country of origin. The work seems thus to have been completed by 1539: but on 6th September, 1607, the

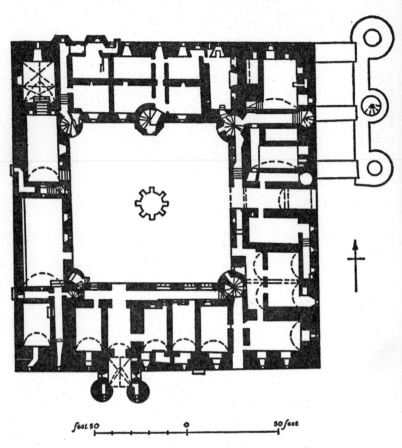

Fig. 23   Linlithgow Palace, ground floor plan
(*By courtesy, Ministry of Public Building and Works*)

north "quarter" fell, "rufe and all, within the wallis, to the ground". This range was rebuilt between 1618 and 1633, in the then fashionable neo-classical style, under the direction of the master-mason William Wallace. The work of James V, which has stamped its character on the rest of the palace, shows the

Dirleton Castle, East Lothian

Huntly Castle, Aberdeenshire

Craigievar Castle, Aberdeenshire

Caerlaverock Castle, Dumfriesshire

quaint mixture of Gothic and Renaissance detail characteristic of the same monarch's buildings at Stirling and Falkland. The palace forms a quadrangular embattled structure, with square towers, not projecting, at all four external corners, and in the angles of the courtyard round stair turrets carried up from the ground. In the centre of the courtyard is a most elaborate fountain. By Scottish standards the palace is indeed a striking building: yet we may well believe that King James V's Queen, Mary of Lorraine, familiar as she was with the châteaux of the Loire, must have been using the language of courtesy to her husband when she declared Linlithgow to be "the most princely home she had ever looked upon". In the palace, on 8th December, 1542, their daughter, the hapless Queen Mary, was born. On 1st February, 1746 the palace was burned through the carelessness or malice of Cumberland's troops, quartered there during the Jacobite rising. Thus throughout its entire history Linlithgow Palace has been associated with the House of Stewart, and perished in the final ruin of that ill-starred dynasty.

From the High Street of Linlithgow the palace is approached on its south side through an outer gatehouse or "fore-entry", hard by the western tower of the noble fifteenth-century parish church of St. Michael. The entrance to the palace itself lies through a second gatehouse. This is a poor dumpy thing—the one piece of inadequate design in the entire palace. On three sides its basement contains the ample vaulted cellarage and kitchens requisite for a royal household: but the north wing, as rebuilt by Wallace, contains unvaulted living rooms on all floors. On the first floor the east range contains the Great Hall, or "Lyon Chalmer", with its own "court kitchen": in the south range is the chapel, with an ante-room beyond it: while the private apartments of the King and Queen occupy the western range. Originally the entrance was on the east side, defended by outwork towers and approached by a drawbridge: but this was blocked and the entrance transferred to the south under the new arrangements of James V. The "old entry", as it was thereafter called, had a richly decorated "frontispiece", with canopied niches of castellar design, containing symbolic statuary, all of which has long since disappeared. Apart from the two entrances, the principal features of the external elevations, which are stern enough, are the five lofty dignified windows of the chapel on the south front, and on the north

14

front an exceedingly beautiful oriel—the sole survivor of three.

Inside the courtyard the most spectacular thing is the highly ornamented face of the "old entry", on the east side. Its principal feature is provided by three canopied niches, which once contained, respectively, statues of the Pope, a knight, and a labourer. On the south side is a long corridor, the work of James IV, with windows and decoration of Tudor fashion—perhaps the work of an English mason who came north with Queen Margaret, a daughter of Henry VII. Above the new entrance on this side was a magnificent portrayal of the Annunciation, of which the statue of the Virgin together with her Pot of Lilies, still remains. In the west front the visitor's eye is at once caught by the unique window of fourteen lights which serves the royal Presence Chamber. The north façade, with its neo-classical detail, is finely conceived, and gains added dignity from the three-sided stair tower midway in its length. The pediments of the windows are carved with emblems illustrating the Union of the Crowns.

Space forbids us to describe the many splendid rooms in the palace. We shall content ourselves with giving some account of the Great Hall and the Chapel. The Great Hall, or Lyon Chalmer, measures 100 feet by 30 feet, and with its hammer-beam roof and the vast triple fireplace at its dais end, must have been—as indeed it still remains in ruin—a noble salon. At two levels in the west or courtyard wall are mural galleries. Between each pair of windows in the chapel are canopied niches, once containing statues.

The castles dealt with in this book are mostly bare, windswept ruins. For the modern mind, it is hard to furnish them anew. But Linlithgow was a royal palace, and so, in the public records of the kingdom, we encounter many references to its "plenishing" under the later Stewarts. We read of the gorgeous tapestries and "Arras cloths", and the "chapel grayth" which were carried around from palace to palace as the monarch moved about among his royal manors, consuming his rents (payable largely in kind) upon the spot, supervising his estates and keeping a watchful eye upon the public administration. We read of the royal beds, canopied and upholstered in silk and velvet; of carved oak chairs of state, covered with coloured velvet; of hangings heavy with cloth-of-gold and cloth-of-silver; of window curtains of crimson damask; of richly-fashioned oaken coffers; of tables and table cloths; of fragrant rushes spread upon the floors; of gold and silver plate; of kitchen utensils; of foreign wines and home-brewed ale.

XV

The Tower-Houses

SCOTLAND is *par excellence* the land of tower-houses. Probably no country in Europe has rung the changes more extensively upon the theme of the tower-house as the "fencible" residence of a feudal baron, be he king, great magnate, or just one of the ordinary run of lairds. In the ingenuity of their planning, in the skill with which the conflicting demands of comfort and defence are harmonized, and in the economy which is studied in all these structures, large or small, the practical common sense, logical outlook, shrewdness and frugality of the Scottish character is protrayed. Purposeful planning, ingenuity of contrivance, and that sense of style which invariably accompanies the achievement of fitness in design, are the hall-marks of our Scottish tower-houses. They represent a contribution in the general field of medieval domestic architecture of which any nation might be proud.

We have already glanced at one or two of the plain rectangular tower-houses dating from the fourteenth or fifteenth century: Lockleven, Threave, Dundonald, Spynie. And we have noted at Craigmillar an early example of a tower-house on the L-plan, where a wing (or "jam", as it was called in Scotland) is appended to the main structure. The earliest dated example of the L-type of tower-house, which became so popular in Scotland, is David's Tower, in Edinburgh Castle, partly demolished by English cannon during the siege of 1573, and subsequently englobed in the Half-moon Battery, where its battered remains were discovered in 1912. The Exchequer Rolls show that the tower, built to the order of David II, was in course of erection between 1368 and 1379.

Rather than to proliferate notes, which could amount to little more than an inventory, of even a selection from the numerous Scottish tower-houses of the fifteenth and sixteenth centuries, it seems to be better to provide a fairly full analysis of one of the most characteristic and charming of the species, which illustrates, as vividly as any, the *ethos* of these fascinating structures.

Over against the battlefield of Prestonpans, in the middle of an ancient fruit-garden, stands Preston Tower, a robust and martial little structure on the L-plan, measuring about 40 feet by 34 feet over the long sides, with walls nearly 7 feet thick. The re-entrant angle looks north. The original structure (which was afterwards heightened) contains three main storeys, of which the two lower are vaulted. In each of these a loft was provided. The basement is entered by a door (secured by the usual outer door of wood and inner iron gate) and contains in the main building a cellar, with a "pit" or prison in the "jam", now entered by a door forced through from the cellar, but originally only from above. The "pit" is furnished with a sink and drain, and has a ventilation chink in the roof. Otherwise, it is totally dark! On the first floor is the hall, entered directly through the main door of the tower, which is on the east side and was secured by a draw-bar. In the hall are two deep-embayed windows, a fireplace and a mural closet. A trap-door communicated with the loft in the cellar below. In the south-west corner of the hall a newel stair winds up to the summit of the tower. From the hall also, a passage leads through to the lord's private room in the "jam". This is vaulted at a lower level than the hall and is neatly fitted up with a fireplace, small windows, a wall-press, and a privy. In the floor of the passage was a trap-door, beneath which a most curious narrow concealed stair leads down to a small mezzanine prison, apparently a place of less rigorous confinement than proposed for the unfortunates consigned to the "pit" below. From their prison, the "pit" itself was entered by a trap-door. A third trap-door communicated between the prison and the private room above—so that, we may imagine, the laird could enjoy the luxury of inspecting his victims without leaving the secrecy of his own apartment! The top storey is disposed in the usual way, with a large upper hall in the main building and two little rooms one above the other, in the "jam", which thus contained five cells from basement to battlement. The tower is crowned by the

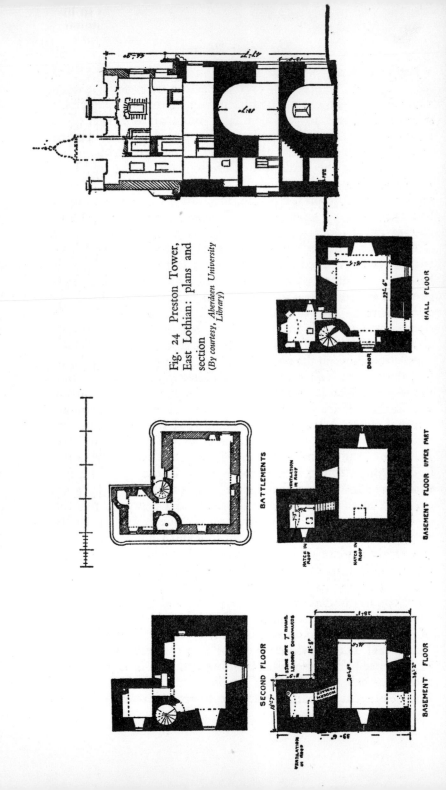

Fig. 24 Preston Tower, East Lothian: plans and section
(By courtesy, Aberdeen University Library)

usual embattled wall-walk, with angle turrets and a machicolated jutty over the entrance. The latter defensive contrivance, however, must have been put out of action by a timber hoarding later applied to the south-east angle of the tower. This oversailing gallery appears to have been reached by a movable ladder on the south front, and before turning the angle towards the tower portal a wooden door, or iron gate, had to be passed, for which a recess, to receive it when thrown back, is provided in the south face of the tower, close to the south-east angle.

In 1626 Preston Tower was enlarged. Determined to maintain the tower-house theme to the last, its owner chose to do this not

Fig. 25   Preston Tower, East Lothian: view from south-east
(By courtesy, Aberdeen University Library)

by building on to his castle, nor by extending apartments round the barmkin wall, a fragment of which remains. Instead, he added a couple of storeys on top, and carried these up from the rear wall of the battlements, a fact which gives the tower its striking "telescopic" aspect. Being in an advanced Renaissance style, with classical pediments and obelisks, and a mock crenellated battlement, the addition creates an effect truly startling. The total height of the tower, as thus added to, is over 70 feet.

This most interesting little castle belonged to the Hamiltons. It was thrice burnt—once in 1544 by the English, again by Cromwell in 1650, and finally by accident in 1663.

The mightiest of Scottish tower-houses is Borthwick Castle in Midlothian, built under a licence granted in 1430, and still inhabited. Here there is not one "jam" but two, both set on the same side of the tower, which thus assumes the plan of the letter E with the middle bar struck out. This immense structure is entirely faced, outside and inside, with ashlar masonry. It has been calculated that the castle must contain no less than 12,000 tons of hewn stone, and that the entire weight must be at least 30,000 tons.

A further planning improvement in these L-towers was to provide for the spiral stair in a square or round tower occupying the re-entrant angle. It is thus taken entirely out of the interior of the building, the whole area of which is thereby available for the competent planning of the required accommodation. Balvaird and Innerpeffray, both in Perthshire, and Leslie in Aberdeenshire, are examples where the stair tower is square: at Tillycairn and Braemar in Aberdeenshire it is round.

In the older tower-houses defence was conducted mainly from the wall-head. The loopholes at ground floor level were designed mostly for air and light. It is not easy to shoot through a mere slit in a wall six or eight feet thick. The defenders of the castle assailed their foes either from the "bartisan" or open parapet, or from oversailing timber wall-heads, such as we have seen were provided at Castle Kisimul. With the introduction of small firearms—hand guns or harquebuses—in the sixteenth century, the axis of defence shifted from the vertical to the horizontal. Instead of defending their tower from the parapet, the garrison now defended it through gunloops at ground level. So the "jam" or wing, instead of being set at right angles to the main structure, is built *en échelon*—that is to say, it is set out diagonally, so as to command two sides of the main building. Hence we arrive at what may be described as the double tower, or "two-stepped" castle. The wing or "jam", thus echeloned to the main structure, might be square, as at Scalloway Castle in Shetland, or might take the form of a round tower, as at Pitfichie in Aberdeenshire.

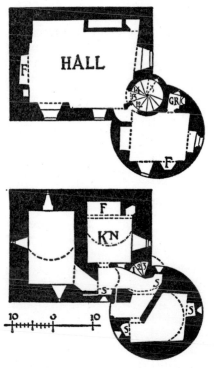

Fig. 26 Pitfichie Castle, Aberdeenshire: ground and first floor plans
(By courtesy, Aberdeen University Library)

From this it was but a further step, and to the logical Scottish mind an inevitable one, to build the tower-house with *two* echeloned wings or flanking towers, one at each of two diagonally opposite corners. Each tower commands two faces of the main house, while the latter in turn enfilades the towers—so that it is impossible to approach the castle from any quarter of the compass without coming under fire. We can surely admire this canny Scotch device which thus economically makes two towers do the work of four by commanding all four faces of the castle. Moreover, since the flanking towers held on to the central structure, as it were, by their finger-tips, they interfere as little as possible with its lighting. And thus we reach the final and perfect stage in the development of the Scottish "house of fence" equipped for firearms. We may call it the "three-stepped" or Z-plan. Such castles seem to face the spectator with an air of sturdy and repelling strength—like a boxer with one arm on guard and the other withdrawn for a punch.

The flanking towers of a Z-castle may be either round, as at Terpersie in Aberdeenshire or Muness in Shetland; or square, as at Glenbuchat, Aberdeenshire, or Hatton in Angus. Sometimes one tower is round and the other square, as in the fine Aberdeenshire castle of Harthill. The two most imposing ruined castles on the Z-plan in Scotland are Drochil in Peeblesshire and Noltland on the remote island of Westray in the Orkneys. Drochil was built as a hide-out by the Regent Morton, and left unfinished on his execution in 1581. Here the flanking towers are round. The plan of this castle is unique in that it is built as a double tenement, with a central corridor. This is an essay in the French plan *"tout une masse"*, then popularized by the famous architect, Jacques Androuet du Cerceau.

Even more remarkable is the grim castle of Noltland in Westray, where the flanking towers are square. This also was built as a hide-out, by one of the worst scamps of a wicked time, Gilbert Balfour of Mountquhannie, a ruffian deeply implicated in all the dirty work of Queen Mary's reign. Like Drochil, it was left unfinished by its founder, who in the end fled the country, only in due course to earn himself a well-merited doom in Sweden. No castle in Britain, perhaps in all Europe, exhibits a more lavish provision for artillery defence than Noltland. Its massive walls with their tiers of yawning gunloops have been compared to an old-time man-o'-war's hull. Over seventy embrasures can be counted in the building as it now survives. All this martial provision was not devised to repel the poor fishermen and crofters of Westray!

One of the most remarkable and fascinating Z-plan castles— in spite of its prosaic name—is Claypotts on the outskirts of Dundee. Though uninhabited, it is roofed and floored, and carefully maintained by the Ministry of Public Building and Works.

Here both the towers are round, but above they are corbelled out into square oversailing, gabled caphouses, producing a highly bizarre effect. The building bears the dates 1569 and 1588. At ground level it is well furnished with wide-mouthed gunloops, and on the two free angles of the central building are open turrets connected with short lengths of wall-walks. Such castles as Claypotts, Noltland and Drochil must be considered as hall-houses rather than tower-houses. On the other hand, Harthill Castle is emphatically a tower-house. Thus the Z-plan is equally

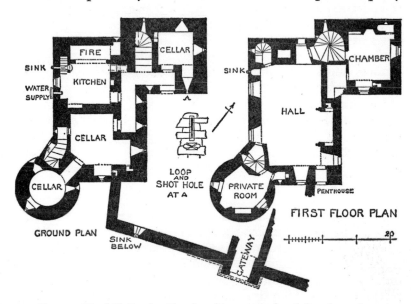

Fig. 27 Harthill Castle, Aberdeenshire: ground and first floor plans
(By courtesy, Aberdeen University Library)

applicable to both the current types of Scottish "house of fence". Indeed, it could be applied to a courtyard building, as in the remarkable castle of Tolquhon in Aberdeenshire, built between 1584 and 1589, but incorporating a tower-house of the fifteenth century. This older structure, however, does not project externally from the corner which it occupies in the new mansion, two of the angles of which are defended by towers, one round and the other square, placed *en échelon* to the central building. This castle is of further interest by reason of its spacious forecourt, with "bee-boles" in the outer wall, and because it retains the decaying remnants of a fine pleasance, with a cruciform pattern of yews and hollies.

The earliest form of gunloop in use during the sixteenth century seems to have been wide-mouthed, with a splayed in-going and a narrow circular throat. The outer ends of the embrasure were square, or else rounded off. But this type of gunloop soon proved itself dangerous to the arquebusier within: for the leaden bullets of those days, striking upon the smooth bevel of the embrasure, might easily be guided inwards, to the scathe of the defender serving the gunloop. This risk it was sought to counter, in some cases, by replacing the smooth bevel or splay with a series of stop-ridges, forming what is known as the "redented" gunloop. This type of embrasure seems to be of German origin. A more usual method of meeting the danger was to turn the gunloop inside out, as it were, so that the splay is on the interior of the wall, and externally the opening appears as a plain circular orifice. In Aberdeenshire, and particularly at Tolquhon, we find very curious gunloops of doublet and triplet patterns: but these must be accounted largely ornamental in design. The type appears, surprisingly, at Muness in Shetland—the northmost castle in the British Isles.

An inexhaustible amount of ingenuity is displayed in the planning of our Scottish tower-houses. One of the most extraordinary among them is—or rather was—Elphinstone Tower in East Lothian. Unfortunately this unique structure became so dangerous, by reason of subsidence due to old coal workings, that it has recently had to be in part demolished. As can be understood from the plan and sections, the tower contains a bewildering series of mural galleries, closets, and stairs all hollowed out in the thickness of the walls. Yet when the whole is carefully studied and analysed, it resolves itself into an extremely well thought out, and indeed basically simple theme. In the hall, the stair ascending from below enters at the screen end, while the stair leading to the upper floors enters from the dais. Hence anyone going upstairs would require to traverse the whole length of the hall, and his movements could be watched from a concealed post in the flue of the hall fireplace. In the storey above the hall, the lord's private room, occupying the eastern half of this flat, has an impressive approach along a wide gallery or waiting room. The same arrange-

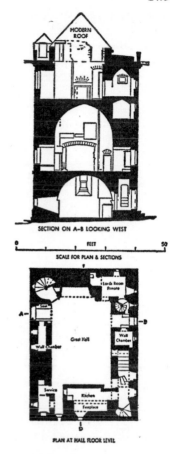

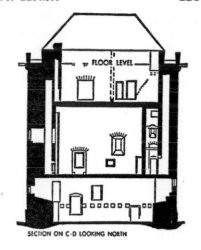

Fig. 28 Elphinstone Tower, East Lothian: plan at hall level, and sections

(*By courtesy, Ministry of Public Building and Works*)

ment, though on a far more magnificent scale, is found in Lord Cromwell's great brick tower-house at Tattershall in Lincolnshire. The lord's private room would benefit by the heat from the kitchen "lum" in its gable wall. These are the main principles of the plan; all else is elaboration of accessories.

As a typical example of a Border Tower we may select Hollows Tower, better known as "Johnnie Armstrong's Tower", in the pleasant valley of the Dumfriesshire Esk. It is a simple rectangular building, vaulted in the basement only, where the walls are well provided with gunloops. Above this are three storeys and a garret, the latter having crow-stepped gables and rising within a wall-walk carried on an ornate parapet with angle turrets. Only the hall and the lord's room above it have fireplaces. Since these are both in the north wall, only this gable requires a chimney. On the other gable is perched a beacon-stance. "The Mersemen in our age," writes an old Scotch historian, "against the suddan entring of the ennimie, to lat sie quhan danger is, thay kendle bleises in tour heidis, or heicher places."

Johnnie Armstrong's Tower, otherwise known as Gilnockie Tower, is famous in Border history as the residence of the clan chief who with his followers was hanged by James V in 1530, during his punitive expedition through the Western Marches. After vainly appealing for mercy, "it is folly to seek grace from a graceless face" cried Johnnie bitterly, and so submitted himself "very proudly" to his fate, which aroused widespread indignation throughout the Borders:

> "John murder'd was at Carlinrigg,
>   And all his gallant companie.
> But Scotland's hart was ne'er sae wae
>   To see sae mony brave men dee."

In the Scottish tower-houses the doorway was usually protected by a double defence. First there was a wooden door, constructed in two thicknesses, the outer boards running vertical and the inner horizontal, and the whole being clinched with large iron nails. Just behind this door was a gate of open iron work. Thus the wooden door could not be opened until the iron gate had been swung back behind it. If the door were burned or broken up, the iron gate could not be burned, and the defenders could shoot out between its bars. These iron gates, or "yetts" as they are termed in Scotland, are constructed in a most remarkable fashion, which is not found south of the Border. The bars penetrate each other, and the mode of penetration is reversed in opposite quarters—or, to state the matter in another way—repeats itself in diagonally opposite sections of the "yett". The strength of this mode of construction will be readily understood by anyone who has examined these yetts. The "grilles" or iron gratings which protect the windows are contrived in the same fashion. It is a notable tribute to the ingenuity and skill of our old-time Scottish smiths.

An English narrative gives us a vivid picture of the capture of a Border tower in 1547:

"We came there about an hour before day; and the greater part of us lay close without the barmkin. But about a dozen of the men got over the barmkin wall, and stole close into the house within its barmkin, and took the wenches and kept them secure within the house till daylight. And at sunrise, two men and a woman being in the tower, one of the men rising in his shirt, and going to the tower-head, and seeing nothing stir about, he called to his wench that lay in the tower, and bade her rise and open the tower door and call them up that lay beneath. She so doing and opening the iron door, and a wooden door without it, our men within the barmkin broke a little too soon to the door. For the wench, perceiving him, leaped back into the tower, and had gotten almost the wooden door to. But we got hold of it [so] that she could not get it close to. So the skirmish arose, and we over the barmkin and broke open the wooden

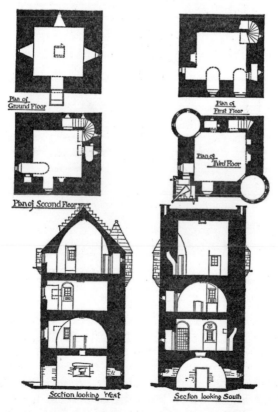

Fig. 29a   Coxton Tower, Moray: plans and sections

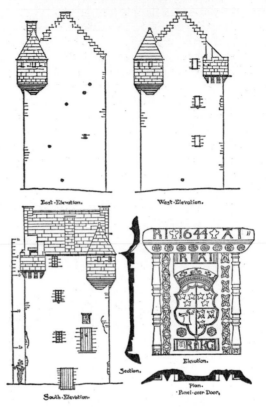

Fig. 29b   Coxton Tower, Moray: elevations and details
(*By courtesy, Aberdeen University Library*)

door. And she being troubled with the wood door left the iron door open: and so we entered and won Lochwood!"

Here then, at Lochwood Tower, we have the tower, within its barmkin wall, which also sheltered a house or outbuilding, wherein serving women lay. On the Border such fortalices were called "peel-towers" or "peel houses", from the Latin word *palus*, a stake—meaning originally the palisade by which (as we saw in the case of Breachacha Castle) such towers were surrounded. Later, the word came to be applied to the tower itself.

Perhaps the most astonishing tower-house in all Scotland is Coxton near Elgin, which bears the date 1644. It was therefore built in the midst of the Civil War, which bore with particular

Crichton Castle, Midlothian

Macmillan's Cross, Kilmorie, Knapdale, Argyllshire

hardness upon Morayland. The tower is vaulted on every floor: it is thus an all stone building, and therefore fire-proof. In each of its four storeys the axes of the vaults are reversed, so that all this weight of masonry is distributed equally on the four walls. The topmost vault is pointed, and carries the stone slabbed roof. The door is on the first floor, and was reached at first only by a ladder, though now by a modern stone forestair. There are the usual defences of an outer wooden door and an inner iron yett, and the windows are strongly barred. The tower has crow-stepped gables, and on the two front angles are turrets, one round, with a stone helmet, and the other devised as a square open post, from which the door could be commanded, or a parley held. Coxton Tower was the residence of a branch of the Innes family. The last laird, who died in 1708, is described by a contemporary as "one of the first gentlemen in Scotland, being a graceful person and a fine nature". So we have to think of one of the first gentlemen in Scotland, as late as the eighteenth century, living in four rooms piled one on top of another, in a tower into which his graceful person could obtain access only by climbing up a ladder! No building in Scotland more startlingly illustrates the long and stubborn native devotion to the tower-house as a suitable plan for a small laird's residence.

XVI

The Crowning Glory of Castellar Construction

IN England, the age of castle-building may be said to have
closed with the advent of the strong-handed Tudor dynasty,
which broke, once and for all, the hydra-headed power of
feudalism. Henceforth the only fortifications to be tolerated in
England were works of national defence, like Henry VIII's artillery
castles on the channel coast. Probably the last castle, in the old
sense as the private stronghold of a feudal magnate, to be erected
on English soil was Thornbury in Gloucestershire—left unfinished
by Edward Stafford, Duke of Buckingham, on his execution, as
an "over-mighty subject", by Henry VIII in 1521. On the other
hand in Scotland, where the power of the Crown remained
chronically weak until the Union of 1603, and where, long after
that event, the old bad habits of feudal strife and clan warfare persisted, fortified dwellings, well equipped for defence with the new
small-arms, continued to be erected until far on into the seventeenth century. Nevertheless, for all this endemic anarchy the
well-being and civilization of the country continued to increase;
and, so far as the castle-builders—that is to say, the landowners—
were concerned—these reached the height of their prosperity
during the last decades of the sixteenth and the earlier part of the
next century: until the outbreak of the great Civil War in 1637
put a virtual stop, for at least a generation, to fine building of any
kind.

What were the reasons for this new-found affluence of the
castle-builders? In the first place, the lairds were in funds as they
had never been before, for into their greedy hands had fallen
most of the landed wealth of the ancient church. Secondly, many
of them were now beginning to turn their backs upon the old

wild life of sturt and strife, and sought now to improve their position by honest trade—like "Willie the Merchant", "Danzig Willie", who built himself the glorious castle of Craigievar in Aberdeenshire, and founded the baronial family now represented by Lord Sempill. And in the third place, paradoxical though it may seem, the government of Scotland was far stronger and more effective now that the King had removed himself from Edinburgh to London, and so was free from kidnapping by baronial factions and bullying by the rabble-rousing "Presbyterian Popes".

Inevitably the new wealth of the lairds found vent in a prodigious outburst of castle building. It was a time when, coincidentally with the various modifications of plan at which we have glanced in the preceding chapters, corresponding changes were being wrought out in elevations and in internal decoration. All the external improvements were by way of converting originally utilitarian or military features to domestic or aesthetic purposes. The old open parapet on the wall-heads was now omitted, and the pack-saddle roof, resting between picturesque "corbie-stepped" gables, was lit by quaint dormer windows, often highly enriched with neo-classical motives. The simple corbel course, formerly requisite to carry out the parapet and leave the whole wall-head free for the roundway, now became developed into a highly ornate cornice. This enriched corbelling became one of the most striking features of the later castles, being introduced in riotous exuberance without reference to structural needs. The old open turrets for flanking defence were now roofed in to form turrets with gabletted or pointed roofs. And the "weepers" or spouts which carried off the rainwater from the former open parapet or angle turret, being no longer required for such a purpose, reappeared as imitation cannon, often stuck on in impossible positions, far below the wall-head, and therefore where there was no rainwater to discharge. In these latest castles there is a marked contrast between the bare severity of the lower portions and the profuse adornment above. This is well illustrated at Amisfield Tower, Dumfriesshire, built in 1600, where the ground plan is still that of the primitive square keep, but by an effective use of corbelling the upper part is worked into an intricate skyline of gables and pinnacles. This last and richest development of castellated architecture is known as the Scottish Baronial style, and flourished especially at the beginning of the seventeenth century. It is important to remember that all the major characteristics of this beautiful style are native in origin, being directly traceable back to practical features from which they have been evolved by a logical development. There is no question of the style being imported ready-made from France, as has often been asserted.

In north-eastern Scotland, where there is a veritable galaxy of these late castellated mansions, we find them to be the work of a vigorous school of native master-masons, the Bells and the Leipers, and doubtless others whose names we know not. True indeed it is that for their internal decoration artists were imported from south of the Border, and to them we owe beautiful plaster ceilings such as we find at Craigievar in Aberdeenshire, Muchalls in the Mearns and Glamis in Angus. But side by side with these imported craftsmen were working a famous school of native artists in tempera work, covering the plastered walls and the beams and ceiling boards of the principal rooms with glowing colours—formal patterns and figure subjects derived from the lays of the troubadours or from the tales of classical mythology.

It is no accident that the choicest specimens of Scottish Baronial architecture are found in Aberdeenshire and the adjacent counties. Here the Reformation was slow in making its way: the breach with the medieval past was less complete, as may be seen by examples of the *Arma Christi* in carved or painted work dating from far beyond the middle of the sixteenth century. Thus in this remote and conservative district we encounter a kind of Indian summer of Gothic art, gradually blending with Renaissance motives so as to produce a most charming composite style. Into what this style might have burgeoned forth, had not the Civil War and the Puritan Revolution so balefully intervened, is anybody's guess.

Happily, most of the masterpieces of Scottish Baronial—Craigievar, Midmar, Castle Fraser, Fyvie, all in Aberdeenshire; Muchalls, Allardyce and Balbegno in the Mearns; Glamis in Angus; Earlshall and Kellie in Fife; Cullen in Banffshire; Pinkie and Wyntoun in Lothian; Ballindalloch on Speyside—are still intact, and, with one or two exceptions, well cared for. Following the pattern of this book, let us now turn to look briefly at others which survive only as stately ruins. First among them we shall place Huntly in Aberdeenshire, the chief castle of the "Cock o' the North", the head of the great family of Gordon. In 1594 the fourth Earl of Huntly, having taken part in the last rising on behalf of the ancient faith, incurred the forfeiture of his estates and fled overseas. His castle was dismantled by James VI, gunpowder being used to blow part of it up. Three years later, however, the Earl made his peace with the King, and in 1599 was created first Marquess of Huntly. Forthwith he began the restoration of his ruined home. The splendid row of oriel windows, with which he adorned the south front of the castle, are obviously inspired by those of Blois, of which *château* the Marquess is said to have been governor. On the opposite or courtyard side, the grand "frontispiece" with its wealth of armorial bearings and sacred imagery has been justly saluted by the present Lord Lyon as "probably the most splendid heraldic doorway in the British Isles." Equally fine are the carved fireplaces in the state rooms. It is probable that not only the inspiration of this splendid work, but also some at least of the craftsmen, were imported from France. One of the masons in Lord Huntly's service was called Ralf Raleine, which does not look like a Scottish name. At the same time, the plastered interiors of the castle were richly decorated by the Edinburgh painter John Anderson, who was also employed at Edinburgh Castle and Falkland Palace. He was an uncle of George Jamesone, the famous Aberdeen portrait painter.

At the north end of the sunny Howe of Angus stands the stately ruin of Edzell Castle, once the home of the Lindsays of Glenesk—that gifted, gallant, turbulent, gay and tragic race, whose pitiful decline and final foundering has been so movingly portrayed in *The Lives of the Lindsays*. The oldest portion of the castle is a noble, early sixteenth-century tower-house on the L-plan, the "jam" containing the staircase. To this was added, later in the same century, a quadrangular mansion, never completed. Finally in 1604, Sir David Lindsay, Lord Edzell, appended to his castle a walled pleasance to which there is no parallel in Britain. The walls are divided by pilasters into a series of compartments, which are adorned in two alternating ways. In the first, the central part of the wall-space is taken up by a gigantic representation of the heraldic fess-chequy of the Lindsays, consisting of three rows of recesses arranged chequer-wise, and dished so as to contain flowers. In its heraldic colours, the blazon is: *gules* (red) a fess chequy *argent* (silver or white) and *azure* (blue). The deep red sandstone provides the *gules*, the solids in the fess chequy would be painted *azure*, and the flowers planted in metal basins in the voids would supply the *argent*—or *vice versa*. Above this the seven-rayed mullets or stars which the Edzell Lindsays adopted from their predecessors, the Stirlings of Glenesk, are carved in relief, the centre of each mullet being pierced with an opening into a nesting box in the wall. In the alternative scheme there is one large oblong recess, dished for flowers. Above both schemes are a series of sculptured panels, displaying, on each of the three sides of the enclosure respectively, the Planetary Deities, the Liberal Arts, and the Cardinal Virtues. These sculptures are of German *provenance*, and the Planets, all save one, are copies of engravings by the Nuremberg artist known from his initials as Meister I.B. Their presence on this garden wall in Angus is explained by the known Nuremberg connexions of Lord Edzell.

At the fine ruin of Crichton Castle in Midlothian we find un-doubted work of foreign masons. The nucleus of this castle is a plain fourteenth-century tower-house, which by successive stages was enlarged into a quadrangular mansion, enclosing a narrow courtyard. The most spectacular feature of these additions is an arcaded range, the upper frontage of which is wrought with facetted stone work, well described in *Marmion*:

> "Still rises unimpaired below,
>   The courtyard's graceful portico;
>   Above its cornice, row on row,
>   Of fair hewn facets, richly show
>   Their pointed diamond form."

The capitals of the arcade carry the monogram of Francis Stewart, fifth Earl of Bothwell, and his wife Margaret Douglas, together with the insignia of the Lord High Admiral of Scotland, an office conferred upon him in 1581. Lord Bothwell had returned that year from Italy, and it is probable that his diamonded façade was inspired by the *Palazzo dei Diamanti* at Ferrara. The capitals on his main staircase are undoubtedly of Italian type.

Even in Scottish history, there is no more extraordinary character than "the wild Earl of Bothwell". He stands before us as a cultured ruffian of a true Renaissance type—as Italianate as the diamonded façade with which he adorned his castle. Earl Francis, however, finds a close parallel in his kinsman, Patrick Stewart, Earl of Orkney, whose unrelenting tyranny is still to this day a bitter memory in the Northern Isles. When in 1615 justice at long last overtook him, he was found to be so ignorant that his execution had to be respited to give him time to learn the Lord's Prayer! Yet to this savage we owe the building which has been claimed to be "the most mature and accomplished piece of Renaissance architecture left in Scotland". Earl Patrick's Palace opposite the great Norse Cathedral of Kirkwall, is distinguished alike by the competence and subtlety of its planning and by the masterly refinement of its architectural details. Notable features are the great oriel windows, quite in the French manner. Yet Earl Patrick's master of work was Andrew Crawford, and his master-mason was John Ross. These men were surely Scots.

From the standpoint of scenic architecture, perhaps the most beautiful piece of pure early neo-classical design in Scotland is the *façade* of Nithsdale's Building at Caerlaverock Castle in Dumfries-shire. I use the words "scenic architecture" advisedly: for the first Earl of Nithsdale's work, which bears the date 1634, is in the strictest sense a *façade*—its fenestration is most imperfectly adjusted to the apartments inside. Yet alike in its main theme and in all its details, the master-mason has combined robust vigour with delicate grace in a way truly admirable. There is much about the design that is individual, and affinities with other work are ill to find. A notable feature is the absence of stringcourses defining the storeys, as is usual in Scottish work—for example, in James VI's building at Linlithgow. On the other hand, Nithsdale's *façade* shows none of the articulation of the different storeys by pilasters or columns which is so characteristic of English work. Nor does it show the English fenestration of large mullioned and transomed windows. In both these respects, Caerlaverock should be contrasted with the contemporary work at Kirby Hall in Northamptonshire, which Inigo Jones was remodelling at the same time. Yet the work at Caerlaverock, though it was probably not designed by an English architect, has no exact parallel in Scotland. The pediments of the doors and windows are enriched with carvings either heraldic or culled from classical mythology. They remind us that the noble builder was known to his contemporaries as "the Philosopher".

Caerlaverock Castle is one of the most splendid examples of baronial architecture in Scotland. It includes masonry of every age between the thirteenth and the seventeenth centuries. Its gatehouse is the most impressive in Scotland: and Nithsdale's "dainty fabrick" is a rare blossom of that early flowering of the New Humanism, which was blighted by the chill blast of the Covenant. A watery cincture, which always so greatly sets off a ruined castle, completes the attraction of the scene. Few castles offer more of interest to the technical student; few more enchant the lover of the picturesque; few appeal more to those over whom the deeds of other times have cast their glamorous spell.

XVII

West Highland Crosses and Grave Slabs

AMONG the ecclesiastical monuments upon the island of Iona, by far the most interesting, as it is also the most beautiful, is the ruined Benedictine Nunnery. To begin with, it is the only substantial remnant of such a building in Scotland. Then it has not been restored: for while the rehabilitation of the Abbey Church (and later Cathedral of the Isles), and its recovery for religious use, is in every way a praiseworthy achievement, the result has inevitably been a certain loss in archaeological verisimilitude. Moreover, it is clear that the Abbey buildings, and above all the church, had been extensively reconstructed in the later Middle Ages; and the chronological problems thus involved are of great perplexity. On the other hand, the Nunnery retains a very large proportion of the original work of about 1200. It is a building of high distinction, the work of an extremely able master mason. Evidently he came from Ireland, and it is clear that he was thoroughly conversant with the distinctive and charming Romanesque architecture of the sister island. This primary work at the Nunnery seems to have been the model imitated by the late medieval restorers or rebuilders of the Abbey. The Nunnery, in fact, is the architectural key to the development of the Abbey; and also (or so it would seem) to the other two major ecclesiastical monuments of the Hebrides, Oronsay Priory and Rodil Church.

Even more important than the ecclesiastical buildings on Iona is the unique assemblage of carven crosses and grave-slabs. These form a collection of early Celtic and late medieval art to which there are few parallels in Europe. The collection forms an epitome, available for study in a single small locality, of a corpus of medieval art peculiar to the Western Islands and Highlands, the monuments of which, elsewhere than on the island of Iona, have to be sought for, at the cost of much wearisome travelling, in the remote and scattered churchyards where they now lie mouldering in neglect, or buried altogether beneath rank grass and the kindly moss which preserves the beautiful details of the carving. In these Hebridean monuments Scotland possesses a heritage of which any cultured nation would be proud, but to which the modern Scotsman is almost completely indifferent.

Prominent among these, not merely in the physical but also in the artistic sense, are the great free-standing High Crosses of Irish *provenance*. The finest of them all, the beautiful and awe-inspiring St. John's Cross on Iona, dating from the tenth century, has twice been blown down by the raving winds that beat upon the island. Its fragments are now packed away in crates, awaiting a more civilized age. Scarcely less lovely, and of about the same period, is the Kildalton Cross on Islay. Iona itself possesses, fortunately intact, the well-known St. Martin's Cross, belonging to the same early group; as well as the fifteenth-century Maclean's Cross, which illustrates the later Hebridean type with a solid central disc from which the head and arms of the cross emerge. Macmillan's Cross at Kilmory Knap, Argyllshire, and the beautiful Lerags Cross at Kilbride, just south of Oban, are other examples of this most striking form of monument. Lerags Cross is dated 1526.

But the vast mass of the Hebridean monuments take the form of recumbent grave-slabs. Both these and the later free-standing crosses display foliaceous scrolls and other patterns derived ultimately from the Anglian vine-leaf. They also illustrate a remarkable peculiarity of this late West Highland art, namely the revival of early motives, such as the dog-tooth, nail-head, and billet ornaments. The claymore, or two-handed Highland sword, war-galleys, carved ivory caskets (of which some originals survive) mirrors and combs, grotesque animals, and scenes from Holy Writ or Christian mythology, figure on these facinating monuments, the intricate beauty of whose designs leaves the spectator fairly breathless. Most interesting of all are the recumbent effigies of warrior chiefs, portraying the characteristic martial panoply of the Hebrides. We see these fierce-looking island potentates with their pointed basinets, hoods of mail, quilted tunics, and greaves probably of hardened leather (*cuir bouilli*). For weapons they carry the claymore and the lance, and defend themselves with smallish, heater-shaped shields, upon which are displayed the chief's heraldic bearings. Similar equipment is displayed on the tombs of Irish chiefs. Only in one or two cases in the Hebrides do we find a figure clad in the normal plate armour of the mainland. One of these is the so-called MacLeod of MacLeod tombstone in Iona Abbey. This monument is further remarkable in that it was a brass, of which only the matrix now remains, showing that the figure was a plate of metal by itself, while other strips formed the inscription round the margin of the slab.

At Rodil Church, Harris, Alasdair Crottach, the eighth Chief of MacLeod, who died in 1547, provided for himself, so early as 1528, a remarkable monument in the form of a canopied altar-tomb, displaying in high relief sacred subjects, as well as a hunting scene, the MacLeod Galley, and our earliest known representation of Dunvegan Castle. The Chief's effigy is clad in plate, with the exception of the camail or chain hood and a hauberk, the skirt of which is seen below his surcoat. In a more central district, this armour would be assigned to about the end of the fourteenth century. It could be the same suit as the one depicted on the Iona brass. We must presume that in the Hebrides such a suit was a prized possession, which descended from father to son, and that it was to be found only in the hands of powerful chiefs with mainland connexions, like the MacLeods of Dunvegan.

By contrast, the monuments of ecclesiastics in the Hebrides do not seem to differ much in their vestments and concomitants from those on the mainland. Among those on Iona, space must be found for some account of the tombstone of the Prioress Anna, who died in 1543. When complete, as depicted by Pennant, it must have been one of the most remarkable ecclesiastical monuments in Britain. The Prioress is portrayed as a sleek-looking, self-satisfied lady of ample proportions, clad in rochet and cloak. Her hands are clasped in prayer, and her head, which is covered by a hood or coif, rests upon a pillow, which is smoothed down by a couple of angels. On either side are her two pet lap-dogs. Over her head are three tall towers with oversailing parapets and high pointed roofs, as well as a mirror and a comb. The figure of the Prioress occupies only one half of the slab: the other half, now mostly broken away, contained a figure, set "heids and thraws" to the Prioress, of the Virgin Mary as Queen of Heaven, with the Holy Child on her arm, and accompanied by the sun and moon. At her feet is inscribed a prayer from the Prioress. "*Sancta Maria ora pro me*": while round the whole slab ran the inscription "*Hic iacet Domina Anna Donaldi Terleti filia quondam priorissa de Iona, que obiit año M° d° xl°. Eius animam altissimo commendamus.*" Like the other late Gothic inscriptions on the island, this legend is rendered in competent "black letter".

On Iona alone there are some seventy surviving crosses and grave-slabs: but only a handful of these are now given shelter in a small museum which the Ministry of Public Buildings and Works has contrived out of the ruins of St. Ronan's Chapel, the medieval parish church of Iona. The greater number of them lie exposed to decay, mostly in the famous island cemetery, the Reilig Orain. None of these are in their original places, and the so-called "Ridge of the Kings" and "Ridge of the Chiefs" are bogus. The stones were arranged in their present positions by the Iona Club in 1868. No one would wish wholly to disfurnish the Reilig Orain: nevertheless, it remains one of the most urgent needs of Scottish archaeology that the best of these priceless monuments, here and elsewhere upon the island, should be placed under shelter in a museum provided in Iona for the purpose.

The Ministry of Public Building and Works likewise preserves, though not under shelter, collections of these monuments at Ardchattan Priory and at the churches of Kilmartin and Kilmory Knap, as well as at Kilberry Castle—all in Argyllshire. Others in the Ministry's custody are at Rodil in Harris. Another collection, not under national keeping, is at the Augustinian Priory of Oronsay.

The Royal Commission on the Ancient Monuments of Scotland is at present working in Argyllshire, and in due course will thus record and publish all the West Highland monuments in this county, which contains the greatest number of them. But it is a race against time.

The same intriguing revival of Romanesque and early Gothic motives, which we find on the Hebridean tombstones, meets us also on the capitals and other ornamental work of Iona Abbey and Rodil Church. It is also found in the castles of the western seaboard, as at Castle Stalker and the now restored Castle of Dundarave, on Loch Fyne above Inveraray. Here the doorway is surrounded by dog-tooth ornament, and flanked by grotesque sculpture, including the splendid figure of a piper. Over the lintel is the date 1596, the initials of the builder and his lady, and the pious legend: *Behold the end: be nocht vyser nor the Hieste*, together with the family motto, *I hoip in God*; while above is the empty panel for a coat of arms, enriched with the dog-tooth, billet and nail-head ornaments.

XVIII

"The End of Ane Auld Sang"

IT was the Great Civil War of the seventeenth century that really gave the *coup-de-grâce* to Scotland's national architecture. For thirty years fire blazed and the sword was bare throughout the land. Comparatively speaking, little building could take place during this unhappy period. For example, George Heriot's School in Edinburgh, began under such fair auspices on 1st July, 1628 (as recorded on the foundation stone) was not in a habitable state until 1650—and then only to be promptly commandeered by Cromwell and turned into an army hospital! When settled conditions returned with the Restoration of 1660, the old generation of master-masons, bred in the national style, had mostly disappeared, and the way was opened for the predominance of the pure classical Renaissance.

Yet the traditional modes of building died hard, particularly in the burghs, where houses with stair turrets and crow-stepped gables continued to be erected until far on into the seventeenth century. In Aberdeenshire, Leslie Castle, "FUNDED: IUN:17, 1661" as appears on a stone in its wall, is still built on the traditional L-plan, with a square staircase-tower in the re-entrant angle, and is still provided with redented gunloops and the old-time paraphernalia of angle turrets: but the gables are no longer crowstepped; and instead of a single large "lum", there are triple chimney stacks seated diagonally, in the English manner. And at Keith Hall, the seat of the Earl of Kintore, also in Aberdeenshire, the large addition made, in the last decade of the seventeenth century, to the ancient "three-stepped" castle of the Johnstons took the form of a plain flat *façade*, devoid of angle towers or turrets, and capped with a classical balustrade set between low pavilion roofs of Dutch type. On the ground floor it contains a great central hall, of quite medieval proportions: but this no longer forms the common living apartment of the household as the old hall of the Johnstons did: nor is it even the lord's dining room. It has degenerated into a mere vestibule, though a noble one—a hall in the modern sense; and its door, instead of being placed at the screens or lower end, as it is in the Johnston hall, is now found midway in the side wall. The door thus delivers the traffic directly into the centre of the hall, an arrangement making it useless for festal purposes. The same disposition is found in Charles Maitland's addition of about the same period, to Hatton House in Midlothian—one of our most interesting old Scottish mansions, unfortunately destroyed by fire in 1952, and since then allowed to go to wrack and ruin.

The nucleus of Hatton House was a powerful L-shaped keep of the later fourteenth century. At the hands of James II it stood a notable siege in 1452, when all the resources of the military art of the time—including a "sow" or movable penthouse to protect the *latomi* or quarrymen engaged in hewing their way through the walls, and a "great bombard"—no doubt the renowned "Mons Meg" now at Edinburgh Castle—were employed to secure its reduction. The tower was enclosed by a "mantle wall", of which considerable portions, including a round angle tower, still remained. In the sixteenth century a hall house was added to the ancient tower, projecting from its south side. This work was probably done pursuant to a licence granted in 1537. Then after the Restoration, Charles Maitland, afterwards third Earl of Lauderdale, who had acquired a fortune by swindling the Mint, completely remodelled the mansion, converting it into a large quadrangular structure, with round towers at all four corners— the ancient keep occupying what might otherwise have been an open courtyard. On the east side was the large vestibular hall already noted, while south of this was a dining parlour, with a drawing-room in the sixteenth-century hall-house. Though Renaissance features appeared in certain external details, such as the balustrading, and internally in much of the decorations, the general design of the house, with its angle towers capped by their high conical roofs, was Scotch enough. The broad terrace on the south side of the house, having in its centre a fountain, and terminated at either end by a garden house; the semicircular bath-house; the stone arbour or "belvidere"; the fine classical gateways; and above all the spacious grounds, once extending to 240 acres, with their stately avenues, walled gardens and artificial lake, presented an unrivalled picture of the dignified leisure of high life in the eighteenth century.

"Here", wrote the late Sir John Stirling Maxwell about Hatton "we find all the comfort and much of the splendour of houses of the same period in England, but it is the work of Scots heads and Scots hands, and in its broad lines, as well as in every detail, we are conscious of a national style. One cannot but deplore the loss of so fine a tradition. Can it be recaptured?" The same comment would be true of Drumlanrig Castle in Dumfriesshire, the magnificent palace of the Dukes of Queensberry, built between 1676 and 1689. But in the primary work at Haddo House in Aberdeenshire, built in 1732 by the second Earl of Aberdeen, from the design by the elder Adam, we have a brilliantly successful essay in the pure Palladian style: and with this, we may say that the native Scottish manner has finally given way to the architectural modes of contemporary western Europe.

In the field of ecclesiastical architecture the collapse was even more speedy. The poverty of the Reformed Church, its summary rejection of the ancient ritual and indeed of all the graces of worship, and the impact of English Puritanism, all combined to turn the churches of the seventeenth and eighteenth centuries into mere preaching boxes. Yet here also old traditions died hard. During the two Caroline episcopacies a few buildings were erected in a style somewhat recalling "Oxford Gothic". Examples are Dairsie in Fife, erected in 1621, and still in use as a parish church; Michael Kirk (1705), near Elgin, now happily preserved as the private chapel of Gordonstoun School: and the Tron Kirk, Edinburgh (1637–47), whose fate now trembles in the faltering hands of Edinburgh Town Council. Such lovely buildings survive as "memorials of a brilliant failure": "a vast project—even that of covering Scotland in the seventeenth century with such church edifices and services as England has retained."

Nevertheless, it would be a gross injustice to suggest that the rank and file of Scottish parish churches erected in the seventeenth and eighteenth centuries are devoid of architectural merit. On the contrary, many of them possess a quiet dignity all their own, and share in addition the quality of perfect fitness for the simple, unadorned form of worship for which they were designed. So long ago as 1886 the late Dr. Kelly, in calling attention to some of the ruined post-Reformation parish churches in the north-east of Scotland, observed with truth that

"straightforward and simple in their construction, they have the rare virtues of truth and quietness, qualities which, in these days of restlessness and self-assertion, we have the greatest difficulty in attaining . . . The general style of the churches of Fetteresso, Drumoak and Midmar is that of the second half of the seventeenth century: fortunately at Midmar the date 1677 is incised on one of the door lintels. It may safely be concluded that the style belongs to the period covered by the Second Episcopacy (1661–1689). It may be that the influence of the dominant party had some share in giving churchlike character to these buildings. But perhaps changes in church government were too frequent in those days, and opinion too unsettled for the formation of a style either Episcopalian or Presbyterian. They, in the middle of the seventeenth century, were much nearer the Reformation than we are. Habits of building, the unbroken inheritance of centuries, cannot be lost and completely forgotten in two or three generations, especially in remote country districts. The Reformation and the Renaissance with all their combined power had not as yet destroyed all superstitions and traditional canon . . . Therefore, on the whole, it would be strange if we did not find the post-Reformation churches as they are; if not Gothic, yet Gothic in spirit and feeling, and in general form and proportion. For the rest, they are quiet, unpretending, and refined examples of vernacular Scotch building. Masons, even late in the eighteenth century, were men of some education in their art; and not seldom possessed of much feeling. Witness the headstones and other memorials of last century [the eighteenth] which beautify our churchyards. Both in freshness of design and refinement of execution, many of them leave nothing to be desired: and put to shame the intolerably crude productions so common in our suburban cemeteries. In these buildings of the seventeenth century, the proportions of the windows; the delicacy of the splays; the picturesque and natural irregularity of jointing; the accentuation of the springing of the gable outline by these singularly natural, simple and expressive spur-stones; the short, refined fillet to the corbels; and the thoroughly sensible way in which all is ordained, make us have the highest respect for the true thoughtfulness and uprightness expressed in work so harmonious and stable."

16

In such churches the windows are mostly found only on the south side and in the gables. The pulpit was usually placed midway in the south side; and sometimes a gablet and gushet roof were provided to accommodate the lofty sounding board. Thus the minister did not have the sun in his eyes, while the congregation could enjoy its warmth. The blank north wall could be used for memorial tablets—as well as for the heating stove! The pews were arranged on three sides of the pulpit, often with galleries at the east and west ends, and, when the width of the building permitted, or if a north "aisle" had been added, on that side as well. Hence the minister, instead of being a priest set apart to celebrate mysteries in the chancel, was now the father of his flock, having them gathered all around him and leading them in family prayer, as used to be the fashion in Scotch farm kitchens until well on into the last century. It is a great misfortune when Presbyterian churches, so arranged in perfect fitness for the worship for which they were designed, are nowadays turned eastward in such a way as to ape Roman or Anglican ritual.

At Midmar in central Aberdeenshire we have an east window of two lights, divided by a transom, quite in the Gothic tradition. South doorways are the rule: very often there is one for the congregation, and another, further east and near the pulpit, for the minister. Occasionally special windows and even private doors may be provided for an important pew: at Midmar, for example, one such door bears the initials of a laird of Midmar and his lady. Often the galleries were reached by stone forestairs.

Tulliallan in Fife is an excellent example of a parish church built in 1675, but alas! abandoned, unroofed and hastening to decay. It is oblong, with a north "aisle" and a western tower. The windows are typical seventeenth-century Gothic, but the quoins are rusticated and the tower is of quasi-classical design, with a rusticated doorway beneath a pedimented panel, round arched belfry windows, and a concave pyramidal slated helmet. Drainie Church, near Lossiemouth, built in 1666, was of the same plan as Tulliallan, but remained more purely Gothic in detail, with simple pointed traceried windows; two doors, also pointed, on the south side; crow-stepped gables; and a fine belfry at the west end. The north "aisle" was separated by a wide stone arch. Long neglected, this picturesque and charming ruin, for generations a landmark in the "Laich o' Moray" was at last demolished because it was found to be a danger to low-flying aircraft from the R.N.A.S. Station at Lossiemouth.

One of the most striking ecclesiastical ruins in all Scotland is the former parish church of Thurso. Its cruciform shape does not reflect its medieval origin, but is the result of successive additions to a post-Reformation fabric. Nevertheless, the lower part of the east end is of Romanesque date, being a semicircular vaulted apse within a square end, like St. Margaret's Chapel at Edinburgh Castle. Its two windows, east and north, are mere slits, without a check for a frame or glass. The south "aisle", like the northern one at Drainie, is separated by a great stone arch from the "nave". In the angle which the medieval chancel makes with the latter is inserted a most remarkable and highly picturesque staircase tower, rectangular on plan but set obliquely in the angle. The tower is tall and tapering, and has curious semicircular buttresses rising to the first floor level, where the stair admitted to a session-house built on top of the Romanesque vault. The gables are crow-stepped, with Renaissance finials, and have plain basket-traceried windows, with transoms: in the south gable the window is of great size, containing five lights and two transoms. This window forms a most impressive feature in the ruined church, and clearly has been designed to catch the sun. There are porches on the south side of the "nave" and at the east corner of the north "transept"; while forestairs admitted to the galleries in all four limbs of the cross. The tower formerly bore the dates 1636 and 1638. Apparent from its Romanesque chancel, the medieval origin of this fascinating church is confirmed by its dedication to St. Peter.

One of the most perfect examples of eighteenth-century arrangements in a Scotch Presbyterian church is the old parish kirk of Glenbuchat in Aberdeenshire. It is now abandoned, but well cared for by the County Council. The church, dedicated to St. Peter, dates from 1473, and embodies some masonry of that date: but it has been twice reconstructed, once in 1629, under the First Episcopacy, and again, towards the end of the eighteenth century. On the east gable is an ornate belfry, removed hither from the west end about 1857. It houses a Dutch bell dated 1643. At the apex of the west gable is a stone bearing the date 1629 and the initials of the then incumbent. On the corner of this gable is the stance for a sundial. In either end wall is a tall oblong window, and in the south front are two windows and two doors. The north side of the church has no openings. Internally the little kirk is a model of primitive but comely decency. Its walls are plastered and so is the coved ceiling. Between the pews the floor is cobbled, and the alleys are paved. The pews are arranged on three sides of the pulpit, which is midway in the south wall, and is lit by two skylight panes in the roof. Over the pulpit is a sounding board, and beneath it in front is the precentor's desk, with a double forked mounting on its breast for him to display the card anouncing the psalm tune. The manse pew is of the box type. Most interesting of all are the box pews on the north side. Each contains a small table. The partitions between the pews can be lifted out: while ledges are left on the ends of the tables so that the partitions can be laid across between them, in such a way as to provide one long table for the yearly communion. At the east end of the church is the "laird's loft" erected in 1828, and displaying on its breast the tinctured arms of Earl Fife. In the eighteenth century the church was thatched with heather.

Situated amid Highland scenery and in a well-kept churchyard that displays some fine eighteenth-century tombstones, Glenbuchat Kirk is in every way, outside and inside, a little gem. Its preservation, due to the combined efforts of an enlightened County Council, the Ministry of Public Building and Works, and private generosity, is an example that might well be followed in the case of other fine old parish churches now hastening to decay in every Scottish shire.

Our tale is nearing an end: but before it closes something must be said about the military works erected by the British Government to secure its hold upon Scotland in the seventeenth and eighteenth centuries. These works fall mainly into two periods: those erected under the Cromwellian Protectorate, and those built by the Hanoverian government during the period of the Jacobite Risings. Of the Cromwellian forts at Ayr, Leith, Perth, Aberdeen, Inverness and Inverlochy, little now remains, since they were all dismantled at the Restoration; but in far away Shetland, Fort Charlotte, built to defend Lerwick Harbour against the Dutch in the reign of Charles II, still survives virtually complete. Burned by the Dutch in 1673, it was reconstructed in 1781, and given its present name in honour of the then Queen. The fort, which covers about a couple of acres, is of pentagonal design, with the usual angled bastions, or demi-bastions. Much more important are the Hanoverian works of the eighteenth century. These include the ramparts of Edinburgh and Stirling Castles, and also Fort George, the most splendid example of eighteenth-century military engineering in all Britain—distinguished alike by the complexity of its defences and by the architectural quality of the buildings inside. Since Fort George is about to be abandoned by the War Office, its preservation, intact and in its entirety, becomes a national duty from which the responsible authorities must not be allowed to flinch.

After the Forty-five, two ancient castles in Aberdeenshire, Braemar and Corgarff on the Dee and Don respectively, were repaired and garrisoned as a means of controlling the military road built from Perth, over the Mounth and through western Mar to Speyside and Fort George on the Moray Firth. Round each was thrown a wall with a salient midway in all four fronts, the whole being closely loopholed for musketry. More interesting than these are the fortified barracks erected in the Highlands during the uneasy period between the two Risings—at the time when General Wade had begun his great scheme of opening up the disaffected area in the way that the Romans had understood so well: namely by road engineering, bridge-building, and garrisoned check-points. These are Inversnaid in Stirlingshire, and Fort Augustus, Bernera, and Ruthven-in-Badenoch, all in Inverness-shire. Of these only shattered fragments now exist, save at Ruthven, where the building, burnt by the Jacobites in 1746, survives as a vast shell which, standing on the immense *motte* of an early castle of the Comyns, must rank among the most imposing of British ruins. The two barrack blocks face each other across a large quadrangular courtyard, at each of two diagonally opposite corners of which are rectangular flanking towers. This arrangement must not, however, be regarded as a salute to the memory of the traditional Scottish "three-stepped" or Z-plan, since the original scheme provided for a tower at all four corners, but two were omitted for reasons of economy. Built in 1719, Ruthven Barracks is for ever famous by reason of its defence against the Jacobites in August, 1745, by Sergeant Terence Molloy, with a garrison of only fourteen men. The stout-hearted sergeant's report to Sir John Cope is one of the gems of British military literature.

Index

Index to Places

PURSUIT TILL MORNING

PURSUIT TILL MORNING

by

ALAN WYKES

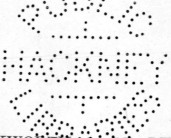
GERALD DUCKWORTH & CO. LTD.
3 HENRIETTA STREET, LONDON, W.C.2

Printed in Great Britain
at the BURLEIGH PRESS, *Lewins Mead*, BRISTOL

THIS STORY IS FOR

MURIEL

MY WIFE

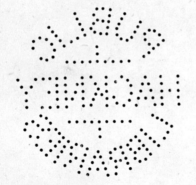

PART ONE

1

ONE by one he dropped the things in the suitcase. Shirts, pyjamas, socks, the handkerchiefs—a dozen, linen, his initials embroidered in silk : L.K. A pardonable vanity, she did them so beautifully. Yes. He was still thinking of her entirely without bitterness. He thought he was hungry and his tongue tingled as he thought of trifle and whipped cream. Why that ? he wondered. From so long ago. *My sweet tooth.*

The bell rang and he went slowly down the stairs, straightening his tie. The house was empty, its emptiness rose up to meet him. His footfall soft on the carpeted stairs, the coloured reproductions passing the edge of eye and mind as he descended : Degas, Manet, Degas again and his everlasting dancers.

It was a boy with another wreath. Carnations and iris, delicately arranged. Among the wired green leaves he saw the card and the name: Mr and Mrs Bonnamy, wondered who the hell they were. He put the wreath with the others, standing it against the wall, tenderly, smiling, with the thought that they would stay there for ever. Standing back he looked at them : circles and crosses. Symbols, he supposed. A circle, endless, everlasting life. A few days ago he would have thought—indeed, said—That's what they try to kid you with : religion, symbols. Now he did not think anything except how hungry he was.

There was meat in the larder.   Slicing it on to a piece of bread he felt the sickening in his throat.   Turning away he went up the stairs again.   Degas, Manet, Degas.   Behind and below him the wreaths stood in the hall, the cards with their black edges.   Sympathy, your terrible bereavement et cetera. . . . Solemn and amusing.   Yet he felt neither emotion.

The wardrobe door swung back and with dispassionate surprise he saw himself mirrored there, stubble on his chin, his clothes unpressed and soiled, his shoes sodden with the rain through which he had walked, his hair unbrushed.   It seemed like looking at himself from the outside, watching inward upon something that was happening to him. Watching himself close the suitcase, open it, take out one of the handkerchiefs with the silkwoven initials and put it in the breast pocket of his jacket with the L.K. showing on its little white pyramid, close the lid of the case again, the locks going *snick snick*.   He didn't know where the key was.   What the hell did he want to lock it for, anyway ? Nevertheless he looked.   The most likely places.   Her jewel-box—empty except for a red bone dog on a tinny gold pin.   He held it against his breast as he had seen her hold it when she was uncertain about wearing it.   Woolworth's, obviously.   Putting it in his pocket he tried the small drawer of the dressing-table.   A bag of lavender, rustling dryly ; and, right at the back, a gold locket with a portrait of her mother, faded and dry as the lavender. Funny, he had never seen it or even known she possessed it. In his pocket it tinkled against its chain like a tiny bell heard miles distant.   He looked in other places but there was no key ; and presently he forgot what he was looking for and stood the case down on the floor and lay on the bed with his legs swinging gently above the white sheepskin rug.   The things he had found in the small secret places pressed against his thigh through his pocket and later, when

he rose, he put them all back where they belonged, each in
its ordered place.

Lying, staring up at the ceiling at the moving shadow of
the lightshade. His eyes hurt, open or closed they hurt,
stinging as if slivers of ice were falling upon them ; but it
was the inanimate and unshed tears of yesterday that
pressed on them. The room was so quiet ; and suddenly
the folding travelling clock ceased its movement. Eight
days, he thought ; it must be eight days since it was wound.
Six-thirty. The timetable, departure column, gave the
time of his train as seven-ten. At six-forty he left the
house, carrying the case and walking swiftly toward the
bus-stop. Behind curtained windows lips moved, watching
him, speaking of him as he went, saying how strange it was,
that he must be mad, that no normal man would bury his
wife on a day different from the one on which the flowers
were delivered, that it must have gone to his head, but
there, one and another had offered to help, had been to him
and been rebuffed, rudely, so that it was no wonder that
after a time people got tired of trying to help. And there
he went, his own sweet way, and good luck to him, and the
devil take the hindmost, for it was plain to see sympathy
was the sort of thing such people did not understand. No,
nor never would. So let him go. And when the milkman and the paper-boy and the postman call, well that'll
be just too bad, for where help's offered and refused (and
rudely) nothing's up to anyone except to mind their own
business, which is what they were all doing all along, just
trying to put out a helping hand. So now just watch him
and smile a bit to yourself and thank God that at least you
had the decency to offer if he had the rudeness to refuse.

Standing there at the bus-stop he felt the eyes on him,
scores and hundreds of eyes watching, wondering about
him. He could almost share their amusement. So
strange it must seem to them. The small details : the

1*

house, the milkman, the opened windows, all as if he meant to return in a couple of hours.

He did not mean to return in a couple of hours. His face hardened fleetingly and he felt the pain of his eyes. Looking at his hands he felt and saw the lines traced with the day's dirt. He remembered that he had not washed or shaved and that his clothes were creased. Also, he had forgotten to put a hat on—a thing he never did ; he hated being without a hat. But this time it seemed not to matter.

In the bus he searched his pockets for fare. He had seven shillings and four pennies ; he put the two half-crowns and the florin in his pocket. It would be enough for train fare, he knew. But not for a meal as well.

The conductor said : " You look a bit cheesed, mate. Feeling all right ? "

[Answering, Yes, without knowing to what question he was giving an affirmative, he watched the suburban road with its trees and lace curtains and aspidistras slide by ; watching the scene change to shops, pubs, an old man playing a tin whistle in the gutter, two men arguing and gesticulating outside a pub, lights coming on in the streets, men walking homeward with their little cases and their day's worries graven on their faces. Outside the cinema people stood in silent ranks, their mouths mumbling on words he could not hear. A man, a lean man smelling of onions, pressed up to him on the seat and whispered : " I've got a cert for Gatwick. Two-thirty to-morrow. Half a dollar. Interest you ? "

" Gatwick ", he said, and again, " Gatwick ", the syllables dissolving into nothingness in his brain. He looked back at the man. " No. No, I don't think so ". Then he added words that made the lean man certain of his madness. " Where can I sleep ? " But there was no answer to that. The bus ground on through the curling wind of evening. He could see the wind through the window, rustling the corner of a poster stripped from a hoarding, twisting straight into a line of washing suspended from an iron balcony behind a row of shops. He could see the washing for a long way : it diminished slowly until it was the size of scraps of paper torn for spills. Then a woman came out on to the balcony and gathered it in, folding it over her bare arm as she reached out over the balcony. He could see all that : then the bus rounded a curve and he could see it no longer. He could see nothing, though he knew the conductor and the lean man were looking at him ; they were talking all the time too, asking him what was the matter, did he feel okay, oughtn't he to have those eyes seen to, pouring as they were ?

"Sleep", he said. "I need some sleep". And immediately he said the word it became the greatest need in the world. The conductor and the lean man watched him cross from the bus to the sloping road leading to the railway station. He was no longer walking swiftly as when he had left the house. It seemed that something had overcome him at last.

Yet there was no sleep awaiting him in the warm and crowded train. It was an electric train and in the flying and gathering dusk speeding backward past the open window he could see the intermittent flash of sparks from the conductor-rail. As if, distantly, a gun shook and flashed its warning in his brain.

Sitting pressed between two silent and outraged women whose conversation he had cut off by squeezing himself between them (it was the only seat) he stared over the five heads opposite him without absorbing any details of the impact of what he saw. Indeed, he saw nothing : only, as the train gathered speed, the green and disembodied flashes. His hands were in his lap, the case trembling in the rack above his head. Even the hunger had left him now : just the train's noise and the unseated and elusive agony screamed through his brain—that inviolable part of his brain that waked, and, waking, screamed at him to sleep.

Time and time again up to the morning of this day he had told himself : You know exactly what you are doing, you are calm and collected. *Calm and collected, she used to say, and me het up as I can be* and you have made all your plans for the future. You have watched her end, you have seen the clean horror of her death and were completely detached about it. Because you could be nothing else. You know full well this is numbness, that a part of your brain does not understand yet ; so while this is so you plan, you make your arrangements. You cause it to be known that the burial will be on Friday the 25th, just twenty-four hours too late. No-one will come, but there will be flowers, wreaths, symbols, black edged cards, beautiful poems and epitaphs. You think this is exactly the right touch. And you go to the burial yourself, without flowers, for naturally none have arrived and you can never think of her in terms of flowers, so you don't buy any. At the graveside there is a little scene you have already almost forgotten : a scene in which you have fallen and two men are raising you to your feet and brushing clods of yellow soil from you. They murmur words, words that you have certainly forgotten because they meant nothing at the time, mean less than nothing now. That was the first time. You didn't know exactly what you were doing. But afterward, when you returned to the house, you knew then ; and you planned in your brain what you would do, while all the people kept coming to the door and offering you things—meals, money, clothes —help, can we help ? they said ; and were most upset when you said to get the hell out of it ; like stupid children, almost weeping with chagrin. But they went away in the end and stood in little groups outside their houses, groups of one two or three, arms folded, lips murmuring and sliding over the words you had said to tell them to go away. Yet another time, watching and hearing those same words, in that same and unvarying order, on some foot-lit stage or beam-lit screen, they would laugh, laugh, laugh, and tell each other, but in another way. But that was different. So you wandered the familiar floors of the house all that day, and without knowing it you suddenly came furtively and secretly upon another day, locked round the circular face of time, upon which two vain angles formulated some design of light and darkness and uttered certain especial and inviolate hours in which it was time to wake or sleep. But this time you ignored their invitation and warning and returned the glare of unmitigated malice with which the blank and symbolic face seemed to watch you. And it was quietly and unobtrusively *this* day, this very day upon which you were glad of yesterday's preview of the brain's chilled un-recognition ; and were able to dispense with plans and thought and desire and any emotion whatever. You paced the familiar floors, but ignored completely now the angular division of time's symbolic face. This was the period of shocked anaesthesia and you could do nothing but what you planned to do yesterday. Yesterday, yesterday, yesterday—and you wondered with one vague and unreal part of you exactly the definition that another equally vague and unreal part of you placed upon the word. Until suddenly it hissed through the window with the green flash blooming flowerlike upon the spreading darkened countryside and you knew with childlike and opening wonder that it was nothing but the wheels' circular and everlasting song. So you closed your eyes then upon the pinhead pricking of pain. But did not sleep ; for all sleep had vanished down some dark and mazelike quandary of anguish.

At Victoria he sat on in the empty compartment. The other occupants flowed past him to the thin din of their voices. They looked at him strangely but took no other notice. He might have been poured there, graven in some quiescent and silent mould with miraculous perfection of imitation ; a waxwork. The porter who reminded him of the attainment of his destination gazed at him for some brief period of time, wondering if at last he had stumbled on the propped body, the lifeless and staring corpse of fiction, but when he entered the compartment and said with emphatic and regretful appeal : " You've 'ad it, mate. Victoria. The end, the terminus ", he felt relief that the young man was not indeed a corpse but merely a young man a little bit simple and wild-looking, poor young feller, something to tell the missus, anyway. And " Terminus ", he said again, though the young man had gone, slowly along the platform, towards the barrier under the high and dusty bulbs and the blackening smoke and belching steam spewed forth by the thundering juggernauts at the rails' end.

Coming now out into the traffic maelstrom he felt his feet cold on the paths of centuries and in the footsteps of those who had gone before him : and knew, with that urgent and remindful part of his brain that uttered warning after warning, that he must find somewhere to sleep, a stone in the wilderness on which to lay his head, some unsculptured sky at which to gaze.

It was late summer, a night on which autumn hung in remote suspension above the city and was written on the faces and in the eyes of those whom the streets harboured ; and fluttered among the trees of Grosvenor Gardens, touching their already diminished leaves with subdued and reminiscent malice—malice of winter and the touch and caress of the season of cold and death. So that those upon whom the burden of age had descended turned inward to the teaching of the heart and of childhood for consolation and found therein a question as eternal as their own for answer : *To what end ?*

Crossing Grosvenor Gardens he passed the homeward crowds, patient at the sign at which, at some new angular utterance of time's symbolic face, the juggernaut wheels would bear them on their day's-end way. *Home*, he thought, and thought of the house abandoned in the quite suburban street, again with that solitary dispassion to which now was added some vein or thread of amusement as the curtains and the lips began to mutter within his vision, the wreaths in the hall to fall slowly and irrevocably to dust upon the dry chatterings of umbrage and the mock-words of sympathy.

And now : Move on, he thought, and plainly and simply came the answer to his question : Ask a policeman. Which he did—the first he saw, a man huge with health and the fruits of encyclopaedic knowledge, a man who showed no surprise at his question, a man, obviously, who was asked hundreds of times in a night, Where shall I sleep ?—a man to whom such a question was no question at all—a man who said, without emotion of any kind whatever : Take this turning this turning and that and knock upon the door of a certain house and the door shall be opened to you—for sixpence if you have it, or the chopping of some wood if you haven't.

So, following the syllabic directions, he went, and found that it was so.

2

WITHIN this room of mauve porcelain, black panels and stainless steel Mr Arnold Katesgrove stands shaving himself.

In the garden the lake is full of the morning sun. Pleasant. Everything familiar surrounding him : the self-chosen colour scheme, the furnishings from Maples, everything the very best. Perfection in attention to details : Arnold Katesgrove's religion. Even to the choice of the washers on the bath-tap he had given twenty minutes of his valuable time, examining figures, statistics : such-and-such a percentage of leather washers fails in such-and-such a time, such-and-such a percentage of rubber washers lasts so long : and so forth. So that the house, his home, had been built up around him in this fashion, detail upon detail, characterizing the timeworn bricks and once weed-strewn lawns with what Arnold Katesgrove called the perfection of accuracy.

The face in the mirror looked smoothly back at him as he skimmed the razor through the snowy lather. Always while shaving he thought, A successful face, broad capable hands, I could turn them to anything. The hands and the glimmering blade—it was an open razor, the most efficient under analysis—caressed ponderous chin and wide thin upper lip (strangely the bottom lip was full and sensual: the effect of two different mouths) as he thought of his sisters waiting for him downstairs.

He liked always to think of his sisters—anybody—waiting for him, dependent on him. Dependent for advice, decisions, everything.

Carefully he skimmed the last of the lather. There was no blemish on his skin. He rinsed his face and rubbed the alcohol lotion into the skin, slowly, carefully, with the circular movement his hairdresser had advised. Arnold Katesgrove accepted advice as well as gave it. The expert's opinion, the experience equal to his own in its own particular sphere.

The heated towels and the scented water in the bath-room surrounded him with their aura of luxury. He always regretted leaving the bathroom, the cunning contrivances and designs, the personal monogram inlaid on the cork floor

beside the sunken bath. Elsewhere others shared beauty
with him.

In the dressingroom Bourne had laid out the summer
gray. He hovered unobtrusively, folding things. He was
a man worn smooth with service, unreal as a shadow.

" A beautiful morning, Bourne ; but there's a touch of
autumn somewhere ".

" Exactly, sir. The Harris ? " He was already holding the tweeds over his arm, running his dry fingers along
the ties. " This one, sir ? "

They understood each other completely, these two.
Arnold Katesgrove liked to surround himself with people
he understood and who understood him. Anyone else
was beyond his ken, mistrusted—unless they remained
silent. Inanimate things invited no comprehension :
books and pictures and music—they were on the surface
of the mind, they appealed by being easy on mind, eye or
ear. Nothing else. Experts directed one's opinion if one
wasn't sure.

He dressed slowly, carefully : Saturday : the day he
liked best. Sunday was next, but there was church.
After forty years of churchgoing he still couldn't remember
the collects and responses without looking at the prayer-
book : and at Communion he always wanted to say the
wrong Creed. Dimly, he hated himself for this solitary
weakness of memory, as he would have scorned it in
another.

But Saturday : the casual, reflective day : the evening
and night with Nollys (even to himself now, after seven
years, he thought of Elise as Nollys ; just as she had grown
convinced that she had not anagrammed her Elsie), the
journey back, solitary in the Sunday morning train, the
morning mist and the Sunday papers bundled on to empty
platforms. He hated that : something thorned his head,
crucified him to the morning : loneliness, he called it,

putting away the decay of the viler analysis, deep in the mind's dustbin, shut tight against contemplation's gaze upon the ghoulish truth.　Truth is at the bottom of a dust-bin.

The morning was the penultimate breath of summer. Summer lying in lingering snatches, lying out there in the lake in gold smurrs, pressed within each fold of cloth as he slid his body into the suit.　Warm, he felt—then suddenly he was cold, in a breath, the flesh pricking on his arms, It was a warning, but he could not acknowledge it as such. An old wives' tale : somebody walked over your grave. Yet he had a feeling all was not well with the day.　Swiftly to his mind swayed each possibility : Elise the weak link, he could never be fully sure ; yet he made so certain, there was nothing else he could do, nothing, a complete change of identity was the only real and final answer : he did that, even to the extent of wearing other clothes—other clothes into which had been stitched tags carefully and indelibly marked with the name *Lucian Trent*—and of adopting, slowly and certainly, week by week, until now, so many years later, the Mr Hyde change and transformation were inviolable and natural as they could possibly be.　Even to the other name-tags for his clothes *Arnold Katesgrove*, which he carried always and sewed into the suit each Sunday morning with the needle and thread he carried for the purpose.　It was detail again, the utmost perfection. But there was yet the millionth possibility of chance, the coincidence, the unintentional word or meeting, the single sandgrain on a limitless shore upon which some near or prying finger might be placed, the chance meeting with someone so near as to be able to decry the dark glasses the unfamiliar clothes and the stooping stick-assisted walk that were Lucian Trent's.　Tying the tie he thought, with smile secret and immense, of the risk—implicit in the dark and murmurous gathering of blood in the veins.

He descended now the stairway, leaving behind him the
folded and softfooted noises of Bourne, passing at the first
landing the stained window rich with its gleams of colour
and the rigid and tranquil flowers, his footsteps slow and
deep in the carpet's richness as he reached the hall and the
walls gleaming too with their brass and copper bright
against the polished oak and the silence and stillness of the
house.

His sisters awaited him, president at the long breakfast
table in the sunny room, their hands wafting among the
coffee odour and the silver dishes.

3

In the morning, wakening to the light of the cold gray
silence wherein he had slept, cold and tranquil and deeply
forgetting, thrust in the iron bed uncaring with that re-
ceptiveness that is the body's last stand, when it is thrust
to beyond feeling by the mind—to breaking point. So he
had slept. And with that miraculous recovery that too is
the body's he found, waking now, some quality of refreshment in sleep just left that was a sojourn in some sequestered arbour of childhood, that was part of that experience
before there was experience, when there was only future,
the pending hour, the evening—nothing beyond.

Leaving the place he took with him that feeling amount-
ing to buoyancy, that attitude in which he now had two
separate minds—one to enjoy and one to grieve, the joyous
mind having come upon and overtaken him with sleep,
from which he had emerged retaining its happiness and

humour while not yet forgetting grief and its cause ; but
he had formed now his plan.

He walked quickly along Vauxhall Bridge Road and on
into Victoria Street thinking of the feeling respondent to
the act of washing and shaving. In a public lavatory he
did this, spinning the water over his head in cold gushes.
Shaved, he looked younger and griefless, a boy almost, the
water flattening hair to skull and coursing the lines of his
face, trembling on the eyes' brink—the eyes dark and dark
with secret humour and some quality of calm and barely
visible vindictiveness lying dormant now as the pebble
that, sinking, had rippled the surface.   A grouch, one would
have said ; he has a grouch—but he is taking his time ;
pondering, one might have added : but he's maybe the
more dangerous for that.

The streets gleamed in the poignant and unutterable
regret of late summer. He noticed now how people had
absorbed the advent of autumn into their eyes and glances :
as though, with disconsolate surprise, they waked suddenly
to the end of a visitation.

It was early.   The Post Office was closed, but looking at
its heavy doors he felt no annoyance : rather, an opportunity.   There was the park.   It lay spread between the
roads and the traditions, the musing statues and mast-
draped flags, harbouring its mendicants and birds, its grass
soiled flat with bodies' brief and animate controversy, its
close and ordered terrain, the morning sky scissored with
the skyline's unstereoscopic darkness and antiquity chal-
lenging origin as who should say : Created by creator's
creation.

This was the time of recollection.

Arnold to whom I am going.   Arnold the eldest, Arnold
the shining light and the public figure, the director and
formulator of taste within the solidity and character and
rolling lawns of Hartney Fold.

Here at this juncture of thought and reminiscence a man came and sat beside him; a man stark and angular holding in his hand a paper bag mottled with grease from which he drew with regular and despotic insistence crusts of bread that he tore apart between his long and gnarled fingers and threw into the air to fall upon the ground at ever decreasing intervals. Birds fluttered and pecked at the crusts, their bright eyes cocked against violation of trust, bright with inherent distrust of the human hand.

In a while the man spoke and the birds rushed upward in a long and gathering paroxysm of fear at the sound of his voice. Their wings beat and beat against the morning stillness.

" There is nothing so beautiful as the flight of birds ", he said. His voice was soft, gentle and cultured; and touched faintly with some quality of madness.

" I could talk of things as beautiful ", he answered. He was not trying to be argumentative : he really was recalling things as beautiful.

The two voices were speaking at once in perfect consonance.

" Yes ", the bird-man said. " No doubt you have a wife ? "

" Yes ", he said. " No. No, not now. Until Thursday I had a wife. Today is Saturday. I have no wife ".

" You have a wife ", the bird-man went on as if he had heard nothing. " I, on the other hand, have nothing but a badge ". He drew from his pocket a circle of tin : it was not a badge, it was nothing—perhaps the top of a coffee tin. He turned and turned it in the bony fingers. The sun was in it and, as it faced upward, the smear on its shining surface of the flight of birds, reflected. " Any time I like I can enter any of the Royal houses without challenge. I am a member of the Royal Society. Buckingham Palace,

Holyrood, Windsor—all of them. We could walk across
the park to the palace now ; you could watch me go in.
You see, I have studied the flight of birds for so many years
now ".

"And that makes you important ? "

"I have watched birds flying since I was a child ".
(He saw the bird-man turning skyward to endless and
countless flocks of birds.) "As others have : but they
have seen nothing but the possibilities of imitation : and
in imitating they have created what they are pleased to
call a new beauty—a new beauty they call this thing they
have created !—a thing of tin and wood and sparks
and vapour flowing in little pipes ; and having created
it they find a new use for the force of gravity. I can
never understand why men watch with greater ease
the slow curve of bombs on their houses than stand
and ponder the flight of birds. Perhaps you can understand that ? "

"No ", he said : "I cannot understand it either ".

The morning sun swept over the park and the limp flags
and the bemused statesmen on their marble pedestals.
The birds, their flight broken by song, circled and swung in
the air. Looking at the bird-man, his badge, his mania,
he thought : It is true : I do not understand it ; there is
very little I, we, understand. Very little.

I understand this : the warm and sleepscented hand
flowerlike in its immobility upon the pillow ; some speechless beauty that I have seen sometime and recollected in
tranquillity. Freda—your warm form hand body scent
breathing here beside me. Then no longer your breathing.
No longer you. Days up to that *no longer you* days and
nights in which we said Thank God we *know* we are happy,
stickily sentimentally happy perhaps, *how* happy is surely
immaterial *Freda you said that once : how, meaning in what
manner, is completely immaterial.* You said that once ;

and I said Yes that's right completely immaterial. How
we used to fight when I said the wrong thing and upset
your mental age which we decided was twelve. I said it
was a nice age. Some people are happy and don't know it.
We knew. It wasn't for any reason ; just because we
liked each other, I suppose ; we liked being suburban and
cheap, holding hands in the pictures and twining arms as
we walked along. It was all we were good for, you and me.
Arnold said that, didn't he ? That you were all right as a
milliner's needlewoman, embroidering hats at so much a
dozen. That's when you used to say you were het up,
thinking about him ; and I sat and listened to you, calm
and collected and making you angrier because I showed
no emotion. Yet it was there : you just couldn't see it,
hidden away under my smile. Arnold should know you
pretty well, shouldn't he ? He had every opportunity.
Snakesoft Arnold : a man as good as his word : his
word as rotten as a fallen apple. You waked from sleep
some faraway night screaming his fear into my ear.
You think I liked that ? In some cold dim dawn you
shivered, remembering him : soft warm smooth vile
cunning rich disgusting Arnold. You said. Hating him.
Hating you because of him. Hating. So now it is that I
have absorbed that bright legerdermain of hate, I that will
add bead by bead to the chain of invective, I that will
watch his descent to the pit from which surely he must
have sprung. I that will send him there. The Monte
Cristo Touch. I smile grimly inside the inside of my inner
mind : a melodramatic touch, one you would have
thoroughly approved, my silent darling. I smile grimly
dimly a little primly as I ponder my plan—a plan without
superstructure as yet for as my beloved idol said, The best
laid schemes of mice and men fall in the privy soil sometimes. So there is to be a building up, a superstructure,
rivet and word and deed and thought, slow upon slow and

sure upon sure, until something falls, my brother, upon your gross and useless body. " That is what I understand ", he said aloud, his voice startling the birds to flight. They rose again in a noisy scatter.

The bird-man was leaning forward. All the crusts in the bag were gone. His boots were odd : one laced, one of buttoned kid ; the corner of his overcoat fell in a worn triangle over the buttoned boot. He was a man grown old with the pursuit of unattainable beauty. Grown old now with mania. " My name is Shula Horn. Any time I want I can walk in—" with a lost and muttering air he began searching in his pockets.

" Yes, yes. You told me. You've a badge. My name is Laurie Katesgrove ; not Lawrence—Laurie. I can walk into Hartney Fold whenever I want to—now. That is where I am going ", he said. " I am going there now ", hammering the words in though he did not move from the seat. He felt his mood refracting and scintillating on the facets of the bird-man's moronic passivity. It crossed his mind that there was an odd but certain link between them. He felt cold in the sun, cold in his mind, cold in his heart, cold in every murmur of his teeming and subconscious blood. I am going to kill him. *I am going to kill him.*

He got up, rising into the sunlight, into the solitude and the morning, aware of himself, alone, an unknown and unmarked pursuer, a journey before him, an inarticulate and actionless journey. It is now morning, he thought ; and with brilliant and reasonless clairvoyance he saw in vision the ultimate moment of the journey. It was in some dark place shadowed by high walls and rungs of lightless windows. There was nothing beyond that : only, distantly, the dawn of some remote and farflung morning. *In what unhappy distance and at what future hour will it be ?* he thought and discovered himself thinking with veiled surprise, Why did I think that ? Nevertheless, he took the first step.

When he looked back the bird-man was still there, signatory and dedication, a confederate almost, a figure black with immobility and patient with silence, surrounded by the vast unending movement and squawking of the birds.

In the Post Office he spent a long time over the composition of the telegram to Arnold. He stood at the counter thrusting his head into the frosted-glass cubicle. He pulled the forms from their container one by one and wrote message after message. All the time the case containing his clothes stood beneath the counter at his feet and he kicked his toe against the hide at precisely the same moment that each message-form was scrawled across with its heavy lines of cancellation and screwed into a ball. After a little time there were more than a dozen of the little paper pellets at his feet and an attendant came across to him.

" You're using plenty of the forms, aren't you ? They're not put there to waste, you know. Nor to write love letters on ".

" Believe me ", Laurie said, " this is no love letter ".

The attendant went away and stood watching, his hands linked behind his back ; a tall and pugilistic man with two rows of medal ribbons on his uniform. He watched three more paper pellets fall to the floor and started to walk across to Laurie again. But he was already crossing to the clerk.

He handed the message to the girl and stood there watching her count the upside-down words.

" Tenpence ", the girl said. She held out her hand, the form pinned down by her pencil-point.

" Knock off ' Surrey ' ", he said ; " it can't be necessary ; everyone knows it's in Surrey ".

She scored out the word. " Ninepence ".

He counted out the pennies.   All the time his eyes were smiling, he was thinking of Arnold reading the telegram. Picking up the case he walked out into the sonorous street, pale-bleached in the sun.

4

CALM.   Coming into the room with all the calm of years. Perfectly composed.   The pale sun on the table the very essence and reflection of his perfect composure.   His sisters with all the formality of their attitude, sitting there awaiting him, acknowledgement of his status implicit in their every movement.   He must, remembering the warning of the day's beginning, have shown some discontent or desire, for Elspeth, nearest the window, was already pulling the crimson twisted cord.   The heavy curtains moved silently and the sunlight was briefly gone from his place, marked with its monogrammed plates and silver, at the head of the table.   " No ", he said, and instantaneously with that spoken, whispered word her hand had grasped the other cord and the curtains admitted the calm sunlight once again.   " I like the sun " he said and seated himself. " This morning I think we need it ; there is, somewhere, a touch of autumn ", shivering again within the warm and caressed folds of the tweed and the Fair Isle pullover he always thought of himself facetiously as ' sporting ' on Saturdays.

" Yes, Arnold ".   Elspeth, a sparse and twisted woman, branchlike with that similarity to wood long sapless and useless except as a perch for canary or budgerigar, a woman touched with the reflection of man's un-desire and grown, not bitter but, rather, humiliated in the manner of children tormented by fear of loneliness. Elspeth too was haunted by this fear that on some groundless and terrible occasion she might speak and receive no answer. She therefore honeyed her words and actions that others might think her pleasant and easygoing, delightful conversationalist or receptor of confidence and intrigue. And she said, with repetition of that desire to please : " Yes, Arnold ".

" But it's been a long summer ; there must be an end ".

There must be an end : thus the warning that slid through his bones and brain ; and swiftly and unaccountably upon the warning the threat and horror of pursuit. Yet there at his table was everything normal, of normal countenance, the upper halves of his sisters sawing the air toward their food, rhythmic and with that precision and deliberateness to which he was accustomed ; the flat unfurled sunlight between the curtains held the spinning and countless motes of summer and beyond, in the garden, lay pooled and touched with the smoothness of silk within the pallid marbled precincts of the lake.

He could hear his sisters breathing, a haunt and echo of warning within the sheer sunlight. The sound worried, irritated him : a distant fretful plaint of servility coming, it seemed, from that memory wherein dwelt the cause and conception of unease. Yet no comment was possible without vulgarity, rancour or irony.

He did not speak. The paper—of course it was *The Times*—lay folded with its white borders enhancing the pillars of print at the side of his plate : In Memoriam, Personal, Properties For Sale, Public Notices. He unfolded it and propped it barrierwise before him, not reading but allowing his eyes to traverse the print, thus suppressing his unease.

Behind the barrier Christine began to speak, a long tirade about servants and the Women's Institutes and her jade, her everlasting jade. Arnold did not bother to listen. The bacon lay in congealed tatters on the dish, but the coffee was warm and sweet on his chill stomach, he drank it with the relief of a drunken man drinking champagne on the morning after some insignificant debauch.

In due time, a time in which no inkling of his unease could have penetrated the barrier, he rose and left the table, still not having spoken, and went into the garden.

At the lake's edge he looked down at his serrated image imprinted on the water : a dark and distorted shadow athwart the smurr of sunlight. Around him lay the garden in its gleaming and tended beauty. He strode the precise and ordered paths, hands looped behind him in posture of fleshed and heavy serenity. All was serene. A flight of swallows rose suddenly in silent movement across the sky and fell briefly beyond his vision like a scatter of burnt paper. Some petal of memory unfurled in his mind and revealed engraven there words heard faintly in youth, square and neat now as the carved inscription on tomb or plaque : *When the swallows homeward fly*. A flutter and echo of memory to which for the moment he could attribute no origin but in which nevertheless there clung some forbidding likeness of a signature pendant upon some writ or deed to which it seemed certain that in due time he must depend or listen. But the speaker or occasion of the words escaped him. Only their portent gloomed among the invoked calm of his thoughts. So that furrows deepened suddenly between the heavy-lidded and elephantine eyes.

He did not pause as he walked amid the garden's deep scents. Pauses and admiration were for moments when he was observed. None could pause or say with greater

admiration and effect than he : These roses bear my name,
here are delphiniums of unequalled size, in my hothouses
there are orchids. But an audience was necessary. There
was no beauty in the things themselves. *I* give them
beauty, he thought, my name is their cause and their
existence. With perfect composure he stopped at a rose-
tree. A single late bloom lay folded within the cool green
leaves, deep red. Without violence he plucked it and,
without looking at it, crushed it in his soft white hand,
feeling the crushed semi-liquid and blood-coloured mass
(yet with colour and quality deeper and more passionate
than blood) rendered into pulp and exuding the veins of a
living organism that had lain embalmed and invisible
within its deep red heart and the curved and luscious
beauty of its petals. He crushed and crushed his fingers on
the soft petals that now fell with the scattered abandon of
wind-blown blood-drops. From the heart of the rose a
frail and yellow stickiness like pus spread over his hands.
He looked at his fingers with distaste and wiped them on his
handkerchief. The stain smeared on to the white linen as
though a woman had wiped her lips on the folds, and he put
the handkerchief away in his pocket, half wondering
whether to throw it into the incinerator. But he remembered, a constant and irrevocable thought, that they cost
money. And continued his monotonous and measured
promenading of the garden, keeping always to those paths
and those parts of the lawn where the sun lay in lambent
and cooling pools, reminiscently with a faint and calm
apprehension of autumn.

A little later when Rose the parlourmaid came with the
telegram she found him again at the edge of the lake.
Above them the sun lay imprinted on the ivory sky in
medallion gold, its light refracting from leaf and bough and
water, across which his squat shadow spread like a thumb-
print whorled by the impress of the water's quiet rippling.

" A telegram, sir.   It just came ".

So there was the crux and magnitude of his fears, confined within the flimsy seal of a pink envelope, his name blandly written on the shiny surface without either prefix or title, as though a formula to decide his name had been extended to the most infinite fraction.   Of the wording and import of the telegram he was ignorant.   For a moment he allowed the thought of destroying it unread to ponder his action.   But that would be worse than useless.   Besides, it might be of no importance.   From his broker, perhaps.

He screwed the envelope into a ball with the same kneading motion that he had used for the rose.   The crimped pink paper floated a little way on the lake then opened out like the uncurling fronds of some exotic flower.   Moisture had smudged the indelible pencilled writing into a stain that spread in an opening retina of purple across the thin pink paper.   The scrap of paper moved suddenly into a cluster of tall reeds and hung there.   Beside Arnold Katesgrove stood the girl, watching him read the telegram, neat in her black satin, waiting.

" There is no answer ", he said.   She walked back toward the house between the passive and sundrowned flowers and even beyond the thought and fear that now glowed fiercely in his brain he was aware of an inert sensual consciousness of her hips and legs.

But that was deeper, anonymous.   He read the telegram again.   He tried to imagine it was impossible.   He looked up and away into the distant curling spaces of the garden and to the house, mellowed red brick, Georgian windows, noble proportions, the windows polished bright with sun, no curtain stirring behind their immaculate brightness, the servants going with gliding and emasculate movement about their tasks.   Elspeth and Christine shadowed and tight within the solid and mellowed walls.   He saw them, the scene unrolling like a rising curtain upon the retina of his senses. Real, solid. Then he looked again at the paper in his hand forcing himself to believe it was lies, impossible, a trick, a forgery, non-existent. Yet it was there. The paper rustled slightly between the cared-for fingers softened with rosewater lotion. He looked down, believing it to be impossible, reading the words again, though already they lay in cold and inviolate print upon his brain, etched there with the acid and stylo of some stronger agent than ink or vitriol. Yes, it was still there, beyond and apart from any form of fear now. As if, from within the husk or shell of some other being he looked upon himself with compassion and some inscrutable knowledge of time space and distance that rendered non-existent the fear that he bore now within the living self at which he looked. So that the telegram was without purpose now. Nevertheless he did not destroy it as he had destroyed the envelope. He stood there for perhaps a full minute reading and re-reading the syllabic message: FREDA GONE STOP WITH YOU TODAY—LAURIE and at once there entered across the sundried memory of childhood the small and screwed-up figure of Laurie reciting at some party or soirée lines of verse or prose in which he said *When the swallows homeward fly*. So the thought, wild and anonymous, had had some import after all.

He could not see himself yet he knew he was without composure in his appearance. He felt sick and turned toward some sequestered corner of the garden. He bent double in the corner but he could not vomit. Alone, he listened to the depthless silence and knew he was without friends. There was no-one. There had never been any-one. And though he had cared less than nothing, for a moment now he was terribly aware of the loneliness into which he had thrust himself.

Leaves moved in the dark arbour in which he stood concealed; moving surface to surface in the long ecstatic whisper of living, mocking him with the infinitesimal murmur of their presence within the arbour.

He came out from the arbour dabbing his lips. He was swaying a little, his face still white. Walking back to the house he knew his fear had disappeared beneath the assumed composure.

Calm. Coming into the room he had so recently left with all the calm of years. The room was empty, the long table bright under the sheen of polish and flowers. He came through the open glass doors and the heavy curtains, glancing obliquely at the mirror, at himself. Normal now.

Ascending the stairs past the waxy turgid flowers before the stained window he thought with irony : Saturday : my casual, reflective day *Freda gone ; with you today* Gone. *Gone ?* GONE ! So the word shrieked in his brain. The bitch. The little bitch. *Death is too good for her. To clutter up my life with her insignificant shopgirl's bitchery of death.* And Laurie coming here. *Laurie !*

Memory remembering this (remembering in a spool of pictures unwound in the presence of memory in some remote and darkened corner of the brain ; remembering in less than the instant wherein one soft and polished shoe leaves the thickly carpeted tread of the stair and alights with furtive and deliberate calm on another), remembering :

On a summer afternoon she came into the shop. He saw her through one of the tiny holes he had himself drilled in the walls. (There were many of these, one in the ceiling of the ladies' room.) Through this hole he saw her as she came in, very young (perhaps fifteen ? he thought), with neither poise nor happiness nor any beauty that he could discover in her pale countenance. But her body, her body, he thought, is . . . delicate. . . . And he could see within the secret folds of his darkened mind the erotic and phallic symbols of his pleasure. In his office he questioned

her. So you are Freda, he said. She sat timidly, but
below the desk he watched the brief swirl of her thighs as
she sat and crossed her legs, then, remembering perhaps
some reprimand for immodesty, uncrossed them and sat
perfectly straight, her hands sculptured in her lap as she
looked toward him across the desktop, ignoring everything
but his eyes, into which she looked with some quality at
once passive and terrified.   Your name and age and address
and father's occupation : questions to which he knew every
answer but nevertheless scribbled figures and words on a
pad the while he watched below the desk at her bare and
rigid legs.   You will have to wear stockings, of course ;
you understand that ?   She had not unbuttoned her coat,
and in a moment he told her to do this, saying that the office
was very hot.   She immediately loosed the buttons, not
speaking, and in a moment he asked her again about the
stockings.   Yes, she said, I must wear them.   I think we
understand each other, he said again.   Then : You can
start on Monday ; tell your father I am employing you.   I
like my staff to be here five minutes before nine o'clock,
he said.   Then she asked the only question she had voiced :
May I go now ?   Yet she did not rise, but sat there as he
stood beside her brushing his fingers lightly together with
the dry sound of rustling paper, sat there awaiting his
assent, speaking the four words without looking at him,
without even moving to watch or to bring within the range
of her apparently inert hearing the snakelike hiss of his
hands : May I go now ?   At which interrogative he smiled
with innate stealth and said, Yes.   So she went then,
Arnold watching her go as he had watched her arrive,
speaking to no-one, walking straight out of the shop into
the street and the musing sunlight and the slow gathering
of people in the streets of the hot town.

Memory ceases then in that fractional mote of time in
which the polished brown shoe hovers between the deeply

carpeted stairs ; ceases ; yet leaves in its wake the deep-rooted menace of its significance. So that with the immediacy of cause and effect another thought springs trapwise upon the ceased memory : Laurie is coming here about Freda. So much he knew, had read in the impersonal print of the telegram. But to what purpose he was coming only the bodiless fear that now lay rolled with the inescapable inference of a net over his mind gave import.

Bourne was hoving, mothlike. " Is everything all right, sir ? You look a little . . . strained ".

" Yes ", he said. " Yes, everything will be all right ". He was speaking to his own questioning mind.

" Did you say you *were* all right, sir ? "

" Yes ! " he shouted. " Blast it, man—get me a drink ". Bourne's impassive face faced him. " I'm sorry ", he said. He spoke quite normally now. " I just received some unexpected news. Mr Nollys wishes me to meet him earlier than usual in town. It crossed my mind that he may have bad news. His father, I believe, ails badly ". He added, as if to give some conviction : " He may need some help ".

He felt an echo of the friendlessness of the arbour and knew that Bourne did not believe him. Bourne had turned away, perhaps so that he could smile unobserved. That was the depth of the understanding between them.

He stood at the window. Down in the garden Christine was moving among the flowers. She was dressed in a yellow tussore coat and a floppy hat ; her hands were gloved in rough leather as she snipped off the roses one by one and laid them in the flat basket she carried. She laid the blooms in the basket carefully, regimented neatly as matches in a box. All the time she moved among the flowers he watched her, hearing each *snip* of the scissors punctuating Bourne's furtive movements as he packed.

And again, as if in confirmation, he felt the flesh pricking
on his arms. *Laurie. A weakling. A weakling morally
and physically. He can do nothing.* Child of a harlot, he
thought consciously, a frilled and beribboned pansy
standing in some dark and shrinelike corner whispering
through womankissed lips, When the swallows homeward
fly. *Then why do I fear?* the secret pricking of his flesh
whispered. But there was no answer to that, no answer
to which he could give even silent utterance ; for every pore
sweated in the knowledge of pursuit.

Money, he thought suddenly. I shall need money.

He went to the tallboy and took out a cashbox. In it
there was a roll of notes and he took all but five of these.
With what design or purpose he left those five he could not
have said. If asked, he would have thought and said,
Against some future need. Nor did he lock the cashbox ;
and again he could have stated no reason.

Buttoning the coat across the sporting pullover he sat in
a leather chair watching Bourne pack. He sat with his
ankles lightly crossed, his hand encircling the glass of
barleywater, a man at ease, a man unfeared and unfearing
(he thought), watching the tall mirror in which he sat em-
panelled. But Bourne was thinking, There is something
wrong. He is afraid, Bourne thought ; and said aloud :

" I've packed your usual weekend case, sir. There's
nothing else you'll be wanting ? "

The man in the chair drained the barleywater. " No.
Why should there be ? " He put the glass down. The
imprint of his pendulous lower lip was smudged on the
glass. He took the handkerchief from his pocket and wiped
his lips. Then he crossed and dropped the handkerchief
in the linen basket. Everything normal except the time
of his departure.

Nevertheless, Bourne thought—perhaps smelling fear
as an animal smells fear in a man—he is afraid. Without

watching he could see the figure in the chair, how it bore, with neither reason nor expectation, that quality of collapsion ; so that within the suit of fine wool and the linen most impeccable Mr Arnold Katesgrove no longer exuded any semblance of refulgence, no health of body mind or estate ; but, rather, appeared now in need of some help other than earth or heavenly. Collapsed, Bourne thought : he looks collapsed. And was about to ask again if his employer was all right. But he had done that already with what result he knew. And between them there was no affection or understanding. He gives me no confidence, Bourne thought ; he tells me nothing but what is known to all. He kids himself we understand each other, he thought. But he tells me nothing. I don't care a damn about him, he thought : he pays my wages : that is all. He pressed his knee on to the lid of the case he had packed, rather from force of habit than from any necessity, and locked it *snick snick*. He took it and tested its weight.

" That's ready, sir ".

The other took it and put it on the floor. He was standing by the window again listening to the faint mocking repetition of the scissors as Christine cut the flowers.

It was nearly noon, the sun marking irrevocable passage of day and season. There was a faint stirring of leaves in the garden and the sun dimmed under a huge white cushion of cloud. Again the pricking of flesh along spine and back and the faint pellucid tremor of fear.

Leaving the case in the hall he sought his two sisters.

" You're going so soon, Arnold ?   Before lunch ? "

" Yes," he said.   " I have had a message from my old friend Nollys——"

" Ah.   The telegram ", Elspeth said.

" —he asks me to meet him earlier than usual. For what reason he doesn't say. But I am going to accede to his request. I have known him a very long time ", he added ;

and it was the first time they had heard him attempt to justify any word or action.

" Of course, Arnold ".

The two women stood before him, thin and dry, their faces suggestive somehow of a suppressed and emotionless greed.

" You'll be back as usual for church to-morrow morning ". It was neither statement nor question : a mere ghostly and repetitive phrase.

" So far as I know ".

In turn they leaned toward his cheek, their dry lips brushing the ivory flesh. From the door they waved to him as the purring of the car rose and sighed fitfully away in a bodiless and abstract mesh of gears. And from the dove-gray upholstery of the car he in his turn watched through the square of sidescreen as he turned the car into the road, seeing them stand in the entrance with the open door and the soft oblong of darkness behind them, standing as they always stood with the unmistakable suggestion of outraged piety clinging to their beshawled outlines. He waved too, and they were gone behind the speeding backward motion of the trees.

Away, he thought ; I am away. And smiling : First blood to me.

In the mirror above the windscreen he saw the dark, speeding road. There was no other vehicle in sight. Without conscious reasoning he pressed his foot on the accelerator.

It was an avenue of beech trees. Far above him the leaves arched and mingled across the road, shutting out the light. Presently, when he left the avenue he found the sun had faded in the autumnal sky, lying faint behind drifting clouds that moved softly in a last suspiring breath of summer.

At the station he parked the car and enquired the time

of the next down train.   He was told it was in forty-three minutes.   His own train to London left in twelve minutes.

In the train it occurred to him that the two trains would pass.   He began to work out at what time and place this would be.

He was alone in the compartment and he sat crouched in the corner.   When the two trains passed he threw himself to the floor, although he had drawn down all the blinds, and listened to the deep and shattering terror of his heart as it cried beneath the tumult of the train's passing.

5

SITTING in the other train Laurie was thinking, with some assumed ironic nostalgia appropriate to his present mood, of Hartney Fold.

He was not alone.   In the compartment with him there were other people with whom he had exchanged neither speech nor glance.   With the incalculable reserve of people making a short journey they gazed from the windows or examined with pretence of interest the lithographed holiday scenes that met the gaze of their eyes.   There was a woman and two men, the woman perhaps a suburban schoolteacher, austere and bespectacled in a highnecked blue dress, the two men uniformed and carrying square metal toolboxes which they held fast on their laps with the rigid and patient devotion of men long skilled and without fear of uselessness.   Laurie did not look at them.   He sat in the corner, diagonally, one leg lying along the checkered plush seat.   He had not bothered to move the leg when the other people got in and through closed eyes he sensed with some distant breath of amusement their indignation. He did not move, but sat there in feigned sleepfulness, aware with a combination of the senses other than sight of their outraged and silent sufferance.

He started now to remember and wonder about Hartney Fold. He found he could remember the face of one of the porters at the station to which he was going, a man ruddy with beer. Also some of the children with whom he had played at some period of his childhood now vague except for the thin and grubby faces and the misty recollection of the school playground—a square of concrete ringed about with iron railings curved at the top. Dim and nameless features jigsawed up and down in his brain. And during a moment of the utmost quiet within his mind there arose a memory of a gathering of children—silent now in memory, with that similarity to a row of portraits long hung in a deserted and darkened gallery—and silent too at that time to which memory recalled him, as they sat with that austerity that only children can assume at times of imposed silence, while he, Laurie, spoke, from a throat trembling with suppressed tears, words over which he had pored in punishment for some misdeed of which he had not even then been aware. The words—he could not recall them— had been concerned with autumn.

At that moment Arnold's train passed them and he opened his eyes and dreaming senses to encounter the steel-throated scream and backward rush of the blurred windows. The uprushing tumult scarred through his brain like a screech of derision. The frenzy of steam and speed was gone as suddenly as it began, and without warning, leaving the cluttered suburban terraces rolling past the train without haste.

The scene unemotional. Smoke twisting idly from chimneys across the now smokecoloured sky, a scurry of birds rising suddenly from the arrowing roar of the train. Laurie thought of the old man in the park, Shula Horn, and his passion for beauty as he sat amidst the careless circling wings. The passing of the trains had absorbed in chaos all the desire and purpose of his journey. He felt suddenly empty, a vacuum withdrawing all mind heart and fleshly need. Opening his eyes he saw and heard the two men discussing football in a frenzy of suppressed anger because of the schoolteacher's presence. Shutting his eyes again he felt the loneliness that stretched to the farthest reaches of solitude.

The train slid into a station and the two men got out. As soon as they had closed the door their voices rose in anger. About a centre-forward, Laurie thought : nothing more ; they will presently come to angry silence—perhaps blows—because one of them says that a man neither of them knows and is never likely to know cannot kick a ball in the approved style.

The schoolmam looked out of the window. No-one else got in. Just before the train started she half rose from her seat and put a hand on the doorlock. But the guard had already blown his whistle. The train began to move forward into a hiss of steam. The woman lay back, watching Laurie. He could feel her gaze on his face. She turned away and looked out through the window.

Presently he asked her permission to smoke and she said in a faint harsh voice :

" No, I don't mind at all ".

All the time he could see her wondering what action she could take in the event of any of the things she was imagining actually taking place. He could see her reasoning with herself, telling herself.

The blue haze of his cigarette smoke lay on the air and added to the dreamlike quality of the sequence in which the woman had suddenly began to prick at his memory.

The train slowed at a signal and Laurie saw that they were leaving the suburbs behind. There were fields lying between a rash of villas. The train slid forward, gathering speed. He said :

" We must be getting near Hartney ? "

The woman leaned forward, thrusting her loveless face close to the glass. He could see that she thought it best to humour him. He smiled a little, twisting his cigarette stub to the floor.

" Yes," the woman said. " Four or five more stations. I'm not quite sure where—" They slowed into a station. " O yes. Yes. Sunnymede. Four more stations. Hartney is the fourth station from here," she added. Her hands in her lap twisted blue string gloves. Behind the thick spectacles her eyes trembled. " You know Hartney ? "

" Yes ", Laurie said. " I know Hartney. I know Hartney Fold ".

" O. The big house ".

" You know it too ? " he asked.

" O yes ", she said. He could see that half her terror was gone. He smiled deep within himself, turned away toward the window and said, " It's my home. Was ", he added.

" O— " she was about to speak. Her hands fluttered. " I know it so well. The two Katesgrove boys—" she was smiling but she suddenly ceased. " You must be one of—"

" I am," he said. " I'm Laurie ".

" But I thought—"

He said. " Yes. Of course you did. Everybody did ".

" O. I'm sure I didn't mean—"

" No ".

After a silence she said : " I'm a teacher at the Central School. My mother was there before me ".

" I remember you ", he said. " You used to come and meet your mother in the evenings while you were working for your teacher's certificate ".

" That's right ", the woman said. All fear had gone from her now. Her eyes were bright with the happiness of recognition. " How did you know ? "

He shrugged, not speaking. In a while she opened her lips to speak again, but she said nothing. Her breath expired. At the station he got out without either word or gesture of farewell. The woman looked after him through the window, drawn into a shell of indignant umbrage. He saw her as the train slid away, watching him from averted eyes.

The station was the same, as he remembered it: Stephen's Ink, Waverley Pens, Bovril, Huntley and Palmers Biscuits: the tin plates were still screwed to the wooden walls of the booking-hall and the fence that bordered the platform. There was a basket of pigeons on the platform. While Laurie watched, a porter came on to the platform and opened the basket. The pigeons rose in a mutter of cries, circled and flew away. The porter, a youth of about eighteen, emptied the basket on the platform; there was a scatter of corn and muck, gray and white. In a moment the porter went into the booking-hall and returned with a stiff broom. He swept the platform, a cloud of dust rising about his feet.

" You a stranger here ? " he asked.

" Yes ", Laurie said. " Yes. A stranger ". He said: " Where is Hartney Fold ? "

" The big house. Mr. Katesgrove's place. You go on up the hill out there. You keep left all the time. Even when you come to the three roads and there's two on the left you take the left of the two. You see ? "

" Yes ", Laurie said. " I see ", thinking, It is amusing to have someone direct you to a place you know: like filling in missing lines in a drawing.

" You c'n getta bus. They're every hour. From here ".
In a moment the porter said, " It's a tidy walk ". He
lifted the broom and a curling of dust rose over his boot.
" They start from there. At the end of the approach ".

" Thanks ", Laurie said. " I'll walk ". He said : "I
like walking ".

The road curved away between high banks to distant
hills. Nothing had altered. The town lay away in the
opposite direction round a flick of road. He could see the
chimney of the brickworks and a few roofs flattened like
postage stamps to the hillside. Laurie started to walk
toward the town, conscious of a profound need. His
thought checked his steps : Later. I can return there
later ; and he turned without halting and retraced his steps
past the station thinking of the woman in the train. He
remembered her, even in those days she was severe and unsmiling, a child old before her time, coming to the school
each evening at an hour predetermined by habit to meet her
mother, an ogress with a black velvet band encircling her
neck.

Freda would remember her, he thought. *Would* is the
operative word there, he thought. He stopped and put his
case down on the dusty road and lit a cigarette, thinking
of Freda remembering the schoolmam. It was the last
cigarette and he tossed the packet away with some violence.
Then he walked on. Arnold will have some, he thought ;
if only for visitors. Or perhaps he gives them cigars ? he
thought.

She would remember her, he thought, seeing her laugh as
she remembered the schoolmam, adding the details he had
forgotten : *Yes, and she wore one-bar pointed shoes and
worsted stockings, even a girl of that age* laughing, collapsing
completely presently in helpless laughter as she recalled
the girl. Thinking this without bitterness or regret, as if
in a moment the scene would come true ; thinking, even

when realizing its impossibility, still with no sadness ;
and bitterness had now become a cause, no longer an effect.

He ceased thinking of Freda. Of a sudden a horse and
flat cart had overtaken him. The driver was brown-
skinned, a face riven with wrinkles beneath a faded and
shapeless Panama hat. On the cart were piled vegetables,
fruit.

" You want a lift, son ? "

About a mile ahead there was a junction of three roads.
Already there you were on a hill and, turning, you could
see the road by which you had ascended flicking back
between the steepsloping banks to the town, visible now
as a jigsaw of roofs, the road leading to it like a trail of salt
spilled idly between the hills indicative exactly of the sort
of place you would find at the end of the saltlike trail, the
very manner of its spilling somehow faintly presaging the
destination to which in due time you would come. As if
the signpost, standing with gibbetlike angularity at the
road junction gave written inventory below the single word
and figure HARTNEY 3 of all that might be found in the
town.

It was this that Laurie remembered : that there was no
single surprise ever to be found in the town ; at whatever
day or hour one went there was always an apathy without
solution, an awaiting ; strangers coming to the place
thought that they had been there before ; it was a con-
densation and typification of a hundred other towns, without individuality or style or architecture : a sprawl among
the green hills. It had sprung funguswise from a hamlet
which had long ceased to be its nucleus and now was spread
like a jilted and outflung overflowing at the edge of gray
and red and green roofs, looking at a High Street that fifty
years ago had been a lane edged with black- and elder-
berry, and the grim barnlike façade of the Baptist Chapel.

" Amazin' how it's grown ", the man said. He looped

the reins over the brakepedal. Beyond his faded pellucid eyes floated some recollection upon which he smiled. " I mind the day when there was naught there but a string o' cottages an' a Post Office. Mist' Arnold Katesgrove's certainly done a multitude of good to Hartney. A church, a school, a chain of shops—"

" You come from Hartney ? "

" No ", the old man said. " But I seen it grow. You come from hereabouts ? "

" Hartney Fold ", Laurie said.

The man looked at him without surprise. " A showfer, I dessay. You've summat to do there ".

" Yes. I've summat to do there ".

The cart rattled away down the right-hand road. The sky was uniformy gray now : no hint of summer was present in its flat screenlike depthlessness. A distant train crossed the valley drawing the eye to earth and all that was left to indicate the musing season of sun and life : the trees and flower-scattered hedgerows already whispering under the caress and burden of autumn.

From here, as Laurie turned into the avenue of beeches, there was an increasing familiarity : as one who, listening to well-loved music comes with each phrase and cadence and unravelling of melody to that emotional climax to which the music, note by note, has taken him.

With inward cynical bemusement he thought of Arnold reading the telegram : the Levantine ivory-dry and waxen-pallid face absorbing guilt and terror as the blood drained from its paleness. *It ought to have been a winged messenger instead of a telegram-boy*, he thought ; *some Mercury bearing with outriders and trumpeted fanfare a scroll from which he read in a voice of thunderous brass a denouncement and accusation and followed the strident tones of voice and trumpet with a volley of leadtipped arrows spun from taut and golden bows, the arrows sinking with barbed and accurate vindication into the soft pale useless flesh yet leaving no death but only the horror and anticipation of pain and death never to come but to linger a breath outside knowledge and pain forever.* Yes, he thought, that would be too good for you, my brother. He thought with sudden infinite regret that apart from butchery and similar unpleasant methods there were few deaths suited in the circumstances. He possessed no weapon nor any knowledge of the infliction of death beyond crude and repulsive butcheries. He had not till this moment considered plan or method. Even now he did not consider any plan. It had not occurred to him that Arnold might have flown. If it had he would not have worried or cared. *It is now a matter of time—of second mounting upon second to the ultimate moment of the journey.*

And the mounting seconds brought his feet now to that spot where through the glinting trees he could see the outline of the house, dark from where he stood, for it also was fringed with trees, poplars standing erect and unswept about the laurels and yews that bordered drive and entrance.

Confirming memory the wide green gate swung back over the gravelled drive, hinges shiny with oil, the gate perfectly hung, opening to the touch, the name engraved on the topmost bar, carved into the wood and filled with gold-leaf, the letters gleaming with their own quality of lustre : HARTNEY FOLD. Farther on, round the curve of the round clipped yew he could just see the other exactly similar gate at the far end of the drive ; and, as he walked on to the golden gravel each particle of which had that appearance of being new-washed, the house stood before him with the precision of a cutout silhouette dropped immediately into place in the blank page in memory. Yes, he thought : the same (though he had expected no difference), and looked immediately upward to the tiny gable and curtainless window that shone with slanted darkness at once familiar to the point of immediacy—as if he had just left the room and come down into the garden to depart and looked up at the window with compassion for the lonely room and the two or three silent pieces of furniture.

There was no movement. The house lay quiet and stark, glooming under the haze of autumn. Then suddenly there was movement. Behind the tall stained window above the entrance-door Laurie saw a figure move slowly downward and across the squares and segments of bright glass, moving in diagonal silhouette without apparent movement of limb or trunk, like a figure on an escalator. And at once he thought : Elspeth : because of some secret and inherent stamp of posture or stance whose individuality was perceptible even through the thick coloured glass and with only that motionless gliding downward movement that took her from his vision almost before the thought entered his head, even though she moved slowly (as he remembered) having neither need nor ability for haste ; thinking that in a moment he would see the embodiment of that motionless yet moving shadow and wondering with sudden shaft of oblique cynicism : I wonder if she will drop dead with shock ?

But it was not she to whom he could say when the door opened inward like a crooked smile : I am Laurie ; remember ? I am come. For he had momentarily forgotten that in this house there were servants ; and it was with equally momentary surprise that the door's crooked grin leered open not upon Elspeth, whose thin dry form was for the moment the subject and expectation of eye and brain, but upon the immaculate tail-coated and striped-trousered (but nevertheless senile) figure of Manning, major-domo and /or (according to education and outlook) head cook and bottlewasher. But already the words were half spoken.

"I am La—"

Manning bowed, a movement related to bowing only by suggestion. He was old, with that livid lifelessness of a waxwork that Savile Row tailors have dressed. He was beginning to close the door. " You are Mr. Laurie. I regret, sir, my instructions were, when you went from this house, that you were never to be admitted again," saying the words with the exact intonation of un-surprise, almost as though Laurie had left the day before and was expected back in defiance of banishment and for whom therefore words must be prepared, firm and polite, but leaving no doubt as to their authority.

" That's all right ", Laurie said. He pushed past Manning, not with any air of defiance, but with undoubted authority, as though in the instant of his entrance some reversal of superiority had occurred. " The conditions on which you were given those orders are rendered null and void. As from Thursday ", speaking with the cynical cocksureness of a newsman in a cheap flick. " Tell Elspeth I am here. Or Christine ", he added.

He went straight forward, dropping the suitcase in the single movement of stride and turn, opening the heavy panelled door of the lounge.

It was the same. Just as the house had fallen into the compartment of preconceived knowledge in his mind, so did this room with its chintzes and wide fireplace, the crossed spears and Morocco daggers fixed in inviolate and impotent possession of death to the walls, the beaten brass gong and the hunting prints, and the intricate glass-cased mechanism of the 365-day clock.

He did not sit down : he stood at the fireplace looking across at the door. Standing in the creased and sleepworn suit in the pocket of which only the fine linen handkerchief with the silkwove initials made any attempt at luxury, or decency even, and the shoes still raindulled, smoothing back with one hand the rumpled dark hair that he thought of with annoyance as being uncovered since his departure.

And suddenly, from somewhere deep in the house came a smell of food, bringing with it the memory of hunger. There were apples in a silver bowl on the table. He took one and ate it, quickly, with no assuagement of hunger. Then, from without the door he heard the soft bodiless foot-falls of women and watched the door open inward toward him revealing the dark straight spaces of the hall and, now, within the room, the two withered and twiglike women who faced him across the tickless and timeless annunciation of a moment of reckoning.

"You've come back, then? In spite of what father said——"

It was Elspeth who spoke, with that same quality of expectation and apparent ignorance of any passage of time with which Manning had spoken ; as if, at the moment of Laurie's departure his return had been anticipated with rehearsed words and gestures pondered and pondered from day to day during the mounting years of his absence, ready at any time of day or night for his appearance, cherished and thought on with malicious joy and spoken now with all the years' accumulated spite, certain in their pronouncement of effect. Yet she spoke too with some revelation of fear, as if from the sapless husk of her body she had updelved some spark of determination, steeling herself by virtue of the knowledge that with Arnold away she must not weaken.

"—In spite of what Father said—"

He turned away, but he could still see them in thought : thin dry women wearing gray gowns and cashmere wraps.

"I suppose it wasn't enough to drag Father's name through mud. For you, it wouldn't have been enough to know everyone treated him with derision as well as pity when they knew—" Christine came into the room.

It was she who spoke now. She sat at the table, but it was as if she could not bear to be below his height, even though he was not looking at her. She rose. She was not a tall woman but she invested the movement with some degree of authority. " Even though he paid for your education—" she paused again in mid-sentence. He still did not turn to meet her anger, which was dry and bloodless as if it too had shrivelled within the clothes and suppressions of years. " Even though he certainly fed you and, in all probability, your—your—lover ".

" Shut up ", Laurie said. " Shut up ".

In the cool silent room the three stood mute : the two be-shawled women quite still, thin dry lips parted, even the rustle of their gray silk gowns suspended ; and,

" Shut up ", Laurie said again, the words bitter with narrow-eyed and purposeful fury. And as if the two women had been blade-pierced by the words they remained silent. " O yes ", he said. Fury had died from his voice now. He came toward them, round the table. It seemed that they shrank a little from him, though there was no actual movement. " Yes. You can use a word that means nothing to you except a definition in a dictionary. You can use it about a girl you never even heard of except by name. Maybe you read it in a library book ? What are you reading now ? " he said. " Marie Corelli ? " He was remembering the red-bound moralizing, the Hall Caines, the Charles Garvices. " Yes. That is the word you'd use ". He turned away, toward the window. " Freda ", he said quietly. " You remember Freda . . . no, you can't remember her. You never knew. But you knew I married her, didn't you ? And that Father— Arnold—it doesn't matter who—forbade me the house because of it. Yes. I think you remember that all right. Your disappointment shows in your face ".

" Disappointment ? "

" That I didn't come back and beg to be let in. Like a slinking cat. You'd have enjoyed that—you, Christine, Elspeth. Wouldn't you ? "

" What's that to do with—"

" —with coming back now ? " Elspeth said. She was thinking, If only Arnold were here ; it needs a man to deal with a man. She could feel her heart, fast. At my age, the thought, such a shock. . . .

" Ah. You want to know the reason. You want to know why I've come back now. Isn't that it ? I can tell you that ", he said. He half turned. They could see his eyes, tender, smiling a little. Then not smiling : hard, cold. Involuntarily the two women pulled their wraps closer. " No ", he said. " There isn't any need for me to tell you why I've come back. I could've sent you a post-card ", he said. " You'd have known just the same. But you wouldn't have known what you'll know before I go ". It was as if he had forgotten what he had started to tell them ; then as if he suddenly remembered, " Freda's dead ", he said.

Outside, afternoon sunlight fell aslant the garden.

Dead. Thinking, There are those in whom some faith has reached such proportions that intimate immortality ; in whom is gladness that their beloved has at last passed to those sightless regions in which faith may be tested. I am not of these, he thought : I trail no clouds of glory. The rose is blown, its glory gone. Tomorrow has become today. Not for me the protestations of belief. Remembering her, he said :

" Yes. Dead. Where is Arnold ? "

Christine said : " You will never find Arnold here on Saturday at this time ". If only he were here, she thought. In the pocket of her dress her fingers enclosed one of her pieces of jade. It was cold to her touch. It was always cold. But there was no comfort in its texture now. " If you'd lived here . . . it was your right to live here until you chose to live with—"

" Marry ", he said. " I married her. Didn't you know that ? Didn't you believe it ? "

" If you'd stayed here ", she said, " you'd have known that Arnold always goes away on Saturdays. You'd have known he visits Mr Nollys in—"

" Nollys ? Who the hell is Nollys ? " he said.

" A friend of Arnold's ", Elspeth said. There was a timid delight for her in telling this, as if, even though he had come for some nefarious purpose (neither of them doubted it) he must rely on them for information. She was seated on a spindly chair of dark mahogany that seemed by its very construction to be matched to her fragility. " Naturally you wouldn't know him. We are in Arnold's confidence ", she said, and Christine added :

" Mr Nollys sent me one of my finest pieces of jade as a gift ". (From its coldness now she seemed to gather some strength, as if she knew what he was about to say.)

Laurie crossed to the door. His hands were pushed into the soiled jacket pockets. " You'll want to know—pleased or otherwise—that Hartney Fold is now mine. Mine ", he said, and could see that the import of the words had not yet touched them. " Because Freda is dead. I was kept out—cut off—whatever you like—while she was alive. P'raps you'll want to see proof of that—that she is dead. Here ". He took from the pocket a folded paper. He opened it. It was printed in pink and bore a stamp and a florid signature. He threw it on the table. " A death certificate. You may never have seen one. But you've got no need to worry ", he said. " I wouldn't live in this place now if the world was a wilderness. Christ found a home in the wilderness. No doubt I can do the same—"

Their indrawn breath was sharp in the silent room.

" —that makes you suck your hollow cheeks, doesn't it ?

To take the Name you've lived and sheltered in all your lives ".

" Blasphemer ", Elspeth said.

He shrugged. " You're too useless for me to bother about.   Arnold, on the other hand, needs a lot of attention. From me.   From me *for* others.   He isn't useless : he's evil.   Yes.   O yes, you can look in his life and smile ; you can sit there in shawls and ignorance and look appalled ; but it doesn't alter the fact ".

After a moment he said : " I'm going up to Arnold's room ".

He turned from the room leaving Elspeth and Christine sitting in the chairs like mutes.   He had spoken in a metallic tone that seemed unanswerable.   And now they were left alone in the room.   " If only Arnold were here ", Christine said, at last aloud ; and across the trembling silence of the room she heard her sister say, " Yes, If only Arnold were here.   But it's not Arnold.   It's Laurie ".

He mounted with single purpose to the room.   It was empty now.   Bourne was below in the kitchen, stretched in a chair, sleeping.   The room was like an empty stage, waiting, after the curtain's rise, for the entrance of whoever was to start the play.   It bore that resemblance in the disposition and tidiness of its properties.   The walls were smooth with the sliding doors of built-in cupboards ; they had the look of smooth efficiency, that they would open with a touch.   Laurie crossed and slid them open, one by one : clothes—twenty-seven suits (he counted them idly), disposed in order of shade and design, linen in glassfronted drawers—day-shirts, sports-shirts, dress-shirts, underlinen in neat pressed piles.   Without conscious expression or anger (actually he was smiling) Laurie took a silk undergarment from one of the piles.   Bending, he glossed it over one of his dulled shoes, not with any real attempt to polish the leather, but rather as a gesture of which in normal

circumstances he would be incapable ; though even now, as
he tossed the soiled garment aside he was aware of no conscious contempt by playacting.

In a corner was an open bureau : neatly docketed letters
from churches and social organizations, receipts for subscriptions, a photograph of a group of boy scouts, appeals,
a checkbook with stubs made out to church and temperence
causes.   He picked each item up separately, thinking, This
is what he wants people to see.

On the other wall the sliding doors were locked.   The bed
was a peninsula of sprung and feathered luxury between the
fastened doors.   Turning back the covers Laurie saw a
wedge of silk sheets, pillows monogrammed in yellow silk.
Above the bed at the exactly correct angle a readinglamp
was secured to an extending arm ; on a table at its side
was a photograph of Christine and Elspeth, beside it a pill-
box labelled BISMUTH TABLETS and a Morocco dagger
companion to those on the lounge walls.

The room was ostentatious, sensual.   To it clung, without visible or even tangible evidence, the effluvium and
definitive quality of lewdness : as of some recent nympho-
maniac orgy.   There were three etchings of cathedrals and
some mural diaglyphs of religious subjects : nothing else
pictorial.   Only the soiled silk undergarment lay in a
corner like a smudge on the room's bland innocence.   But
there is a smell, he thought, a stench of rotting and garbage
thoughts.

With neither passion nor attempt at concealment he
picked up the ornate dagger and levered at the locked doors.
They flicked open.

If he had listened he would have heard the faint and
surreptitious approach of the two women, would perhaps
have known by acknowledgment in thought if not in word
or greeting that they had entered the room.   As it was he
knew without knowing : like this *There, my brother, behind*

*these doors lies all that you would conceal, that, with due and
sufficient warning you would have suppressed or destroyed as
the General of a retreating army orders the destruction of all
documents, but which, lacking that due warning* How he
must have trembled, he thought, when he knew I was coming here *you must perforce abandon and leave to my perusal
and that of your beloved sisters who are surely here at this
moment to see and understand something they can neither
understand nor believe* thinking this as it were with cynical
wishfulness, but beyond all conscious thought reasoning and
knowledge and looking suddenly toward the door and seeing
them standing there, as from a dream of great rarity one
may sometimes wake to know with certainty and pre-
knowledge the nature and consequence of all one's relevant
actions.

" So you not only come here with the definite intent to do
evil—"

" —but before you're in the house five minutes you're
already robbing like a common housebreaker ".

" Interfering with Arnold's most precious possessions—"

" His books—"

" His first editions—"

" Even we are forbidden to touch them ", Christine said.
They were standing in the doorway.   They had entered and
stood exactly like shadows, with the same lack of dimension.   Their thin harsh voices too were bodiless in that
same way.   They watched him, wondering.   There was
terror in their wonder.

Beyond the closed windows the afternoon lay dormant.
Nothing had moved.   Then suddenly Laurie began to
take books from the revealed shelves.   They were thin
sumptuous copies monogrammed in gold.   He tossed
them one by one on to the bed where they lay with leaves
outsplayed.   He no more than glanced at them.   He said :

" Pretty, aren't they ? But not quite what you expected,

are they? Are they?" he asked again. He turned holding in his hand a thick book he had taken from the lower shelves. "In German. This is quite a noted work on eroticism. But brother Arnold has had it translated for his own pleasure—even to the most obscene words". In a thick gold-edged album were photographs. The two women could see them; yet they still could not believe what they saw. Laurie went on: "But of course Arnold is heavily engaged in welfare work for young people: he must have some reading for his moments of relaxation". Behind the books was a bundle of letters—receipted accounts for the rent of a flat in Mayfair. "Shepherd Market", Laurie said. "Arnold flies high". He took one of the bills and cut off the portion bearing the printed address. He cut it carefully with the gilded dagger; then he slipped both blade and paper into his pocket.

The two women watched him, saying nothing. They still said nothing as he came round the bed toward them. They seemed to stand entranced. But Elspeth was thinking now of Arnold, wondering where he was. "Ahhhhhh," she said. Quite suddenly she sat down on the bed. There must be something, some explanation, in a minute she would think of it. "I know", she said. "He has taken them from—from—"

"Yes?" He had stopped at the tallboy and pulled open one of the drawers. "Maybe he's taken them from the Boys' Brigade library so they shouldn't blacken the boys' minds? That's what you'd like to think, isn't it?"

"I can't think," Elspeth said. "It's so—"

"Of course there's a reason, Elspeth", Christine said. She was thinking of the opportunity given her now to be strong. She was thinking that at last someone depended on her, someone was listening to what she had to say. And there was nothing to say but what she knew Elspeth expected her to say. "Arnold would hardly be likely to

tell us about such things, where he found them . . .
why . . ."

" No ", he said. " You're right there ". The cashbox
lay on the top in the drawer with the five pound notes in
loose disarray. He pocketed the notes, slipping them into
the breast pocket behind the embroidered handkerchief.
Then he stood between the two women.

" Why don't you ring for Bourne ? " he said. " For
Manning ? " He looked at the books on the bed. The
album of photographs lay open. " For the Minister of the
Baptist Chapel even. No doubt he'd be interested to see
Arnold's collection ". He smiled as he saw Christine's
hand move toward the bell-push. He smiled as he saw her
think, No ; what am I thinking of ? this is something I
—we— must bear alone. She was thinking too, In the
morning he will be back ; there is only one thing to say, to
do—what Arnold would wish. What would he wish ? she
thought. And strangely then the thought of death
flickered in her mind : as if Laurie's purpose had been laid
bare before them. Looking at Elspeth she thought *She
knows too. There is nothing we can do.* And she did not
speak. Perhaps it was not necessary. Perhaps she knew
even then that there was no word or deed of theirs that
could alter the course of events which, without either statement or inference of speech they knew to be implicit—by
his very gesture or stance, perhaps by the subtle implication as he slipped the blade into his pocket the while he
tossed the excreta of Arnold's mind upon the silk covers
of the bed. Anyway, they knew ; also knew, without
yet being able to believe it, that about Arnold which was
too monstrous to believe.

" What are you going to do ? " Elspeth said. It was as
if someone had told her she too was about to die.
" Arnold. . . ."

" Do ? " he said. " Do ? " He passed them and they

watched him, heard him as he strode quickly toward the stairs. " I'm going to find Arnold and pay him for my education. I suppose he'll expect payment. He always does. No doubt he'll be prepared— " But now his voice had faded to silence—a silence heavy and ominous with threat, a silence into which presently fell the mark of his departure : a softly closing door, a footfall close on the gravel, descending into the mist and presence of horror as the two sisters stood listening dumbly to the dying footsteps of him who went in pursuit, standing in the complete revelation and recognition of guilt and death, standing in the omniscience and false luxury of the bedroom and the waning minutes of time. The waning minutes of time.

PART TWO

6

NOW it was late afternoon. In the waning light of summer Laurie arrived at Waterloo Station. He strode forth under the vast gaunt dome of curved and dirtied luminosity that is not light nor indeed anything resembling light but is, rather, the lessening of the years' scum and filth by the thousand star-scattered light-bulbs that bloom in symbolic and useless profusion.

He had changed the first of the banknotes when buying his ticket at Hartney station. The same youthful porter who had set free the pigeons did duty now as clerk, cloak-room attendant and adviser of the hour and destinations of trains.

" Ah. You found the Fold okay then ? "

" Yes," Laurie said. " I found it. Now I want to lose it. London ", he said.

" You want a single or a return ? "

" A re—No. A single. There'll be no need for me to come back ".

" Please yourself. It's one-an'-three-'apence difference. If you don't get it now an' you want to come back it'll cost you one-an'-three-'apence more. With the cheap day tickets—"

" Thanks ", Laurie said. " I know what I want to do. I know I don't want to come back here. I'll deposit this suitcase, though ".

" Well, if you don't want to come back—"

" All the same, I'll leave the case ".

The porter, now beyond the wire grille of the ticket window, shrugged. " Well, I suppose you know what you're—"

" That's right ", Laurie said. " Where do I leave it ? "

" Cloakroom. The door over there ".

And it was the same dusty youth, his chin flowing back to the grim knotted tie who emerged from the office with its serried rows of green pink and white tickets and crossed the dank and dusty hall to the advertisement-plastered flap that, unlocked and squeak-hinged, made a counter across which in observance of regulation this that or the other the case was passed and examined and a grudgingly- and laboriously-written receipt tendered.

" If you aren't coming back I still don't see—"

" Don't you worry ", Laurie said. He thrust the slip of paper into the pocket from which he had earlier produced the scrawl-signed death certificate that only at this moment he remembered having left on the lounge table. " If I never come back for it you can take it to the police and with your own hands produce the woman's limbs that are carefully packed inside. Mind the blood ", he said as the porter took the case and plastered it with the duplicate of the label. " What time's the next to London ? "

The porter held the case suspended above the ground for a moment in horror—just an inch, as though by the profound simplicity of the suggestion he had been convinced and frozen. Then he dropped it, suddenly, without ever once smiling or altering the dumb and vacant expression of his narrow chinless face. " Enquiries ? That'll be across at the Booking Office ", and he pointed back across the hall to the grille behind which, after the ceremony of uphinging and locking the cloakroom flap, he reappeared in due time, having stopped on the way across the three or four intervening yards of space to look from the door up and down the long gleaming rails, not in apprehension or expectation of any train but, apparently, in order to encompass some subtle change in identity before he could appear with satisfactory demeanour for the purpose of answering enquiries re trains.

" Five-eighteen.   Stops at Bret Park, Holt Castle, Raymondsworth, Sunnymede—"

" Yes ", Laurie said.   " Does it stop at Waterloo ? "

" Ah.   It's got to stop there.   You see, it's a termin—"

" No ", Laurie said.   " No.   You're fooling me ".

He went out on to the platform.   It was four-fifty then. When did I eat ? he thought ; and couldn't remember.   It became suddenly necessary that he remember—not the actual impact of food on tongue and palate but the mere occasion even, so that in the recollection there might be conviction that for many hours yet he would not faint or grow giddy with hunger.   Yesterday, yesterday, yesterday ? and with all the yesterdays slithering backward through memory with the blurred likeness to white palings speeding backward through darkness he came *My sweet tooth* at some appointed hour to a table over which he was just tall enough to peer, to see clustered and gleaming upon the damask all those bowls plates and dishes forbidden with dry and dire threat and in voice in which he was yet too young to be aware that there lingered the breath and invitation of disobedience.

That was at Arnold's party.   Arnold was twenty-one. It was the day on which Arnold, having become by convention and presentation of paraphernalia and legerdermain, a man, imbued Laurie, who was to remain unaware of the fact until he himself had come almost to manhood, with the spirit of wonder and fearful defiance that marked the change from infancy to childhood.

He was three ; that age tender and sexless in which

influence predominantly feminine has had that effect of emasculation resulting in woman-clinging, parrot-like imitation of women's inane and gurgling cries less childlike than any child's have ever been, and womansmelling—as though in prophesy of lifelong feminity. Only with him there was no woman. Unless you could call Mrs Stranks and Elspeth and Christine women. Mrs Stranks who from the moment of her arrival and in the solitude of her scrubbing of floor yard and closet—a solitude broken only by the presence of the child, of whom she could not have taken less notice if he had been non-existent—would talk and mutter to herself all the obscenities of the gutter from which she must have been dragged—a narrative eternal, remorseless, without beginning or end, concerned only with that obscure past from which she must have come, though she seemed possessed of neither past nor future. It was of course Christine and Elspeth who (as they said) made themselves responsible for his care ; but they, even at that teen-age in which girls are normally full of gawks and giggles, were in many ways less feminine even than Mrs Stranks. They kept him clean, took him from and put him to bed, fed him and attended with maniac insistence to his religious education— even at that age when good and evil were merely embryonic qualities inexplicable and at times unattainable ; and sin hell and damnation were completely meaningless.

So when, on that day on which he was to attain certain knowledge that he was later to know as childhood, he peered over the edge of the table and saw the jellies and whipped cream lying there in solitude bereft of ownership or invitation he was only supplying the immediate needs of salivation. Right or wrong did not enter his thoughts. He began immediately to eat the jelly, holding it close to his face and sucking it into his mouth with tongue and teeth, quickly—perhaps because even at that age there may have been some deep and unrealized knowledge of crime and punishment. But not quickly enough : for before he had swallowed a twentieth of the anticipated quantity he already felt the shock and surprise of a blow that made him spew back the half-swallowed jelly into the bowl and look up with momentary tearless wonder—like the penultimate breath before birth—into the face of Arnold.

Then, after that immense suspension of breath, he began to cry, to scream in pain as the realization of the blow bit through to his nerves and he saw through the haze of tears Arnold's raised arm prepared to strike again.

" That — will — teach — you — perhaps — to — treat — what — doesn't — belong — to — you —"

But by then he was insensible—he was aware only of the alternation of meaningless words and painmeaning blows up to the time when he at last collapsed like a stricken animal, needing only that solitude of isolation to bring to fruition the knowledge he had gained. He was only three, but on that day he learned the first fact of life, cruelty : accepting it after the first revolt of pain as something whose recurrence would be as automatic as food sleep or light.

He was locked in the bedroom *the tiny gable and curtainless window that shone with slanted darkness* not, he was told, as punishment—for punishment had already been dealt out to him by Arnold's flying and brutal arm— but to give him pause to ponder and seek forgiveness : a pause that was to follow him even to manhood, to that age when he came at last fully to realize that his soul's awakening was not really what they sought, but merely his soul's humiliation.

It was his father who came to the room to see him. Felix Katesgrove was a man with an everlasting odour of decay about him. He wore black—black snuffstained suits, a black knitted tie threadbare with the knots of years — his eyes dim and damp with the unshed tears of the world's wickedness. He cringed still to the memory of his first wife—a woman he had ensnared with a gaudy printed religious tract, and from whom he inherited no less than the house and seven acres of Hartney Fold, a marital relationship of passionless but convinced submission and, on her death three years later (from pneumonia contracted while trying to sell the idea of Souls washed in the Blood to stevedores of East India Dock), an inheritance of thirty-four thousand pounds. The money was too great a temptation for his fanaticism. He floated a company to print and distribute the gospels. Within five years he had doubled his outlay. When he married Esther Coulter he had some underlying hope that history would repeat itself. He had ensnared his first wife with the certainty of redemption. He thought it would work again. But she was too strongly bound to the streets from which he had, as he termed it, rescued her.

When Felix Katesgrove came into the room it was evening. From deep within the house—and so faintly that they might have been on another planet—came the noises of the party. The child lay on the cot—not asleep, but apparently so, for that very day he had learned deception. The man stood in the open doorway, pausing a moment as if within his secret self lay some scruple or doubt. Behind and below him the mutter of noise rose and drifted. He carried in his hand a candle, for he would not permit the gas being wasted in any room not actually in use, and the flame, like a squat lemon worm, thrust back the long smudge of his shadow on to the bare scrubbed floor beyond the door. He stood thus for a moment, the threadbare frockcoat worn grudgingly over the years falling loose about his thighs, like the drapes in some empty room moving without sound at the chill wind's touch. Then he came into the room, his foot pressing a loose board, and stood over the child's cot. As he stood there the candle swealed brightly and the room was unfolded from the petals of light.

Till then the child had kept his eyes fast closed. Now he knew it was useless. He opened them, looking up at his father with neither invitation nor fear for so long as he could look into the leaping and guttering source of light. Then he turned away toward the wall. As if the man too were uncertain he turned away from the cot, placing the candle on the chest of drawers which, with the cot and the table, were the sole furnishings of the room.

Then he sat down on the caneseated chair, balanced precisely on the frame, leaning slightly forward away from the downblooming of light, his hands a twin glim on the dark shiny serge,—leaning forward toward the still and unexpectant child with that resemblance to wraith or cadaver enhanced and typified by the shroud of light as, now ceaselessly, as if with a brief unfettering of speech he must say some certain quantity of words, he began to speak : speaking not as to a child but as to a full grown man :

" You are here, in solitary confinement, as you should know, because you have committed a sin :—a sin that is beyond the pale not only of recognized convention but is —far worse—heinous in the sight of the Lord.

" You have stolen. You are a thief. That would be heinous enough if your motive had been good : but it was greed : the mere carnal satisfaction of your belly's lust for food. Tell me—you can speak with perfect truth if the canker of the liar as well as the thief has not already grown in your mind— are you ever hungry ? "

The man paused for a moment and it may have seemed to the child that his voice had perhaps been lost among the shadows, for he watched with widened eyes toward the

3

flamewashed walls. Anyway, he spoke no word of comprehension or acknowledgement and in a moment the man
said again, " Well, are you ? " and this time the child,
divining knowledge of the question without having understood one word of what the man had said, shook his head.

" No. Which leaves me some hope that the flame of
Ananias has not yet been kindled in you.

" But the absence of one sin does not outweigh the
presence of another ; nor does the birth and life of one
God-inspired son outweigh the faults of a child of the
devil.

" Arnold your stepbrother has from the day of his birth
been an example and shining light in the dark days that the
Lord has seen fit to utter as my cross. Born of a woman
who gave her very life in the Lord's cause he has been
worthy of her blood and of the Blood of the Lamb.

" It is perhaps your misfortune that you were born of a
woman with the inherent evil of the harlot—a woman
whom even my prayers and protestations could not prevent
sinking back to the bed of depravity from which I had
dragged her. But that that misfortune should be your un-
doing I have not any intention of permitting. I will first
see you scourged—as in his wisdom Arnold saw fit to
scourge you this afternoon when he caught you in the midst
of your greed and theft. But that is not sufficient. Two
more requirements are the composite of every sin : contemplation and forgiveness. That is why you have been
shut in this room, alone, for five hours ".

The voice ceased now, without finality or cadence, as
though in that space of time that had now elapsed that
certain number of words scheduled for that time had been
spoken and there was now due a pause that was like a suspension not only of speech but of time also. Then at once
the voice began again, still in mid-cadence and without
apparent intake of breath, side-flickered by the bare

windows' reflection of the candle's yellow leap, steady and toneless, bare as the room's inscrutable shadows.

" So now the opportunity if not the intelligence has been given you to contemplate your sin. There remains only its absolution. For that purpose I am going to teach you —I hope, though there is violent doubt within me—for the first and last time—how to pray for forgiveness. Get from that bed to your knees on the floor ".

The father now loomed high over the child, cruciform— as was his wavering shadow on the wall, so that for an instant during which the shadow remained still there was no token by which to distinguish man and shadow, and the child lay looking up with the hot bright eyes of fearful wonder waiting for whatever punishment was to come.

" Get up ", the man said ; and took the child from the cot and stood him beside it. " Now get down on your knees as your stepsisters and brother and father have taught you ".

The man knelt then and began to speak, but in a voice now hushed with awe, his hands suppliantly clasped and mimicked in monster and leering skiagraph upon the wall.

" O Lord forgive this child its wickedness, open thou thy heart to my supplications on its behalf, make clean the heart and mind within the opening flesh, show clear the path of righteousness to thy paradise awaiting all men who live in the style and likeness of thy teaching. Grant this child repentance and humility and the knowledge and love of thy goodness and its imitation here on earth at all times and in all places. For thy dear Name's sake. Amen.

" Now get up off your knees ", he said ; " and go and find your stepbrother and ask *his* forgiveness. It was he whom you wronged. Go ", he said.

So then the child went down in search of the only person he knew to whom he could look for comfort. But at that hour of the day she had long departed. In the dark stone scullery he stood calling her name. It was dark but he was certain that in a moment he would hear her come, clatter and clang of mop and bucket. He stood calling her in the darkness again and again. But it was Arnold who stood presently in the doorspace, beyond which, through an endless succession of darkened rooms gleamed the pale light of the lounge, shadow-crossed by the moving guests.

"Stop making that row", he said. "Why are you calling Mrs. Stranks? Is that what Father told you to do?" he said. He was leaning backward into the distant light like a snake preparing to strike. Then he curved forward and picked up the child. "Did he,? did he?" His voice too was snakelike.

"Forgive", the child screamed. "Forgive! forgive! forgive!—"

That was in the evening of the day on which the child stole the jelly from the table. It was February. By summer the flower of fear had bloomed in his heart; but in winter it died, furling close to the bare stem of contempt. Because:

In the hours in which he was permitted to turn from the catechism and gaudy illustrated parables he amused himself among the weedstrewn acres of Hartney Fold. There was a grove of young oaks standing in what appeared to be complete abnegation of all that was enacted beneath their now gaunt and lacelike branches. Here the child became for those granted hours of pleasure giant, hero and prince— all those characters of whose existence he was aware not from any normal method of perusal of illustrated fairy stories but from the few sentences addressed solely to him by the erstwhile obscene charwoman. The rest he filled in by imagination, mixing character and incident to form one great phantasmagoria in which and to which he escaped in his daily revels beneath the oaks.

One day, concealed among the scrub he heard footsteps approaching. He had then learned the value of deception and he remained hidden—not because he was afraid of punishment but because he knew he would be forbidden to visit the spot again, not by word or threat, but by extra catechism and prayers. He crouched within the bush. He could not see out but after a while the voices became loud and he knew it was Arnold and Mrs Stranks. He did not think it strange : there was no reason known to a child of that age why they should not walk and talk together. Inside the bush he tightened his body. Thorns pierced his skin but he kept silent. He knew that was the ultimate need of the moment if he was to keep secret his lair. He heard the voices grow louder, coming toward him like a threat.

" —here's the place. Nobody could see us now from the house, even with a telescope. Where are they ? "

He heard them stop right beside him, so close that their bodies were like a curtain drawn across the interstices of light.

" I got 'em in mi stockin' ", the woman said. " Look the other way, can't you ? Yer Father'd—"

" Never mind about him. Where's the photos ? "

" Wait, can't you ? Wait . . . ? "

Beyond the screen of latticed light and darkness rose the scuffle and mutter of finger-smirched flesh, the small intrinsic noises of a mock struggle.

" Arnold. Stop it, can't you. You are—" then the soft impingement of hand on cheek.

" You bitch. Hand them over. Or do you want me to tell Father just what he'd like to know about Lily Stranks

—that Lily's no right name for you, for instance.   Do you want me to tell him that ?   Do you ? "

" All right ", the woman said.   " All right.   I'm only teasing you, Arnold.   You know—"

" I know ", he said.   " Where are those photos ? "

" Here.   Can't you— "

Silence then ; and after a few minutes Arnold laughing softly.   " Christ, they're good.   Where did you get these— London ? "

" They're   French ",   she   said ;   " genu-ine.   I   got 'em—"

" Never mind.   My God, look at that one—"

In his hiding place the child could hear them both laughing now, not with any amusement but with that serpentine quality of infamy kept apparently for this or similar moments ; so that in that instant the child's hate and fear of Arnold died, furling its moribund fronds away from the newblown flower of contempt.   Without understanding one iota of the conversation or purpose of their meeting he knew now that he never need fear Arnold again, that indeed *he* held the instrument of fear and was no longer its subject—knowing this with neither knowledge nor understanding of its use : yet aware that in due time and place that knowledge and understanding would be given to him : aware of all this in his child mind in the fleeting instant wherein was enacted beyond the spaces of light between the twigs of the bush the first breath of that snakelike laughter of lewdness.

" Christ, yes.   Can't you imagine— "

Then the woman :   " You'd best let me keep 'em, Arnold.   If your fath—"

" Keep him out of it.   It's only for a while ; he won't be here much. . . ."

" What do you mean ? " she said.

" Never mind.   Give me those photos.   You'll see ".

" You aren't—? "

" No ", he said. " Nothing the old fool doesn't deserve. Fanatical old— All right, I'll take them ", he said.

And the next day it was there too : the memory that meant complete disavowal of fear : the knowledge that, in his awareness of Arnold's deception he, a child eighteen years his stepbrother's junior, held that coronet of fear hitherto encircled about his own head, that it was his to wield as and when he pleased. It did not for an instant occur to him that he was wholly without guile, that speaking of his knowledge would and could lead only to disaster ; he did not think of the way he would wield the palm of fear, he thought only of its power secret within the cloistered depths of his mind, a fact to which he clung and which gave him henceforth the embryo and soil of avengement. It was there : Yesterday, he thought, yesterday I saw Arnold and Mrs Stranks in the wood ; and for days and months it was Yesterday . . . until at last in the darkness and solitude of an endless tunnel of years knowledge and desire grew to fruition in a bright bloom of vengeance made manifest in the green suave shape of an automatic vending machine standing before the child now grown to identity knowledge manhood and grief as he thought *so that in the recollection there might be conviction that for many hours yet he would not faint or grow giddy with hunger* when did I eat ? —having as it were between thought and thought visualized in camera the whole of that incident in which he grew from infancy to childhood, that day on which he learned both pain and duplicity and that other day in which came knowledge and power.

Thinking, Arnold, my brother, your hours are numbered, he looked at the clock's cryptic enigma : four-fifty. Nearly half an hour, he thought.

And now walking beneath the latticed gloom of Waterloo Station amid the seethe of deathless humanity presided

over by the impersonal bodiless voice of the train-announcer
and the plumes and pistons of steam and speed, walking
from the gloomed translucent semidark into the waning
afternoon he came to a small café used by truck- and bus-
drivers. Thinking, I had better eat now, he entered.

Behind the moisture-ringed counter sat a woman
dressed in a stained overall, rising from between the twin
gushes of urn-steam like a genie transformed from nothingness. Behind her in the gloom clatter and effluvium of the
kitchen a man in a once rigid and pleated chef's hat spun
dishes through scumthick water and whirled them quickly
between the folds of a towel to which clung grease and filth.

He sat down at the marble-topped table on which re-
posed the stained askew crockery of a finished meal and
ordered coffee and steak pudding. The woman came and
cleared the table, wiping it off with the corner of her overall.
Around the table's edge, like an heraldic shield's indenture,
were the burnmarks of countless cigarettes. On a shelf
high amid the fumes and flyblown posters a radio played
softly, a song endless endless and enigmatic, a voice un-
nurtured and sexless, like the fading dissolute themesong
of a debauch already dawnflushed and gravebound.

Laurie took from his pocket the packet of cigarettes,
the cellophane wrapping from the chocolate he had eaten in
the train, and the two slips of paper. A tiny breath of
draught blew in suddenly from the whine of traffic's wheels
beyond the open door; the breath fluttered the paper
slips, moving them like blown petals across the burn-
scarred marble; he took the ornate dagger from his pocket
and weighted the slips with it; under the blade's gilt
and glitter the fronds of paper and the cellophane up-
curled. He lit one of the cigarettes and with the match
held delicately between finger and thumb he ignited
the cloakroom ticket at the same instant that he pulled
it from beneath the dagger's blade, watching the slow

creep of flame as it obliterated word and figure in a curling of black ash upon which, ghostwise, remained the faint sheen and indentation of print, shrivelled now and fallen to a black skirmish of dust upon the table as he crushed the ash between his fingers. I will have no further use for that, he thought; nor that. And with another match he ignited now the printed heading he had severed from the receipted bill he found in Arnold's room, watching, with eyes screwed against the drift of smoke slanting across his face, the slow caress of flame and dissolution of words and figures as the paper charred between his fingers: 1A GRANTHAM MEWS, SHEPHERD MARKET, MAY-FAIR, W.1.—conscious now as if the flame had burned the words and figures on to retina and brain that no printed or spoken word could ever be necessary as a reminder of his destination.

From an adjoining table two men watched him. They were bus-drivers, their uniform coats unbuttoned, their caps pushed back from sweatbeaded foreheads. They seemed to consider him with some amusement. He began to eat, slowly yet viciously, as with some remote antagonism against food and feeding: As if he's in a hurry but don't really want to be, the two drivers thought. But it was not that. They sat watching him, jetting smoke from their nostrils, their cigarettes held concealed by their cupped palms and taken from and placed to their nicotine-stained lips with exactly that care and touch they might expend on thin tubes of blown glass. Beyond the open door the clash and clatter of wheel and gearwhine reproduced and amplified in a thousand rushing vehicles mingled with the now fading now blaring sob of the radio and the faint hiss and sibilant bubble of steam and tea within the urns.

Slowly, Laurie ate the food. Without tasting it or being even aware of its nature—whether it was flesh or root—

3*

he felt its warmth and weight settle slowly inside him.
The warm rank coffee ballooned outward through artery
and pore until presently he took the care-folded handkerchief and wiped it gently across his brow, pausing in mid
descent of the now soiled linen to remark again the silkwove initials L.K. and to think, A pardonable vanity, she
did them so beautifully. Then flicking the long cylinder
of ash from the table he turned to the two bus-drivers and
said through the haze and sob of music and traffic-whine :
   " Mayfair. What number bus do I get from here ? "
   Cupping the cigarette away from his face one of the men
told him.
   " Thanks ", Laurie said. He stood now in the doorway,
a pause and suspension of thought activity and progress,
balanced on one of the dulled shoes to one of which clung a
thread of silk, the creased and shapeless suit hung about the
flesh and life which hung for that brief moment poised and
immobile within the fluttering cloth. Then, as if the pause
had been for no other reason than consideration of the overcast sky he stepped into the street even as, behind him, the
twin voices to which he immediately turned sounded from
within the catafalque of radiowhine and urn-bubble :
   " Ain't you forgotten something, mate ? "
   So turning he saw with the immediacy with which he had
heard the voices the gilt blade lying bland and still amid the
cold scummed coffee and the disorder and glitter of chipped
china.
   " O ", he said. " Thanks ". He slipped the blade
point downward into the pocket and, it seemed to the
watching drivers, disappeared at last into the crush beyond
the door with the intent and hope of ultimate destruction,
after he had said once again over his shoulder and integral
with the movement of departure :
   " Thanks. I shall need this ".

7

*You. Sitting there my darling on this westward-rushing
vehicle sitting amid the chaos confusion invective of your mind
heart physical well being (you should never have eaten steak
pudding on an empty stomach : didn't I teach you anything?)
sadly neglected now your Freda (I, I, I, I—you hear me?)
is no longer there to pine in absence to worry in presence to
look after you morning noon and night mind body and estate
your clothes aired your food cooked every mortal thing done
for you and what do you give me in return (One of my natter-
ing moods, this) yes darling yes all right all right : your love :
I know it really but sometimes I choose to forget just for the
sheer damn' pleasure of hearing you remind me like you do,
like this : What the hell? really Freda, I—and you look at
me like the old man of the mountain or something with that
gleam in your eye nearly pompous only then you remember
we live in a suburban terrace (my heart's delight) with folk-
weave curtains and china dogs and things you laughed at
once but don't laugh at now because you've got to like them too.
Always china dogs in my life, Laurie,—not always folk-
weave curtains but always china dogs, sometimes antima-
cassars and always (after most of the china was gone, irre-
placable among the years of depression) a milkbottle and
sardine tin on the table. Before you. Before I'd even
spoken to you except perhaps in that far distant childhood
before anything.*

He listened to her, her voice, presence, ethereal impingement on the smooth blank lakelike and darkened mirror
of his mind as the bus bore him westward amid the clash
and shatter of traffic. 1A GRANTHAM MEWS, SHEP-
HERD MARKET, MAYFAIR, W.1. *You see honey-
bunch that too is only a street* thinking, Perhaps not even a
street, it sounds like one of those stables converted into

flats, reached by a rickety wooden stairway, full of cushions
and bric a *brick gutter and peeling paint, heritage apparently
of a thousand cloistered iniquities : an English village, my
sweet, with everyone not knowing the place saying, How
picturesque, it's growing too—almost a small town now.
Remember ?   Then it actually reached, by status and designation the dignity of township with even a Mayor* The golden
chain of office looped around your neck Arnold my half-
blood brother *when one day there was established even a local
paper The Hartney Herald, remember ? and in the Post
Office appeared that card, royal arms seal and all complete,
the thick black letters inanimate yet livid with that foreboding :
The correct form of address for this Town is . . . the word
bearing the implication of evil—as plainly as if the letters had
been transcribed.*

So it was that passing threadwise through the bright
harsh streets he perceived (but with the perception of
grieving rather than of knowing) those other quiet savage
raindark streets, that house (that house that he came to
know with the familiarity of visitation—broken gutters,
worm, rathole and odour ; but from this session of sweet
silent thought he summed up, dramawise, only the piecemeal remembrances of words and deeds not born of his
own knowledge but of the retailment of others' ; word
sentence and scene—as if he himself had lived the story,
had been cast among the characters, had written with his
own pen dialogue and direction, had conceived in his own
mind pause climax and ultimate close (though here he was
indeed present in the flesh).) that house wherein she had
been conceived born and nurtured ; seeing it with an inward turning of retina upon brain : thus :

Through the somehow peachcoloured haze of the warm
calm afternoon the street straggled between honeysuckled
cottages, an evocation of picture-postcard beauty, smudged
with the smut and soot that clung in the corners and

invisible places, the eternal sooty tears of the brickworks chimney, the dirt and muck that would become suddenly visible beneath the turned back petal of convolvulus or woodbine, that hung in light spatters in each window corner, even though the windows might be cleaned every day, like black forgotten remnants of tangible odour—a breathing over of some breath like that of the fabulous dragon's brimstone. It was like that always ; so that the women of the place came continually on dirt smears in airless corners and stairs' turns. When they had lived there for years they accepted the smoke-blackening, accepting it as they would accept death or injury. It was a slow process of dirtying. They knew they would never be free from it now. So when strangers said—as they often did— that it was a lovely village, so picturesque, so English, they did not even bother to argue, as a child will see neither reason nor sense in arguing with a man speaking of some incomprehensible notion.

There was a single main street running through a cobbled square in which stood a rustblistered pump, derelict since the brickworks had brought water to the village. From the square and the street there were narrow blackwalled lanes and alleys leading off to river quarry and siding, always running between walls on which was neither designation nor indication of destination, but only the tattered stains of moss or ivy and green brassknobbed doors leading to patches of open fallow land wild under torn bushes and windblown weeds.

From the square, looking eastward up the smooth curve of a green hill, Hartney Fold was visible, and part of the thin stringcoloured road unravelling in a long winding flick past station and brickworks, and snipped suddenly by the down-crushed edge of the hill.

It was along this road that the two men came. One of them was Arnold Katesgrove the other an older man—

seemingly middleaged, perhaps because of some quality of grief or loneliness that seemed stamped not only on his features and hair but in the manner of his speech and gait. He was a frail man, and the fact that the sleeve of his patched jacket hung loose did not cause any surprise in the beholder's eye. He seemed so frail that the impression he gave was that the limb might have been snapped off in any high wind or sudden twist or motion. He was dressed in neat patched clothes, no garment matching, so that the effect was slightly bizarre ; even his socks, visible as at each slightly hesitant step his trouser cuffs rode above his too-large shoes, were darned by some apparently un-skilled hand with wool of a contrasting colour. His lean frail face that in twilight or lamplight would bear that translucent quality of taut parchment bore for the moment no expression : he might, but for the steady fixation of his eyes, have been deep in sleep. His name was Albert Thornton.

The other man, Arnold Katesgrove, was younger. He was dressed in dark clothes that might have been made by any good tailor ; his chamois gloves and silver-knobbed cane added no mark of distinction ; face, stride and manner were faintly redolent of a shifting superimposition of repellancy and unaired flesh ; as though he strove consciously to over-throw some ghostwise caress of wanton iniquity. He spoke, a voice profligate and sanctimonious :

" It'll all work out for the best. You see ".

" That's easy to say ". The older man now spoke. " You realize that, I—"

" Of course. But wait till I show you the figures. That's all I ask. Just wait till I show you the figures ".

" Figures ", the other said.

" That's right. Figures can't lie. Not this sort ".

Thornton shrugged faintly. It was impossible to tell what he was thinking. Presently he fumbled in the jacket pocket and found a cigarette. They walked on, silent. After a while he asked the other for a match.

"You know I don't smoke", he said. He added with faint sanctimonious petulance : "A sin. Polluting the air."

"Sin or no sin", Thornton said. He stopped and swung his arm across his body to the other jacket pocket. "Blast". The pocket was empty. The younger man smiled. He was of those to whom malice is wit.

When after a while they came to the village street they had not spoken again. They entered one of the houses, a room clean and dark, smelling faintly of earth and polish, a room through which they passed quickly into another, larger room. Here ribbon-caught curtains hung motionless at an open window beyond which a small yard sheltered a wooden privy and a mass of purpling clematis. Thornton went at once to the kitchen range and lighted his cigarette. The empty sleeve swung forward as if possessed of some motion and desire of its own.

"You know my position". The two men sat now at the small plushcovered table. Between them a potted fern trembled in the disturbed air of their speech. The silver-knobbed cane and chamois gloves lay across the table's corner in comic implication of a photogravure advertisement in a magazine. Katesgrove's forefinger arrowed on a scrap of paper torn from a notebook. "These are the figures. As you see, we both stand to gain a handsome profit within three years. Believe me, if it was all my own money—"

"If it was all your own money you mean you wouldn't hesitate ? "

"Exactly. I wouldn't hesitate for one minute. I mean, I wish it could be all my money. I shouldn't have to share any of the profits then". He smiled, without amusement. His fingers were steepled together. "We have to remember it is our duty as Christians to help one another ".

Thornton got up and walked to the window. The cigarette burned between his fingers, the blue thread of its smoke withdrawn by the heavy motionless air through the open window. " So because your father goes off to China teaching what he's pleased to call heathens, leaving you not enough money for your liking, I'm expected to help ".

Katesgrove rose still smiling. " Haven't you got it rather wrong ? You are not *expected* to help ; you are being given an opportunity of a good investment, which, considering the fact that you will not be able to work again, and considering the fact that you have received a comparatively large sum in compensation for your injury, will be of immense advantage to you. The capital itself would soon dwindle to nothing : you want a sure investment, something that will bring in a comfortable income for you and Freda, something you can live on always. You can rely on any proposition of mine being thoroughly dependable. I am very careful about such things. I have an analytical mind ". He made a mark on the paper, a nought.

" No doubt ", Thornton said.

" This place is going to expand ", Katesgrove said. He said : " I am going to expand it ".

" What's that ? I—"

" Nothing. Nothing at all ". Handled properly, he thought, there is money in everything : there is money in expansion, there is money in religion, there is money in shops ; there is even money in a limbless man's pocket, he thought. He looked up over the white steepled fingers : a face already fleshy, the lips like two different mouths. Living in a hole like this, he thought ; already falling to pieces. He looked across the cracked ceiling darkened by the years' smoke. An appalling place. In a cheap vase standing on a corner whatnot were blue and yellow flowers ; on the high mantel a pair of grinning china dogs sprouted paper firelighters from their hollow backs. There was a silent clock with one hand, beside it a ball of pink knitting-wool thrust through by two glinting needles.

At the window a breeze stirred the curtains, faintly, with some reminiscence of a long-empty room. Thornton turned, the empty sleeve of his jacket now stirring with what seemed to be an emotional rather than a physical correspondence. He came near the table, his eyes now quickened perhaps by the same emotion. The smoke of the cigarette threaded slowly across the room to the open window. " Just because I know you in church doesn't mean I have to—"

" My dear fellow ! "

" —it doesn't mean even that I've got to consider your proposition. Nothing means I have to consider it. There's no connexion between us that implies that I've got to do what you tell me, ask me. I'm going to do this solely because I think it will be a good way of investing the few hundreds I've got. I mean, have to come. I'm thinking for Freda. I may as well tell you this : I ain't thinking of you, of helping you, Christian or no Christian. I'm think-ing it's a good way to help Freda, to make sure of her future. I'm thinking you've got the ability to start the business, to make it go. I'm risking that. Any business is a risk. But I'm with you when you say Hartney's going to expand. The brickworks'll mean more workers, more workers means more houses, more shops. Now this company's opened the new quarry they'll treble their out-put if they can get the men. And the men—"

Later that night Thornton sat down in an old leather armchair. He had signed a paper. Katesgrove had gone, taking the paper with him. His frail body sat poised in the chair and when presently he rose to light a cigarette, the chair regained immediately that vacant quality of smoothness, unimpressed with any weight or design of occupation, as if only a shadow had sat there.

Upstairs there were two rooms. One of these was Thornton's. It contained an iron bedstead with brass ornamental knobs, and a few nondescript pieces of furniture. There were texts and oleographs on the walls, a pink cardboard hairtidy hanging beside the cold eternally lifeless fireplace ; in one corner a clothes cupboard had been roughly contrived by hanging a flowered cretonne curtain from brass hooks screwed into a triangle of wood. But the room contained beside these an unmistakable odour of wallflowers, and the memory of Thornton's dead wife. It was a memory that was with him always, like the frail flesh stretched over his bones. He could not avoid it. She was a woman who in life had escaped him always : now he could not rid himself of the wallflower odour of her presence.

He lay on the bed, fully clothed, smoking. He was enmeshed in memory ; doubt. Freda came to the door *Twelve years old*.

" Well, I've signed it ", he said.

" Have you ? " she said. " What does it mean—your death warrant ? "

" Practically ", he said. " If Katesgrove doesn't make a do of this shop. It's my money going down the drain as well as his. Mostly mine. Well. I've been an' gone an' done it now. God

speed is what this bus wants ", he said aloud. People turned, looking. Ahead traffic lights flickered, flicked. Lights were coming on in the windows now, the vast omnipresent skysigns spilled Nicholson's Gin, ruby scintillations of Sandeman's Port, the man with the glittering cape and toreador hat, the Wrigley imp wriggling-present-absent under the flat pale autumn sky. Where are we? he said, not aloud, himself speaking to himself. He looked downward through the window (in the corners a light web-like spatter of dust, slow erosion of muck) into The Strand endless shoreline nerve strand of people faces colour mass threadlike eternal erosion abrasion of noise noise noise noise shatter squeal whine (Sandeman outflickering) song laughter scream

downcurtain of silence within the mind, a lonnnnnnnnn-nnnnnng suspiration . . . . . . quiet.

A woman leaned toward him, a strong vigorous woman, blotchfaced, tremulous cherries in a black mazelike hat.

" You all right, mister? you look a bit peaky. I thought you—' '

" I'm all right ", he said. " Must have dozed off . . . one of those splitsecond nightmares ".

" Split what? " she said. " Groanin' to yerself, you was. Groanin' ".

" I—I haven't slept much lately. I suppose—" The cherries genuflected across the bright letters of TEN MINUTES TO WAIT SO MINE'S A MINOR. " I know just how you feel, my dear. Insommia, they call it. My daughter Elsie—that's the married one—she had it chronic. The doctor described lordnum for it. So many drops each night. It was a business ".

" Pardon me, sir ". A small man with spectacles caught on a black ribbon leaned forward from behind Laurie. " If you suffer from sleeplessness I can recommend an effective cure. From my own experience. Two five-grain aspirin tablets taken in a glass of warm milk immediately before retiring. A most efficacious remedy. Most effi—"

" Thanks ", Laurie said. " Sleep is a thing I have to

avoid—tonight. But I'll remember ", he said. " Excuse
me ", he said ; " I have to change buses here ", lurching
between the rows of curious faces, tandem, like a street of
lamp-posts, he thought.

Standing at the intersection, whirl and clangour of
traffic, downpouring of light from the chiaroscuro that hung
above the city.

Light caressed his face in long suppliant waves. Above
him daylight was beginning to vanish, to muse and ponder
among the yet unseen stars and the quiet pale sky, a
warning pause brief and bereft, season to sad season. To-
morrow it will be autumn, he thought. On the seats in
Trafalgar Square the strange ruminant figures sat clasped :
a gray ageless woman eating with infinite care something
from a twist of newspaper ; the statuesque immobile
figures in their attitudes of agony and death spun over with
the fountains' flicker and the fading day and brightening
night. The lions mused at the base of the tall column,
resting in their stone grief, surrounded by those small
groups of people to whom one could put no name—the
gazing, the lazing and the mute, their eyes touched with
that anonymity of destination and purpose, like people
set down at mid-juncture of their journey and awaiting
with the inborn and consummate patience of their kind
those events to which in due time and place they would
submit.

He is waiting, Laurie thought ; and conjured into his
mind for that moment a vision of the Bohemian luxury
flat. Arnold skulking in a corner awaiting, amid the
cheers of the audience, certain retribution in the person of
the strong handsome hero already hammering at the bright
flimsy door. Like a film, he thought ; and saw the children
and the loving-couples gripping hands and seats in their
excitement.

Yes, like a film. We sat through some lovely films, didn't

*we, honey? But you don't know how this one's going to
end up.*

*That day. I was twelve. It meant nothing to me that day
because Dad had signed a paper. He was laying on the bed
all among the wallflower perfume Mum left behind. He told
me and I didn't know what it meant; only that it was something to do with his compensation money that he got from the
quarry when he lost his arm. I'd never heard of Arnold
Katesgrove then, only the way people say Mr Katesgrove this
and Mr Katesgrove that. He was just a name. Only I
think right inside me I knew something even then though he
was only a name. He left something behind him in the cottage,
something I couldn't put a name to either; but it was him.
Like an animal leaves fur or smell or something in the chair it
sleeps on. It was like that. So that even I, at twelve years
old, knew about it. Though I couldn't have said about it,
not to explain what I meant.*

Yes, Arnold was always like that, he thought; you
could always tell where he had been by speaking to people,
touching the things he had contaminated. For it was a
form of contamination. Even Mrs Stranks, who one might
think was beyond any corruption,—even she appeared
after a time to have sunk below some hidden zero; like one
who, clinging to the last remaining grain of self-respect, is
told suddenly that there is nothing left to cling to; and
lets go, with realization of truth too late.

Now in the faint afterglow of day the city flowed round
him in long thunderous approaches of hollow scintillant
sound. He stood waiting for the bus. He had not
thought of sleep since the morning, but now he thought of
it as something chimerical. Beside him a boy in the
uniform of a foreign army encircled the waist of a girl. On
the girl's cheeks were two rougespots; her lips scarred into
the pale waxy flesh as she stood looking up at the soldier's
dark quiet furious face quiescent in suspense between two

emotions. My Freda, he thought, you are with me always; you linger in the long arid dusk between day and night—thinking this with neither interest nor compassion nor sentiment, as though viewing a sorrow unfolded by another, some story that he could read or not as he willed. It was as if he stood outside himself, watching, awaiting with detached interest his own next move.

He took the bright blade from his pocket, holding it delicately between the fingertips of both hands, watching himself, disinterested, a man considering a purchase. Beside him people stood watching with askance curiosity. Only the soldier and the girl ignored him. They stood now eating sweets from a crumpled paper bag.

" Nice bit of work ", the man beside him said. He wore a tight doublebreasted suit and carried a briefcase. A pearl stickpin shone like a tear in his tie. " Nicely chased. A paperknife ? You can pick up some nice things at dealers' places. I remember once—"

" A paperknife ", Laurie said. " I don't know. I hadn't thought ". He looked down at the blade. " I suppose it is. I wasn't going to use it for that, anyway ".

The man with the briefcase sat next to him. It was a seat near the front of the bus. Chains of lighted windows pulled them along. There were lights everywhere now. The sky was a flat blankness like a tent pegged down with a million lights. The man with the briefcase began a long story about a Dutch Vase of blue delft.

" As near as you go to Shepherd Market ", Laurie said.

" Curzon Street ", the conductor said. " I'll give you a shout ".

8

THERE is this about a conscience, Laurie thought : it is like a dustbin : you can put all the rubbish in it, time after time, adding, adding, adding.   The things you don't want to see.   They go in, deep.   To the bottom.   That is truth : that which you want none to see.   Shove it in and put the lid on, quick.   It's all right if there's nobody looking.   But someday someone peers round the corner of your mind.   You're finished then Arnold.   You're rumbled, twigged.   That was the day I saw you and Mrs Stranks in the oakwood at Hartney.   There was nothing you could do to me after that.   You—the Sunday School student and teacher looking at dirty postcards, procured by a woman you professed to abhor, of whom you said to father, when you had finished with her, She is profligate, unfit to enter this house.   But it was she who gave me my small delights, to whom I fled for comfort, from whom I heard those words I was later to know as kindly; for then I knew them only as different.   From no-one else did I ever receive any love emotion or speech that was free from Father's fanaticism.   In Christine and Elspeth there was only the humility that is not true because cowardly.   In you there was cowardice and cunning.   In me there was nothing, then— nothing but a vast plain of longing, a null null void, awaiting the touch of knowledge.   It came that day in the oakwood.   I knew then that there was nothing but pursuit. That just as I had followed you into life, so I would follow you to its darkening.   I knew this because it was always written on you, within you, within your mind.   And the mind gets full after a time, doesn't it, Arnold ?   You stuff it and stuff it with the filth and iniquity, taking bits out to look and gloat.   Until there comes a time when you are alone with it all, when the mind's dustbin is full, when

it bursts in your head and you must look, look, look ! but
this time there is someone else looking too ; this time you
must speak, reveal ; for contemplation is no longer enough.
You have come to that time when you must share what is
in your mind.   Because you know (you had forgotten this
truth : it is at the bottom) it is time to die, Arnold

to whom now through the swift outfading of unstarred
night the rise-fall-whine of vehicle bore him, pausing
tremendous between the serried and runged city's lights to
outfling men women and children upon the lightpooled
dark and tumult of tragi-quasi-comedy, the briefcased man
(his story told, his Goodnight brief) upon that exact spot
where later a newsboy was to stand shouting, Tragedy
Tragedy in the East End.   Arnold who, in that harsh
silken room lying formulate with every detail and intricacy
of waiting between day and night, was already saying :

" Mad. Of course he's mad. He thinks—imagines—
I've done him some wrong.   I tell you, Elise, he's dang—"
he ceased speaking.   Then in a moment he said : " I must
get away ".

It was a small room, converted from some loft or stable
the identity of which remained implicit behind the silk
drapes and erotic prints.   There was a divan furnished in
red and purple silk, some chairs of red leather and chrom-
ium, a bookcase littered with magazines, records for a
portable gramophone.   Beneath the single window's red
velvet curtains a cocktail cabinet stood, open, the ranked
glint of the glasses bearing some bland reminiscence of a
fairground.

" I must get away ", he said again.   But he did not
move, standing there in the precise centre of the small
room touched with that garment of fear to which now, after
the several hours of his presence, the woman to whom he
spoke had grown accustomed.

" Get away ? " she said.   " Don't talk so silly, Luce.

What've you got to get away for . . . from? What's wrong with you? You just keep on and on ". She was a woman of some age obscured by art and device, indeterminate. Her blond hair hung over her shoulders and lay across her forehead in a yellow procession of glinting curves, like printed brackets :))))))))). She wore a peach-coloured wrapper. She lay, posing, across the divan, like a slash of light across the red and purple silk. Watching Arnold, whom she knew as Lucian Trent, she thought, What's up with him? I've never seen him like this before, not all the years. " Come here, sugar ", she said ; " come and tell Elise what it's all about ". Her voice was harsh, bore that same implication of fairground that characterized the room.

But he began to speak then, turned away from her in the farthest corner of the room where he stood in the down-shaft of light from the redshaded standard, speaking as if in communion of reasoning with the light itself.

" There was nothing wrong about it. Right from the beginning there was nothing wrong—I can swear that. It was a simple business proposition. Heavens, there are thousands of them completed every day. This one was no different. Why should it be? After all, it was my money as well as—"

The woman interrupted. " Tell me by all means if you want to get it off your chest, Luce ; but for God's sake put names to people and things. What money? What man? "

" Thornton, his name was. He lived in a decrepit little cottage in Hartney. He was a sidesman in the church I went to. Father drove us to it. I was a sidesman also. There was nothing but church ; four times on Sundays, three times during the week. He—Father—was a fanatic, a maniac if you like. My mother was his convert ; she died leaving him wealthy and he married again, thinking perhaps to make another success. I don't know. He converted her all right,—she was a street girl ; but within a year she had left him. Laurie was her son.

"But Thornton. That was a simple business proposition. It had to be. Father went to China—a missionary —and I was left at Hartney Fold with Christine and Elspeth. He left me an income of eighty pounds a year— useless. I always had ambitions, to be successful, to carve a way for myself. I had it in me. But eighty pounds a year—

"Then came the accident at the quarry and Thornton lost his arm, his right arm. He was useless after that.

"The firm paid him a few hundred pounds in compensation, but there was the daughter, this girl Freda— he had to keep her and himself.

"That was my opportunity. And his too : that's the thing you must realize : his too. It wasn't only for me, it was for him too. Could I help it if there was a commercial depression at the time ? Could I help it if all the money went in overheads ? It's the sort of thing you risk, everyone in business risks. Right from then they were against me—him, Freda, Laurie, all of them. Right from that very day. I went round to tell him. Although he knew more or less I still went round to tell—

That day there'd been a thunder

"Thunderstruck, I was : the way he took it

storm over Hartney. Going down from the house. Past the station the water whirling in the ditches gray dark violent my heart as I went toward the house. Knowing how he would be. Knowing. Yet knowing I must go. Meet it. Finish. Thornton. The girl. As if I cared a sou for them, what they felt, lived, did, as if

"It was my fault ; of course that was the first thing he said. I should have known. People are like that : ungrateful for all you do for them.

*We sat.   Between us the table, trembling wilting fern.
Outside, the yard, a diagonal flood of water seep seep seep into
the agedark stone whispering beneath the already rotting house
rot in roof rot in floor rot in wall.   But good enough.   For
them.   A man, useless, his daughter a bitch ; but a pretty
bitch, her body secret, deep, murmuring desire beneath the
pale skin my desire my desire my desire shrieking throb throb
throb within my pulse heart and beating brain ; and a smile
within the mind that watched thinking smiling at the column in
the Sunday gutterpress : Man Assaults Girl : and in smaller
type Under age of Consent—smiling the while I watched
myself resist, thinking, Later, watch and wait watch and
wait.*

*So we waited.   In the quiet gloomy Sunday room we waited.
The girl watching me, waiting for her father to speak, to break
the silence that was more terrible than fury—the silence that
gathered about my words when I told him he was penniless.
Because the girl.   It was she I wanted.   Otherwise would I
have gone down there ?   Would I ?   To hell.   They could
find out for themselves.   But the girl.   Yes.*

"The girl just sat there.   She said nothing except
' There isn't anything left at all, then ? ' and when I said,
' No,' she just went on sitting there looking

*at me with that dark furious smiling womansilence that I
hate, that goes deep like a knife.*

"But Thornton.   You would have thought I had deliberately swindled him.   He said as much

*sitting there with his one hand clenching and clenching on
the cigarette that with his bare fingers he had twisted to
blackened and stinking pulp, whispering again and again,
' You bastard.   You thieving bastard '.*

"Though he'd signed an agreement that said he was
willing, that lent me his money to do as I thought fit with
in the business, to be repaid by me within a certain time
provided—and this was the point he wanted to dispute

now—the takings reached a certain figure in that time.
And because they hadn't and he would have to wait a little
longer for his loan to be repaid he was accusing me of
swindling him. It wasn't that. As God's my judge it
wasn't. I was simply asking him for a little longer to
repay his loan. The business was bad then, but I knew it
would be a success in a little while.

*Bad. Well I called a profit of three thousand bad. So
would any business man. Why should I bleed myself to
repay him? Wait. Let him wait. I wanted all that money
just then. There was that property deal. People were getting
to know me, to expect benevolence, subscriptions : a public
figure, a cornerstone of empire. And Thornton worrying
about a paltry five hundred. There was too much at stake.
Prospects. Every day someone coming to me with a proposition, money in all of them*

*and Thornton watching me now too both of them the girl
Thornton watching until mad I*

*leaned toward me and said (his face paper-pale only his
eyes fixed burning and livid) : ' And what do you think we're
going to do, live on? What do you think? '*

"So when Thornton asked me for help—"

"Asked you?" the woman said. "You mean after
calling you as good as thief he *asked* you for help?"

"Surely". In the motefilled light of the harsh livid
room Arnold now turned toward her, spreading before him
the soft white expensive hands in that posture of
benevolence, that attitude of saintly martyrdom, beseech-
ing. "Surely. Wasn't that just what he would do?
Isn't that the human way?—to belabour our benefactors
and then plead for help? And what could I do but help?
As a Christian—"

"Let's get this straight". The woman also stood now.
They stood facing each other, peering through the savage
downpour of light. Around them the room waited, as if

for some dooropening and revelation that had until this moment remained outside comprehension. " You mean he accused you of God knows what and then said—"

" Yes. He begged me to help him. Anyhow. And there was a way. Freda was ready to start work ; she'd left school some time before and had been seeking employment ; but there was none in Hartney. Times were bad ".

" Yair. You said that. Bad for Thornton ".

" And for me too. That's what nobody seems able to grasp. But the Christian attitude implies help. So I offered employment to Freda ; at a small wage, true ; but it would be better than nothing until such time—"

" Employment ? In the shop that had gone bust ? "

" No, no. The business had not collapsed. That is what a non-business man or woman cannot understand. The business was doing as well as could be expected ".

" You mean it was just his, Thornton's bit of it that had bust ? "

" Precisely. You see—"

" Yes. I see." The woman appeared to be no longer interested in the conversation. She went to the window and looked down on the stoneflagged courtyard. It was not yet quite dark. Above the embattled roofs the glow of the city merged with that coalescence of rainbow or horizon into the prone tranquil sky unflowered by moon or star and lying flat with the promise of rain and autumn above city world and universe.

The man's voice continued, freed now from its quality of restraint, because with the woman behind him he need no longer act and determine that posture of performance that sought her understanding and pity.

" So Freda came to work for me. *That afternoon when she sat looking at me across the desk, her legs knees thighs and swirl of skirts visible to me as I bent to pick something from the floor. That day when in the office I told her the exact*

*colour and design of her underclothes and showed her the
holes I had drilled in the wall of the ladies' room. A mistake.
I should never have told her about that. It was a mistake —
the only one I ever made in connexion with my private life.*
To have her in the shop was a mistake. It gave her the
opportunity to be grateful which she immediately conceived as an opportunity for what her father had persuaded
her into thinking was a justified avengement. It was soon
after she came to work in the shop that she began to spread
tales about my treatment of her—tales that only my
reputation in the town and my connexion with the church
could silence. But about such stories there always lingers
a flavour palatable to gossipmongers and old wives. It is
these—the small casual distilled words of idle speech that
now fertilized by my own stepbrother, have proved too
much for me. Laurie has always hated, been jealous of
me. Now, convincing himself that I have been the cause
of Freda's death, he has found an outlet for his jealousy.

" That is why I must get away. Because there are
reasons—very strong reasons—that have convinced him of
my guilt—"

Still the woman did not speak. He moved from the
light to where against one of the chairs was poised the
silverknobbed cane. Moving from the light to what there
was of shadow in the room his face passed likewise through
a change of expression, of countenance. His features (they
were still broad, ponderous-chinned, two-mouthed by virtue
of the differing lips) bore now no blandness or sanctimony.
It was now that he began to exude through every pore that
panic of conscience and fatalism at last accepted. It was
now that he began properly to tremble, standing within
reach of the stick yet unable to grasp it for the complete
and possessive shudder of movement that held him. He
was like a man seen on the flickering screen of a pioneer
cinema. He could not control the trembling or find word

of answer as the woman now commenced to speak, her
voice without variant or emotion as if she too had come
suddenly upon some stultifying knowledge.

" Yes. Reasons. I can imagine them too. The same
as I can imagine what happened to Freda. Listen, Luce
(That's funny : I've known you all these years and I
probably don't even know your right name yet) : you've
been reasonable to me. I haven't expected more. You've
paid for me, my body, and that's what you got. Methods
by the way. I've got use to it. But now, suddenly,
right out of the blue I begin to find out a few things about
you : not from anyone else's lips : from your own. And you
should know ; and I guess I should too. No man can fool
me the way you've tried to fool me these last few minutes.
Your tale don't hold, Luce : you ain't told me the half of
it : it's the other half you're worried about. So would I
be if I had your tendencies. I know you pretty well in the
line of business, Luce. You've got to admit that. I
don't know what any of these geezers—this Laurie and the
rest of them— are really after you for ; but if my guess is as
good as I think it is, they've got reasons. I don't want to
know any more about it—I'm no Mother Confessor. I've
nixes against you myself, but I'm dead set against getting
mixed up in the trouble you represent. I've a respected
name in Shepherd Market. As for this place—it's pretty
and I like it ; but I can take it or leave it. There's others
just as good ; and freer-spending men than you, my Luce.
And I guess you know something about curtains, as the
saying is, or you wouldn't be telling me all this, letting me
in on a setup you've kept me dumb to this seven years.
Not that I wanted to know. Curiosity was never a big
portion in my nature. My living's all I want and that
you've given me. I've never worried my gentlemen friends
for information. A man's life's his own, I always say : let
him live it. But when it comes to things that smell

faintly of muck beneath the outer skin—then I'm through. Of course there's different grades of muck and different grades of stink. But there's something shone through you tonight, Luce Trent. I don't know what it is, but it's something I don't like ". Her voice still dispassionate, quietly impersonal, as though she held convocation with herself. She had been mildly surprised at first, even a little disgusted, but that had died off like a fading leaf. She was a woman whom no man surprised for long ; but she could not be venomous without cause. She pulled the peachcoloured wrapper closer about her and tied the girdle. In the movement lay the inviolable closure of an incident.

" What am I to do ? " he said. The trembling had ceased. He spoke like a child.

" Do ? Do I know or care ? " She looked at him as he stood before her leaning on the stick. The expensive clothes, the manicured fingers, the care-soft flesh. No guts, she said, not quite aloud, " You'd better do what the flicks say : Get the hell out of it. Where, don't ask me ".

" Will you do this for me ? " he asked. There was a sheen of sweat on his face. His eyes watched her with a plea at once faint childlike and mute. " We've had some good times together, Elise ; haven't we ? Haven't we ? " he said ; and when she did not answer he went on : " And I've given you some nice . . . presents. Will you do a little thing for me ? If Laurie—if anyone—comes here, seeking me, put them off my track. Will you ? Will you do this . . . for me ? "

" Christ ", the woman said. The word and its formation were like the gesture of spitting. " I never knew a man could be so yellow, white and every lily colour of liver ". She turned and pulled back the curtain. " There's a man coming under the arch now ", she said, and turned to see him possessed by the cold outpouring of sweat again.

She laughed then, a sound bright hard and savage as the light in which she stood. " Snakes aren't in it with you ", she said. She was still laughing.

" But will you ? Will you ? "

" Get down on your bended knee ", she said, laughing. And in a moment she watched, sickening, the beginning of genuflection. " O my God. So bloody bloody gutless. . . ." She spat, directly on to the groomed and homage-postured head. " That for your gutlessness. Now get up and get out ". Slowly the man got up. He did not look at her again. As he moved toward the door he covered his eyes with a pair of dark glasses. That was all. With his own hand and movement he seemed to write Finish. The door closed, quiet as a turning page. In the room in which the woman he had called Elise now stood alone the print and designation of his presence remained, like the smurred impression of a thumb on glass. In the corner the divan stood with the concavity her body had made marking its smoothness. On the now closed door the movement of his departure had left a creased frock on a lop-sided hanger swinging, scarcely perceptible, a motion faintly redolent of a shadow swinging from a gibbet. In a moment his footsteps in the stone corridor ceased, and with their cessation the metronome movement of the shadow came also silently to rest. The woman had not moved. She seemed to be waiting for complete silence. When it came she crossed to the gramophone and played a record. It was Hawaiian music, languorous, stemming. She turned out the light ; then she went to the window and drew back the curtains.

In the courtyard below the man crossed slowly toward the archway. He was like a figure being moved slowly across a checkerboard of light-dappled darkness. She watched him. He was like a man lost. Long after he had disappeared beneath the archway she seemed to see him,

4

walking the streets beneath the slow submergence of lamplight and morning; in the empty and vanquished streets
to the end of night—a man lost and alone.

9

Now it began to rain, a soft monotony of thin drizzle. In
the streets people began to appear in waterproofs and up-
turned collars. The rain fell on the city with that haggard
runnelling like a woman's tearstained face. In a little
while the streets began to gleam. In the parks the trees
grew heavy and sombre, the grass beneath them stretching
darkly away from the wet glim of the roads. People
sought shelter in doorways and arcades, groups of two and
three, waiting for buses and taxis, or against some planned
or identified moment when they would be joined by other
people, or would part, to resume, with that anonymity of
destination and purpose stamped on their rainwet faces,
their endless walking.

When Arnold Katesgrove came out into Piccadilly he
was, felt, completely alone : not only with the physical
companionlessness of the lone man, but with the state of
mental despair to which he had now come. He did not
know what to do. He knew there was no-one else to whom
he might turn, speak even ; he was afraid with that horror
of the intangible that since the morning had begun to
manifest itself. It was not only of Laurie, of retribution :
that, in itself, he had thought on, had considered with his
habitual analysis, had brought, as it were, to the light of
reason. If I see him, he reasoned, it can be in a crowded

street or place where I can invoke aid ; even he will
hardly dare to attack me in a London street in the midst of
any thousand or so people who by average will be in the
vicinity at that same moment.   He thought of it in this
way, even working out some plan of movement that would
take him to the most crowded places at the busiest times.
Then he considered night.   But at night, he thought, there
are hotels, keys that will lock doors.   There is even police
protection, he thought.   He did not think of how in any
city a man can remain hidden for years : it was as if the
moment of meeting, the end of pursuit, was an accomplished or certain fact.   He will find me, he thought, had
been convinced from the moment in which he read the
telegram ; and no word or deposition could have swayed
him ;   wherefore he made no attempt at concealment.
He knew it would be useless.   Out of this certainty had
grown his fear.   But it was that other, greater, intangible
fear to which he could find no answer.

This was of course himself.   There is no answer to guilt :
only the deeprooted fear of the unknown, that it may conceivably be worse than the known ; so that the mind,
seeking refuge, comes to terms with the known, belittling
it for the sake of confidence to face the secret unknown.

He began to walk, to drift along the swarmed pavements.
He was still wearing the dark glasses and almost without
thought he had automatically adopted the stooped gait
that for years now he had assumed with the identity of
Lucian Trent, which identity he lost—and as in a few
moments he would lose again, finally, irrevocably —in the
lavatory at Piccadilly Circus tube.   Between Shepherd
Market and the tube he called nowhere, spoke to no-one.
At that place and time each week his Saturday nights
began.   It was a routine, safe, orderly.   His sisters thought,
vaguely, that he visited an old friend at Tufnell Park—
Nollys.   He told them nothing else, not even the address.

It pleased and flattered his vanity to think that for a few hours each week he could fool people completely, that they would never find him nor even begin to look for him except in some vague suburban area under a name that did not even exist.   So there was added pleasure in the schoolboy touch of dark glasses and assumed name.

But there was no pleasure now.   He turned watching, people's face as they passed him.   There was no recognition anywhere.   All strangers.   He walked close to the bright windows.   For a moment he imagined a man looked at him searchingly ; he turned to a window and stared at a display of coloured scarves knotted round plaster throats. The suave featureless faces looked back at him like mocking and broken reflections in water.   He put his hand to his own throat, to the linen collar now limp with rain ; pulling at its constriction the button broke and the tie slipped awry.   But the face of the man he thought had watched him had gone.   There were a hundred faces in its stead, swimming past him like masks carried on poles.   He lifted the heavy knob of the cane suddenly, wanting to batter madly at the faces ; but the urge of rage passed before he had lifted the cane higher than his own shoulder and he felt empty and fearless : as if wakening from a fever-ridden sleep.

Then the fear came drifting back.   Elise in the room looking at him with that glance of abhorrence and amaze that she might have bestowed on some vermin or maggot. He had forgotten her completely until this moment.   Now, with the effect of outfading anaesthesia he remembered.

So there was really no-one now.   It is true, he thought : even she has turned against me—she, a pander and a harlot, a paid body with no rights but those of payment ; and I went from her room, from her insult, like that, like a mongrel cur to its lair, he thought.

But indignation was useless.   For a moment, with that

clutching at straws which is the adjunct of cowards and liars, he imagined the whole story without truth : as if Freda was just a name in a book, a printed and meaningless word on paper—not even on paper possibly, perhaps just a word, a name possessed by some girl unknown. For it was her, he thought; if only I had kept clear of her. But how was I to know that Laurie would marry, actually marry, with ceremony fee and ring the girl whose body alone was a mere outringing of desire for me ? That was the beginning.

It had begun on that summer afternoon when Thornton had signed the agreement. It had begun then, for although he had not seen her or even known she existed except perhaps by the word Daughter, desire had begun.

It was female : that touch of feminine finger and presence that lays its mark on any residence, room or mansion ; that was there, like a mark of trade or inheritance, symbolized in the ball of pink knittingwool on the mantelpiece, in the odour and reminiscence of mop and polish that pervaded the room, in the very disposition of pot pan and utensil that lay in ordered (perhaps not even ordered : but with that unmistakable womenhandling) array on the shelves ; so that at once, without hesitation or thought, one could say on entering the darkened quiet parlour with its hushed grasses before the cold fireplace, its cold dusted and unused furniture and its faded and untrodden carpet, A woman lives here. That much was certain. So that when Arnold Katesgrove left that afternoon he took with him, beside the deed for which he had come, the definitive formulation of that licentious desire never long absent from his senses and now evoked by his eroticism into a near-mania that must see, know, the girl.

He had not long to wait. There were a dozen excuses he could and did use to get into the house : queries about the business, the agreement, details about which he would not normally have considered consulting Thornton but which now were the keys that gave him entrance.

The first time was on a Sunday. In church he looked through his praying hands to the pew in which Thornton sat alone. Simply because she was not there his desire was stronger. Beside him his sisters sang and mumbled. He thought of them with derision—for their meek sexless humility and their straight formless clothes. They were both still young yet their youth was lost beneath their rigid garb and formal attitudes. He watched them singing, their faces bent toward their hymnbooks. When they kneel, he thought, they are like sacks tossed to dry on the pews, collapsed, without thought or pleasure. They think of nothing but what they are told, he thought. This was true. He took joy in his own secret lust. He had already had lovers. Since Felix Katesgrove went away Arnold had found many opportunities to visit London. Till now he had never flaunted his profligacy nearer home than that. Lily Stranks he did not count : she revolted him but she was useful : it was she who had started his collection of erotica. But now there was Freda—a girl he had never seen but who yet was the cause of longing.

It was summer. Inside, the church was cool, permeated with the air of vaults and the touch of stone. When they came out Arnold felt the heat in him, rising. He walked through the village with Christine and Elspeth without seeing Thornton. Then he saw him, ahead, alone, striding.

" Excuse me ", he said to Christine. " There's Thornton. I must go and speak to him. He looks so lonely. I noticed it in church ".

" Of course ", she said. " No doubt you will catch us up. We will walk on, slowly. If not, we will see you at lunch ".

" Yes ", he said. He caught Thornton ; by then he was

hot and breathless. " I had to see you ", he said. " If there's anything we can do—my sisters and I— "

" Do ? " the other said ; " do ? "

" Well, perhaps—I don't know—household duties. . . ."

" My daughter looks after the house ", Thornton said. " You knew that, didn't you ? "

" Of course. But isn't she a little—well, young. We have a very good parlourmaid at the Fold. Perhaps sometimes—"

" No," Thornton said. He drew on the cigarette he was smoking. The blue thin haze of smoke lay above his head, unmoving in the breathlessness of the air. " She does all right. She's going on for fourteen. She wouldn't welcome any parlourmaids here. No more would I. This is no place for parlourmaids. Look at it : pretty as a picture, they call it ; they can't see the bedroom ceilings, the walls peeling with damp. Come in ".

He went in and Thornton showed him the tiny flowers of mould on wall and carpet, the dark stains on the ceilings upstairs, the paper peeling from the walls in dark corners. All the time he could hear the girl moving about in the house, humming to herself. Hiding, he thought. So that was it : like a game. Hiding, she is hiding herself from me ; and it became fact because he thought so. So that above the inherent carnal desire arose the conscious and already formed (because already desired) feminal knowledge and vision : woman, female, having no relation to fecundity or procreation, but only to a monstrous and overpowering obsession with flesh and coition.

She was there now. They were downstairs again in the stale airless room. Beyond the doorway into the scullery he could see her, moving against a background of steaming pots and steamdrenched walls. He went out, Thornton following.

" So this is Freda. The little housewife. Well ".

She turned, watching him coolly.

" Hallo ". she said. She was at once a child and a woman, with that overblooming of womanhood come too early upon childhood, neither pretty nor beautiful nor even superficially attractive, but with that (to him) latent possibility of fleshly sinning manifest in the curves of breast and thigh, in lithe and sinuous movement and in the mockery with which she regarded him. She was dark, thin, and suppressedly agile, as though constantly remembering some early admonition to seek grace, translated now into an epicene quality of movement that might have belonged to man woman or even robot. But to him she was merely youth urge and desire—and female.

" That's her ", Thornton said. " Looks after me damn' nearly as well as her mother did. That's saying something. But it's probably different to the looking after you get ", he said. He was bitter. Moving about the room he seemed invested with bitterness against death, domocile and his own helplessness. He began to cough presently and when he took the cigarette from his mouth there was a red line along its length like a strand of cotton. He drew the back of his hand across his lips and replaced the cigarette.

" Charming ", Arnold said. " Quite a domestic scene. I can see I was wrong in offering you help ; everything, all your domestic affairs are in capable hands ". He smiled, but the girl had already turned away from him.

That was the first time. It was like a minute awakening in him. He was then more than twice her age and he wanted her. He fed his desire with thought and erotica in his locked bedroom at night. He lay thinking, planning how he would see, lead her.

It was simple. Each time he went he came to know more about their domestic habits. He learned that Thornton went into Sunnymede, the nearest town, alone, on Tuesdays. He found this out early, but for weeks he did not

call on a Tuesday.   He pretended always to be engrossed
with Thornton.   There was a chipped mirror on the mantel,
sentinel beside the silent clock, and in this he observed her
moving about, watching him, puzzled at his attitude, his
silence, so clearly different from what she had expected
after his first visit.   He knew she had perceived then his
desire, had expected its flowering, had been ready with
scorn and disgust.   Instead, now, she saw (and he remarked this too) he ignored her, perhaps saying Goodday
or Goodbye, for weeks and weeks nothing else.

Then one afternoon she came and sat near him while he
discussed some problem with Thornton.   She sat with some
needlework in her fingers and he watched the womanness
working in her, drawing his attention to herself.   She said
nothing : merely moved her body and her legs several
times ; until Thornton said suddenly :

" Keep still, Freda.   You're not a child now.   Go out
if you can't keep still ".

Presently she went out into the scullery.   The two men
could hear her moving about behind the door that she had
closed noisily behind her.   " She gets a bit above herself
sometimes ", Thornton said.   " She's got no-one of her
own age to mix with ".

" A pity ", Anrold said.   But he did not pursue the
subject.

The next day he called again. It was a Tuesday.
" Dad's out ", she said.

" Yes ", he said.   " I called to see you ".

" What can you want with me ? " she said.   She had
changed her dress.   It was almost as if she had been
exepcting him, someone.   " Come in ", she said.

They sat in the musty and unused parlour, in the semi-
dark of summer's end and dusty plush furniture.   Arnold
felt the cold damp touch of another season in the armchair
in which he sat.   He leaned forward, his hands folded on

4*

his cane.   Opposite him the girl sat in the wash-faded and too-small frock poised on the edge of the chair companion to the one in which he sat watching, smiling at her, companion even to mouldbloom and dustodour, the two of them sitting there in the remote Surrey summerlight poised as it were on two opposite and trembling brinks across a chasm through or into which in a moment a word would propel them.

" I have a little gift to make to you ", Arnold said.

But that was really only, if not actually the beginning, an early stage.   He began to take her about, to make her presents, to begin what he called a fatherly interest. Always with Thornton or, if not with him then in some place where they could easily be seen.   People began to talk, the kind of talk he intended : that Mr Katesgrove was doing a power of good to the Thornton girl, giving her presents, dresses and that ; taking her to places with her father, taking him out of himself a bit, which is what he wanted, miserable he's been since Mrs T died, such a tragedy, and they say he's got the silicosis or worse which means the girl's as good as . . . well, it does work out that way far too often, really, doesn't it ? and of course he's a partner, well a sort of partner, with Mr Katesgrove now, They've started up that dress shop in the High Street, it certainly adds tone to the place and we did want a shop like that—save us going to Sunnymede every time ; and although of course Thornton's not really a partner in every sense of the word—well, it takes a man with education to run a shop, now doesn't it ?—but his money's in it, though I expect Mr Katesgrove was really thinking more of an interest for him than anything else, some sort of responsibility to take that bitterness out of him, well, that's really the best possible thing I always say.   For of course Mr Katesgrove would have got the money without bothering about Albert Thornton's few pounds, but they say it gives him pleasure, and Albert certainly does need an interest.

So there it was : that attitude for which he never even had to strive, that was present in populace and individual, that was already deeply engrained centuries before he was born, a feudal mode not only of mere existence but of living too : an acceptance and imbibing of a mass dope and anaesthesia reduced to a formula sustaining and impregnable : money, property and religion.

On that day in which lay the seal and abnegation of Thornton's ruin he said he would lay bare the rot to other people's eyes.

But it was useless. Even before he started to tell people he knew it was useless.

He went in the evening to the pub in the village. It was darkening now. The pub stood back beyond a rain-pooled green above which its sign leaned, beaded still with a fringe of raindrops. The shops of the single main street crescented away from the pub like the darkened coaches of a train. The street itself, the wavelike surface of cobbles, curved through the darkgleamed floodwater. There was no traffic. The road was completely empty, still, silent, but for the long faint hush ssssssssssh of the engulfing flood.

Thornton crossed the green, his head stooped forward, not passively, but as if impugning some secret arraignment. He was wearing Wellingtons and an old raincoat.

He sat in a shadowed corner beneath an aquatint *The Roast Beef of Old England*. He knew everybody present but he did not speak ; nor for the moment did they address him. The landlord leaned on the zinc bar, his head following with metronomic precision the flight of darts.

They were taciturn men ; but they watched him. After

a while the man opposite from him across the wooden bench spoke. He was a man Thornton had known all his life, with whom he had worked at the quarry.

" Well, Albie ", he said ; " I hear you're in trouble ". It was disinterested, impersonal, casual.

" It's got around quick enough ", Thornton said.

" Things do ".

Thornton drank. The empty sleeve of his coat lay on the bench. He put his glass down but he did not release it : his hand clenched on the glass as if from its cold mute abstraction he gathered some force, some strength of purpose. " The bastard ", he said quietly. " The thieving bastard ". His face was thin, frail, shadowstubbled with blue.

" No good taking on, Albert ", the other said. " Ain't Mr Katesgrove's fault y'know. Not like I heard, nohow ".

" Heard ", Thornton said. " Heard. That's all you can bloody well talk about. What you heard. You don't know a bloody thing ". His knuckles gleamed with the whiteness of long unfleshed bone.

" Maybe ".

" Listen ". His voice was even quieter now, a long indrawing of breath upon which the whole room seemed to wait, turned toward, watching him now, awaiting that moment in which they could turn on him. For already they knew : climax outcome and purpose, the turning upon the man, the individual, with that pragmatical affluence of design that is the beginning of mob authority, against which there is nothing : the lone defence and purpose of the soul : nothing more. " Listen ", Thornton said. His voice was less than whisper. Round his lips a thin surfeit of saliva gathered. " You think Katesgrove's a wonder, God almighty. Because his father's a missionary, because he goes to church, because you see him there, he smiles at you, speaks. You think that. Because he is up and

coming, a man of property, of means. A saint because he
is building a chapel, a miracle because in a hospital there is
one bed with his name carved on a plate above it, he gave it
—bed, plate and child ; and probably the pain that *is*
because the child's there. You see that, his name in the
paper, a public figure, a man of means and kindness, you
think. You think because he wants you to think. You
haven't found out yet. He hasn't taken your money,
abused your ignorance, led you on with false hopes. ' Open
a shop, Thornton. This place is expanding. The ladies
are the ones to aim at—a dress shop. There's a goldmine
in it, Thornton. With a little more capital than you've
got—' So there it is : the thing for me to do. Golden
prospects. A proper harvest. He does the business, I
put the money. Put and take. I do the putting, that
bastard does the taking. A businessman's—he even called
it a gentleman's—agreement. For what it's worth. But
then there's the day when he comes to see you, sympathetic
look, balance-sheet and bloody all—"

There was a gathering, a sort of slow determinate coagu-
lation of the men in the bar. Without moving they seemed
now to clot toward the wound of his voice, the long slow
furious tirade, begun as scarceheard whisper, louder now
as in the shadowed corner from which he spoke he tautened,
springlike, beneath the downpressure of his own gush of
words.

"—So comes today. I knew for a long time now. I've
seen bills, figures. I don't understand. ' What is it ? '
I've asked him. ' Is it all right ? ' ' Don't worry,
don't worry, don't worry. It's going to be all right.
Business is going to be good '. That's it : that's what you
put in him : faith : all your faith. Because you don't
know what you're at. Figures. Debit. Credit. So one
day he comes and says, ' Finish, Thornton : your bit's
gone, mine's all right : yours is gone '. And that's it.

Out of the ruins he picks your daughter and says he'll take
her and give her thirty bob a week : *and* commission, he
says. That's your Mister Arnold bloody Katesgrove.
That's—"

But it ceased now : the volley of words, furious and
bitter, hot, arid, staunched suddenly as he began to cough,
as at the same moment someone seized and pinioned his
arm, thrust him downward, rigid, on the bench.

" Shut it ", someone said (it was the man who had spoken
a few moments ago) ; " shut it.   Libel, it's libel—slander ".

The landlord, a short stubborn man with a gold albert
pendant across his open waistcoat, thrust through the
group that enclosed Thornton. " On Mr Katesgrove ", he
said ; " it's wrong, wrong. A benefactor, a benefactor.
I've knowed him all my life ; and Mr Felix before him.
I've knowed him, I tell you.   Like a friend, he is.   To you.
To me.   To all this place.   I know ", he said.   " And you,
slan—"

Thornton was powerless now.   He did not speak again.
It would be like speaking to an empty room.   " Get him
out ", the landlord said.   " I don't want anyone making
trouble here ".

That was the first thing.   He had known it would be
useless.   He did not speak to people now : not as he had
spoken to them before.   In the shops where he went for
groceries and cigarettes he was received coldly.   He knew
why.   He said nothing, but he felt people pointing, watching.   One evening as he walked along the road in the long
iron autumn dusk he heard his name as he passed an open
window.   He stopped to listen.   Within the lighted room
the curtains stirred with evening, masking the flay of
words " —if you ask me, Albert asked for it ; messing
about with shops he don't understand.   What does he
know about such things ?   What ?   Now he goes about
trying to slander young Arnold.   If you ask me, that's the

last straw : his own daughter's employer.   As if—" He
walked on thinking, So that's it, now I am slanderer, I am
not only as good as thief but slanderer too—in my neighbours' eyes I am not wronged but wronging.

There were a thousand voices and one song :

*If you ask me, Thornton wants to bite the hand that
feeds him.*

Turning against Mr Katesgrove like that.

*You know Katesgrove Limited have bought the cottages in
Emmer lane ?*

*It had to come sooner or later.   They've bought the site for
the new Baptist Chapel.*

What a businessman He—

*And now Thornton's got a new landlord he's objecting to
paying the increased rent.   On and on about repairing the
place for years, now he's got the chance he objects to paying a
bit more.*

*How can Mr Katesgrove do it without ?   The places are
falling to bits.   It'll cost hundreds—*

*They say Mr Katesgrove's adding a new wing to the
cottage hospital.   There's some talk about a new cinema in
Hartney too.*

*The place is expanding.   Mr Katesgrove 's doing wonders
here—*

*Thornton's trying to blame his illness on to the dampness
in his cottage.   There's not a medical man in the place will
back him up.   They can see through it.   Vindictiveness,
that's all it is.   Naturally, Mr Katesgrove's going to fight
shy of doing his cottage up—*

They say Thornton's trying to prosecute Kates—

*The fool.   Why doesn't he try to forget about the bit of
money he lost—*

*Katesgrove Limited won their case.   Who expected any-
thing else ?   He even offered to forego damages.   Who says he
hasn't a heart of gold ?*

And after all that he still keeps that girl on in the shop.
Paying her wages—

Throwing good money after bad, if you ask me.

The girl—

The girl. . . .

THE GIRL!

The girl whose body alone was a mere outringing of desire for me.

The was the beginning, he thought, recollected.

Now he was a lost lone figure in the brightness of the tube station. Around him the crowds milled, the escalators poured away into the violent airsurged depthless bowels. A policeman traversed the bright harsh light, watching him, watching everybody, floating away like a piece of kaleidoscope. The clatter of movement, noise, humanity, filled the place, the small scooped lightlivid place beneath the earth's surface. I am alone, he thought again; and entered the cold whitetiled booth, the admonition to cleanliness LEAVE THIS PLACE CLEAN—DIRT MEANS DANGER in bright print at eye level side by side with the outpouring of filth and obscenity from the cesspool minds controlling the secret pencil of predecessor and contemporary—an iniquitous mural of word and hieroglyph daily obscured and daily reiterated in a long eternality like lightless streets down which through all the years he had followed, in town village and city, in office garden and church—a long endless subterrane that had brought him now, hunted, pursued, as it were to the beginning, the startpoint, of his mind's preoccupation : as if now, offering him the yet unheard signal, it said, grinningly, savagely, and with expectant hatred : Begin again.

But there was no beginning again. He stood embraced by the cold white walls. He had removed the spectacles and with the automatic repetition of the years' endeavour became again Arnold Katesgrove. It is useless now, he thought, looking at the nametabs : *Lucian Trent* that by habit he had been about to tear out ; deception is useless. He stood for several minutes in the glazed and dream-like aspect of man of whom memory has spoken, said, It is finished.

He left the toilet and strode up the ringing granite between the disinfected tiled walls into the mill and surge of the station : and up and on into the street.

It was still raining as he walked back down Piccadilly — a long downsigh of soft gleams lying bright on traffic, roof and road. He walked heavily, not fast, with that dreamlike quality of vacant amaze that seemed now to have taken possession of him—that vast quiet surrender toward which he thought, felt, he had been walking for all the dark streetlike years ; as a somnambulist, waking roughly, will subscribe in the end to the persuasive ebb and flow of speech.

When he came to the mews he entered under the dark archway and crossed beneath and through the countless refractions of light that sprang bladelike from interstice and surface—light dappling like a multitude of leaves the now wan broken surrendered face, void of all hope fear courage and all else, awaiting as it seemed the imprint noose and violation of retribution ; so that when he stood before the door opened upon the room so recently left, abandoned, saying to the woman who was already standing there in token of unspoken willingness, I have come back, she did not appear to be either surprised or perturbed but simply watched him as he entered, still walking with that dreamlike esoteric dismay, saying again, not in particular to the woman or to the dumb gay room but, it seemed, to all accusers and sympathizers alike who might stand in beyond or about the room in the sum total of their abnegation and signature—saying again to them, to world, hope and hitherto disclaimed justice alike : I have come back.

10

WHEN Laurie stepped down off the bus into the whirl and
raingleam of Piccadilly he sought shelter in a doorway,
the entrance to a shop, the window a pattern of surrealist
designs athwart a central nightmare-vivid showcard and
plaster heads in miniature knotted about their suave necks
with gay scarves and cravats.

He did not seek shelter to consider plan or movement,
since he was bound by neither time nor circumstance, but
rather because it seemed to him that to shelter there at
that given moment now brought to being upon the inexor-
able face of time *was* the plan, the movement to which he
must concede the purpose and motivation of his every
thought and action, as though he followed to a strict
schedule every detail of a secret and preconceived plan. So
standing now on the rain-muddied tiles of the doorway,
hatless still and in the crumpled suit that had caressed his
weary and griefstained flesh for upward of six days now,
he paused, resolute, his face no longer dreamy immobile
or vacuous, but touched with recumbence, like the
deathmask and effigy of some longdead monarch fallen
in battle.

It was a pause, a receptive moment upon which might be
flashed, screenlike, a fantasy, a reliving of years between
rise and fall of an eyelid's flicker. It was the doorway :
with its checkered inset of coloured stones and the besmirch
of footsteps and glisten of wet mud it was the same, so that
he thought, now as then, I am always hanging about in
doorways *I am always hanging about in doorways*, the
thought exact and precise as the breaking of a dream,
juxtaposed with the exactitude of stencil over some sten-
cilled design upon the earlier wordsame thought which now
flooded into that same space in mind and thought that it

appeared was destined for this very place and occasion of reminiscence.

He was at that time still at nightschool. Every evening at the appointed hour he was despatched—perhaps not so much despatched as dismissed from memory—with the exact sum needed for his return train fare to Sunnymede given him by his stepbrother Arnold.

So that on that night when he was to meet her, for so far as he remembered the first time, there was at first no quality of prescience, nothing whatever that might be construed as omen or foreshadowing of the difference of this night from all others.

It began as it always began. After tea, a meal that in common with all other meals he ate from the barescrubbed table of the kitchen beyond which lay the cold darkstained walls of the scullery where years before he had stood in darkness of mind and soul alike screaming, Forgive, forgive, forgive : the while the invited guests passed across the distant drawingroom doorway,—after that he went up to his room and tidied his clothes. There were still, as there had always been, only three articles of furniture in the room : the bed, the chest and the chair. To these had now been added the few books of learning he possessed and, since the very day when he had been able to spell a single word, a Bible mildewed and broken with age, from which he had, ever since he could remember, to learn by heart a passage every day.

There was no mirror in the room. With a brush and broken comb he smoothed his hair. Without apparent intent or care he adjusted his tie (though it was not awry) and rubbed his shoes with a cloth. All his actions were deliberate, calculated, yet without purpose : automatic, merely. His eyes on this as on every other night bore a look of enigmatic calm, as though beyond them lay a terrific motivation in abeyance. As he descended the stairs the house enveloped him, complete, silent, abstract ; yet he knew he was being watched. For as he passed the panelled door of the lounge he heard the words for which he was waiting, confirmation and seal as it were of the hour and destination :

" You will come to me when you return ", the words assuming that same disembodied quality as did his own when he replied to the closed door : " Very well, Arnold ".

It was the same every night. He left the house carrying the small bundle of books that he would need : a youth upon whom no attributes of youth save possibly the single one of years seemed to rest, unsmiling passive and darkeyed yet still, secret and dark beneath flesh and skull, bearing that terrific suppression of energy that was the inheritance of his years, like the sinew and purpose of an athlete.

Only when he had walked the three miles to the station did he make the decision. It was completely sudden, so that he surprised even himself. He had never contemplated such a thing before : not because he was afraid, but simply because it had not occurred to him. But now it was as if the thought had lain dormant for years, as though he had been living all his life for this moment. So that when the thought sprang newformed and complete to his mind *I am not going to nightschool I am going to town* he did not even bother to recapitulate yeas or nays. He merely said, aloud, as if making audience of the quiet road and the evening hills : " I am not going to nightschool I am going to town ", and walked on past the station toward the spatter of lights and the gray starless overcast of evening.

He had never been in Hartney at night before. Although he was nearly twenty years old he had been there only during the day on errands for Arnold or Christine or Elspeth, or to the innumerable services in the church.

He came to the town. With the same decisive raptness that had brought him thus far he knew exactly what he wanted to do. There was a cinema in the town, a converted cornstore standing at the farther end of the main street, a building of yellow brick and stucco to which had been added an iron staircase and balcony giving access to the operating cubicle, and a Punch-and-Judy paybox standing with a kind of outraged decorum amid the lurid posters and glossed photographs of TODAY and FORTHCOMING ATTRACTIONS. It was toward this that he walked, quickly, apparently at the behest of some rendezvous. But it was not that. He had not been inside a cinema before : only stood before that setup of garish stickups and stills and wondered what it was like.

Night was just beginning. He walked quickly along the single street of the town, a figure for whom apparently no other destination existed, feeling with each step the loose coins, their weight against his thigh through his pocket, associating subconsciously the weight texture and dimension of the coins with the idea of illicit pleasure.

He saw the girl long before she was even aware of his existence, let alone his presence within a hundred yards of her. There was a small scrabble of people before the box-office, shifting slowly toward the clotted light from the oval platesized window of the paybox and the entrance door. The girl was the last of these. She stood in the pale semi-dark of the street itself, shifting slowly forward with the line of figures that bore in the evening-hushed street that quality of esoteric despondence of breadline or labour queue. At once, even when he was still too distant to see any detail of her face or figure, save that her hair was dark he thought savagely, violently, God : let no-one come between us : please. Please please please he almost shrieked aloud (but he did not), without faith, true ; so that as he came nearer to the cinema and perceived that as yet no other person stood behind the girl it must have been with perplexity and surprise that he remarked the granting of his prayer.   He could not hurry more without attracting attention to himself ; yet when he reached the cinema the girl was still the last of the line.   He was not breathless, not having hurried, yet his heart leaped.   He saw her, was aware of her now.   Though it was still the halfdark of the street he could have described her with the multiplicity of detail of a photographic plate.   Something had happened to him : some secret and frightening cataracting of the blood within his veins.   As they moved forward toward the lighted window he was aware only of this and of another agony : the fear that he would have insufficient money. He clutched the coins in his sweated palm.

They were at the window now and he heard the girl ask for a shilling ticket.   It was like an enormous relief of suspended terror.   He had a shilling, a sixpence and three pennies.   He followed the girl through the curtained doorway, keeping close to her so that the usherette might think they were together.

The lights had not yet been dimmed.   He sat next to the girl without looking at her.   He did not want to look at her.   It was as if he knew, was certain, exactly what he must do.

All through the performance he sat without once looking at the girl.   Nor did he look (more than one has to look in fascination) at the screen.   He could not have said a moment after leaving the cinema what the film was about. Least of all then, for as they came out into the quiet cold street he spoke :

" What's your name ? "

The girl turned toward him in mute defensive contempt, " I'm sure I don't know what it's got to do with you ", she said.

They were walking together.   But he was not offended nor even abashed.   " I had to speak to you ", he said. " I had to.   I had to ", and again as the outflux of people spun away from them he said, " I had to ". It was final, cold, remorseless, agonizing.

" Why ? " the girl said.

" I saw you there ", he said ; " as I came along the street. I knew something was going to hap— Something was happening to me ", he said.

" Well ", the girl said. " So what ? " she said.

" Just that. I wanted to speak to you, to sit by you. Is that wr— rude ? " he said.

She was walking slower now. " I don't know. I don't know whether it is or not. I reckon it is ". But her voice was quiet, bemused, no longer furious. " Who are you, anyway ? " she said.

" Laurie Katesgrove ", he said. He had not even thought of denying his name. . . . .

The girl laughed, sneered perhaps. " I hadn't thought the town was big enough to hold two people—two men—of that name ", she said.

" You mean Arnold ", he said ; " my stepbrother ".

" Stepbrother or maybe ordinary brother, to a pig ", she said ; " a ripe swine ".

" No, he's my stepbrother ".

" I hadn't meant that ", she said ; " I meant—Never mind ", she said, " One's enough in my life. Goodni—"

" Wait ", he said. He did not force, coerce her. He did not even stop walking. It was she who stopped, listening to the urgency that was more than urgency, that was pain love and desire, in his voice. They were beside a doorway, an entrance to a shop. The window, controlled by a time-switch, was still alight, complete, dustless, dressed with smalltown frocks and millinery draped and girt about sexless and featureless models like stale entombed wax-works. They (Laurie and the girl) stood on mosaiced stone, coloured inch-squares into which had been fabricated a wreathed design about the monogram K.

They stood there in the doorway with the light beating
upon them, touched now by something other than fury or
urgency, subdued, peaceful and triumphant, as though they
loitered, timebound, in a haven of whose existence they had
not till now even been aware.

" Arnold's shop ", Laurie said after a while.

" And don't I know it ". They had not spoken for a
full minute, nor did they speak again until there had
passed an interval of time in which the street emptied,
completely save for themselves,—a long avenue of spas-
modically off-flicking lights leaving their imprint on retina
and brain, darkening and quietening against the sudden
clanking of a distant train and the cold of night. " It
must be nine o'clock ", the girl said. And suddenly the
windowlights went out, a remote click. It was then, seemingly as if the timeswitch controlled also the cataract of
speech so long dammed and subdued, that she began to
speak, her voice high, flat and toneless, her words free and
unhesitant as by rote :

" And don't I know it. Seems as if this might be a time
for you to get to know a thing or two about your brother.
Stepbrother.   Because I've heard about you : not by
name, maybe, though I can't remember even that because
folks always talk about you as the boy at The Fold, as if
you hadn't got any name, as if you were an idiot or something being kept in confinement. Maybe I've even seen
you about, maybe someone's even pointed you out to me,
because if they did the first thing I'd do would be turn the
other way. Because that's how I feel about you—all of
you. Because of Arnold, the shining light and man of
means, who's made Hartney what it is today. The
benefactor, they call him : like they called Edward the
Confessor. But they don't have to work for him, just
because there's no-one else in Hartney to work for now, in
this very shop where we're standing. They've never tried

getting a job in some other place and being told, We'll let you know, meaning they'll find out if it's okay with Mr Arnold Katesgrove. They've never tried suffering under him, being fleeced by him, being alone with him in this shop doing what he calls Book-work, after the shop's closed and there's only you and him there. They haven't tried having him for a landlord, watching him smirk as he goes past the place you live in—if you can call it living to sleep under a roof that's likely to blow off in the next high wind if the rain doesn't wash it away first. They haven't tried sleeping on a bed that wherever you put it reeks of damp, that steams when you light a fire in the room. Nor have they known what it's like to get caught in the clutches of something he calls the law when you won't pay the rent without he does some repairs—a law that works for him but not for us : because he's up to everything, every trick ; and he's got you. Technicalities, they call them, so that he's just on the right side every time. He sees to that all right. He sees to everything, does Mr Arnold Katesgrove. He sees I can't leave without I go without the dole and have nothing to live on ; and he's precious certain not to sack me knowing what I know about him, about the way he is."

" Hate ", she said. " Do you know what hating is ? "

In the darkness beside her he breathed softly, peaceful. " Yes ", he said. " Yes. I know what hating is ".

Presently she went on, her voice quieter now, imbued with rest, fulfilment. " I didn't think it was possible that a man—any man—could treat his own kind—men, women—like that.

" For me, I suppose I can take care. I'm frightened sometimes, when it's not just disgust, when I'm alone with him in that office, when he starts—"

" Yes ", he said.

" But it isn't only that. If it wasn't me it'd be some other girl. But Daddy : it's silicosis from the quarry ;

but there's something else now. He never used to spit
blood before. The doctor says it's the silicosis, that it
goes like that sometimes. That's what they said after
Daddy tried to blame the cottage, the damp, to get some
repairs done. It's just the silicosis, they said ; it'll heal
in time. But it won't : all the healing that's going to get
done was done years ago when he left the quarry. It's
something else now. . . ."

Her voice faded now, died in the quiet cold air. He
thought, This girl, thinking below thinking, knowing,
*This girl whom I love. Love is the word : love love love :
there can be no other* thinking with some surprise and con-
sternation, I am glad I decided, saw her. With wonder
also, that this should happen to him, that like his own
entrance into a play it should happen this wise, without
design or foreknowledge. And then he too began to
speak, to disclose as it were into the very blankness and
intimacy of a journal or microphone :

" Yes. Hating. That is what we have in common.
There must be something secret in a man, something
beneath, apart from, his brain, his will— something that
guides him. Perhaps it *is* God ", he said. " There wasn't
anything I had planned about tonight. I suddenly knew.
Knew. I didn't know you were who you are ; but I knew
it was you I wanted to talk to. Now I know what I want,
what I must do ".

Later, when he thought of it, and even later still, when
they thought of it together, it seemed to him, to them, that
that night was the beginning. But the beginning was long
before that. The beginning was that day in the oakwood ;
even then he had begun to hate, to triumph.

But now he told her about himself, about his life that
resembled that of a slave. " Because Arnold thinks that is
the way. He hates me, my guts, humiliates me on every
possible occasion. And secretly he is afraid. I can see

him being afraid sometimes. A deed is a lie—like a lie : you get fascinated, watching yourself get enclosed in a web of repetition ; you keep on and on, covering and covering until you have to keep on. That's how it is with Arnold : he can't treat me—anyone—any other way now, and he's frightened. He's like Pandora waiting for the box to open ".

" Pandora ? " she said.

" Yes. Pandora. I live in a garret, eat in the kitchen because that is what my father would have wished, but for a different reason, to satisfy his own fanaticism ; and as Arnold wishes for *his* reason : humiliation. Because he is afraid that I shall watch him.

" He knows that I have a talent for drawing, that I planned to take draughtsmanship. So when I left school he sent me to evening classes—to learn mathematics. You see, he knows I shall fail, that he can parade his derision over my failure ".

" School ", she whispered. " Yes. That's where I must have seen you. The central school ".

" Yes ", he said. " That was good enough for me ".

" Miss Biggleswade ", she said, " do you remember her ? She was Missus somebody, but everyone still called her Miss Biggleswade. She had a daughter—"

" —who used to come and meet her every afternoon, wanting to learn about school so that she could take over. A girl of seventeen ".

" Yes. And she wore one-bar pointed shoes and worsted stockings, even a girl of that age ". She began to laugh, thinking of Miss Biggleswade.

Laughing. That very first night I saw her she was laughing : so that presently when the policeman who was trying all the shop doors came along he heard her and said we'd better move along, get home. We walked off out of the doorway, still laughing as if we'd never stop, as if we'd known each other

*for years.   Like a release from something, thinking of Miss
Biggleswade and Miss Biggleswade junior all the way to
Emmer Lane.   Saying goodnight.   Saying we'd meet again.
in the shop doorway.*

*I am always hanging about in shop doorways, he thought,
said to her once.*

When at that moment Arnold passed, hurrying, detached
himself from the Piccadilly crowd and stared at the window,
Laurie could have put out a hand and touched him.   But
he did not.   He merely came from the doorway into the
surge of people and followed.

He walked slowly.   He did not have to hurry.   All the
while he could see Arnold a little ahead, like a cork bobbing
between the mushroom umbrellas and the slanting incessant
rain.   He felt that same power that a man can feel when
he is making quarry of an insect, a worm perhaps, that in a
moment he is going to crush but which for the nonce he
watches with idle curiosity, with-holding the blow, the
deathblow.   He walked with his hand in his pocket,
encircling, gripping the cold immaculate blade.

Freda, my darling, he thought, almost said aloud, his
lips were already formed round the unspoken words.

She was ill then.   The first time.   It was also the first
time he had used any term of endearment to her.   Although
they had been walking together—courting, Thornton
called it—for many months he had called her only by name.
But this time it was different.

He went into the airless sicksmelling room.   Thornton
was with him, trailing behind him, fumbling with cigarette
and match.   He seemed frailer than ever, as if bitterness
had consumed part of his flesh.   " There she is ", he said.
" She's been waiting for you ".

Freda lay in the bed, flushed, rigid, her body outlined
beneath the faded jigsaw quilt.   It was midwinter.
Beyond the closed window he could hear the myriad

whisper of the cold. One of the panes was smashed, blotted out with a piece of rainsodden cardboard. Even as he watched a slow drop of water fell from the ceiling into a bowl on the floor. He found himself waiting for the minute noise of its splash. " She'll have to go to hospital ", he said.

" Hospital ", Thornton said. " P'raps you think I haven't thought, pestered the doctor about that ; p'raps you think that Arnold, being a director, would find room for her somewhere, even if, as he says, there isn't a bed. You think that ? "

" No ", Laurie said. " No. I don't think that ", thinking above hate, I must do something, thinking as it were without consciousness, as on that first night of their meeting he had known exactly what to say and do *There is cyanide, arsenical weedkiller in the garden pottingsheds, there are knives, razors, about the house, why don't I kill him ?* Yet knowing even without knowing why that the time was not yet, saying as he leaned over her, " Freda, my darling, you've got to get better ".

" Yair ", Thornton said. " You've got to get better. Here ".

" We're going to get married ", Laurie said. " I'm free, white and twenty-one when you're ready ".

" Get married ", Thornton said. " And live here so we'll all die of pneumonia. That's a way out, I must say ".

" No ", Laurie said. " I've got a job in Sunnymede. And the offer of a house. You've got to get better ", he said again ; " so that we can go and live in a suburban terrace and have striped curtains and veneered furniture ".

That was what she wanted, what she always pined for. So there was nothing I could do for her better than that.

She got better. She got slowly and irrevocably better, as if the promise he had given her tempted her away from death's door. It was still winter when she was able to get

out, when they walked again among the hills, in day
beneath the slowfading breath and agony of gray hills, at
night beneath the countless constellations of clear cold
stars.

They went as far away from the town as possible, seeking
to disengage from its clutches. It was a borough now,
Arnold the Mayor. Every week his photograph was in the
paper, which he owned, above three-column articles expressing his views, his assertions of brother love and com-
panionship exemplified in the splendid growing activities
of the town. He was seen in church regularly every Sunday morning and evening and, lest anyone should think his
doctrine too inflexible, he had financed the building of the
new Baptist chapel. There is room for all faiths, he wrote
that week in the paper that carried news of his beneficence.
But he did not write that the contract for the building had
been given to a man who had promised to use a certain
percentage of soft yellow bricks rejected by the quarry.
Nor did he write that he was indirectly robbing his own local
government in whom he expressed so much faith by regularly falsifying his income-tax returns. He did not write
in the advertisements of Katesgrove Limited that he was
employing in his shop, as a milliner's assistant trimming
hats at so much commission a dozen, a girl, daughter to
the man he had robbed, whose money had ironically enough
been the cause and cornerstone of his activities and which
now with equal irony, had grown—on paper if not in actual
fact, cash—to such figures which to that same man whose
money it had originally been would have appeared astronomical. He simply wrote, inferred, that he considered
himself now as a philanthropist as well as a benefactor,
that he would open his heart and his purse to any charitable
cause that used his name in its institutions and publicity.
He mentioned nothing of the slum property for whose purchase he had negotiated through agents from a distant town

or of the rents he had increased. Instead, he wrote
violently about the alcoholic habit and the Sunday opening
of cinemas ; but that was under another name.

They could have gone on being together just in the
evenings and at weekends for a long time. They were
quite happy, not impatient, content to watch for the
future opening like a flower in the sun. But Laurie's hand
was forced.

One day in February he returned to Hartney Fold in the
evening. He seldom saw Arnold now. There had been a
day when he went to him and said : " I am giving up nightschool, leaving. It is useless ". Arnold looked, watched
him from beyond the desk. The desk lay between them
like a continent, neat, clean, immaculate, letters and papers
folded in piles, light glinting on orderly boxes of pins, clips,
on the Morocco paperknife *In the rain his fingers slid noiselessly into his pocket, the flesh trembling along the blade's
edge* on Arnold's flesh itself, pallid, obese, satiric. " Yes ",
he said. " I was wondering how much longer I should be
fool enough to waste money on you, to try to educate the
son of—"

" You needn't try any more. I have already given my
notice of termination in ".

The quiet, satiric, idollike face watched him. " And may
one ask what you intend to live on ? I need hardly add
that any support I have been humanely forced to give you
until now will cease forthwith. It was, as you know, con-
ditional upon my every wish being fulfilled ".

Laurie stood immobile, dissociated entirely from the
room and the man to whom he spoke, with that reminiscence of forsaken statuary at once poignant and futile.
" I've got a job. In a shop ". He was motionless, taut.

" A job ". It seemed that the older man weighed the
words carefully. Yes. A shop. And would it be asking
too much to enquire what shop in Hartney has had the

audacity to employ you without even seeking my consent ?"

" I didn't say Hartney ".

" Ah ". The pallid hands came up now on to the desk. The room was airless, warm, arid. " You didn't say Hartney. So one may presume another place is what you mean. Am I not right ? "

" Yes ", he said. " Yes ". He turned, moving toward the door.

" Wait ", Arnold said. When Laurie turned he saw the other's fingers twitching on the edge of the desk, his lips drawn back from teeth the exact colour of flesh. " I don't think I gave you permission to withdraw ".

" I don't need it any more ", Laurie said. " You forgot something. The date. It's my birthday. My twenty-first ". His lips twisted into a smile. " I don't have to ask your permission for anything any more ".

There was almost-silence in the room : only the faint sucking and cracking of the fire. Then Arnold said :

" In that case, and as you say you have sought and found employment in some place other than your native town, it will not be asking too much of that place to lodge and feed you ; as from—" he turned so much as was necessary to glance at the clock " —as from fifteen minutes from now ".

He went up to his room and gathered his few possessions together. He packed them in a biscuit-tin and left the house, speaking to no-one. He walked to the town and asked Thornton if he could spend the night there. The next day he moved into lodgings at Sunnymede, where he had got employment in the shop of a pictureframer and gilder named Ewart. It was at his lodgings, a yellow brick house in a quiet street with geranium-strewn gardens that a policeman called one day, months later, with a message from Arnold.

" He wants you to go up to the Fold as soon as possible. Seemed like it was something important. We had a bit of bother tracing you. Seems—"

" Yes ", Laurie said. " All right. I'll go. I'll go this evening ".

It was February, dark. The house stood in huge stark bulk behind the inverted fringe of poplars that breathed, suspired softly an insistent whisper of damp, winter. When he went in he stood in the gloomed hall aware of some permeation of cold that was even stronger in the house than outside of it ; as if his absence had made him sensitive, acute.

Arnold sat behind his desk in the study, ordered, precise, his face immediately without the down-funnelling of light from the desk lamp. The room was warm, stifling. From the closed and curtained windows came the faint dripping of the trees. It was silent enough to hear that. Then Arnold spoke, his voice controlled, smooth, ironic.

" You may as well sit down ", he said. " It is likely to be the last time you will do so ". Like a fish in a dark aquarium, Laurie thought : he looks exactly like that, touched with gray shadow, his hands limp and boneless, as if he had just withdrawn them from evil things and washed them without removing any of the lecherous evil into which they have plunged. Or a snake, he thought : that's it : a snake— hooded, waiting to strike. " I wanted you to come ", the older man continued, " for an important reason. I have heard from Father's solicitors : a letter bearing great sorrow ". He shifted in his chair, gross, obese, repellant. " Yet it will doubtless be no shock or grief to you to learn that Father is dead ". His voice ceased, like a broken thread.

Laurie did not move. When he spoke his voice was light, almost facetious. " As you say, it is neither shock nor grief. I had little use and less love for a man I hadn't

5

seen since I was five years old, who the only thing he ever
did for me was to give me a mildewed Bible and tell me to
read my way through it, syllable by syllable ".

The other nodded, a nod less than movement, a mere
breathlike blurring of the ivory flesh. " I had not expected
more from you. From a man—if man you can be termed
—born of a guttersnipe and with all the guttersnipe's
attributes inherent in your bones, your very flesh. Lay
aside any desire on your part to assuage the obligation you
should feel toward the parent who saw in you at least a
human soul ; lay aside any feeling of gratitude felt in common humanity toward a man who sired and nurtured you,
saw that you were tended and fed by my sisters' own hands.
Such feelings of common human decency would be foreign
to you, therefore strange if you had exhibited them. But
insult—insult to him who now lies dead in a strange land,
his hands and heart worn out by good work : that I will
not tolerate. Nor need I ". His voice stopped again.
With a fanglike movement of his tongue he moistened his
lips.

" You can say th—"

" Listen. Wait ". Arnold was leaning forward now,
into the light. " Months ago I took it upon myself to
inform Father that you were—carrying on—there can be no
other than a suburban expression for a cheap suburban
alliance—with Thornton's daughter. A cheap hussy who
is in her right place in my shop embroidering hats at so
much a dozen. A bitch : just such a bitch as you, born of a
bitch, would turn to. I informed him of this. To-day,
mingled with the news of his death—even that you could
not dissociate your lechery from—comes his answer, in his
will and testament, of which I am the executor. The sole
executor ".

Laurie did not speak when the voice paused again ;
and in a moment it went on, slow, smooth, vile.

" Your name is expressly excluded from the list of beneficiaries. I see it was hardly necessary to tell you that.
Nor will it be necessary to tell you who those beneficiaries
are. But it is necessary—as well as a deep pleasure—for
me to tell you this : from today and so long as your
association with Thornton's girl continues you are forbidden
to enter this house of your birth. Is that understood ? "
The voice ceased, the man leaned back beyond the
cone of light. In the fire a coal fell, an upward scatter of
sparks.

" Yes ", Laurie said. He was quite calm, emotionless,
as though he had listened to a weather forecast. He was
even smiling a little. But he did not move, rise from the
chair, for a full minute after he had spoken, leaned across
the desk into the light that flooded now his quiet lucid hate,
saying, without tremor or variation of tone :

" Yes. I understand. I hope you understand too ".

11

UNDERSTAND, he thought ; can you, she, he, ever understand, begin even to believe without understanding, how
close is death : from the cradle, from the womb, from the
very instant and desire of conception even, I am with you,
close, shadowclose, he thought. I am death, he thought.
From the very moment of my delivery into life I have been
death for you, my brother. I am death, he thought again,
now, finding the knife in his hand, unshielded.

He was walking, not fast, keeping the centre of the pavement. People fell away from him, made way like water

spinning round a rock. Above and around him the skysigns and the city lights span in the spangling rain. The
roar of traffic filled his head, echoed in his hammering
heart. Faces fell away, past him, drifting away, dying
like foam, floating, grinning. Grins, teeth, eyes, up and
down on the lightsurface and rainsparkle. From a subterrane restaurant an orgy of people rose up in his path ;
on to the path, spinning, laughing, whiskeysmelling.

" Careful, old chap—"

" —where you're going—"

" Mind that—knife ".

" Want to kill us all . . ." features zephyring away,
inchoate, whiskeysmelling, sad. Not by knowing, he
carried the knife point downward along, close to his leg,
held flat with his flattened palm, walking with light passing
and passing across his face, the red and green traffic
signals' glint at the intersection of roads, the falling rain
like dust on his taut gaunt face, the dark mad eyes and
the dry lips parted on dry teeth and speechless tongue.
I am death, he thought ; and within the spinning lights
of his mind, cunningly, *I am death and no-one has seen
me yet*.

Ahead, perhaps a dozen yards, Arnold was bobbing
among the rainglanced faces, hurrying a little now, it
seemed, peering backward from time to time through the
dark spectacles. *He is the only one that knows ; and even
he is not sure, not certain yet.*

When they returned (the dark glasses were gone now,
he noted with some amusement outside himself, as though
a part of him still responded to norm) he was less tense.
He walked easily, casually, watching the same shops pass
in reverse, the vista of lights fading into endless light itself,
like a hall of mirrors, traffic whirring and clotting at the
signal lights, replacing itself as it spread away, endless too.
At the junction of an alley running downward away from

between darkened buildings he paused a moment, listening
to the secret beat of his heart. Pausing, he heard a
woman's garish laughter spread like a stain over the
traffic's and the city's whine and undulation, like the
beginning of all enticement. He walked on, his hands
thrust into the pockets of his jacket. The rain had soaked
through to his shirt, touching his skin with a finger of cold
faintness. But he was not aware of this. He was not
aware even of the direction in which they moved, journeyed.
All sound smell and sight had been subdued, whittled, to
the fine bright dimension of the crowded rainlaced faces
crowding into and out of his vision flanked by the inter-
minable vista of light, the Saturday night happiness brittle
and laughlimned on the mouths and in the voices of those
that passed, foaming away behind him, leaving ahead of
him the vast disseminating perspective of Saturday night
in Piccadilly London England down which I, he thought,
I and my quarry walk alone, fugitive and in silence, to the
beginning of morning. *In some dark and sourceless place
shadowed by high walls and rungs of lightless windows* It
will be there, he thought.

They had come to the Ritz. Ahead (he watched,
motionless, timeless and quiet as the shadow in which he
stood) Arnold paused, looked back (in the shadow, he noted
the torn collar, the awry cravat) and crossed quickly to the
central street refuge, ponderous, elephantine ; and again,
as if with suddenly realized terror, to the far side of the
street.

They were precisely opposite each other now. For a
second, between the beadlike vehicles, Arnold looked
directly into the shadow in which Laurie stood, leaning his
shoulder against the gray wet stone, quiet, carven, smiling
now in that attitude of wonder and childlike pleasure that a
watcher might construe as reminiscence of some remote day
in childhood or youth, or even of emotion recollected in

tranquility, but which no watcher, human or magician, could have known as hate, or even threat.

Standing there with his suitpockets outbulged by his bunched hands, the smile on his lips quizzical, faint, elusive, passed and passed by faces and voices at every flicker of time. With the incarnate and incalculable smile of death overfilming his eyes and throned within his mind.

Death, he thought, seeing again for an instant across the shining ceaseless street his quarry, his brother, though not by blood alone, turn and disappear finally now into the dappling of light and shadow beneath the high garish and brillianced buildings : death. The word one with the smell, the overpowering odour infesting with the magnitude of darkness, of night, the small cold rainseeped room wherein stood in shadowed solemnity the gaunt iron creaking bed, coldbloomed and moist to the touch, and the effigial shape of the man, frail to the point of fleshlessness, above whom Freda and he stood watching, tearless and exhausted, beyond midnight, beyond any time place or dimension whatever, it seemed to them, merely watching.

It was Thornton. He died in winter, at that hour timeless in itself, when nothing in the whole world, it seems, bears any relation to living.

They had watched in turn, sleeping fitfully in a chair beside the bed, for three nights. On the third night they watched together.

He had eaten, drunk, nothing but the brandy they forced between his teeth since Sunday. It was now Wednesday, the night in which he died ; or perhaps he was already dead before that, before death came into the room, perhaps he was too tired, too bitter, to wait even for that ? Laurie wondered then.

They had heard midnight strike, and one, and two, from the clock in the belfry of the new Baptist chapel. There was a light scurry of snow falling, invisible amost, drifting in the quiet yet whispering street like the confetti aftermath of a long forgotten wedding ; it fell across the uncurtained window like dust, slowly, smurring the dark glass. No fire burned in the grate. Above, where the chimneystack thrust through the ragged birdinfested thatch the bricks were crumbled away leaving a gap through which a spark would have set the roof ablaze in less than a minute. From time to time a fine powdering of soot and a few flakes of snow fell into the dead, rusted grate. On the table beside the bed a small brass oil-lamp glowed, turned dim, spinning upward a faint thread of smoke across the garish text that hung with profound abstraction in the centre of the dampstained wall : GOD IS LOVE. The whole scene—room, watchers and watched —was redolent of a Victorian oleograph. The Dying Father.

Then Laurie became aware of death. He was standing, his hands linked before him, looking straight across the bed not at but completely through the girl who stood on the far side in exact formal repetition of his own stance and demeanour even to the gaze which in turn looked through and beyond him, so that to a third watcher it would have appeared that their apparently uncomprehending fixations of gaze met and crossed in midair, like twin foils, above the motionless figure on the bed.

Then was the odour, the effluvium of death rife in the room. It is like earth, he thought,—corrupt, sodden and corpsestrewn : earth long forgotten and unturned, reviled by even the Golgotha in which it might be found, fouled and decayed in and by all the long generations since the formation, the birth, of even earth itself. It stinks, he thought : putrescence unbounded.

Together, as if actuated by identical pulses, they leaned over the bed. In the room the cold stirred the drawnback curtains, twisted the thread of lampsmoke into frayed black breath.   The snow fell on past the dark glass, cease-less, terrific ; and suddenly, as Freda held the lamp slightly askew above the face that looked now exactly the same as it had looked for three days but into which now without a doubt death had breathed, Laurie crossed to the window and drew the curtains.

" Yes ", she said ; she seemed to be speaking to someone outside the room, quietly, almost as if she had not intended to speak at all, nor even knew that she was speaking : " yes. And this will not be the end. Will it ? " she whispered to the cold still face yet speaking not to it but to some power or thought beyond thought, beyond even comprehension ; and again, whispering, " Will it ? will it ?"

That was the first time he had seen, smelled death. (For her it was not the first time : she had watched her mother ; but that had been sudden, violent.)   He told her afterward of the stench, how he could not rid himself of its memory. She said : " With Mother it was wall-flowers : she loved them and their scent stayed always in that room until something else took its place : the rot that was natural and worse than natural because a man caused it, watched it, let it be ".

On the day Thornton was buried Laurie and Freda took what things they wanted from the cottage and went, with the few small ornaments and keepsakes packed in a card-board box, to Sunnymede.   There he had found lodgings for her in the same street of yellow brick houses in which he himself lodged.   In the *Hartney Herald* there was a three-column spread photograph of Arnold, like a headstone to an article in which he expounded full details of his plan for the complete redecoration and part rebuilding of Hartney Fold as A Permanent and Worthy Memorial to the memory of Felix Katesgrove, who died in God's work, January 19—. R.I.P.   They read the article as they sat in the train, read it without comment.   Laurie read it first and then passed the paper across, already folded to show the photograph and the word OBITUARY, underlined, between picture and columns, an implication that appeared to have struck no-one. The train ran on like a bead falling slowly down the long necklace of rails, between the gray dead fields under the long opaque sky, and presently, as they approached Sunnymede, between the garbled roofs and neat arrayed gardens over which gleamed tawdry washing and facetious ornaments, the creosoted fences and tidy outhouses in and about which children ran in the gardens, muffled against the cold. They seemed to have been travelling for ever. Though it was but an hour since they had watched the dark sodden earth scatter among the bright odourless flowers dusk was already coming. They thought of it, without speaking, without putting life to their thoughts, spreading over the cemetery and the freshturned earth—a dark intensity not of design but rather of un-design, a purpose enfolded and with-held to which only in a like dusk or end could an answer be found. Before they ran into Sunnymede lights were coming on all over the town, in all the windows, one by one, it seemed in evocation not of the day they would replace but of night. They could see people seated at tea, images in miniature, tiny by distance, surrounded by the impedimenta and folk-weave of their station, quiet, speechless, neither gay nor sad, behind windows like a thousand prosceniums in which an eternal repetition of theme was played out. Looking at the houses, at the random erratic windows, Freda said : " There. Like that. That's where I've always wanted to be. In a house like that ".

" Yes ", he said. The train was slowing, stopping. " That's where you're going. To a house like that " *was what she wanted, what she always pined for. So there was nothing I could do for her better than that. But it was too late.*

5*

But it was too late, he thought, coming like shadow itself from the shadow in which he stood seeing again for an instant across the shining ceaseless street his quarry turn and disappear finally now into the dappling of light and shadow beneath the high garish and brillianced buildings.

His hands still bulging his pockets he moved, seemingly melted, without haste, into and through the traffic, stopping without stopping at the central refuge with, as he poised there for an instant, that definite semblance to preying hawk or osprey manifest now in that fleeting poised stooped shape, carved, talonlike and statuesque before he was already in movement again, hasteless, plunging, to the road's far side. He could still see Arnold. As if his eyes were directly drawn by some magnetic attraction he saw him again, at once. He was ahead, walking not fast but heavily, among the shadows of high buildings. Then he turned away, slow in vanishing, into a side road, the road curving, with a central linkage of taxis along its smooth rainy surface. When Laurie reached the corner the road was deserted save for the slow surrendered figure of Arnold. He watched him walking, moving from light-pool to lightpool, tiredly, between the high lamps of the quiet street. Then again he vanished beneath the high stone archway entrance to the mews. The street was quite empty then, like a long dampgleamed slate.

He followed, silent among the shadows. A car turned into the road, raking the long vista of brownstone houses and tinelike railings with its lights, passing him, speeding ahead. He walked on. At the stone archway he paused. He was deep in shadow. Then he passed beneath the pale glim and into the courtyard. It had ceased raining. He stood there, quiet. He could hear the faint surge of traffic and even, in deepsilenced pauses between the sullen dripping of the rain from branch and cornice, voices speaking, laughing. These were in the mews, subdued behind curtained windows. He watched the windows, the faint stirrings of laughter. Two boys came from an upper door and clattered down the iron fireladder ; he could see them, turning across the confettisplashes of light ; they reached the courtyard, giggling and talking in falsetto voices. They linked arms and crossed the courtyard towards him, and as they passed he smelled perfume. But they were past him then ; it was as if he just smelled the rain, the wet earth and the long gleaming highlights in the street, and then, when they were long past and faded to a querulous silence, the zephyr of perfume.

Because he was thinking, looking up at a darkened windowshape, thinking, with the certainty of clairvoyance, That will be the one, in a minute he will be there, framed in the lighted glass, a fleeting glimpse that one might have of an inebriate or madman, gazing calmly, cunningly, from the light brightness of his sanctuary.

(In a moment he was to see that very happening : the window suddenly alight, the womanshape peering down through the glass and, like a Hydra, Arnold's head peering too, down into what was to them unfathomable darkness.)

But now he thought : Only it won't be any sanctuary, he won't have but a minute's peace because he will know I am watching, waiting. He will know that, he thought, he will know that—as he has known it, secretly, always.

He stepped now from shadow into a broken fragment of light, the light coming from behind bars, a basement window, lying across him like mimic bars itself, like tautened lyrestrings, golden across half the flesh of his mad weary face, a pellucid caress of tenderness as he watched upward to the window that now shone with light.

12

SHE had not switched on the light again after he left.
The music had long ceased, the record playing to its end
and then circling with the needle in a dead clicking groove
until the spring ran down.   But she did not bother to stop
it, she was hardly aware of the faint ticklike motion until
it had actually stopped.   She sat in one of the red chairs,
in the darkened room, wondering if he would come back.
Then she knew he would come back.   Because there is
only me, she thought, thinking *Men rotten stinking lousy*
men why the hell do we me any girl suffer them?   All our
lives tied up with them.   " You blasted men ", she said aloud
in the small quiet room.   *You men that can't even keep to*
the small bodily evils the simple things that don't hurt anybody
but yourselves but you've got to go all the time for busting some-
thing up, somebody else's fame and fortune, and then the one
that gets busted wants to come and bust you too so it goes on
for ever.   Listen.   Why can't one of you just stop, break the
circle so it won't go on for ever?   Why can't one of you do
that—so then all the others'd be so dumbstruck they wouldn't
even know where to begin again.   Somebody said that once :
turn the other cheek—Jesus or Shakespeare or Gladstone or
one of those guys.   But nobody's tried it yet, they're all too
busy twittering about why you can't do it, why it's wrong, why
it ain't practical, why it don't mean anything at all, that it
was just one of those quotations those guys make up to put
in a book or something, for some wise geezer to wag his head
over and say That's it that's the answer but nobody'd better
try it in case it blows somebody up or something.   So no-
body's ever tried a word of it in case they start something good
instead of something rotten and manstinking.

Yes, he will come back, she thought, because that's
what they've done for God's thousand years : come

back looking for somewhere to snivel on : a sanctuary :
if it's only one they pay for with their rottengotten
money.

So he was that : a plain swine, robbing, thieving, living
on a reputation he got for going to church regular. And
coming here these seven years and me a blasted fool trying
to thing he's just a kittenish old codger catching up with a
sowing of wild oats, me taking him to the Caravan Club
because he says he wants to complete his education, me
watching him as he sits there watching the high spots the
nigger and the white girl the nigger girl and the mule and
the eunuchs and the lesbians from the Caspah watching it
all when there's me nearly sick and him sitting there with
his eyes glaring like lights and me never tumbling never
worrying because I guess I'm paid to put an approval stamp
on all that and all the time him with a double life and a
single life as straight as a donkey's back leg leave alone
his double life which is my business and which he pays me
to make double as I can which I wouldn't mind if I could
think he even went home or about some place and made
even one person happy during one minute of the seven days
before he comes to see me again, crawling, craving for anything that's got filth written on its label. You'd think a
man's going to get tired of all that muck cluttering his
mind. But not Luce Trent. Ain't nothing sacred in
womanhood to him : not a thing.

A landlord. But a swine. And once a swine always a
swine. Because with a mind like that he hasn't even got
room for a conscience until something, somebody, catches
up with him. *In revenge.* This Laurie, after him, watching, waiting, because of what he did to the girl. And then
he's all conscience, fear, sweat, without even the guts to let
himself believe there's nothing likely to happen to him
half so bad as he's made others suffer. But the other
fellow, Laurie, there's nothing he can do now to bring the

girl back *so there's the other cheek, what the guy said.   But it
wouldn't be no use telling him, he'll go on to the end the beginning round the circle.*   O these men, she thought, o these
damn' men.

It was quiet in the room.   But beyond the door that
bore her name (You've got to have style, a name that
sounds something) : *Elise Brooks* in copperplate characters
on a small white oblong of pasteboard pinned with a tack
to the red wood was the sound of laughter, women laughing,
some bacchanale which normally she would likely have
been attending but which now merely irritated her.   Standing at the cocktail cabinet she poured herself a drink.
Whiskey.   In the dark she took more than she had intended.   There was no soda or water : there was some
limejuice but she didn't bother.   She just took the drink
and crossed to the window and stood there, with the glass
in her hand, not drinking yet, looking down into the light-
quilted courtyard, seeing without the seeing registering
in her brain *so it is not raining now* hearing the faint dying
laughter like the echo of a thousand lost generations, dying
in its own afterglow.

Then she saw him come in under the archway, seeing
(also beyond knowledge) his face *My God his face look there
at his face* his steps body and mind surrendering to whatever might be waiting anywhere, slow, foreshortened as
he crossed the curling spaces of light, then again his face,
seeing now, comprehending, thinking, My God, his face, it
looks like the end of the world, as if he'd really found out
about himself, or perhaps it's only stinking lilyliveredness
yair that's it sure as fate because he couldn't see how rotten
he was if the damn' mirror he was looking at broke to
pieces of seeing, receiving, his rot.

So when outside the door he lifted his hand with the key
ready to give him entrance she already had the door open,
the room dark behind her, the stone-flagged corridor in

which he stood lighted by a low-current bulb at its far end with an effect somehow squalid and evasive, as if regretting even the thin coating of light it gave to the walls and the brilliant doors inset like grins; with him standing there until at that moment when he was about to enter and looked over the threshold into her pellucid eyes with a little glance of something that might have been thanks or just plain selfpity, and then walked straight into the room (even then she did not turn on the light) saying to judge hope jury or whoever else in his mind was audience, " I have come back "; so then she knew even a little more about him than she had feared she knew. So then she was quite certain.

" Yair ", she said. They were like two shadows suddenly made substance in the dim room. The woman still held the glass in her hand and now she began to drink, fiercely, like a man. " What else could you do but come back ? " Even in the darkness she knew he was trembling now. " You'd better have a shot of this ", she said.

Even when he drank he could taste nothing. Then it burned, livid in his inside like hot wires. So it has come to this, he thought : I who could and did hold a town of seven thousand people at my beck and call, doing my bidding and reading my word, trusting and looking up to me as to a king in miniature ; to be skulking in a shadowed room with a woman who is feeding me the alcohol I abhor in others and have never trusted in myself, because I am held at the behest of fear that began less than twelve hours ago, that came with the chill touch of morning forgotten by summer, that will linger now, that is part of me now, permanent and peremptory, burning my inside with the rot I had better have let free within me forty years ago.

Forty years ago I started out in life with nothing in my pocket but a Church Lads' Brigade button and a few coppers. I had a good father. All you boys had good fathers. It's

*up to you. Play the straight bat. Run the straight race.
By God's good grace. A clean life : the door to success :
that's all there is : one door to success : a clean life, Steer
clear of vice, temptation. Look at me : a life of continence :
alcohol, tobacco—they're the devil. Sport, clean living, God
at your side.* " That's what I told them ", he said. His
eyes were burning, turning.

" Told who ? Told who what ? "

" The Chur—the Church Lads ", he said. " It was the
first time I spoke to them. No. It couldn't have been
the first time. The last. On the fifteenth. I don't know.
Can't remember ".

" You ", she said. " Talking to the Church Lads.
God ! that's rich—rich ! " Laughing, she turned on the
light. When she turned he was standing, swaying a little,
the glass in his hand. " And now you're bitched. With a
dram of whiskey inside you ". Light glinted on the bright
fringe of her hair, on the tinsel ear-rings. Her eyes were
bright, hard, like two dead stones watching him. She
watched him. The glass tilted, spilling whiskey and he
bent forward watching with the intent calm of a child the
slow trickle from his fingers. " Take a look in that
mirror ", she said. " See if you can see what I can see.
Get a good laugh. Christ ! " He turned toward the
mirror, slow, paunched, debauched, flesh sagging within
the rainsoaked suit. He could see nothing, nothing at all.
Then a haze, a nebulous shape that he knew, told himself,
hard, hammering the words into his own brain : That is
me, that is how I look. But it was only something that he
thought he should see that he saw. Not what the woman
saw : the tilted drooling head stupidly smiling, the glass
downturned at the end of the limp arm, the dark whiskeyreeking stain on the crushed tweed.

The woman went to the window and looked down.
" Here," she said. " Come here ". She took his head

and pressed it to the glass. " There ", she said. " Can you see what I can see ? "

The glass fell from his fingers. The woman looked at him with the dead cold stone eyes. Then they lighted, like filaments glowing behind opaque glass. She touched him, a faint fingerlight touch that she might have given a curtain or an already closing door. He swayed, rigid as tumbling statuary, into the chair ; even then he did not become pliant : he sat stifflegged, the legs in their stained and whiskeyreeking cloth sticking out in front of the chair, his whole mien redolent of a robot laid pendingly to rest in the slightly too-small chair. His head lolled. The woman struck him ; his head stiffened and relapsed ; she struck him again, quickly, on the cheek, a blow vicious and weightless, such as a mother might bestow on a child. She stood before him, standing between his outpropped legs lightly, almost lithely, with the veil-like wrapper falling about her body as she struck at him, first with one hand and then the other, a succession of the light vicious weightless blows that seemed both hating and pitiful ; then she began to belabour him with her muled feet, on the stiffened legs, not ceasing to strike his face but interspersing the blows with her foot like the offbeat of another rhythm. It was quite regular. Then one of her mules came off and she stopped striking him. But she still slapped him, the blows regular, insistent, sharp. She still watched him though he was quite beyond knowing whether she watched or touched him —still watching and slapping him with that mute hating pity that when he began to vomit over her staccatoing hands did not even register disgust but only the remote almost vanquished echoes of some tears that would not flow or retreat, that stayed brinked behind her eyes.

That was at nine o'clock. She ceased quite suddenly and turned away and moved toward the bathroom. When she had washed her hands she returned and sat in another of the red chairs. She did not look at him. She turned out the light and went to the window. In the shadow of the archway she could see the less than shadow of Laurie's bulk. She could see the live end of his cigarette, motionless, like a dead star, waiting. She thought, He is smiling, actually smiling, waiting there. Arnold had begun to snore. She walked round him and moved toward the divan; then she lay down, relinquishing, thinking, He is waiting, because this is not the time; nor is it the place. But he will wait, she thought; even till morning.

So it was that Laurie, watching upward to the dark windowshape that had lighted and showed him Arnold's and the woman's faces peering down at him and then a few minutes later had darkened again, thought, But it won't be any sanctuary because either he's drugged or drunk and won't know or he knows and is trying to make himself not know; and either way the drugging or the drunkness or the forced ignorance will fade away and then he will know; and anyway it isn't time yet, he thought; and this isn't the place either, he thought.

He was standing under the archway now. He might have been waiting for a lover. Somewhere a clock struck, nine *It must be nine o'clock, she said. Don't get so het up, she said. Honey honey honey, she said. Don't get so het up, she said.*

Because there is this: a beautiful memory. Always a beautiful memory. The memory of you. In my solitude you haunt me. In my solitude you taunt me. All the sticky floppy songs you loved: moons and Junes and yous and blues, two gardenias at your plate and don't forget dinner's at eight. But it wasn't. Because you said if there's one thing you wanted appreciated must have it's a good solid meal midday like a tramp or a navvy or a shop assistant or a clerk. Which all right. I agree. What don't Igree? Is ever anything you want I don't agree.

Is ever anything you want you can't have say the word if in power Post Office savings bank ninety-three pounds ten and fourpence. After the furniture. After everything. After we settled. Then start.

It was a house attached on one side to an exactly similar house in a street dotted along its entire length with pairs of the same bland tidy smug houses. The street was a thousand streets and differing only in name from them— and perhaps not even in name, for even that was as stereotyped as the road and the houses themselves. There were trees, maples, alternate with lamp-posts, silver-painted and curlecued. It was in Frampton, a town across the other side of the county, where Ewart had opened a shop and offered Laurie the managership. He said he thought it would be best for Laurie to get as far away from Hartney as possible. Laurie did not know it but Ewart opened the shop mainly because he wanted Laurie and Freda to have what he called a chance. He was a sentimental man. But Freda had set her heart on Sunnymede. " Wait till you see the Frampton place ", Laurie said. " It's got a metal draining-board over the sink and green tins in the kitchen cabinet, all labelled Rice and Sugar and Coffee so you can keep Paraffin and Aspirins and Petaldust in them. It's a honey ", he said.

" You're a honey", she said. She was there, *looking into all the rooms, poking her nose her small soft body incurved my arm standing close to me close close close with all the happiness in the world in her eyes because now she was among all the things she really wanted the sentimentality the pots and pans keeping the place for me home home home the little housewife no talk no reading but Peg's Paper and Silver Star no entertainment but once a week to flicks dance or pub* " Because that's all I've ever wanted," she said.

So it was given to me to make one person happy like the motto says You'll pass through this world but once so do

it now because you won't be up this street again.   So that
was our little hour.   But you had that much, my darling,
which is more than some have.

And then it was over.

And then it was beginning.

At the Registrar's office that day.   No witnesses.   Only
our two selves.   And the Registrar a kindly man saying as
he'd said a hundred, perhaps a thousand times before,
Your full name and age and state meaning bachelor or
spinster, and, Put the ring on please, and, Sign the register
here, please, and, I do hope you'll be very happy.   Then
shake hands and thank the witnesses, who were two passers-
by and even more embarrassed than we were only then we
asked them to come and have a drink and they said they
were Elim Foursquare Gospellers and didn't drink anyway
and thought it was frightfully heathenish to get married
outside God's blessing but were really too astounded about
finding each other—two Foursquare Gospellers outside one
Registrar's office in the same street in the same town at the
same moment and not even knowing each other until we
caused them to be brought together—that they couldn't
be angry with us because we'd blasphemed and offered them
alcohol.   We laughed about them all the way home.   Because that was what you were made for : laughing.   So if
there was nothing else to laugh at you laughed at me and if
I wasn't there you laughed at you.   So sometimes you
waked in the night laughing. And then it was something
else : it wasn't laughing : it was thinking of what was too
close to you because I hadn't got you away from it long
enough.   There would never have been long enough.
There isn't time enough in the world to get away from it.
But mostly you laughed.

Beside me. Curled. Whispering lovewords you got
from glamour magazines somewhere. Whispering. Honey,
honey, honeybunch. Beside me. At night. In the

opposite armchair. All on the nevernever. The true
suburban way. Me watching. Wondering. You watching. Not wondering. Because you had in you my darling
no capacity for wonder : only acceptance. And in me was
all the wonder for both of us : seeing you unfold, become
something, something you weren't before. Seeing you
become a child. Seeing me become something I never was
before too. With nothing. With nothing but a house and
a girl and a bus to catch each morning. With nothing but
those. Day after day. Night after

night was complete now. A long lone wind curled
through the street touching the thin tenuous raingleams,
stirring them like silk. It was a completion, an abnegation.

He stood in the shadowdappling, twisting and twisting
cigarettes between his fingers, lighting one from another
and tossing them away, none of them smoked more than
halfway down, so that now they littered, glowing, about
his feet and in a moment died, one by one, like stars at
dawning. The buildings of the mews hung like a back-
cloth.

Perhaps at one moment of this, the beginning, of his silent
vigil, it occurred to him that he might enter the mews and
go up to the room in which sat lay or watched his quarry ;
perhaps he even saw himself move as it were across the
shadow gone from his body and walking slowly ahead as he
watched from where he was standing, the shadow invested
with its own eyes nose and ears finding the door, mounting
the cold stairs to the corridor, walking slowly along in the
faint glow of the bulb, looking at each door without knowing for what he was looking then suddenly coming on the
red door with its grubby card bearing the name that he (in
shadow) might know at once was the name and place he
sought ; perhaps he watched himself enter the room and go
straight to the figure standing lying or watching somewhere

within the room, watched himself lift and plunge the knife again and again ; perhaps he even thought for a moment that that was what he should do ; but as quickly he thought again, No, this is not the time. Nor is it the place.

The long wind touched his face. It had music, a song. Far away the traffic shifted suddenly along crowded horizons. He felt himself far away from it, high above it, looking down. He moved from the archway into the long deserted road with its infrequent lamps and gleams of rain, standing watching down the long polished road that led now like all roads only to one : the shadow above himself watching himself go down that quiet street in morning and return in evening not even knowing he was happy not even knowing until it was too late that there was nothing else to have.

Every week they went out, together. It was on Wednesday, the early closing day, they went to the cinema most times, but occasionally it was a dance in the local coöp Hall, or in the summer it might be a picnic. If it was the cinema they sat holding hands or with his arm encircling her shoulders in the manner of the very young. She came to think of the cinema, the plush seats and deep carpets, as luxury ; and as if he partook not only of her body but of her ideas too he came to think the same way. They went once, in summer, to Hartney. No one remembered them there, or if they remembered they showed no sign of recognition. There were posters about the town advertising a Youth Leagues Convention at which the President, Mr Arnold Katesgrove was to speak, to inaugurate a great recruiting campaign. The world needs youth, the posters said. They bore the picture of a Bishop who had promised his patronage, side by side with the President's portrait, the two faces seeming to watch each other with calm remote hypocrisy.

They had tea in an imitation Tudor Café where the waitresses were all middleaged reduced gentlewomen with pastel overalls and careful gray hair. Over the door a sign swung on an iron arm : Ye Warmynge Pan. A man who shared their table told them that the town was enjoying unprecedented prosperity, a boom, all thanks to one man. He looked at them, beaming, munching toast. " You'd never believe it if you hadn't lived here as I have. I've seen him do it. That's why I was proud to join him ".

" Join him ? "

" I'm a director. Katesgrove Limited. I have the greatest admiration for Arnold Katesgrove. I certainly have ".

" And his cottages in Emmer Lane ? "

" Those old places ? Why, they're not worth a light. Uninhabitable. No-one lives there now. We built a fine new block of workers' flats over the other side of the quarry ".

" At his terms. And his rents ".

" Sure. That's the way business is done. Anyway, what do you know——"

" Nothing, Laurie said. " Nothing at all ".

" Anyway, what do you expect a business man to do ? Take people's own terms, whatever rents they offer ? Why, things'd be—"

" Yes ", Laurie said. " They would, wouldn't they ? " They finished their tea and went. " Come on ", he said. " Let's get out of here ". When they got home it was late. " I never want to go there again ", Freda said. " I feel sick when I go near it. As soon as you're in the place you know he's about, somewhere, contaminating something ".

" You're getting quite a deep thinker ", he said.

" It must be Mrs Bonnamy next door ", she said. " Her husband's a freethinker or something. He doesn't believe

in—well, anything, really. Perhaps she's made me a bit
. . . cynical ", she said.

He laughed. " Cynical ", he said. " Says you ", he
said.

That was the first year of their marriage. They did
not go to Hartney again. The road always led somewhere
else : every week it led to the cinema or the dancehall or
the bus-stop. It was a pattern : every morning one way
along the road, every evening back along the past same
houses in reverse, Good evening Mrs Brown Mrs Smith
Mrs Robinson Mrs Jones what a lovely day what a lousy
day what awful weather what lovely weather isn't it hot
isn't it cold isn't it wet isn't it that's Mrs Brown dear she's
going to have a baby be nice to her dear lift your hat say
how do you do that's Mrs Jones dear she tells me her
husband's got a bonus this year and a five shilling increment
on his wages as well of course you could ask Mr Ewart
after all he's never given us anything ecxept those three
pictures which you liked so much *Degas Manet Degas* so
really he could afford it because you have increased the turn-
over out of all proportion since you've been there because
he must have an end in view in making you manager. . . .
An end. But there was no end to the road : backward and
forward, morning and evening, day, month, year. And I
was happy, because *To what end ?* did not bother me, did
not once enter my thoughts, which ran in the same groove
as my feet, every morning to the bus, every evening from
the bus, paper under my arm, umbrella swinging from the
same arm, turn at the corner, wave, look down the road,
down the long

road was no longer deserted. He could hear footsteps.
Then they died away. There was nothing, nobody, only
the chain of taxis at the distant end of the road where the
traffic clashed and the lights spun. Nothing else. Nothing
is so deserted as a quiet road in a city. Then a policeman,

slow, ponderous, walking with that unhurried precise and measured step. Far away a clock struck ten. The policeman had not seen him yet. He stood now in the courtyard, as if he waited for someone who would appear at any minute. It was exactly that attitude. The policeman entered the court and saw him. He said nothing. He walked slowly round the mews shining his torch upward. The beam played over the walls and doors like a spot of sunlight reflected in a mirror. Then he went away, Laurie thinking, Now he has seen me.

He might never have moved. He stood under the archway with that bearing of an awaiting lover. He flicked away the last cigarette, watching it curve.

From the window, the woman watched him, thinking, There. He is waiting. Like I said. She turned on the light and went to the bathroom and fetched water in a pitcher. Arnold was still rigidly asleep in the chair. She stood the pitcher on the cocktail cabinet and began to clean off his vomit-stiffened clothes. She did it carefully, almost tenderly, standing all the time outside herself, watching herself perpetuate the tender careful movements, thinking ceaselessly, Christ, and now it's me ; now it's me playing the little mother or the big sister or some damnfool thing. Why do I do it ? she thought—why, why, why ? All the time she was thinking what she would do, how she would get him away, thinking at the back of thinking, knowing, *I have planned this all along, since he came today with that horror painted in every pore of him, that horrible fear that I loathe and spurned him for and that I am now condoning, pardoning—even aiding and abetting because I cannot help myself, because there's something in a man that a woman must help and it's something that is only in the kind of man you must hate too because in the other kind you love them or something—something that is different from hate— and you can say Get the hell out of it, knowing they've got the*

*guts to get the hell out of it so you can forget them : but this
kind you couldn't ever forget : you'd always remember them
and think of them looking like an animal—reproachful.*
" You curséd men ", she said aloud. " You damn'
men ".

She knew just what she would do. After that it's up to
them, she thought; I ain't going to stand like a shield while
that feller shoots my body first.

When she had cleaned him up she began to bathe his
face in the cold water. But it wasn't any good : he was
too far gone. You'll have to wait awhile, she thought ;
otherwise they'll think you're already dead when they
take you out. " Could you beat that ? " she said. " They
might blame me. Well, it's early yet, pal ; four hours'll
see you through. And for me some shuteye ". Once more
she turned out the light. Standing at the darkened window
she looked down into the courtyard. She could see nothing.
He's run out of cigarettes, she thought ; and he's got a long
wait. Why don't I throw him some down ? she thought.
I'm nuts about men—nuts about them.

Then she went back to the divan and lay looking up at
the quiet dark ceiling. She did not sleep. After an hour
or so she poured herself another drink. She could not
sleep. At midnight the lamp over the archway went out.
It was not till then that she realized how much light it had
given to the room, which was completely dark now.
Standing by the window she imagined lights going out all
over the city, leaving a dark chaos of stark buildings. She
tried to imagine what it would be like completely dark.
But she could not. She lay down, listening to the minutes
tick slowly away. There was no other sound, nothing at all
but the minutes ticking slowly away in the darkened room
in the darkened world.

13

MOVING silently he crossed the courtyard. He had no means of knowing the topography of the place yet he went at once to the single spot where he could observe without being observed. Thinking, I must not be there when the bobby returns, he moved straightaway, not with any undue effort at silence or concealment but rather as if, of all possible destinations, his feet moved of their own volition without thinking or consideration to that one place where he could watch, from which, when the time came, he could act. Although he did not yet even know in what manner he would confront, kill— since he could not have known Arnold's design or movement, or even for certain if he was still in the building—he did not bother to consider alternatives. With a certain knowledge that was entirely animal and in which thinking, circumstance, bore no part he moved to the place that of all places was the one suited to his purpose. Possibly it was an instinctive cunning ; likely such an absence of design becomes a design in itself, succeeds to the intransient and impoverished schemes of logic, circumstance, succeeds even to thought itself when thought has become frayed, volitionless. His movements too had become invested with that animal quietude which could not be learned in a civilized lifetime yet which lies beneath a veil of thought, of thinking. So that he moved without thinking, with no particular reason or purpose for being quiet, since there was none who watched or cared, yet moving with that completeness of silence that surprised even himself, so that he found himself momentarily thinking, wondering, I was there and now I am here but I do not remember moving, did not hear my-self move. He might have been a stirring of darkness itself as he crossed the courtyard. There was still a

dappling of light on the stones from windowchinks and door-
fames. But a watcher would have said, thought, seeing
him cross, A trick of the imagination ; there is nothing
there. It was like a merging of obscurity with darkness,
fluid, innate, concealing ; a complete relinquishing of
thought to sentience. Perhaps during that moment
memory fled back twenty-five years past the tiny relevant
happenings that would in his mind at that moment have
become triumphs and defeats attended by all the posturings
and fantasies of great events ; perhaps memory fleeing
in the moment took him to that other place across a
quarter of a century wherein he lay concealed waiting for
the man for whom hate was already conceived, embryo,
and for whom after that moment in the oakwood would be
formed, inviolate ; perhaps it was that that exalted
sentience in him : but likely not : likely hate bloomed on
the same stem as madness, without cause known to him.

It was a small cupboardlike space contrived from what
had once been an alcove for a purpose none but the con-
triver could have known and which anyway now had been
abandoned, for it was empty. A door, glasspanelled and
too large by inches had been roughly hung on leather
hinges, and to take the weight a furniture castor had been
secured to the bottom edge of the door so that it opened
almost noiselessly. It was in a corner of the courtyard
below the stairway.

— With that same profundity of need that had made him
come to the place he knew that no one ever looked there,
wondered or bothered or wanted to enter it ; that, for the
time during which he had to wait, he must be there and
there only.

It smelled dark, fecund, as if things were growing there.
When he entered he found that with the door shut he had
exactly sufficient room to stand, flattened, and to move his
head to the side of the glass panel if anyone should look

toward it. Yet he knew that this would not be necessary, that no one would look.

He stood there with the door a little ajar yet, so that he could still smell the night, the dark, the rainwet leaves of the limetrees in the courtyard. Far away, with a part of him that no longer—possibly never had—grieved or hated he could hear the surge of the city, the cymbalclash of a distant radio, the voices and laughter that muted by distance were no more than whisper.

Above the archway the trees loomed in even convex bulk, faintly refracting specks of light that had that quality of itself being material, as if flung on the trees in actual speckshaped and tangible glitters. Through the dark arch standing stark and massive with its reminiscence, by trick of shadows' depth, of Doric columns, he could see the road, deserted save for the trees' shadow passing and passing like scraps of burned paper, rapassant, across the trellis of light. Across the courtyard, the buildings rose in monstrous evocation of lightless decrepitude, as it were lifted and tumbled in wrecklike profusion against the prone sky's ordered vanquishment.

Within the alcove he could feel the dank walls, airless and sunless. Memory fled, so that with the touch of his hands on some slimed fungoid growth between the ooze-smooth bricks he found himself thinking, Well; the old scullery at Hartney Fold, beneath the sink where Mrs Stranks kept her mops and buckets; thinking, It is the same : in texture odour and similitude ; and beyond think-ing, knowing *Perhaps even then I knew that redolence would be with me always, even to this moment, so that in the one place I would always remember, or wot of, the other* and thinking, smiling with that joyless percipience of the inane, Well, well, well ; who ever would have thought it ?

He closed the door now. In the alcove he did not crouch or skulk ; save for the closed door there was no

effort at concealment in his stance. He had that poise of a
man playing some game of hide and seek with children or,
anyway, in which the consequences of his discovery might
even be mildly funny.   He was even smiling a little ; and
although—or perhaps because—during five of the previous
six nights neither mind nor flesh had known calm or rest,
he bore no touch of weariness. Standing perfectly still
now : not rigid : peaceful, flexed, his palms pressed flat
against the wall behind him, receiving into his flesh the
dank and infinitesimal organisms of slime, through the
grimed window watching, aware only of waiting, of the
need to wait, of a time at hand, in the farflung morning.

Above the archway the trees moved now in the long
wind, stirring and glancing against the deep sky.   In the
alcove he heard the long wind, the whisper of it.   Nothing
else : the radio had ceased, the voices hushed beneath the
whisper of autumn.

Memory lifting now, fleeting, streaking, fleeing amongst
the risen winds, companioning the dawnflush and lightless
streets of childhood once again, as if in conjuration of some
final cryptic scena in which too would be the vindication
and balance, the final and irrevocable evidence of hate, the
surfeit and undamming of accusation, bitter then and
bitterer now with weight of years and cause.

It was at a party. He could not remember whose or
even where.   Probably he would have no cause to remember it at all but for the reason of seeking since there was
never a party given for him nor for his pleasure save when
that pleasure was merely incidental.   It would not be
Arnold's for he then would be too old for such things,
except possibly to organize them.   Probably it was in
connexion with the church, since there was nothing in his
childhood that was not adjunct to religion or punishment.
Anyway, there were children there, and Arnold also.

It was a room less than room, made over for the occasion,

perhaps a schoolroom or church hall. The walls were varnished pine for half their height and then an ochreous panelling of plasterboard to the rafterstrutted roof. Verdigrised gasbrackets on the walls, lightless, folded against the panels ; at one end a stage, dusty and derelict with that stoic and decayed emphasis of static improviso long glossed with dust, framed by curtain and pelmet of shoddy velvet. The sound of children, rootless and nebulous too as that less-than-room in which they played, peekfaced, about the frugal and barescrubbed tables, their play surrendered to the intense longing repressed and repressed until it had become at once focus and refraction, dominant silent and threatful while they waited to be told they could begin to eat.

Arnold and the clergyman were there. He watched them watching the children, gloating, delighting because they could with-hold the word. " They are poor children ", Arnold said. " We must do what we can for them ; a few luxuries, a cake or two ". The buns were piled on cracked plates on the table, crawled by flies. Arnold and the clergyman did not give the word. The children hovered, impuissant, sad, waiting for the word, the prayer to begin.

He was there. Not among the children : secluded, on the dusty stage, peeping through the dusty folds of the curtain, awaiting the word, another word, thinking, wondering, with childknowledge and sadness *They want to begin, to eat*, thinking *They are hungry : why can't they eat first, why can't they ?* Yet knowing that the triumph must not be theirs, knowing even before he could write his age with two figures that only defeat surrounded them.

Through the curtain he could see them. Arnold raised his hand, *Silence children silence* amid the immediate hush and the clergyman's eyes like flattened marbles behind aqueous lenses breathing from beyond broken teeth the gloating sibilant pronouncement *And now dear children we have a treat for you artistic pleasurable profound depths of poetry the greatest art in which I never myself excelled ha ha ha* the toothbroken brown breath *no pleasure like poetry no gift so great and in smaller meed that of interpretation one so young as he to whom you will be delighted to listen before our Godgive repast stepbrother to our greatest patron Mister Arnold whom you all love glad to have with us today in these ah festivities therefore waste no more time in introducing our young performer Master Laurie Katesgrove* He's going to make them wait, he thought, the thought and hate strong to tears now because with his prescience and identification he yet could not know that the children had learned with hunger and poverty that attribute of defeat that in some future year may be triumph : patience : and that other Christlike quality of humility through which it seems that all Christborn men must stumble before even defeat is learned, before even its crown is worn.

So he thought only of them hungry, wanting to eat, hating him because now it was upon him that hate fell, coagulated and intensified in the eyes watching him with what he thought was, must justifiably be, hatred, but which was in fact the mere patient bemusement of children of their station, to whom even the delayed eating of food was a mere adjunct to pleasure in the same way that to an adult of their station the awaiting on carnal knowledge would also delight, bestir.

He thought at once, I must hurry it *miss out some verses* so they can eat. If they die, he thought *seeing them fall like ninepins, scattering starved accusative* their mothers will say it was my fault, that I kept them waiting. He thought even that in his frenzy.

But they did not die, he thought now, remembering, pondering the thought. *It was I who died, seeing saying scanning the verses When the swallows homeward fly, all the lines committed to memory sweated into me by threat hate and punishment sweated into me so hard that even to eradicate one word was now more agony than learning saying by rote.*

But to flagellate myself was all I could do wanted to do become noble heroic and entirely limelit in my sacrifice. But I didn't know that then. I wanted them to eat. Myself their saviour.

And then he saw them laughing, perhaps not laughing so much as repressing laughter. He had no means of knowing that the Fauntleroy suit and buckled shoes were not part of the task, the very fact of having to appear there at all. He could not know that it was at these that their derision was aimed, that the abnormal was the only thing at which they entitled themselves by virtue of the birth that allowed them no other privilege, to laugh. Nor could he know that but for a subdued snigger from Arnold even their solitary privilege would have been held in check at least until they had eaten ; for the children understood only that authority had laughed in lonely state at something they did not understand but that it was a golden opportunity to release their own privileged amusement.

Perhaps only now do I know, he thought. I, wanting to make a sacrifice, to ridicule even myself because I thought they were hungry ; and Arnold deriding me, leading their derision for looking like I did, how he had made me ; and I thinking *the suppressed tears the broken voice the dying and the agony of humiliation* I had made my sacrifice, ennobled myself for them, being happy because of it ; and later knowing it was in vain, that there was no sacrifice : only ridicule and hate engendered.

So memory erasing now, obliterating the walls of pine, the grubby ochreous panels, the solemn lean and mocking faces, the false gaiety, the tormentors and the vainglory ; leaving only the imprisoned hate—the long reign and apotheosis of loathing, made bright and fanatic with the caress of mind's madness, the grief and inward turning, the knowledge and the presence here above him in that darkened room (it was as if he smelled, had transient clairvoyance of Arnold's sleeping body), the hour and the magnitude of night—in which he twice had scented death and now seemed to his watching self its very brief and breath. I am death, he thought : and within the spinning lightorgy of his mind, cunningly, *I am death and no-one has seen me yet.*

He had not moved. He felt something of a oneness with the earth, the soil on which he stood, the sad slimed wall his palms caressed, feeling even in the vaultlike dying some fecundity, some promise.

The wind had risen. Through the glass he watched the trees, a scatter of leaves like blackened snow on a photographic plate, falling through the lightspaces and the Doric shadows ; thinking, Falling leaves : not an end and demarcation of summer but a pause, an advent of rest and quiet, a peace within the mind, he thought ; the pause before morning ; and again, cunningly, *I am death* and no-one has seen me yet.

He was standing there when the policeman returned on his beat. It was then about one-thirty. The policeman entered the courtyard and flung the spot of light from his torch over the doors. He did not bother : there was nothing to bother for. He crossed the courtyard and stood beneath the iron stairway. He was humming a little, a thin tuneless drone like an insect. He moved away. He had intended to light a stubend of cigarette and smoke it there, but he felt suddenly chill, the need to walk. Laurie could have touched him as he strode away, ponderous, squeakstepped, toward the archway and the road, the blue and bulky symbol of law and order, justice for the masses, kindness to old ladies. You are a symbol of something I belonged to, he thought : for those years of my life I spent with you, my darling, for what the great reporter Kipling would entitle the happiest years of my life—then I too was part of that order, with its policemen and its children, its puppies and its kittens, its nymphs and fauns and all manner of godwottery in its tiny Sundaytended gardens, its clean svelte roads and its bright parks and buses. I too was of it—a salesman in a shop, selling pictures, pseudo-culture for the masses, the new cult, Degas, Monet, Picasso because they are things to have because you don't under-stand art but you know what you like and these things are so . . . so . . . very. . . . Talk, he thought : that is all you could do : talk and say nothing, simultaneously, with that great vacuity of mind that was yours. The tongue in lieu of the brain, only gossip and idle chatter to sustain your days ; the backyard fence across which to ponder and reconstruct in your own little fashion the lives of others. In this manner :

" My dear—right from the start I was . . . well, no, I couldn't honestly say *suspicious* and yet, well, I don't really know what it was ; something *funny* . . . I said to Ted, ' Mark my words that young fellow's *different* '— how different I couldn't quite put my finger on. Not then. But I knew. But it was some time later that Ted said, ' Charl, you're imagining things : young Katesgrove's as normal as he can be '. And he ought to have known, be-cause they caught the same bus, morning and night, right to the end.

" And I came to think he was right—even though I still had my bit of womansense that sometimes whispered things I didn't quite get.

" Because she was the nicest little thing. We even used the same post to tie our clotheslines to, and it was washdays we had our longest chats. We used to take it in turns to make elevenses and then she'd come into me or I'd go into her. I got to know quite a lot about them, really, in those little chats. I always think other people's lives are so interesting, so different from one's own.

" Not that there was anything startling about Freda's or young Katesgrove's lives. Most of it was a bit sad in a way. But she didn't seem to make much fuss. She glossed over it, as if the way she was living now made up for everything else.

" But with what she told me and what I put two and two together and made five of I got a pretty good idea of the sort of struggle they'd had.

" She used to sit there with a cup of tea and one of my homemade biscuits in her hand and sort of smile, as if she was thinking all the time of the future while she spoke of the past. She was that sort of girl : I could never imagine her being vindictive—not actively ; but there was something going on in her mind the whole time. You could see that.

" She wasn't a pretty kid. She was too little, too wispy, and she always wore her hair in that child's bob that would really have looked much better piled in a few curls on top to make her look a bit taller. She had a sort of heartshaped face and those green eye that can be like flashes one minute and ice the next.

" And when she told me about that filthy beast—well, In a way I could understand it : not the disgusting mind he must have had, but the way he must have . . . wanted her, my dear : I can't think of any other word for it.

" They came from Hartney, you know : it's a pretty little place out Sunnymede way. I can see her now, sitting in my chair telling me about it—how she and her parents lived in a thatched cottage, her hands quiet in her lap with the fingers curled and the palms upward, as if she ought to have some sewing in them or something.

" The place—this cottage—was about four hundred years old, and there was a row of them in a lane with a wall the

other side that was as old as the cottages themselves and
once bordered an estate, Hartney Fold, the big house where
this Arnold, Laurie's stepbrother, lived.

" Well, at four hundred years old you couldn't expect
the place to be much.   It seems that before Freda was born
the whole village was much the same : a cockeyed place
with a square and one of those communal pumps where
everybody has to go to draw water. Most unhygienic,
my dear.

" The cottages themselves didn't belong to anybody in
particular, as far as I could make out.   When the estate
had been carved up a couple of hundred years or so ago
they seem to have been left in the hands of some trustees—
people who just collected the rents and did what repairs
were necessary once in a while.

" But they'd got beyond repairing in four hundred years.
Well wouldn't you, my dear !—and were palmed off on
some of the quarry workers who made bricks, which was the
only thing the village had in the way of an industry.

" Freda said she couldn't remember any time that the
place wasn't damp. They were about a hundred yards
from the river, which used to flood at that spot every time
there was a heavy storm, and years of rain and flooding
had seeped into the walls, rotting and crumbling them.

" Her mother was the first to go—though with her, poor
thing, nothing in the world could have stopped her falling
down the stairs and breaking her spine.

" She told me about that so glibly that I was a bit
shocked. I thought she couldn't have cared much.   But I
came to know later that it was the way she told things, a
sort of pose to cover up what she really felt.

" Because when she told me about that stepbrother
she was—well, casual, really ; as if she was telling me
about a schooltreat or something.

" But it was no schooltreat.

" ' He was a swine ', she said ; and I said,

" ' Aren't they all ? ' thinking she was joking ; and she said,　. .

" ' No.　Not the way he was ', and I said,

" ' O ', just like that, not knowing quite what she was getting at, and she went on to tell me bit by bit how after her father'd lost his arm in the quarry and couldn't work any more, how this Arnold twisted him into a business proposition that was as straight as a question-mark and made away with the only bit of money he'd got in the world —the five hundred he'd got for compensation.

" He—Arnold—was one of these goody-goodys who run the church and the town and everything else, including a mind that's like a drain.　He was the big noise all right— church and benevolent funds and youth organizations ＇ antivice societies—the whole setup that people fall when it's in their own town and can see only one side of man—the side he wants them to see.

" ' But it was the other side Laurie and I knew ', she said, and I said,

" ' You don't have to tell me if it hurts, my dear.　But you can bet your life it won't go a step further than my ears ', and she said,

" ' If only it could ', just like that, with just that bitterness that made me think she'd put the whole thing in the papers if she could, and I said,

" ' Well, dear, if it relieves you—tell me ', because I'd got to like the girl by then.

" So she began to tell me how she had to go to work for this Arnold after her father's money'd all gone.　It was a hat and dress shop, my dear, that he'd had the downright effrontery to carry on with after swindling the one man we know of and probably countless more, on *his* money, and then took the daughter to work in his shop.

" Well, with that sort of man it's difficult to tell.　She

just sat there and spoke of some . . . well, actually I couldn't begin to repeat some of the things she . . . well, no, she didn't *say*, but you could understand a lot more from what she didn't tell you than from what she did.

" Mind you, I'm pretty certain that it was *all right* ; you see what I mean . . . yes, absolutely ; but it was the trouble she had . . . pestering her . . . she wasn't the only one, but of course he hadn't the hold on the other girls he had on her ; for by this time his word was pretty well law in the town and other people hardly dare say too much for fear of upsetting him, because he had that much of a hold on the town that really amounted to something.

" Then she got to know Laurie. It was as if all along they'd been intended to meet. Both hating the step-brother like they did ; and Laurie with as good cause as any, for he'd been humiliated and hated in his turn ever since he was a tiny kid.

" So when they came together they knew they were strong. In their hatred, my dear, if in nothing else. Those were the very words she said. She said,

" ' We were united in hatred if nothing else. But there was something else '.

" And I didn't have to ask what that something else was because the whole road knew they were as devoted a couple as ever married.

" So then the next thing there were two of them to bear it. It was her father's death and this time it was no accident. It was plain deliberate neglect of that cottage that Arnold owned, and crookery on his part—raising the rents of the only alternative accommodation just a shilling or two beyond exactly what he knew they could pay— that gave the father lung trouble that hadn't been helped by silicosis from the quarry and had been downright aggra-vated by pneumonia that he caught lying in a damp bed in that damp house.

" She didn't tell me that she'd had rheumatic fever herself too. She cleared it, being young, but it left a weak spot.

" After the father died—that was just before they came here— they got married. The lived over at Sunnymede for a bit until Ewart opened that shop in our High Street here and gave Laurie the managership.

" When they came, it seemed like they were all set up for a new life. And I for one would have said they both deserved it as much as anyone ever does in this world.

" But things don't work out the way we think they're going to work out.

" She'd come into me, and there was never any need to ask if she was happy. They were as different as chalk and cheese, the two of them : she was just a simple little thing like you'd expect to find in a country village somewhere and he was quite a clever type—not that you ever knew it from the way he spoke or that he threw his weight about ; but he was *quiet*, intellectual type, as they say. And you could see he adored her.

" ' Laurie's a dear ', she said, ' we fight sometimes, but we're, well, as I tell him, stickily, sentimentally happy. Like two kids ', she said, and I knew when she said it exactly what she meant.

" You wouldn't have thought there need be an end to the simple sort of life they led.

" But if I'd known about that rheumatic fever I could've told them. But I never knew a thing about it till one evening Laurie came in and asked me if I knew the doctor's phone number. And I said (I was that shocked : I'd been shopping with her that morning),

" ' What's the matter ? Has she got a bad head or something ? ' thinking it was just that or some little thing that I could put right with a dose of chlorodyne or something, and he said,

" ' No. I think it's more than that '. He didn't have

to tell me any more. I could see by his face : quite calm, it was, but as if you'd wrung every drop of blood out of it.

" The doctor came that night. He said he daren't move her to hospital, though that was where she ought to be. It was then he mentioned about the rheumatic fever she'd caught in that wretched place through the evil of that man. And of course, it was a recurrence.

" It must have been then his mind began to turn.

" There's no other word for it. Of course you can understand the young fellow's being worried. But it went beyond that. Ted was going to the office every morning and passing Ewart's shop, unopened, with the three assistants waiting at the door for Laurie to come with the key ; and when he sent round to him for it—my dear, I thought I'd better go myself, having been so friendly. He never even came to the door, so I walked in. He was there in the dining-room. He didn't even know me. He looked as if he'd slept under a hedge for a month. He was standing by the fireplace, and when I went in he just turned toward me and said,

" ' Who—? I've been out in the rain to find her but she's gone ', and before I could say anything at all he said,

" ' Who the hell are you ', and I said,

" ' Laurie ', I said, ' I'm Mrs Bon—' and before I could even finish my name he said,

" ' Get the hell out of here ', not as if he was in a rage, but just quiet like I've said it. And I was so shocked I couldn't say a thing, and already his mouth was working, not saying anything this time but twisting and twisting like a mute's mouth will, framing on words he couldn't put a sound to, but just standing there with his face all unshaved and dirtstreaked and his clothes crumpled and I could not do a thing but put my hand to my mouth and sort of scream and run out of the house.

" We sent for the doctor and he came and gave Laurie

6*

a sedative and said that Freda was doing as well as could be expected in that way doctors have when they know there's really no hope. So it seems to me that Laurie already had it fixed in his mind that she was gone even while she was still breathing because it seemed like he couldn't bear to go near her, that he was completely unbalanced.

"They got him to the bedside at last. But it was like I said : he'd already given her up for gone, as if he'd known.

"Heaven only knows what happened after. No-one heard a sound of him. And then on Sunday Ted went for his usual walk out to the common and saw him there, just walking, like a tramp, with still the beard on his face grown longer now and all the dirt of days.

"He didn't even look at Ted. Ted says he not only didn't look, or look right *through* him in the way some people have, but it was even different than that, as if he was looking at someone else where Ted was, someone he'd get his hands to their throat sooner or later, quiet, empty, and quite quite mad. Ted came back as white as a sheet for all he's a big man, saying something ought to be done, that it wasn't safe, him being about like that, that he might do himself or someone else harm.

"But the next day it seemed all right. Because someone saw him, washed and shaved and dressed quite sprucely and looking as he always did except that he didn't speak ; but this someone who saw him says he went to the under-taker's to arrange about the funeral, so he must have had some of his wits about him.

"And so I thought I might risk another call. I wanted to make sure about the funeral, to send flowers from the neighbours, all of us in the street.

"And when I called he seemed in a way quite himself, because when I got in he invited me to sit down, and he said,

" ' It's on Friday the twenty-fifth ', as if he knew before I even asked, and I said,

" ' O. Thanks,' just like that, and he said,

" ' Yes. The twenty-fifth. Friday ', not looking at me but smiling somehow secretly to himself, standing there with the quiet mad look in his eyes that Ted saw and that hadn't deserted him even though he seemed to act more sensibly now. As I thought, my dear. But I was wrong.

" Because on the Thursday I went into the town to order the flowers for the funeral. Everybody else in the road was doing the same that day : thinking of him and being sorry, because after all we knew what it must be like for him, we've all had our happinesses and we know what it's like to lose them.

" But to come back that day and learn that she'd been buried that afternoon while we were ordering the flowers —well, it took the wind out of our sails. We knew then he must be mad ; and perhaps we thought of him with some compassion when we all offered to help him one way and another and simply got insulted—you couldn't call it anything else to be so rudely spoken to when you make perfectly genuine offers to help.

" So we were dumbfounded, and a bit, well, *hurt*, to say the least ; for we knew he needn't have been *rude*, whatever he felt like, and after all he's not the only one in the world who's lost his wife. Though it must have been awful knowing it was through his own stepbrother, that but for him and his greed and rotten ways she'd probably be alive today ".

Even this very day

now stirring in the womb great motherness of night beyond those windstirred trees beyond that mute and massive arch beyond the pale sad glow of the city's sleep-flushed hush beyond the animate drowse of neversleeping

beyond beyond beyond, he thought, beyond even the

memory now of happiness that once was yours, my darling, my cold deathscented darling curled there among the myriad earth as once you curled warm sleepscented in my arms saying, Happy happy happy does it matter in what manner? and laughing within my sleep with happiness that is gone now too, stale and forgotten as yesterday's bread yet pined for longed for and awaited, here for this little while, these little hours of justice, avengement, the Monte Christo touch. And then my darling no longer waiting no longer beyond no longer anything but us. Together.

After a while he thought of time, of hours and minutes during which he had stood in solitude.   He thought of them as moments he would have to account for, to someone, to her.

He could smell the dark, the long cold iron dark.   It pressed about him, intense, arraigning ; and he thought, knew *Yes yes it will be all right by morning. Not longer* because already then as if in answer to probe and accusation an oblong of light fell suddenly on the courtyard, intense, bare ; and he looked up toward the lighted window already thinking even as retinae and brain coördinated in the awareness of light *It will not be long now.*

Once he saw the woman, brasshaired, eyes sleep-swollen, stand before the window peering down into the courtyard. Then she passed, shadowed on the courtyard. He did not see her again. He could have been hewn from stone, yet still without that rigidity of stone, as he waited ;   and when in a little while the taxi spun into the courtyard, circled and drew up at the foot of the stairway, two feet away from him, from the door behind which he sheltered, watched, he was still thinking, No : it will not be long now.

PART THREE

14

NOR was it.

To him for whom in this crisis a minute or a month would have seemed a mere division of time it seemed something less than, entirely apart from, time itself. He and the other protagonist of this less-than-drama might have been suspended entirely without their own watching selves in some spaceless and timeless limbo in which neither dawn nor dusk nor high noon played or possessed any part.

Yet he was still aware (though nonetheless without its having any bearing, influence, on whatever would or might take place) of the quality of night. It was as though with a part of him he stood and approved the presence of dark and of those trivia of circumstance that might make his task easier, yet with another part of him he could scorn all such incidental aids with the certain knowledge of what he might call (insofar as he needed it) success.

For he could not have known (beyond what he surmised was her intention : to procure Arnold's escape) what plans the woman had made. He could not even have known with any certainty that she was not actually on his, Laurie's, side, that she might not, in fact, abet him,—save that if the thought had occurred to him (which it did not) he would immediately have answered it with another : No ; she is a woman : in this case her sympathy will be with the hunted rather than the hunter ; because even she, by virtue of her abasement to him, has participated to a certain extent in his sins ; because even she will feel in a certain measure guilty ; and the compassion of the guilty is for the guilty. But he would have forgotten one thing : he would have forgotten that her compassion would be bounded in itself by the compassion she would feel for her sex ; he would forget that, being a woman, she could with ease ride with both hunter and quarry and destroy both with equal unconcern. But even if he had remembered that knowledge that by men is seldom learned until too late it would not have altered his intention. Even if he had known that the woman was later to telephone to the police with exactly the same despotic unconcern with which she had ordered Arnold's escape he would not have wavered, for that too would have seemed a completion of justice.

He believed no less now that this was not the time or place. Even with the taxi within a distance that he could have spanned by stretching his arm he believed that the moment was not yet ; even when after an interval during which he could hear the regular and portentous click of the taxi-meter he was aware that Arnold was being half led, half carried down the iron stairway he still believed, knew, that this was still not the time or place. Because there is still that final torture of hope, he thought—like that tale of the Inquisition where the prisoner is permitted to spend four years of his life digging his way through the earth beneath his prison only to emerge into the daylight and the awaiting arms of his captors : there is still that moment in which he must think, believe, that he has escaped, that he has nothing to fear. That will be the moment, he thought ; and by token of his desperation it will also be the place, he thought.

He did not even have to wonder how he would follow the escaping man. The answer was there suddenly to his eye :

the taxi—not follow : accompany : an ironic inversion of
circumstance that caused him now to smile a little behind
the closed door of his hiding place. Like the man fleeing
from death to Samarra, he thought : only to find death
awaiting him there, on appointment.

The taxi was of the type with a rack at the rear for
luggage. He was already there, crouched, silent and invisible while Arnold and the woman and the taxidriver
were still descending the stairway. He could hear them,
their erratic progress. He had slipped from the alcove
without any noise at all, like a pouring of shadow itself.
He hung to the rear of the vehicle with the ease that might
have surmounted a stone lying in his path, not looking for
foot-or hand-holds but finding them there under his limbs
at the exact moment he needed them. He squatted,
perfectly still, not breathless or even excited. He could
feel the faint shudder of the vehicle's engine, a tremulous
movement like earth over which some distant cavalry
approaches. He had perforce to crouch doubled ; yet he
seemed to occupy no more space than a trunk or box might.
Amid the dense shadows of the courtyard in which the
vehicle itself was hardly more than a vague outline, he was
completely invisible.

He could hear them descending the stairs. By a mere
movement of peering he could see them—see, that is, all
that could be discerned in the deep blackness. By sound
alone he could tell much more.

" His bloody feet and legs are like fagpapers. Christ !
he must'ave had a doing. He must've. . . ." The taxidriver's voice unwound in a long complaining tirade.

" He'll be okay in a bit. When the air's got to him.
See, he's better already. Yair. He's okay now ". He
knew at once it was the woman he had seen at the window,
thought, Even though I know now it must be her, it can
be no other, I know I still would have recognized, placed her

voice even though there had been a thousand other voices
speaking with her ; because that is exactly the sort of
voice I expected her to have—brasslike, harsh, promiscu-
ous, yet retaining that quality of compassion that makes her
woman, regardless of timbre, feminity.

" Stand up now ", the woman's voice said, still speaking
in that same harsh cymbalvoice, " stand up. Stand up ",
then quieter, whispering almost, furious, fury-articulated,
" bastard. Rotten bastard ".

So she knows, he thought, thinking, *I have known all
along she must know* he has told her, by conscience or necessity he has told her, if not all then some part (and likely
leaving untold that part that is the more obvious for being
untold) that has merited, outdrawn, her abuse. Smiling,
thinking, Yes even her he has to tell, to make confidant,
because there is no other ; in all the world no other but a
harlot whom he knows, must secretly admit, will bestow
the compassion his own sin has denied from even
himself.

They were standing beside the taxi now : the little
group of three people that, without seeing as he crouched
at the rear of the taxi he could picture in every posture
and movement.

" He'll be all right once we get him in ", the woman said
now. Through the narrow glass of the rear window he
could even make out now in shadowy form the woman's
head ; as if, still unaware of sex or designation he might
still point, in a parade of a hundred such women, to this one
whom he had never even seen save for a moment, and say,
It is she.

" He'll be all right once. . . ." Her voice fading in the
strain of exertion ; and the man's voice rich, deeply humor-
ous with that laconic dryness of the Londoner : " O yes.
Once. Once upon a time I s'pose he had two bleedin'
legs of 'is own. But not now. Get up, f— you ", he

said. " Excuse my French ". And then the third voice at last, slurred, broken : " All ri— all ri— I c'n manage. I c'n namage. . . ." Hiccuping and giggling suddenly, " whassis, whassis ? . . . is it . . . ? "

" Yair ", the woman said. He could hear her slapping at his face, quick light blows.

" All ri— all ri—"

" This is all right, betchalife. In the middle of the night. Playing patacake with a bleedin' drunk. I'm going to ask you for my fare first, lady. I can see I shan't never get it from this 'erb—never this side o' morning an' a Bombay oyster ".

" You'll get your fare all right ", the woman said. " Just help me, for God's sake. I've got to get him awake, make him understand. You'll get your fare all right. But I must—"

He squatted, listening. It was perhaps five minutes. Then he began to hear, to know, that the drunk man was slowly coming round. He began to speak more or less sensibly now, but his voice still loud, louder than the woman's, which was subdued, urgent now.

" Listen, Luce. If you go to this place—"

" What place ? O. Yes. I thought I'd been—No. It was Nollys *Must be careful what saying Nollys Elise Tufnell Park great thing Christine and Elspeth not know where yesssssss yes yes yes. Elise standing there over me hand patapatapata eyes shining down on me and then in my hand the cold cold glass then in my throat the burning burning black black black all black behind before above amid along long corridor of blackness screaming whirling sighing into rest peace final oblivion. Then what ?* but of course you're Elise. I am beginning to remember ", he said. " I am beginning to remember. Yes. I was—"

" Shut up ", the woman said ; " if you don't want to get in a worse state, shut up ".

" Yes ", he said. " If only I could sit down for a minute. If only—"

" In a minute ", she said. " Listen. You're going to the place where you wanted to go ". She was speaking now slowly, distinctly, each word and syllable valued and charged, as if she spoke to a child of some trivial matter that must be conventionally kept from listening adult ears. " To the place where you wanted to go. Do you remember? Do you? Do you understand? Here's the address. I'm giving it to the driver. He will take you there. When you get there these people will help you. They will help you to get where you want to get. Away. Now do you understand? "

" No. I—"

" Christ ", the taxidriver said. " Now he don't even remember. Get away—put away, it ought to be ".

" Ah, shut up ", the woman said. " Here's the address. Written down. Can you read it? "

" Not in this bleedin' darkness of light I can't, so 'elp me. Give us the bloody paper, lady. I'll read it right enough when I get down the east. At this bleedin' rate it'll be bright noon by then. Cable Street, you said, didn't you? "

" Yes ", she said. " There's some friends of mine—of his—there. They'll take care of him. They know. They'll know . . . I've put a note in his pocket. It'll explain. Just take him there. That's all. Here's the fare. It won't be more than that ".

The conversation was carried on with the quick precision of a musichall act. He could hear the taxidriver reading the address (he had walked to the front of the car and held the paper in the light of the sidelamp). Between them the woman and the taxidriver had got Arnold into the taxi.

Quite suddenly they were moving. The movement seemed to have sprung from nothing at all, not even from the tremulous engineshudder of the vehicle. It was as if he had slept for a moment, crouching there on the then still and now moving vehicle, a movement during which the woman faded (even of this he could not be sure) in a remote staccato tap tap tap up the iron staircase out of his vision (insofar as she had ever been in it), out of his thoughts and out of his life for ever. But even of this he was not sure. They were still then they were in motion, without any interim of which he was aware, without valediction. Perhaps he did sleep for a moment; perhaps it was not even sleep: a temporary cessation of awareness, of sensibility; possibly there was in actual fact no more to hear or be aware of than he heard and knew: the sway of the vehicle as Arnold was thrust in, then the woman's heels tapping upward and away, then the movement.

They were passing beneath the arch, the wet limetrees with their convolutions of light. One of the leaves fell, brushing his flesh, he smelled the rain and earth, felt the rich fecund texture in its minute caress. The road fell behind in a long shining ribbon. In a moment they were in Piccadilly, still bright, but empty now, a long deserted space in which, it seemed, nothing had ever lived. As they moved rapidly through the streets he saw from time to time a patrolling taxi, shadows drifting across lighted windows, the twin red and green glints of trafficlights on the shining roads; then, running beside them, the black viscid gleam of the river.

He was not even thinking; and he had ceased to notice the strain of crouching. He was empty, volitionless. It was as if, being awake and receptive, all thought hung just without the door of his thinking. The city sped by, enclosing, scattered with lights, the loom of walls above him, rows and rows of blackened windows then, like a lone bright flag, a lighted window fading and fading, crossed by bulk and screen of masonry and cornice, then a building blazing with light and sonorous with noise, then darkness and narrowing streets.

Then he began to think. It was Freda. They were crossing the river, the lonely lamps sentinel above the slow turgid water. He began to see her even with his closed eyes. They were together, somewhere deep, an arbour enclosed and coiled in twining flowers. A river ran near, they could hear the gentle motion. Birds flew and circled.

There is nothing so beautiful as the flight of birds.

You hear that ? And yet I can think of things as beautiful. You, for instance. He says his name is Shula Horn. The birdwatcher, the friend of kings, the discerner of beauty in the flight of birds. He asked me something I did not understand, but I understand this :

The warm sleepscented hand flowerlike in its immobility upon the pillow ; some speechless beauty that I have seen sometime and recollected in tranquillity *this, this is tranquillity : with all thought and motivation awaiting consequence* Freda—your warm hand body scent breathing here beside me. Then no longer your breathing. No longer you. Days up to that *no longer you* days and nights in which we said, Thank God we *know* we are happy, stickily, sentimentally happy perhaps, *how* happy is surely immaterial *Freda you said that once : how, meaning in what manner, is completely immaterial.*

Thought entered, focussed. They were still crossing the river, moving rapidly, lights spinning behind. A long parabola of necklaced lights spinning in and out of vision.

I that will watch his descent to the pit from which surely he must have sprung. I smile grimly dimly a little primly Arnold, my brother, he thought, thinking you have escaped, thinking you can get away. There's no escape, he thought ; for any of us ; no escape.

Then he began to prepare slowly in his mind details of what had not yet happened, as he remembered preparing

details and little stories of what had happened to him
during the days at the shop. He knew she would want to
know. In the darkness they had lain, nightly, whispering
of each other's daily activities. He knew she wanted this.
Although their days were without variation she would insist on his retelling all the trivial details, as she would
insist on telling him of her own day, of conversations and
expeditions, tiny consequenceless things that delighted her.
So now he began to think what he would tell her. He tried
to capture a simile to tell her how he felt at that moment,
at any moment during the day ; but there was nothing,
no word. When I come to tell her, he thought, it will be
all right then : I shall remember.

They were running between high lightless buildings now,
narrow, leaning athwart the dark night. They rounded a
corner and he could see the narrow grimed fascias of Yiddish
shops : in one of the doorways the vague form of a girl,
beside the momentarily lightslanted glass a file of men,
waiting. The road ribboned backward, flat, empty now,
the infrequent lamps suspended like smudged coins.

Inside my mind you wait, he thought. My silent darling.
Inside my heart you live. My waiting silent darling. In
    side the swift smooth rushing vehicle
    Arnold
    Arnold waiting also
waiting upon the uprush and surge of clarity within his
mind now, remembering, gathering together sense and
swirling vortex of horror, thinking, What did she say ?
About some people, waiting for me, to take care of me, to
take me where I want to go.

But where do I want to go ? he thought.

He looked at the rushing streets. His head was clearer
now. He found he could remember the day, the whole day,
every moment of it as clear as water. Yes, he thought ;
he will follow, trace me, but if I am gone, beyond water, to

some other shore, perhaps then. . . . That is what she meant, he thought. Then he remembered she had spoken of a note. He took it from his inner pocket. It was a single sheet of paper in an unsealed envelope addressed to a man in Cable Street, Limehouse. The note was scrawled in pencil : *MAX. Get this geezer out for me, he'll pay.* All the banknotes that were in his pocket had been put into the envelope with the sheet of paper. To note and money clung the faint odour of femininity, not perfume simply : an evocative state of womanpresence. Stink, he thought : filthy womanstink and lechery. It was a sickening, a turning away even from his own mind. Possibly if he had thought of his own life, his own actions, at that moment he would still have been repelled. He could feel only the one consuming sensation : fear. All else was subjugated to it. By his side was a small mirror, inset into the doorframe of the taxi. He glanced, peered into it : but he could see nothing but a pale moving shape. His hands were dirty : he could feel that ; and when he touched his clothes he could feel, smell, the vomit. He sweated, felt the sweat beneath his arms, cold when he lifted them away from his body. He looked through the rear window. Here the streets were alive with furtive shapes : shadows merely, he told himself ; but once he saw hands and a face, apparently bodiless, among the shadows of a door. Then again : shadows moving into shadows, scythed by the long road, engulfed by the dirty shops and narrow whispering sideroads. He could see no sign of a pursuer, yet he knew that there would be, could be, no such sign. He felt his tongue dry and hard in his mouth. It suddenly became necessary, vital, that there should be speed. He leaned forward and slid the glass partition.

" Hurry ", he said ; " hurry, man ", but there was no response, neither in speech nor speed. They were already travelling fast, past the grimy shops and the somehow obscene Hebrew characters above the window eviscerated of all save the fleeting dark shineslant of the glass, past the grim lightsmudges from the infrequent lamps, past the stunted railings that formed with their jalousied shadows a kind of poignant circumambience wherein crumbled in desolate corruption the grimed threestorey houses, the tattered gonfalons of Hebraic words, the solitude and threat of the countless alleys and courts.

" Hurry ", he said again ; and this time the driver half turned.

" Whaffor ? " he said. " Ain't no hurry I know of. Anyroad, we're travelling quite fast enough for me. And I reckon I'm doing the driving. There wasn't no hurry back there when the lady wanted to get you in. Not a bleedin' move would you make to help yourself. Bide your time ".

" Yes ", he said. " The time. What is the time ? "

" Threeish. Can't be much more. The buses and trams start 'fore four ".

Presently they turned. It was a narrow lane of small darkened houses. At the far end a single lamp bloomed. Its sicklied light fell on four white posts standing on the brink of some apparent chasm.

" The river ", the driver said. " Can't take you no farther. You go down them steps and double back along this way. It runs along them 'tween them warehouses at the back there. Cable Street. Dark as buggery it is, an' about double as narrer ". He got out and opened the door. Arnold could now see him, only a bulky outline.

" All right ", he said. " If you can't take me any farther—" The engine of the vehicle was still running. Neither of them heard anything but the engine. Neither of them saw anything. They were standing with their backs to the vehicle. They saw nothing of Laurie as he trod softly into the road, the shadows, melting into them, watching.

" Down them steps ", the driver said again ; " double back :

don't go straight on or you'll walk into the bleedin' river ".

" Yes ", Arnold said. He felt the sweat on his body, cold. When the taxi drove away, the sound of the engine dying slowly, whining and dying through all the gear-changes, fading to nothing, to a slow and utter silence, he thought, I am alone. He stood without moving, unable to move. On the silence now he could hear the faint seep of the river, a sound viscous, heavy, like muted wind. He thought of eyes watching from behind dark windows. He was certain they were watching him. He turned suddenly and began to run, toward the lamp, the faint distant pool of light. The walls of the houses pressed, lunged at him. He was running, hearing his heart, his sweat, the leap of his blood.

He was running, transfixed, as though with a part of him he stood and watched himself run on, toward the light. He leaned against a wall, listening to the torrent of his blood. The footsteps died and he thought, with the part of him that watched himself run, They are mine : the echo of my own running footsteps. Then slowly the thought screamed into his brain *But they are not running, those footsteps, they are slow, quiet* and he began to run again, beneath the looming silent walls.

After a while his breath subsided. He began to walk, an actual movement and design of limb and brain now, think-ing, as a hunted animal might, If I stopped in a few minutes, suddenly, I should hear, know.

Almost within the pale flowering of light he stopped, suddenly. Behind him the footsteps came on, slow, deliberate. Then they ceased. The pursuer had stopped.

Arnold ran, fast, lumbering. In the light he glanced down, seeing his own legs moving, thinking, Yes, I am moving now, running.

He passed beneath and beyond a lamp. He did not pause before descending the steps to the river. He might have been a man crossing the threshold.

The steps were narrow, deep. At the bottom he found himself on a wooden pier built out over the river. There was a maze of beams and struts. It was in the shadow of one of these that he stopped, listening to his pounding heart. He looked back up the stone steps. Then the footsteps came on, into his terror. He watched thinking, *In a minute now, a second, he will appear.*

Then he saw him standing there at the top of the steps, a figure slight, grim, faceless. Yet he knew at once that it was Laurie. He held the knife in his hand. The light caught the blade, glinted. He was passing it slowly between the fingers of one hand. The figure paused, not in hesitation but in some apparent contemplation, bemusement, that somehow carried the implication of grinning.

Arnold tried to scream, a reflexive, involuntary movement of larynx and lips. But it was soundless—soundless, that is, except for a faint gathering of breath and saliva. He turned, stumbling between struts and timbers that he could not even see. He had forgotten direction. Moving blindly he halted every few paces to listen. There was no sound but the river now. Then he found himself away from the pier. It was a muddy weedstrewn space before a high building, towering walls with rungs of lightless windows. It was less dark now. Against the sky were stamped the lacelike patterns of jibs and derricks, shiprigging, masts.

Halting to listen again he thought suddenly, conscious of bravery, of suicide. The river, dark, gleaming. But he could not face even that. He could think only of his own heroism in the thought. Before he turned again to run he thought of evil, the wasting disease of it, the rot eating at heart and mind and soul. Only it was too late then. It was his last conscious thought : he saw himself, ridden with evil, a monster about to pray.

Then he saw Laurie. He ran, looking back over his shoulder through the darkness he could not penetrate, looking back with his head twisted like that of a doll, running he knew not where.

It was at the wall he stopped, trapped. There was no other way to turn, only towards the oncoming footsteps. The walls of the building and quay made an angle wherein he stopped, rebounded with the force of his running, still looking over his shoulder with that doll-like fixture of head and neck toward his pursuer.

He screamed then, the sound at last unpent, crescendoing upward into the high and lightless rungs of silence, unbelievable, recurring only by the very nature of the place in which he stood, echoing from out the angle of the walls, so that for that long instant it sounded like two voices, through every tone and harmonic, rising together, upward screaming.

Then he saw Laurie again, small with distance, a mere shadow unmerging from the jigsaw bulk of the pier, already invisible again before eye had proper time to remark, segregate the shadow from the high darkness and looming walls.

But he could not scream this time. It was as if his voice, soaring to infinity, had ceased there, lost. He knew without making the effort that he was dumb, irrevocably mute. Yet even that seemed to matter little—less than nothing. He was licking his lips, his tongue moving slowly over the lips like cold porous stone. But his limbs— his limbs would not move, respond. Although with a part of his brain he knew that he was spent, cornered, he still wanted to run—anywhere, even toward the ceaseless unhurrying footsteps. Perhaps he thought in that moment (like the general of a defeated army) that at any rate the old tag of attack being the best method of defence was worth trying ; perhaps it was just that he could not bear more ; perhaps it was an entirely involuntary surrendering of spirit, will, to which he simply and automatically demanded the response of limb and muscle. But there was no response, no movement save the complete collapse of his body, downward to the ground in utter relinquishment. Terror was ended, pursuit was ended, all was ended.

Laurie came slowly from the shadows. He moved without apparent haste or purpose, with the calm impeccable delicacy of an apparition. Far behind him, sourced in the river's remote reaches and the city's vague and terrific outline, the russet stain of dawn spread across the sky. The faint light seemed to creep forward with him, not more quickly but, it seemed, with a greater furtiveness, for there was nothing about his movement to suggest deceit, no quality of covertness or stealth. He moved simply, idly, close to the shadows yet already touched by the dawn flush, moving toward the slumped figure by the wall.

When he came there he stood looking down at the body. He seemed to be waiting. He stood slackly, bearing still that apparitionlike stance, his slow hands poring over the blade. Another watcher, had there been one, and had there been light enough to scrutinize the two faces would have remarked, in the fallen man, the complete absence of anything save horror, as though horror had itself been born into him and had clung there beneath that mask and surfeit of licentious obesity all his life until that moment; and would have remarked the terror-struck and abject posture of the collapsed limbs that in their very collapse had become fear-rigid; and would have remarked with what quizzical contempt the other seemed to gaze down at him into whom at that moment he could have plunged the knife he still held.

Yet he still with-held the knife. He stood, waiting, as he might have waited for the other to rise and challenge him. But it was not for that. His mind, save for the contempt reflected in his features was quite empty and grave. Save for the contempt, scorn, he might have been musing on some pleasant Elysian pasture where presently he would be.   He certainly awaited no rising or challenge, though it would never have occurred to him, even in sane mind, that Arnold might conceivably already be dead.   He was waiting—at whose behest he could not have told—for something which he knew would presently happen, as if he stood at an open door thinking *It will come in a minute and when it comes I shall know.*

Then he thought, I have pursued you now to the end of night.   And life.   Through all the years and the solitude. And it is nothing—nothing that death awaits you in my hand *the bla legleam, the slowly lightening sky.*   It is quite without emotion, he thought.   And you cannot even think, my brother ; you cannot even think on your deeds and pray.   Even that is denied you.   Even the thought to have prayed was denied you by your cowardice.   But think now if you can ; think with your silent gutted brain. " There is still time before you die ", he said aloud.

Moments passed.   The city's skypointed horizon grew black against the morning.   In a little while life would begin again.   But he did not appear anxious, to hurry. Standing tranquil and bemused he waited until at last the stain of moving light had crept along the dark anonymous ground on which he stood.   It touched the grim mildewed walls and slimed timbers of the quay, the weblike rigging and unsmoking funnels of ships, the quiet black turgid river ; and, finally, the fixed tumid countenance lying grotesque and seemingly apart from the twisted and horrortortured body in the shadow of the wall beneath the runged silent windows and the dawnstain of another day.

At last he leaned down over the body.   Even the blade was touched by light now.   Speaking as it might have been to some distant watching presence he said, " It's morning. It's nearly light ", speaking softly, peacefully as he plunged the knife again and again into the dead silent body, watching the slow surge of dark blood unwind like a scarf over his hands.

15

THEY saw him return that morning. Sitting about the Sunday breakfast tables or peering with idle disinterest through the neat smug curtains or wandering pondering within the fenced and loop-chained bounds of their plots of lifeheavy earth they remarked his approach down the still cool road in which those few who had been awake to perceive had earlier noted the peaceful suspension of autumn dawn itself, as though it too pondered and watched.

They saw him while he was still afar, certainly before it could have been possible with any certainty to recognize him. Yet they knew. He might have been a personage awaited and watched by some committee of reception. But although twenty miles away newsboys were already on the streets with special editions of the papers screaming amid the roar of London's traffic, " Tragedy !—tragedy in the East End ! " no news of this had yet filtered into the town to which he returned at an hour too early for there to be anything but idle curiosity and conversation in the air.

Later it was to be more than that. There was to be a special edition of the papers screaming the name Kates-grove in two-inch banner headlines into the quiet Sunday street and the diningrooms in which even eating of the Sunday midday meal was ceased beneath horror-raised brows. There was to be a babble of conversation which but for the walls and thin paths dividing the houses might have taken place in some hall at a meeting specially con-vened for the purpose, for it was on a single topic ; but for the nonce it was mere idle speculation.

Those who were in their gardens hurried immediately indoors. They wished to dissociate themselves from any possibility of spoken acknowledgement of him. The road became completely empty, silent. It was a gray sunless morning in which the earth too lay waiting, receptive. In

the town the buses were not yet running and the streets lay
deserted save for the litter of tinged leaves fallen from the
maples in the central square, and the casual scatter of
bustickets and spindrift of dust eddying in the gutters.
The idle chatter began then, whirling and eddying through
the houses and quiet sedate streets with something of
that same quality of spent summer. Even the children
had it presently, making a game, a chant, of the words and
furtive phrases they culled from their parents, repeating
them merely by rote and without meaning, in their homes
and the homes of their friends and, on the morrow, in the
schools too, so that there clung before the day was through
a presence of something which in later life they would remember and call evil, but which then, at that age presumed
innocent, was to be for them only meaningless and un-
rewarding, in the same way that to repeat what they had
been told were forbidden words had about it that savour of
attraction that savours only because it is forbidden. But
by then it would be common, national, knowledge. Everyone would know everything about everything. All the
comments of all the crime reporters of all the newspapers
would have been digested and brought to that tenth magnitude that is alone the specific of words and rumour ; in
every town in England people would be nudging with casual
relish over other people's wickednesses—at least that : it
would in most cases devolve on questions of principle, of
motive, of opportunity, of the basic insecurity of society
and the impossibility of sending even one's grown children
out alone these days when it came to even the most respectable of men being murdered for no apparent reason at
all ; and in Frampton itself there would be little else but
conjecture, study, and rumour, and bustrips specially run
to the road in which the alleged murderer lived, in which
people would stand in hushed groups, gazing and speaking
as though dragged by their very hair into the presence of

death itself. Then it would die down, of course : the hub-
bub and the scorn and the rumour ; it would fade from their
memories quicker than the scent of a blown rose, fade and
be kindled in little by the reports of trial and sentence and
then fade again like the suspirant breath of summer and the
dying fall of autumn over the quiet musing road in which
folks would still go quietly past the empty house with its
weedstrewn garden and blank unwinking windows that by
then would be deep beneath the memory of unpleasance
and the convolute twinings of hypocrisy.

But now, on that quiet Sunday morning that seemed to
await his return, that seemed to hang crushed and lifeless as
one of its own fallen leaves awaiting banishment, there was
but the faintest augury of what might, could (and would) be.

It was simply their sense of umbrage that made them
turn from, yet watch, him. They wanted to see how he
would behave, hoping perhaps that there would be something else which in their outrage they could deride. He had
spat on convention once ; no doubt he would spit again.
Anyway there was always the hope. Even the things they
knew about him that they had thought of before as admirable were forgotten. Already they were like carrion waiting to pick the evil from his life. So they watched. In
the sparse rooms and low narrow halls of the little houses
they watched, posed like silent masks behind the un-
stirring curtains, pausing in eating, reading, or whatever
household tasks had until then concerned them, to stand
and watch as he came into their vision and then to watch
him ceaselessly with their eyes until he had entered the
house and they had glimpsed, to the renewal of their
chagrin, the mute and dusty wreaths standing like tokens of
forgotten compassion within the dark untended hall ; and
to watch even then, long after the door had closed upon
him, waiting for something to happen—something that
surely must ensnare, trap him. And even that would

come. Later in the morning they would see even that, have even that satisfaction. And greater : the satisfaction of another's evil to console them, to inflate their righteousness. But before tha⁺, before he had entered and closed the door, while he was still beneath their very eyes they could remark what they at first took to be his grief but which (and in actual coördination : so that independent of each other the same idea was occurring all down the road at the same time) before he had taken many more steps they knew to be something else : something about which they could only conjecture horrifically, looking at each other without speaking while they thought (and they still did not know the other fact : that twenty miles away the newsboys were shouting) : He must be, he is, there is no doubt, mad : no longer a figure of speech, a mere metaphor : a fact now, without a doubt.

They looked through their windows on to a road, a stage, already prepared against his coming, over which hung suspended the overbloom and yellow autumn fall of leaves, falling about him with casual recalcitrance as he came now, walking into their vision from the distance where they had first descried and identified him.

He was hatless still as when he had departed ; but that alone would have escaped attention, as would the soiled and creased clothes and the weary unshaven flesh ; cumulatively they gave him the mark of itinerant or beggar and certainly a stranger to such a road as this ; but even that would not have mattered, would have passed all but remark. But the mark of death : that they could not ignore. It was there, about his mouth, a shadow. They had no means of knowing, recognizing it. How could they have ? Yet it was there, lucid and nameless, something imparting horror without knowledge, something intangible, mystic, beyond their grasp. Later, one of their number, speaking of the day, was to say : " You could see in his

face the mark of killing.   It was there, plain as a pikestaff.
Now I know what they mean by a murderer's face".   But
it was not that.   The shadow about his lips was the token
not of the killer but of the vanquished.   But they had no
means of knowing that either.   Grief, avengement, death,
were without their ken when they watched them in another.

So they simply watched, for the moment, and perhaps
shuddered a little—the womenfolk, anyway : the men were
perhaps slower to perceive, respond.

He came walking, unhurried, awful.   Save for the fact of
movement death might already have claimed him.   He still
carried, as he might have carried a cane, the gilded paperknife.   It hung lightly in his fingers, almost as if it were
fixed there, looped to his hand, perhaps, as a policeman's
truncheon might be.   It was bright, glinting and tawdry-
looking, quite free from any appearance of menace or threat.

He had washed the knife, and his hands, in the river.
In this there was no design of concealment : it was a relinquishment, an abatement of purpose.   The water was
dark, oily,   He lay face down in the shadow of a capstan
at the quay's edge.   Behind him the uncoiling ribbons of
blood wound away from the stiff-postured body ; and in
the water they spread out from his hands and the bright
blade.   He lay motionless, without any attempt at cleans-
ing.   His hands merely trailed in the water, holding the
knife.   He watched without seeing them, the wrists
truncated by water, the blade invisible, the long streamers
of darkening red fading and narrowing, fading.   For perhaps five minutes he lay thus, his face, his mind, empty of
all save peace, and the shadow about his lips.   He might
have lain there for longer : he knew no cause to move.
Then, from far down the river the sound of a siren lifted
from the morning silence in stertorous crescendo.   The
sound shattered into his mind.   He rose without haste, his
fingers still holding the knife as though it had now become

7

grafted onto his skin. The siren faded, ceased. He did
not look at the body again. It lay behind him now as he
moved slowly beneath the high grimed building. He
crossed the slimed timbers of the pier without apparent
care, as he might have crossed them daily for years, and
went on up the steps. At the top the single lamp still
burned as if it awaited his departure ; it died now, like a
burned match. He went on up the street looking neither
to right nor left ; nor did he appear to be looking ahead,
but rather inward upon himself, as a man lost in thought
will pass without speech or recognition people he has known
all his life. But there was none who knew him. In the
decrepit houses there were those who saw him and remarked
the knife and who would certainly remember him afterward ; but at the time he excited no interest, no comment
even. Likely those who saw him judged it better to keep
their observation to themselves ; as with those who earlier
had heard a scream rise into the silence. There is a local
wisdom in any part of any city. Here it amounted to a
brief phrase : Keep your nose out. So he went unharried,
marked perhaps as a lascar or mulatto from one of the
ships. He certainly could easily have been one. In the
gray morning that even now was but a pale lightening of
the sky he could have been almost anything. He walked
for perhaps an hour before he realized that he had moved.
Then realization came, slow and heavy as smoke. It was
as if he had opened his eyes to find himself in a strange
place ; as if he had opened his eyes with mild surprise
to find himself somewhere he knew vaguely he should not be.

By then the body had been found. It was found about
ten minutes after he had left it by a member of the crew
of one of the ships lying on the river. This sailor was
returning from a Saturday-night carouse in Shoreditch,
whence it had taken him the remainder of the night after
the orgy had ended to return. Even then his head was not

very clear. He stumbled down the steps with some difficulty and crossed the piertimbers to the quay. He saw the body and the horrorstained face, the slashed garments and the still gushing blood all at once. He stopped, in actual midstride, with his foot held a little above the ground and his knee already flexed to take the next step, exactly like a stilled film.

It was the face. The blood and distortion of the limbs and neck he could have understood, even perhaps appreciated; he was a sardonic man. But the face, drained empty of all save horror—that was too much. He turned, already in motion of running before his feet had concluded the step he had been taking. That was at four o'clock. By four-fifteen there was a crowd of a hundred people on the quay. They watched with fixed curiosity while the white-coated police orderlies bore the body beneath its gray crumpled blanket to the ambulance at the top of the lane. When it had gone they stood in idle speculation watching the spot where it had lain. They watched as the detectives began to take measurements, photographs. Eventually they drifted off in small batches and returned at odd intervals throughout the day, silent, hands pocketed, watching from behind the white tape and the sentinel policeman who strode round the now dried red stains and the sad anonymous ground. They might have been awaiting anything. From time to time one of their number would refer to a folded newspaper, to the photographs of the very spot on which they stood, of their own watching faces, and start a babble of conversation. This went on throughout the day. On the Monday none of them was there. Many of them passed the spot on their way to work, but none paused now. There was a different crowd there now. Sightseers: silent idle folk who had come merely to watch and remark the spot where the body was found. They in turn drifted away and were replaced by others throughout the day. The next day there was nobody. The men working about the quay had forgotten. The place where the body had lain was no longer roped off. The police had made all their enquiries, taken all their measurements, made their arrest. It was finished.

He had not thought of the finding of the body. He had not thought of anything until now. A clock appeared before his face, suspended above a grimy grocery window, flies on the dead empty packages, the faded crépe paper tubes, the rusted pins. Five-thirty. He thought then, simply : Half past five ; morning or evening ? he thought. Surely I should not be here ? he thought. He was not tired. He was not anything. Nor had he any idea wherehe was.

Traffic was thin, the streets gray, lonely, unpeopled. He stood at the kerb's edge, lost. The few who passed or observed him probably remarked that he looked weary, done. But it was more than that : he had that quality of a dying flame, as if at any moment he might disappear into oblivion. He stood there for some time, while the day opened and the traffic grew denser, whirling about him. Then he began to walk again. He was still walking without thinking. It was as if he awaited the turning of another page in his mind, his eyes turned inward upon that slow page of his mind, waiting till they could discern what was written there.

Then it was full daylight. Across the page there suddenly appeared the vision of a bus, a destination-board: VICTORIA.

Victoria, he thought, the thought clicking like a fount of type onto the page : that's it, that's where I've got to get to : Victoria.

The train was practically empty. He was alone in the compartment. He leaned back, watching with puzzled eyes the skypointed horizon sliding backward, away from memory before he could properly designate, justify it. Smoke drifted slowly across the city, across the blank page of mind, of knowing, across the peaceful toneless sky. Autumn, he thought ; summer is ending. Then he began to remember.

The small suburban stations slowed, stopped, passed from vision : the lonely porter, the clanging milkcans, the bundles of papers thrown amid a scurry of minor dust on to the deserted platforms ; the faded posters, the chipped advertisements, the guard's whistle, the green flag tremulous in the morning air. I am going home, he thought : it is time to go home. He was calm, utterly peaceful.

So now, he thought, it is but a little while. At every wheel's turn it is less. Listening to the wheels clattering with dimensionless fury through sealed and solitary decades of time. *With me. And with every wheel's turn it is less. And less*
                                       and
                                                   less
hearing them bear him homeward, to this and that and the other on which he pondered as the bare rigid horizon flung by, the flat gray sky and endless, scattered clouds of like texture, glooming, seeming to wait.

There were no buses running in Frampton on Sunday mornings. He was the only passenger to alight from the train, walking with slow weightless steps down the slope that fell away from the small brick station building, the gleaming rails, the wild and untended chrysanthemums and the empty chalked parking spaces to the dust-sputtered street and the crimped and fading mapleleaves drifting among the anonymous litter of last night, any night.

Above the quiet town now the faint sound of bells drifted. The few people in the streets walked with that downcast decorum of early Sunday toward the faint clear sound. They might have been medieval penitents. He saw them without interest. Passing the church he saw them drift in, swallowed in the Gothic shadows and the now omnipresent clang of bells. He walked on, away from the

sound. It was a three-mile walk to the road in which he
lived, that he thought of as home. He covered the
distance in about an hour, walking still with no sign of
haste. When he was about halfway home two men drifted
from some shrubbery beside the deserted road and followed
him. They were heavy-looking men of whom one would
say at once (besides the obvious designation), They are
naturally kind men, probably with two children each and
wives with permanently-waved hair. Cigarettes slanted
from their lips and they walked with their hands in the
pockets of their belted Burberrys, not speaking. They
kept their distance at about two hundred yards. When
they came to the end of the road into which he had turned
they did not follow any farther. They still did not speak,
but it was as if they had said, Stay : here will be near
enough. They remained there for about an hour after
they had seen him diminish into the distance of the gray
road, come to the house outside which for a moment he
stood poised, tiny by distance, then again turned from out
their vision as he entered the house. They seemed to hear
the faint sound of the door as he entered.

He closed it immediately. In the small dark hall the
smell of dust lingered. Against the wall the wreaths stood
like tokens of long-vanquished heroes, dustfilmed too, the
blossoms withered and dry, drooping from the coronets of
wire and leaves, tawdry, purposeless now, and not even
beautiful, marked by the blackbordered cards, the phoney
sympathy, the words purchased at so much a dozen in the
printers' shops.

He stood for a moment leaning against the wall, the
closed door, smelling the dead odour of flowers, the dust-
rimed leaves, the emptiness. Then he went on up the soft
stairs, Degas, Manet, Degas fading into and out from his
vision slowly as he rose.

In the bedroom the windows stood open, exactly as he

had left them, the curtains hanging without motion, like the tattered banners in cathedrals. There was nothing else to do. Then he remembered the handkerchief, the jewelry, the portrait of her mother.

But they did not matter particularly, he thought ; they do not matter now. Nonetheless, I must take them, he thought. But later. There is plenty of time.

There is all the time in the world, he thought.

Beside the bed the folding travelling clock marked timelessness. It must be eight days since it was wound, he thought. But that was yesterday, yesterday, yesterday. The spurious hieroglyphics watched, mocked him. Of all things I remember these, only these, he thought : the warm form beside me perfumed with sleep *here in this airless room ?* the coming home and the departing, the food placed before me, the mornings you were angry, somehow, not with me, with life. It will be no good, you said ; if he were to die tomorrow he would be honoured and remembered for what people will say, believe, he has done for them. We are the conquered, the little, the vanquished now : because it will go on for always. The trickery and deception, the lying and the swindles, the people to applaud, the fools who see no wrong, the public figure upheld on his own clay pedestal by the stupidity of those that stand and gaze and worship and never look deeper than the refined nose, the aristocratic face, the crested signet, the fine tweeds. The pomp and triviality, the fairground heraldry, the false wisdom and the smile for the child kissed at the profitable garden party.

They triumph now, he thought ; they are the tokens men uphold : honour, justice, corruption—these they flounder in, unable to tell black from white, satisfied with black where white would mean wonder, imagination.

We are the outlaws. With our little moments we live, piecing them together, marvelling at the pattern—the folkweave and the spurious silver, the imitation Chippendale and the lavish kitchenette. We see it and want it and take it and are happy. And then we lose it and there is nothing else. It is gone, vanished down some long vale of dreams, weightless, silent, gossamer,—broken.

He was lying on the bed, looking up at the lightshade's shadow on the ceiling. The knife lay on the table beside the clock. Beyond the open window a light wind curled among the drifting leaves. His eyes began to hurt, as if with unshed tears. He covered them with his hand but he could not sleep. He smoked for perhaps an hour, continuously, until the room was full of the wafting planes of blue smoke. Then the sound of footsteps came up from the street.

Without haste he rose from the bed. In the wardrobe door he saw himself with wild surprise *Well. Do I really look as scruffy as that?* All he did, everything he touched, was without haste. He took the folded handkerchief from his pocket and spread it on the dressing-table. Then he emptied the jewel-box on to it—the red bone dog on the Woolworth pin, the portrait locket, the dry lavender. He folded the handkerchief carefully about the worthless trinkets and slipped them into his pocket. They pressed against his thigh and jingled when he moved. Smiling, he put the knife into the other pocket. They will want that. Yes. Exhibit A.

Then the knocking, brief, hard, shattering. Watching from the window he could see the trembling of curtains all down the road. " In a minute ", he said aloud, though to what or whom he could not have said.

Then the knocking sounded again, brief, peremptory, and he went on toward the stairs. The empty house rose up to meet him, the arid dust, the scentless flowers, the tawdry words, the mocking. They rose up to meet him as he descended softly, completely without sound, past the soft pictures and the symbols of death, toward the door.